THIRD EDITION

Teaching and Learning
THROUGH
MULTIPLE
INTELLIGENCES

Linda Campbell

Bruce Campbell

Dee Dickinson

PEARSON

Boston   New York   San Francisco
Mexico City   Montreal   Toronto   London   Madrid   Munich   Paris
Hong Kong   Singapore   Tokyo   Cape Town   Sydney

KH

Senior Editor, Education: *Arnis Burvikovs*
Editorial Assistant: *Christine Lyons*
Marketing Manager: *Mandy Trapp*
Senior Editiorial Production Administrator: *Deborah Brown*
Composition Buyer: *Linda Cox*
Manufacturing Buyer: *Andrew Turso*
Cover Administrator: *Kristina Mose-Libon*
Editorial Production Service: *Susan McNally*
Illustrators: *Joel Gendron and Denise Hoffman*
Text Design/Electronic Composition: *Denise Hoffman*

Between the time Website information is gathered and then published, it is not unusual for some sites to have closed. Also, the transcription of URLs can result in unintended typographical errors. The publisher would appreciate notification where these errors occur so that they may be corrected in subsequent editions.

Library of Congress Cataloging-in-Publication Data

Campbell, Linda, 1948–
    Teaching & learning through multiple intelligences / Linda Campbell, Bruce Campbell, Dee Dickinson. — 3rd rd.
        p. cm.
    Includes bibliographical references and indexes.
    ISBN 0–205–36390–3
        1. Learning.   2. Multiple intelligences.   3. Cognitive styles.   4. Teaching.
    I. Title: Teaching and learning through multiple intelligences.   II. Campbell, Bruce,
    1945–   III. Dickinson, Dee.   IV. Title.

LB1060.C366 2003
370.15'2—dc21

                                            2003050027

Printed in the United States of America

10 9 8 7 6 5 4 3 2   [CIN]   08 07 06 04

10/25/04

■ ■ ■ ■ ■ ■ ■ ■ ■ ■ ■ ■ ■ ■ ■ ■ ■

*To Dr. Howard Gardner, we extend our deepest thanks
for his thoughtful reading and recommendations as
each part of this book has taken form. The Theory of
Multiple Intelligences has brought about positive
changes in teaching and learning for students and
educators throughout the world.*

*T*his book is dedicated to discovering
the gifts in every student.

WITHDRAWN

ACKNOWLEDGMENTS

This book represents the combined efforts of theorists, teachers, administrators, students, researchers, and interested lay people whose work, questions, and comments have helped us articulate the Theory of Multiple Intelligences.

First and foremost, our thanks are extended to Dr. Howard Gardner for his inspiration and critique of this book. In addition, we are especially grateful to those who shared their expertise with us on the book's contents. These individuals include: Nancy Murphy for her impressive knowledge and suggestions for the logical-mathematical chapter; Lowell Hovis and Mark Wahl who also provided helpful feedback on the logical-mathematical chapter; Kristen DeWitte for her ideas for the linguistic chapter; Sarah Welsh for her beautifully drawn mindmap in the visual chapter; Carol Scott-Kasner for her thoughtful contributions to the musical chapter; Pat Guild for her contribution entitled Appreciating Differences in the interpersonal chapter; and to Kate McPherson for her wealth of information on service learning in the interpersonal chapter.

We also thank those who helped the book take its early pilot edition form: Dorothy Bestor for editing, Roz Pape for book design, and Cheryl Senecal for graphics. We feel fortunate, indeed, to have found Jean Lilley, who as teacher-turned-graphic-artist created the cover and book design for its second version, and to Rhonda Cole, Deborah Brown, Denise Hoffman, and Susan McNally for their thoughtful work on the third and latest edition. We appreciate as well the support for this book from numerous publishers and authors who graciously permitted us to include their work in ours and from those at Allyn and Bacon who consider our work worthy of publication.

Contents

CHAPTER 1

A Way With Words:
Verbal-Linguistic Intelligence   1

CHAPTER 2

The Calculating Mind:
Logical-Mathematical Intelligence   31

CHAPTER 3
Moving to Learn: Kinesthetic Intelligence   63

CHAPTER 4

Everyone Is an Artist: Visual-Spatial Intelligence   93

CHAPTER 5

Tuning In: Musical Intelligence   127

CHAPTER 6

Understanding One Another: Interpersonal Intelligence   153

CHAPTER 7

The World Within: Intrapersonal Intelligence   185

CHAPTER 8

The World around Us:
Naturalist Intelligence   219

CHAPTER 9
Curriculum Development through the Multiple Intelligences   249

CHAPTER 10

Dissolving the Boundaries:
Assessment That Enhances Learning   285

CHAPTER 11
Lessons Learned   323

Introduction
MANY KINDS OF INTELLIGENCE

A Word about the Third Edition

For the third edition of our book, we have included new content based on the evolving understanding of Howard Gardner's Theory of Multiple Intelligences. In the pages that follow, the reader will find updated resources in each chapter, new technology options, information for integrating MI theory into standards-based instruction, and student achievement data from MI-based schools. As with previous editions, however, the goal of this book remains constant. We seek to provide educators with multiple ways of teaching so that students and teachers experience success and enjoyment in learning.

In what ways are your students smart?

Do you have students who create beautiful pieces of visual art? Are others gifted in sports, making complex physical movements appear graceful and effortless? Some may play musical instruments so well that listening touches chords within. A few may thrill to the challenge of mathematical precision. Some may have a special understanding of the natural world while others may love writing and have already learned the excitement of seeing their stories or poems in print. Several may be natural leaders, offering positive role models and

trusted guidance to their classmates. And a few may possess penetrating personal insights into who they are and what they stand for, while pursuing important life goals. Among the students mentioned, who would be the most intelligent? The question is impossible to answer because these examples represent individuals with different intelligences. Each student is unique and all in distinct ways offer valuable contributions to human culture.

A Definition of Human Intelligence

Dr. Howard Gardner, Professor of Education at Harvard University, has conducted substantial research on the development of human cognitive capacities. He has shed the common premise of intelligence theory which adheres to two fundamental assumptions: that cognition is unitary and that individuals can be adequately described as having a single, quantifiable intelligence. In his study of intellectual capacities, Gardner (1983) established criteria to measure whether a talent was actually an intelligence. Each intelligence must have a developmental feature, be observable in special populations such as prodigies or "savants," provide some evidence of localization in the brain, and support a symbolic or notational system.

While most people possess the full spectrum of intelligences, each reveals distinctive cognitive features. We possess varying amounts of the eight intelligences and combine and use them in highly personal ways. Restricting educational programs to a preponderance of linguistic and mathematical intelligences minimizes the importance of other forms of knowing. Thus many students who fail to demonstrate the traditional academic intelligences are held in low esteem and their strengths may remain unrealized and lost to both the school and society at large.

Gardner's research revealed a wider family of human intelligences than was previously believed, and offered a refreshingly pragmatic definition of intelligence. Instead of viewing "smartness" in terms of a score on a standardized test, Gardner (1983) defined intelligence as:

- The ability to solve problems that one encounters in real life.
- The ability to generate new problems to solve.
- The ability to make something or offer a service that is valued within one's culture.

This definition of intelligence underscores the multicultural nature of Gardner's theory.

A Description of the Eight Intelligences

In his 1983 book, *Frames of Mind*, Gardner presented his Theory of Multiple Intelligences that reinforces his cross-cultural perspective of human cognition. The intelligences are languages that all people speak and are influenced, in part, by the cultures in which we are born. They are tools for learning, problem-solving, and creating throughout life. A brief description of Gardner's eight intelligences follows.

Linguistic intelligence consists of the ability to think in words and to use language to express and appreciate complex meanings. Authors, poets, journalists, speakers, and newscasters exhibit high degrees of linguistic intelligence.

Logical-mathematical intelligence makes it possible to calculate, quantify, consider propositions and hypotheses, and carry out complex mathematical operations. Scientists, accountants, engineers, and computer programmers all demonstrate this intelligence.

Spatial intelligence instills the capacity to think in three-dimensional ways as do sailors, pilots, sculptors, painters, and architects. It enables one to perceive external and internal imagery, to recreate, transform, or modify images, to navigate oneself and objects through space, and to produce or decode graphic information.

Bodily-kinesthetic intelligence enables one to manipulate objects and fine-tune physical skills. It is evident in athletes, dancers, surgeons, and craftspeople. In Western societies, physical skills are not as highly valued as cognitive ones, and yet elsewhere the ability to use one's body is a necessity for survival and an important feature of many prestigious roles.

Musical intelligence is evident in individuals who possess a sensitivity to pitch, melody, rhythm, and tone. Those demonstrating this intelligence include composers, conductors, musicians, critics, and instrument makers, as well as sensitive listeners.

Interpersonal intelligence is the capacity to understand and interact effectively with others. It is evident in successful teachers, social workers, actors, or politicians. Just as Western culture has recently begun to recognize the connection between mind and body, so too has it to come to value the importance of proficiency in interpersonal behavior.

Intrapersonal intelligence refers to the ability to construct an accurate perception of oneself and to use such knowledge in planning and directing one's life. Some individuals with strong intrapersonal intelligence specialize as theologians, psychologists, and philosophers.

Naturalist intelligence consists of observing patterns in nature, indentifying and classifying objects, and understanding natural and human-made systems. Skilled naturalists include farmers, botanists, hunters, ecologists, and landscapers.

Gardner is careful to explain that intelligence should not be limited to the ones he has identified. In his 1999 book, entitled *Intelligence Reframed*, Gardner considered potential new intelligences. These included existential, moral, and spiritual candidates. Existential intelligence entails the ability to contemplate the meaning of life and death, but Gardner has been unable to locate its origin in the brain and so it is premature to be considered an intelligence. Moral intelligence involves making of value judgments and because intelligence is value-free Gardner chooses not to credit this capacity as a full-blown intelligence. Similarly, spiritual intelligence enables us to grasp cosmic and transcendent truths but ultimately it depends on affective capacities. He believes that the eight, however, provide a far more accurate picture of human capacities than do previous unitary theories. Contrary to the small range of abilities that many standard IQ tests measure, Gardner's theory offers an expanded image of what it means to be human. He also notes that each intelligence contains several sub-intelligences. For example, there are sub-intelligences within the domain of music that include playing music, singing, writing musical scores, conducting, critiquing, and appreciating music. Each of the seven other intelligences also contain numerous facets.

Another aspect of the Multiple Intelligences is that they may be conceptualized in three broad categories. Four of the eight, spatial, logical-mathematical, bodily-kinesthetic, and naturalist, may be viewed as "object-related" forms of intelligence. These capacities are controlled and shaped by the objects that individuals encounter in their environments. On the other hand, the "object-free" intelligences, consisting of verbal-linguistic and musical, are not shaped by the physical world but are dependent on language and musical systems. The third category consists of the "person-related" intelligences with inter- and intrapersonal intelligences reflecting a powerful set of counterbalances.

Each intelligence appears to have its own developmental sequence, emerging and blossoming at different times in life. Musical intelligence is the earliest form of human giftedness to emerge; it is a mystery why this is so. Gardner suggests that excelling at music as a child may be conditioned by the fact that this intelligence is not contingent upon accruing life experience. On the other hand, the personal intelligences require extensive interaction with and feedback from others before becoming well developed.

Gardner believes that since each intelligence can be used for good or ill purposes, all eight are inherently value-free. Goebbels and Gandhi both had strong interpersonal intelligence but applied it in dramatically different ways. How individuals go about using their intelligences within society is a moral question of crucial importance.

It is evident that creativity can be expressed through all the intelligences. Gardner notes, however, that most people are creative within a specific domain. For example, although Einstein was gifted mathematically and scientifically, he did not exhibit equal genius linguistically, kinesthetically, or interpersonally. Most people appear to excel within one or two intelligences.

This book is about how to create open systems of education to make it possible for the human mind—which can be the most open of systems—to flourish. Not all human beings will become great artists, musicians, or writers, but every human life will be enriched through developing many kinds of intelligence to the greatest extent possible. When individuals have opportunities to learn through their strengths, unexpected and positive cognitive, emotional, social, and even physical changes can appear.

About the Authors

The authors of this book have shared with teachers exciting breakthroughs in learning students experience when instructional strategies engage the eight intelligences. They themselves have been classroom teachers at all levels from elementary through university. Many experiences from their work are interwoven throughout the text as illustrations of what can happen when the repertoire of teaching strategies is expanded and the opportunities for learning in different ways are increased. Brief synopses of the authors' work follow.

As an elementary and secondary public school teacher for 10 years, Linda Campbell, Ph.D., won three teacher of the year awards. Linda began serving as a professor of education at Antioch University Seattle in 1989. There, she has designed and administered teacher education programs for urban and northwest tribal communities. The recipient of a Gates Foundation grant in 2002, Linda currently develops integrated high school and college programs for underserved youth, with a special emphasis on culturally responsive programs for Native American students. She has authored *Multiple Intelligences and Student Achievement* published by ASCD in 1999, and *Mindful Learning: 101 Proven Strategies for Teacher and Student Success* published by Corwin Press in 2002. Linda has won numerous academic and community service awards.

When he taught a multi-age classroom of third, fourth, and fifth grade students, Bruce Campbell used MI theory as the organizing principle. He established eight learning centers, each devoted to a different intelligence. The students spent two-thirds of their school day rotating through the centers and the final third doing project-based work. Their achievement results were impressive, and, as a result, Bruce's classroom was featured in a video funded by the U.S. Department of Education and in *USA Today* and newspapers throughout the country. More recently, Bruce worked as a curriculum specialist for the Marysville School district in Washington State. He consults nationally and internationally and authored *The Multiple Intelligences Handbook: Lesson Plans and More.*

Dee Dickinson is CEO and founder of New Horizons for Learning, an international education network based in Seattle, Washington, and on the Internet at www.newhorizons.org. She has taught on all levels from elementary through university, has produced several series for educational television, and nine international conferences on education. Formerly, she was director of the Seattle Creative Activities Center, founder of the Northwest Art Project, was commissioned by IBM to write the report *Positive Trends in Learning,* and edited the book *Creating the Future.* Dee serves on advisory boards for numerous organizations, including the University of Washington's College of Education, KCTS TV, the Learning Forum, the National Learning Foundation, and ChildResearch Net, and is a Fellow of the George Lucas Educational Foundation and the International Corporate Learning Association.

A Multiple Intelligences Inventory

Before surveying the strategies in this book, it may be helpful to self-assess your use of each of the eight intelligences. Everyone relies on one or more intelligences for successful living and working. Heredity, the environment, and culture all influence our intelligence preferences. It is also interesting to note that as teachers, we likely rely on one or more intelligences in our instructional approaches. Such inclinations may be determined by our individual preferences, our training as educators, and the "cultural norms" of our schools.

The following inventory enables readers to identify their strengths and the intelligences they seldom use. It is organized in a developmental fashion ranging from novice level expression of an intelligence to that of the inventor level. Before completing the inventory, reflect on each intelligence one at a time. Then, log your developmental level of that capacity on the grid. As you do so, you may notice that the task is easier said than done. This is because each intelligence has numerous sub-components. For example, some people may express at the expert level in verbal-linguistic intelligence if they are skilled speakers. Others may be experts because of their writing ability. As you plot the development of each intelligence, you may want to note which sub-component you have in mind. Proceed through all eight intelligences until you have created one snapshot of your cognitive profile.

DEVELOPMENTAL SELF-ASSESSMENT OF MULTIPLE INTELLIGENCES

	VERBAL-LINGUISTIC	LOGICAL-MATHEMATICAL	BODILY-KINESTHETIC	VISUAL-SPATIAL	MUSICAL-RHYTHMIC	INTERPERSONAL	INTRAPERSONAL	NATURALIST INTELLIGENCE
INVENTOR Invents new forms of communication through the intelligence; identifies new aspects of the intelligence or creates original works.								
EXPERT Demonstrates mastery of the concepts and practices of the intelligence in professional or avocational activities. May be viewed as a specialist.								
PRACTITIONER Develops proficiency in the intelligence's symbol system. Understands concepts and skills of a discipline and applies such knowledge in many contexts. Can learn additional skills.								
APPRENTICE Perceives relationships between symbols and objects or events they represent. From role models or instruction, learns symbol system, concepts, and skills of the knowledge.								
NOVICE Learns about the intelligence through exploration of the environment, interaction with others. Observation, imitation, and experimentation instill knowledge and skills.								

After completing this brief assessment, reflect on the results. Are there differences between intelligences used in your personal and professional life? Are there other intelligences you would like to develop for classroom use? How were your areas of strength nurtured as a child and as an adult? How might you go about developing other intelligences of interest? Could you establish a timeline for such work? What kinds of intelligences do you perceive in your students? Which intelligences do you feel are most highly developed in teachers in general? Reflecting on such questions might deepen your awareness of your unique capacities and expand your appreciation for those gifted in other domains.

Intelligent Environments

Not only is it important for teachers to recognize the intelligence in our mind/body systems, it is also important to consider that it is possible to create positive environments in which to live and learn. The new field of research on "distributed cognitions" suggests that intelligence extends beyond individuals and is enhanced through interactions with other people, with books, and with the tools we use to think, learn, and problem-solve, such as pencils and paper, notebooks and journals, calculators and computers.

Take a moment to reflect on your classroom environment. How is it "smart?" Are there sufficient opportunities for students to interact with each other in pairs, small groups, and as a whole class? Are a variety of resources available, including books, magazines, trade publications, bulletin boards, art work, posters, computers, databases, and networks? Throughout this book you will find suggestions for creating environments that foster the development of all the intelligences.

It is well to remember that noted neurophysiologists such as Marian Diamond have discovered that the brain can change structurally and functionally in response to learning and experience—for better or worse. Throughout life we can continue to develop enhanced mental abilities in environments that are positive, nurturing, stimulating, and interactive.

What This Book Offers

Written for educators, this book offers practical classroom applications of the Theory of Multiple Intelligences. Philosophically, the authors maintain that students must have opportunities for the creative exploration of their individual interests and talents while also learning valued skills and concepts through multimodal means. Not all children exhibit the same intelligence profile, nor do they share the same interests. In an age of exploding information, none of us can learn everything; choices ultimately must be made about what and how we will learn. In making such choices, the students' individual inclinations and interests should guide some of their curricular options.

The basic knowledge that many state standards claim all students should master in language arts, mathematics, history, and science does not need to be taught in the same manner for everyone. Frustration and academic failure can be reduced if teachers presented information in numerous ways, offering students multiple options for success. This book assists educators in acquiring "intelligence fair" methods of perceiving students and their talents, of designing curriculum and assessment approaches, and of nurturing individual capacities so that each student may experience academic success and the joy of pursuing an area of intrinsic interest.

An important distinction should be made among academic disciplines and intelligence. In his book, *Multiple Intelligences: The Theory in Practice,* Gardner (1993) explained that intelligence is biopsychological potential. This potential can be used and applied in multiple disciplines or domains. For example, musical performances often tap musical intelligence as well as bodily-kinesthetic and interpersonal processes. Rather than seeking to develop the intelligences for their own sake, it may be more worthwhile to use a variety of intellectual faculties to master each school's academic disciplines.

As you browse through the book, you will notice that each of the chapters on the eight intelligences is organized similarly: each begins with a story of an individual who exemplifies a particular intelligence. This is followed by a definition of the intelligence, suggestions for enhancing the classroom environment, and numerous instructional strategies. The final three chapters are dedicated to curriculum and assessment issues and what has been learned from multiple intelligence school programs.

The authors offer this collection of practical applications of the Theory of Multiple Intelligences to reinforce the fine work that many teachers are already doing and to offer ideas that may be new to some. All of these suggestions are founded on the same goal: to free the learning potential and creative expression of every student in every classroom.

1

A Way with Words
VERBAL-LINGUISTIC INTELLIGENCE

The poet possesses a relation to words beyond our ordinary powers, a repository, as it were, of all the uses to which particular words have been put in previous poems. That knowledge of the history of language use prepares—or frees—the poet to attain certain combinations of his own as he constructs an original poem. It is through such fresh combinations of words, as Northrup Frye insists, that we have our only way of creating new worlds.

—Howard Gardner, *Frames of Mind*

WRITING THROUGH A LIFETIME

The introduction to Carl Sandburg's *Complete Poems* quotes the great poet as saying, "At the age of six, as my fingers first found how to shape the alphabet, I decided to become a person of letters. At the age of ten I had scrawled letters on slates, on paper, on boxes and walls and I formed an ambition to become a sign-painter."

*E*ven though his failure in entrance exams in mathematics and grammar kept Carl Sandburg from being admitted to West Point, he graduated from Lombard College and pursued a brilliant career as a poet and writer. He collected American folk songs into an anthology, The *American Songbag*, and his four-volume biography,

Abraham Lincoln led to doctoral degrees at twelve universities. Yet never satisfied with his writing skills, even into his eighties, Sandburg wrote:

I am still studying verbs and the mystery of how they connect with nouns. I am more suspicious of adjectives than at any other time in all my born days. I have forgotten the meaning of twenty or thirty of my poems written thirty or forty years ago. I still favor several simple poems published long ago which continue to have an appeal for simple people. I have written by different methods and in a wide miscellany of moods and have seldom been afraid to travel in lands and seas where I met fresh scenes and new songs. All my life I have been trying to learn to read, to see and hear, and to write. At sixty-five I began my first novel, and the five years lacking a month I took to finish it, I was still traveling, still a seeker. I should like to think that as I go on writing there will be sentences truly alive with verbs quivering, with nouns giving color and echoes. It could be in the grace of God, I shall live to be eighty-nine, as did Hokusai, and speaking my farewell to earthly scenes, I might paraphrase, "If God had let me live five years longer I should have been a writer."

DEFINITION: Understanding Verbal-Linguistic Intelligence

Sandburg's statement exemplifies verbal-linguistic intelligence in both his keen sensitivity to the sound, rhythm, and meaning of words and in his lifelong passion to express himself in his writing. Gardner suggests that language is a "preeminent instance of human intelligence" that has been indispensable to human society. He describes the importance of the rhetorical aspect of language, or the ability to convince others of a course of action; the mnemonic potential of language, or the ability to use words in remembering lists or processes; the capacity of language to explain concepts, and the value of metaphor in doing so; and the use of language to reflect upon language, or to engage in "metalinguistic" analysis.

The use of words to communicate and document, to express powerful emotions, and to set to music in song, sets human beings apart from other animals. Early in the history of humankind, language changed the specialization and function of the human brain by offering possibilities for exploring and expanding intelligence. The spoken word made it possible for our ancestors to move from concrete to abstract thinking as they progressed from pointing to objects to naming them and to talking about objects not in their presence. Reading made it possible to learn about objects, places, processes, and concepts not directly experienced, and writing has facilitated communication with those the speaker has never met. It is through the ability to think in words that humans can remember, analyze, problem-solve, plan ahead, and create.

Since the normal fetus develops hearing while still in the womb, the foundation of verbal-linguistic intelligence is laid before birth. Researchers such as the prominent neuropsychologist

Marian Diamond indicate that babies who have been read to, sung to, and talked to before birth have a head start on the development of verbal-linguistic intelligence.

The Talaris Foundation at the University of Washington and the National Association for the Education of Young Children stress the importance of creating language-rich environments in which adults engage young children in reading together, playing with words, telling stories and jokes, asking questions, stating opinions, and explaining feelings and concepts. Children should be involved in discussions and provided with opportunities to make meaningful choices and decisions. Small wonder that a child born into such an environment has a leading edge on becoming a competent listener, speaker, reader, and writer.

Classrooms in every subject matter area, at every grade level, can also be language-rich environments where students frequently read, speak, discuss, and listen—and above all are encouraged to be curious. Interest in learning grows when students feel secure enough to ask questions and debate viewpoints Expressing ideas verbally is an important metacognitive exercise, for it is often in hearing ourselves speak or reading what we have written that we gain insights into what we really think and know.

Self-confidence grows when students learn to defend their position in discussions and debates. They understand their lessons more deeply when they have opportunities to teach others what they have learned. Yet observations of classrooms by such researchers as John Goodlad reveal that, in many cases, teachers are the ones who speak the majority of the time—to groups of passive students.

Even in classrooms where students are primarily listeners, that skill is seldom taught. Yet, it is through listening that one learns to use the spoken word correctly, effectively, even eloquently. Speaking is another essential skill that does not develop effectively without coaching and encouragement. Articulate writing requires practice as well as broad, thoughtful reading. These four components of verbal-linguistic intelligence are so valued in society that they appear in most state assessment measures and standardized tests, and more importantly, they are fundamental to learning throughout life.

CHECKLIST: Verbal-Linguistic Intelligence Qualities

Early in the history of our country, in the schools of the Massachusetts Bay Colony, reading and writing comprised two-thirds of the curriculum. Today, the curriculum has vastly expanded, yet reading and writing, along with listening and speaking, remain essential tools for learning in all subjects.

In 1996, the National Council of Teachers of English published standards that identify what students should know and be able to do in the language arts. Not meant to be all-inclusive or prescriptive, the standards support a range of purposes, developmental processes, and community contexts for English language usage. They recommend that students:

- Read a range of materials for a variety of purposes.
- Learn and apply multiple reading strategies.
- Acquire a working knowledge of language conventions, structure, and variation.
- Create written works.
- Participate in active inquiry.
- Use research materials including those available through technology.

- Experience a multicultural language arts curriculum.
- Use literacy skills to pursue topics of personal and social significance.
- Participate in collaborative learning using language skills to promote and sustain a sense of community.
- Use language skills to discover one's individuality and to direct one's future learning and communication goals.

Becoming highly literate requires a lifetime of meaningful interaction with others, with a variety of texts, and with one's own writing. Lists of standards do not imply that literacy acquisition occurs in discrete or fragmented ways. Rather, language learning is dependent on the interplay of multiple skills simultaneously. Literacy is also dependent on context. Educators can tap their knowledge of students to teach linguistic skills appropriately in the classroom.

Below we have listed some qualities of verbal-linguistic intelligence. We recognize that those with hearing, speaking, or sight impairments will develop language and communication skills in other ways, often through the intelligences discussed in later chapters. It is likely that a person with well-developed verbal-linguistic intelligence exhibits the following characteristics.

1. Listens and responds to the sound, rhythm, color, and variety of the spoken word.

2. Imitates sounds, language, reading, and the writing of others.

3. Learns through listening, reading, writing, and discussing.

4. Listens effectively, comprehends, paraphrases, interprets, remembers, and analyzes what has been said.

5. Reads effectively, comprehends, summarizes, interprets or explains, and remembers what has been read; enjoys one or more literary genres.

6. Speaks effectively to a variety of audiences for a variety of purposes, and knows how to speak simply, eloquently, persuasively, or passionately at appropriate times.

7. Writes effectively: understands and applies rules of grammar, spelling, punctuation, and uses a broad vocabulary.

8. Exhibits ability to learn other languages.

9. Uses listening, speaking, writing, and reading to remember, communicate, discuss, explain, persuade, create knowledge, construct meaning, and reflect upon language itself.

10. Strives to enhance his or her own language usage.

11. Demonstrates interest in journalism, poetry, storytelling, debate, speaking, writing, or editing.

12. Creates new linguistic forms or original works of writing or oral communication.

Verbal-Linguistic Learning Processes

Throughout this book, you will find connections between each of the other intelligences and the development and use of language. Although we discuss the four linguistic skills separately as listed below, they are closely linked and can be integrated throughout the curriculum.

Because so much has been written on the subject of literacy, this chapter does not discuss the introduction and teaching of fundamentals, but rather highlights ways to exercise linguistic skills. The strategies here include:

Establishing a Verbal-Linguistic Learning Environment

Listening to Learn
Keys to Effective Listening
Listening to Stories and Reading Aloud
Listening to Poetry
Teachers as Storytellers
Listening to Lectures

Speaking
Students as Storytellers
Classroom Discussions
Memorizing
Reports
Interviews

Reading
Finding Materials
Words in the Classroom
Reading Across the Curriculum
Reading for Understanding

Writing
Categories of Writing
Writing Across the Curriculum
Writing Options for All Content Areas
Getting Started with Writing
The Real Work of Writing
Writing Groups

Technology That Enhances Verbal-Linguistic Intelligence

Establishing a Verbal-Linguistic Learning Environment

■ ■ ■ ■ ■ ■ ■ ■ ■ ■ ■ ■ ■ ■ ■ ■

Verbal-linguistic intelligence is deeply rooted in our feelings of competence and self-confidence. The more children exercise this intelligence in a secure setting, the more easily they develop effective verbal skills. Teachers can provide strong models by playing with words, sharing their favorite written works, engaging in discussions with enthusiasm, teaching important reading skills, and telling stories.

Storytelling is one of the oldest and most engaging of the language arts. It is not used nearly as much as it might be to motivate students, explain processes or events, or simply create a hospitable environment. Stories in the form of parables have been used by every religion in the world to convey important principles and teachings. Myths and legends have been told in all societies to explain scientific phenomena, preserve cultural knowledge, and entertain and inform listeners. The oral tradition is an ancient one, and bears recognition as an effective means of communication. Later in this chapter you will find suggestions for using storytelling in the classroom.

Reading aloud carries the sound, rhythm, and music of language into the ear. Recordings or videotapes of actors interpreting the works of great playwrights, poets, and short-story writers bring the written word to life. Teachers reading some of their favorite written works with enthusiasm and feeling can inspire interest that lasts a lifetime. Students who participate in choral reading or who read to each other before doing so to the whole class can develop greater self-confidence.

Teachers can model effective listening skills by paying careful attention to and asking thoughtful questions of students or guests in the classroom.

Students are encouraged to listen more carefully to others when they themselves are listened to attentively. Ways to develop these skills are described later in this chapter.

Extensive opportunities for individualized reading, writing, and speaking have positive effects on achievement and tend to carry over into leisure-time activities. Students can be guided and motivated to become enthusiastic readers. Their curiosity can be piqued when parents or teachers suggest materials that relate to their interests; however, students must be introduced to other purposes for reading as well such as reading for information in nonfiction texts. Classrooms enriched with a wide range of reading materials at a variety of reading levels can support students' interests and skills.

The study of great stories, plays, poetry, or novels can be complemented by challenging writing assignments. Students can be asked to replicate the writing style of others or to connect a work's content to their lives. They can predict, extend, or critique a plot and write to engage others outside of the classroom.

To make sense of what might otherwise be a fragmented educational experience, teachers can help students see connections between subjects. Teachers of math and science can demand the same high standards of listening, speaking, reading, and writing as do language arts instructors. And teachers of literature may create a meaningful context for reading a book by relating it to studies in other subjects.

Students require a variety of experiences to engage linguistic intelligence as exemplified throughout this book. Exercising listening, speaking, reading, and writing skills leads to fuller human development and to the mastery of skills needed throughout life: thinking, learning, problem-solving, communicating, and creating as contributing members of society.

Listening to Learn

For those able to hear, the human voice provides the first introduction to language. It has been estimated by researcher Lyman Steil, and others, that individuals spend 80 percent of their waking hours communicating, and that 45 percent of that time is devoted to listening. Steil estimates that in many traditional classrooms students spend over 70 percent of classroom time in listening, yet little is taught about effective listening strategies.

Steil contends that the majority of people are inefficient listeners. After hearing a ten-minute oral presentation most listeners hear, understand, evaluate, and retain only half of what was said. They lose another 25 percent during the following 48 hours. In other words, most people retain only about a quarter of what they hear unless they have developed the skills to listen more efficiently.

Keys to Effective Listening

Dr. Steil worked with businesses to help employees improve their listening skills. He eventually developed ten keys to effective listening. Teachers may wish to discuss the ten keys with their students and to practice one or more of them as appropriate.

Since there is a definite time-lag between the number of words the average speaker says in a minute (200) and the average number of words a listener can process in a minute (300 to 500), good listeners use the extra time to activate their thinking. When students are listening to an explanation, a lecture, or a guest speaker, they can put the time-lag to use by identifying the speaker's purpose, main points, and central themes. They can review and evaluate what has been said, anticipate what may be coming, think about what is personally relevant and identify questions they may have. They can also embellish their notes and glean additional information from paying attention to what the speaker is saying through body language. If teachers want students to remember what they hear, it is important for them to discuss the content within the next eight hours.

Listening to Stories and Reading Aloud

Telling stories and reading aloud can engage interest and facilitate learning in all subject areas. For example, a history lesson can be brought to life through anecdotes or the letters or journals of historical figures. Howard Zinn's book, *A People's History of the United States,* offers captivating stories of the making of our nation appropriate for sharing in the classroom. Science lessons can be prefaced with accounts of important discoveries, such as those of Madame Curie, George Washington Carver, or Thomas Edison. For example, by learning about Edison's life, teachers could read selected passages from any one of numerous biographical sources or turn the information into a story. The following illustrates one potential story to be read or told to students.

Thomas Edison: An Inventor Throughout His Life

Thomas Edison began conducting experiments during his childhood. Assuming that birds could fly because they ate worms, Edison cut up worms, mixed them with food, gave the concoction to an unsuspecting woman, and waited to see if she would fly. Another experiment he attempted as a boy was to sit on a batch of eggs to see if he could make them hatch.

While undertaking thousands of failed experiments, Edison eventually invented and patented 2500 items, including the electric lamp and phonograph. He was determined

10 KEYS TO EFFECTIVE LISTENING

These keys suggest ways to improve listening. In fact, they're at the heart of developing better listening habits that could last a lifetime.

10 KEYS TO EFFECTIVE LISTENING	WEAK LISTENERS	STRONG LISTENERS
1. Find areas of interest	Tune out "dry" subjects	Ask "What interests me?"
2. Judge content, not delivery	Tune out if delivery is poor	Judge content; skip over delivery errors
3. Be open-minded	Tend to enter into argument	Withhold judgement until comprehension is complete
4. Listen for big ideas	Listen for facts	Listen for central themes
5. Take notes appropriately	Take intensive notes using only one system	Take fewer notes; use different systems, depending on speaker and material
6. Work at listening	Fake attention	Work hard; exhibit active body state
7. Resist distractions	Are easily distracted	Ignore distractions; know how to concentrate
8. Engage intellectually	Resist difficult material; seek simple material	Use dense material as exercise for the mind
9. Consider options	Agree with information if it supports preconceived ideas	Consider diverse points of view before forming opinions
10. Capitalize on the fact that *thought* is faster than speech	Tend to daydream with slow speakers	Challenge, anticipate, summarize; weigh the evidence; listen between the lines

to "give laughter and light" to humanity, but most people scoffed at him. Without losing hope, Edison attempted over 1000 unsuccessful experiments in his efforts to make an electric lamp. When people told him he was wasting his time, energy, and money for nothing, Edison exclaimed, "For nothing! Every time I make an experiment, I get new results. Failures are stepping stones to success."

Dedicated to making electric lamps, Edison said he'd meet his goal by the early 1880s. In October, 1879, he created the first electric lamp, and in so doing, received enormous praise. His invention was impervious to rain or wind, and brightened the darkness of the night. Just as he had hoped, Edison provided people with light and laughter.

Sharing such biographical information brings people and their work to life. Not only do students see the human side of invention, they also learn about important qualities creative individuals possess. Perhaps they will discover similar qualities within themselves or identify new ones to pursue.

Biographical Resources as Subject Matter

An excellent resource to assist teachers in learning about the lives of others is the book *Great Lives* compiled by Simon Boughton. This volume includes biographies of over 1000 men and women from around the world who have made important contributions to humankind. The book is arranged both as a dictionary of famous individuals, and as a chronological timeline; it includes a subject index as well.

An outstanding resource, if it can be located, is *Cradles of Eminence* by Goertzel and Goertzel, which describes the childhoods of 400 famous men and women. There are also educational series that feature biographies of artists, mathematicians, scientists, and others such as *American Women of Achievement, Black Americans of Achievement,* and *World Leaders of Achievement* published by Chelsea House.

Listening to Poetry

Just as sharing the lives of famous men and women enlivens learning, so too can poetry. Short poems can introduce many curriculum units. Teachers might want to compile and share poems with each other to complement any subject matter area. An excellent resource for poems across the curriculum is Koch's and Farrell's *Talking to the Sun: An Illustrated Anthology of Poems for Young People.* Merry Broughton makes poetry across the curriculum available online at her website at www.ceap.wcu.edu/Broughton/Poetryunit.htlm.

Many students write poems that they will gladly share. Two student poems are printed below. The first was written by a 16-year-old and may be appropriate when introducing a lesson on cycles of night and day or on literary character development.

Dawn
by Yvonne MacRae
The death of a star
Is secretly hidden in
The birth of a day.

The next poem was written by a fourth grade student who had recently learned about the Multiple Intelligences. She wrote the poem "for fun" one evening and brought it to her teacher the next morning. This poem serves as an excellent introduction to Gardner's theory for students or adults. Indeed, the authors frequently use the poem at workshops to introduce MI to teachers.

The Intelligence Rap

by Shawna Munson

The eight intelligences are really cool.
We all have them so no one is a fool.

Linguistic deals with writing and with
*   words.*
We have language—we're not like animals
*   or birds.*

Logical-mathematical doesn't need to be
*   a shock.*
If you study real hard, you'll be smarter
*   than Spock!*

Spatial involves seeing, drawing, and art,
Creating different things and taking
*   them apart.*

In case you didn't know, kinesthetic is P.E.
Get fit and coordinated athletically!

Naturalists are collectors of animals and plants.
They like to press flowers and count little ants.

All of these so far are really neat,
But I like musical 'cause it has a beat.

Sometimes, I feel lonely, without any friends,
But interpersonal skills put that to an end.

Intrapersonal skills are when you want to
*   reflect.*
For yourself, you should always have respect.

Now, I've come to the end of my rap.
Learn in many ways and you'll never be a sap.

Teachers as Storytellers

When resources are not readily available, or when a teacher wants to explore teaching content in various ways, storytelling offers an option that delights young and old learners alike. Any topic or subject springs to life when told as a story. Additionally, people of all ages find it easy to remember information when it is encoded in a story. Even though many of us would claim we are not storytellers, all of us already are! Each of us has stories from our own lives we enjoy sharing, many of us like telling jokes, recounting dreams, or even gossiping about others—a practice that may be the basis for future folktales or legends.

Subject Matter Stories

Where can classroom stories come from? Often from our own life experiences. Remembering our own reactions as students when encountering school subjects can provide teachers with real life stories to share with those learning similar content. For example, many of us remember struggling with long division or learning how to participate in a debate. We can share such stories with students, inviting them to guess how we resolved such dilemmas and then contrast their suggestions with our experiences. Additionally, students are often eager to tell stories about their encounters with academic content.

The Cultural Dimensions of Storytelling

Storytelling is also a powerful way to provide students with insight into history and diverse cultures. Students may be interested to learn that storytelling is older than written history. Before reading and writing were common, stories transmitted the oral history of a culture—including the hopes, fears, values, and accomplishments of its people.

For example, during the time of slavery in the United States, stories served a crucial purpose. Since slaves could not gather in groups larger than five, nor speak or write their native African languages or write in English, they used animal stories to forge a sense of community they were denied. The animal they chose for many of their tales was the rabbit—a creature as powerless as the slaves, but one who knew everything happening around him and yet remained silent. The rabbit was called Brer Rabbit.

Multicultural Storytelling Resources

There are numerous resources available for the teacher who wants to introduce students to other cultures, in part, through storytelling. When multicultural stories are told, teachers can ask students to listen for and gather information about diverse cultures. Upon hearing a story, teachers and students might discuss its structure and meaning as well as its cultural implications. Suggested questions include:

What is the setting in the story?

How do you imagine it to look?

Who are the characters?

What are the personal qualities of the characters?

What human traits appear to be respected in the story?

What did you learn about this community?

Are there stereotypes that the story reinforces or diminishes about this culture?

School and local librarians are usually knowledgeable of a variety of storytelling resources. They often eagerly identify stories to accompany any cultural study. We have included a partial list of multicultural storytelling books.

African American Stories:

Uncle Remus and Brer Rabbit by Joel Chandler Harris
Mules and Men by Zora Neale Hurston
The People Could Fly: American Black Folktales by Virginia Hamilton
Shuckin' and Jivin' by Daryl Cumber Dance

American Indian Stories:

North American Indian Legends by Allan Macfarlan (Ed.)
Native American Stories from Puget Sound by Vi Hilbert
On the Trail Made of Dawn: Native American Creation Stories by M.L. Webster
Native Ways: California Indian Stories and Memories by Yolanda Montijo

Asian Stories:

The Chi-lin Purse: A Collection of Ancient Chinese Stories by Linda Fang and Jeanne Lee
Floating Clouds, Floating Dreams: Favorite Asian Folktales by I.K. Junne (Ed.)
Little One-Inch and other Japanese Children's Favorite Stories by Florence Sakade and Oshisuke Kurosaki
American Eyes: New Asian-American Short Stories for Young Adults by Lori Carlson and Cynthia Kadohata

Hispanic Stories:

Mexican Folk Tales by Anthony Campos
The Circuit: Stories from the Life of a Migrant Child by Francisco Jimenez
Latino Read-Aloud Stories by Maite Suarez-Rivas (Ed.)

Jewish Stories:

A Treasury of Jewish Folklore by Nathan Ausubel
Rachel the Clever and Other Jewish Folktales by Josepha Sherman
Mara's Stories: Glimmers in the Darkness by Gary Schmidt

Female Heroine Stories:

Cut from the Same Cloth: American Women of Myth, Legend and Tall Tale by Robert San Souci

The Woman in the Moon and Other Tales of Forgotten Heroines by James Riordan

Chocolate for a Teen's Heart by Kay Allenbaugh

Collections of Stories from Diverse Cultures:

Folktales Told Around the World by Richard Dorson

Join in: Multiethnic Short Stories by Outstanding Writers for Young Adults by Don Gallo (Ed.)

Wonder Tales from Around the World by Heather Forest and David Boston

Resources on the Art of Storytelling:

The World of Storytelling by Anne Pellowski

Telling Stories Your Way: Storytelling & Reading Aloud in the Classroom by Robert Barton

Listening to Lectures

Although it is likely that there will be fewer lecture formats in classrooms of the future, they are, nevertheless, one effective means of presenting information to large groups of older students. As a result, students should learn effective ways to listen to them. Although such skills are rarely taught, some suggestions follow to sharpen your students' listening abilities.

1. Teachers might present a mini-lecture on an unfamiliar topic. To begin, give the title of the talk and ask students to use the following active listening practices by writing:
   - what they already know about the subject
   - what questions they have about it
   - how they feel about listening to this talk

Then, when the lecture begins, ask students to:
- outline or mindmap the significant points
- underline the most important ideas
- note in some way, such as with asterisks or stars, any point that is unclear or that is particularly interesting
- put in the margin questions they wish to have answered

After the mini-lecture is finished, ask students to write or explain:
- what they learned that was new
- how this topic relates to what they already know
- its relevance to their lives

Respond to any questions students might have after the lecture and suggest they note the answers. Then have students discuss their notes with partners. It is especially effective for some struggling students to discuss and identify key ideas and then add to their notes as appropriate.

2. Another useful exercise is to ask students to listen to a mini-lecture without taking notes or making mindmaps. Immediately following the lecture, request that they list everything they remember, and categorize their information into topics. Then suggest they work with a partner to compare lists and fill in any key points they missed. This exercise develops both listening and memory skills.

3. Teachers can provide students with blank listening guides to complete as information is presented. For some students, it may be helpful to specify the main points to focus their attention before a lecture begins. Such processes can help students think in organized ways, and learn how to structure future presentations of their own. A sample follows.

LISTENING GUIDE

Student name: _____

Speaker's name: _____

Title or subject of talk: _____

Introductory ideas: _____
_____

First main point: _____
_____

    Supporting details or examples: _____
_____

Second main point: _____
_____

    Supporting details or examples: _____
_____

Third main point: _____
_____

    Supporting details or examples: _____
_____

Concluding ideas: _____
_____

Other ideas: _____
_____

Questions this presentation raised: _____
_____
_____
_____

Speaking

Effective speaking involves not only the words we use, but the way we say them, our tone of voice, facial expressions, posture, and gestures. Albert Mehrabian, author of *Silent Messages*, suggests that only seven percent of what we communicate in speech has to do with the words we use, 38 percent has to do with tone of voice, and 55 percent with our facial expressions and body language. If so, then speaking involves all the intelligences!

It is essential for teachers to model strong speaking skills because good modeling has a profound effect on the speaking habits of students. Teachers may make a point of using colorful or sophisticated vocabulary frequently, playing with puns, jokes, and riddles, or eloquently describing a personal experience.

The classroom can provide a supportive environment for learning to speak effectively as teachers create a relaxed and positive atmosphere for students to converse and discuss ideas. These are not classrooms in which the teacher is doing most of the talking! Questions that stimulate discussion should be thought-provoking and not easily answered in a few words. It is also important for teachers to ask open-ended, interesting questions to which they may not know the answer. As a result, stimulating discussions can take place that may lead to surprising insights and new possibilities for learning for all involved.

Clearly, students benefit from practicing and developing speaking skills through such exercises as the following.

Students as Storytellers

Some students will enthusiastically volunteer for opportunities to tell stories to their peers. Others will find the idea daunting. Yet listening to stories involves numerous listening skills, and telling stories requires linguistic stretches. Storytelling, an entertaining and powerful form of linguistic communication, teaches students about the rhythm, pitch, and nuances of language. Educators interested in encouraging storytelling in their classrooms might want to consider the following guidelines.

Storytelling Guidelines

1. *Model storytelling yourself.*

2. *Identify local storytellers to visit your classroom.* You may want to learn whether there is a storytelling guild near you or perhaps, as in Philadelphia, an official storyteller for the city.

3. *Help students find stories*—from class content, dreams, family or school events, stories they already know, anthologies, or interviews with senior citizens.

4. *Teach students some of the skills of storytelling such as:*
   - begin with an interesting opening
   - keep the number of characters manageable
   - make sure the story contains images that listeners can "see" or imagine
   - encourage the use of simile and metaphor
   - animate key points in the story with sound effects, voice, hands, and body movements
   - keep the voice clear, expressive, and well-paced
   - make eye contact with the audience
   - consider whether there will be audience participation

5. *Practice storytelling with the whole class.* The teacher can select one story and read it part by part to the class, asking students for embellishments to make the story vivid and entertaining. The whole class could divide into groups. Each group could be assigned a section of the story to learn and then tell in sequence.

6. *For beginning storytellers, anxiety can be relieved when students tell their stories to small groups of four or five peers rather than the whole class.* Students who volunteer may tell their stories to larger groups. Also, telling stories to younger children often reduces unnecessary tension.

Classroom Discussions

Classroom discussions occur in nearly every subject at all grade levels. There are logistics to address such as the arrangement of physical space and ways to involve everyone in the conversation before discussions will be positive and satisfying. For example, teachers might consider how student desks or tables are configured. Does the current arrangement facilitate or impede student discussions? Might a U shape, desks placed facing each other, or a circle better accommodate interaction?

Human dynamics influence the quality of classroom discourse. Some students must learn to refrain from dominating the conversation. Others need encouragement to participate. It is challenging to keep a discussion on track, to pose higher level questions, and to teach students how to assume greater responsibility for leading classroom discussions. To address these and other issues, some suggestions follow for initiating, implementing, and debriefing discussions as well as involving everyone equally in the process.

The Five Stages of a Classroom Discussion

As Richard Arends (1994) indicates in *Learning to Teach,* effective classroom discussions typically consist of five stages. These stages, when intentionally planned for, strengthen student discourse and reveal where intervention might be warranted. Some teachers assume that discussions require less planning than lectures or cooperative learning activities. Even though spontaneity and flexibility are important aspects of discussions, it is prior planning by the teacher that makes these features possible. When discussions are to be conducted in a classroom, teachers may want to plan for the five following stages to ensure meaningful dialogue with and among their students.

1. *Explain the purpose of the discussion.* Teachers should explain what will be discussed as well as appropriate standards of student behavior. Questions can be posed, issues raised, or a puzzling situation presented to initiate the conversation.

2. *Hold the discussion.* Teachers can ask students specific questions or request volunteers to initiate conversation. It is important to ensure that responses are listened to with courtesy. On the blackboard, a flip chart, or the overhead projector, a student volunteer might list or mindmap discussion contributions. Such processes keep the discourse on track as well as prevent redundant contributions.

Teachers can model effective discussion skills by responding to student questions in diverse ways. For example, to reflect on student ideas, statements such as, "I heard you say . . ." or "that is interesting because . . ." are helpful. In attempting to encourage students to consider diverse perspectives or alternative possibilities, a teacher might assume the role of devil's advocate, or ask, "You have provided one point of view about this topic. Are there other points of view?" "How do your ideas compare with . . . ?" David Perkins, Harvard psychologist, calls such questioning "unpacking your thinking."

Wait time should also be provided. When students are asked a question approximately one minute of time should be provided before responses are considered. The teacher should also observe student participation carefully, encouraging those who are not comfortable speaking and keeping others from monopolizing discussions.

3. *Keep the discussion on track.* Students will often bring up issues not related to the topic at hand. Teachers can gently state that the focus of the conversation has shifted, and that the discussion should revert to the original topic. If many students appear interested in a subject raised by a peer, the teacher may choose to set aside classroom time for students to pursue the other topic later.

4. *End the discussion.* Discussions, like other lessons, should be brought to closure. The teacher may want to summarize what has been said, relate the discussion to other classroom learnings, or use it as a bridge to highlight new information.

5. *Debrief the discussion.* Teachers and students will both benefit from talking about how how the discussion proceeded. Ask questions such as, "How did the discussion work today?" "What would have made it more effective?" "Did everyone have a chance to participate?" "Did we listen effectively to everyone?"

Once students see discussions modeled effectively by the teacher and understand the stages of such discourse, they can then assume responsibility for leading either small- or whole-group discussions themselves.

Involving Everyone in Discussions

In whole-class discussions many teachers find that only a small percentage of students actively participate. The following strategies may encourage equitable participation.

1. *Assign a discussion monitor.* This student keeps track of everyone's participation. If she notices that one student talks repeatedly, she might give that student a note asking that he refrain from speaking until others have had turns.

2. *Provide each student with three or four "talking tokens."* A token must be relinquished whenever a student makes a contribution. When all of a student's tokens are gone, she must refrain from speaking, which encourages others with tokens remaining to enter into the conversation.

3. *Use "talking circles" with students seated in a circle formation. An item such as a feather or stone can be passed clockwise from one student to the next.* Students must receive the object before making their contributions. This process can be adapted by having students remain at their desks but requiring that they raise their hands and receive the object before talking.

4. *Encourage a variety of contributions.* Students who are English language learners or speak nonstandard English can be encouraged to make contributions in their languages. This gives the teacher and classmates opportunities to consider language diversity. Teachers can then restate or embellish what the contributor offered. Teachers might also contrast respectfully the differences between languages used in the community and standard English used in the mainstream classroom.

Facilitating Small-Group Discussions

Many students and adults are hesitant to participate in large, whole-group discussions and prefer instead to talk with fewer people. One way to broaden participation for all students is to use the collaborative strategies offered below.

Think-Pair-Share To encourage student reflection on the content of a lecture, a film, or a provocative question, the teacher can pose a question or raise an issue. Students are given one to two minutes to think individually. They are then paired with classmates to discuss their thinking for approximately five minutes. For the final step, each pair shares with the whole class what they have discussed.

Buzz Groups Teachers can arrange students in groups of three to six to discuss ideas about a particular topic. Each group assigns one person to serve as the recorder who lists all of the ideas suggested by the group. After several minutes of discussion, the teacher asks the recorders to summarize the ideas and opinions expressed in his or her group.

Fishbowls Fishbowls are effective group processes to use during the middle or end of a unit. To conduct a fishbowl, classroom chairs or desks are arranged in a large circle, with a smaller, inner circle of chairs provided for four to six students. Those sitting in the inner circle are in "the fishbowl," and they have the task of discussing a topic while the rest of the students watch. Any students in the fishbowl, after having contributed whatever they wanted to the conversation, vacate their seats. Observers are free to fill any vacancy in the inner circle. The fishbowl continues until the discussion reaches a natural conclusion or the teacher brings closure to the process.

Memorizing

Although memorization has fallen out of favor in many classrooms, there is no better way to free the mind to concentrate on oral presentation or writing skills than to memorize basic facts, a poem, or lines in a play. The fringe benefit is that many of these pieces are remembered for life and provide solace, amusement, or inspiration when recalled.

Young students may memorize nursery rhymes, jingles, or short, lively poems, such as those in Jill Bennet's *Noisy Poems*, to say first as a group to inspire confidence, and then as solo volunteers. Older students may wish to memorize longer pieces, such as Poe's "The Raven" or Langston Hughes' "The Dreamkeeper" to present to the class, perhaps choosing to use sound effects, background music, or costumes. Choral reading at any age develops greater flexibility in range and tone of voice, and conveys the rhythm of language while encouraging emotional expression. Since singing often enhances the quality and flexibility of the voice, it is useful to have the class sing poems that have been set to music.

Poems or jingles can also be written by students or the teacher to use as mnemonic devices to remember information in many subjects such as history, science, or geography. For example, jingles can be made up to remember the order of the planets in the solar system or the process of the water cycle. Medical students have for generations used rhymes to remember the names of bones in the hand and other parts of the human body. Memory tricks can even improve spelling.

Improving Memory

When students are asked to memorize any kind of content, it is important to realize that repetition alone has little value unless accompanied by active student involvement. Information will, quite literally, go in one ear and out the other without strong memory encoding. To help students memorize important information, the following strategies can be suggested.

1. Students might first review the entire piece they are to memorize. This gives an overview of the task and provides mental hooks for later learning.

2. Students can "cluster" or "chunk" portions of the content to memorize it, and create visual images for each section. Their visual images can be drawn or simply imagined.

3. Content can also be set to music to help facilitate long-term memory.

4. Students might tape-record what they want to memorize. They can play the tape back frequently to enhance recall of the content.

5. Short memorizing sessions are often more productive than long ones. Explain to students that memory work should not exceed more than 30 minutes at a time.

6. Review schedules are necessary for information to be retained. Explain that memory is greatly reinforced when items are reviewed the following day, a week later, a month later, and so on.

Reports

Students are often asked to give reports in class. Report-giving typically begins in early elementary grades with "Show and Tell' and progresses to formal research reports often required in high school classes. The kinds of reports teachers assign vary greatly in content, format, and assessment criteria. Students benefit by explicitly knowing how to format their presentations. Typical guidelines for formal reports often include:

Guidelines for Reports

- select a topic suitable for the audience
- organize the presentation
- plan an attention-grabbing opening
- use colorful anecdotes and specific examples
- involve the audience in some activity, and
- plan an effective conclusion

Further points include suggestions for oral reports:

- choose appropriate vocabulary for the topic and audience
- engage the audience with eye contact and body language
- use clear diction and good grammar
- avoid speaking in long, rambling sentences
- use effective and varied expression, and
- avoid using "ahs" and "ums"

To help stimulate interest in conducting research for their reports, students can identify the facts, suppositions, and questions they have about their selected topic. Questions can be posed such as:

What do I know for sure?

What do I think I know?

What do I want to know?

As with peer review of written work, the response of the audience to an oral report should first of all be positive. Feedback can be given in an "appreciation sandwich" format by first specifying what was good about the presentation, then offering suggestions for improvement, and ending with another positive comment.

Interviews

Interviewing others is one way for students to develop oral information-gathering skills. Before conducting interviews, students need to distinguish between an interview and a conversation. Although both are forms of oral communication, conversations consist of informal talk or the exchange of ideas on topics of interest to those speaking. By contrast, interviews have a predetermined goal; the interviewer seeks specific information and avoids topics that may be considered irrelevant. For example, doctors interview patients about their symptoms; reporters interview people to gather information for a story; high school students interview professionals to learn about different careers; personnel directors interview prospective employees. Teachers and students may want to brainstorm lists of interview situations and discuss the purposes inherent in each. It may be appropriate for students to interview those of diverse cultures, careers, or expertise to complement their academic studies. Students should have opportunities to do practice interviews before conducting their formal ones.

It is helpful for students to know what constitutes effective interviewing skills. Some suggestions follow which may be used to prepare for or assess student interviews once completed.

To prepare students for interviewing, the teacher may want to divide the class into small groups to role play different interview circumstances. Perhaps students will be interviewing younger children at their school, famous athletes or artists, community activists, school board members, or even each other. In their small groups, students can brainstorm appropriate questions for each circumstance, as well as role play interviews. While two students role play, other group members can observe the effectiveness of the interview and suggest improvements. Such activities assist students in developing the skills for the real life interviews they are about to conduct.

Reading

Literature serves as the foundation for developing the whole gamut of verbal-linguistic intelligence. Stories, novels, biographies, essays, plays, and poems are springboards for discussion and listening skills, speaking projects, and creative or analytical writing. Literature offers food for thought, models the effective use of language, and stimulates intellectual development.

An increasing number of curriculum planners and teachers are supplementing or replacing textbooks with real books that offer examples of the finest writing in various genres and that may prove to be more interesting and relevant to student interests.

EFFECTIVE INTERVIEWING SKILLS

- Be prepared for the interview. Know what you want to ask and what the purpose of the interview is. You may want to give the interviewee your questions ahead of time.

- Schedule the interview at a mutually agreed upon time.

- Know how you are going to take notes and have the appropriate supplies. If you are tape-recording the interview, secure permission from the interviewee before proceeding.

- Ask open-ended questions that elicit more than a simple "yes" or "no" response. Use question prompts such as "What is your experience or opinion about . . . ," "Can you please describe . . . ," "Can you give me an example of . . . "

- Maintain a friendly facial expression, adopt positive body language, and be polite.

- Be a careful listener. Refrain from asserting your own opinions.

- Keep the interview on the subject.

- Keep the interview within preset time limits.

- Once the interview has ended, review what was said to help retain the information in your long-term memory.

- Write a thank-you note to the person you interviewed.

Finding Materials

A classroom library can supplement or replace reading textbooks. Reading materials can include classic works in fiction and nonfiction and expand to include magazines, manuals, and pamphlets.

Developing a Classroom Library

Teachers can develop their classroom libraries through numerous ways that include:

- working closely with school and public librarians and media specialists

- asking colleagues, professors, and classroom guests to suggest appropriate reading materials

- involving parents in recommending and donating books

- forming liaisons with community literacy groups and newspaper personnel

- meeting with paperback book distributors to work out special price deductions

- having students review, recommend, and catalog materials

- securing a range of multicultural resources that include picture books, poetry memoirs, biographic scripts, classic fiction, "how to" manuals, and contemporary nonfiction works

- introducing students to electronic databases or the Internet to access current information on topics they find interesting.

Even with large classes, it is important for teachers to identify the developmental levels and interests of individual students. Reluctant readers may perk up when they have opportunities to read books about their interests such as hobbies, pets, inventions, scientific discoveries, favorite sports, music groups, or foreign countries. Reading materials should also address diverse reading levels. School librarians can be good allies in helping teachers identify materials for varying ability levels.

Words in the Classroom

In every classroom there are words on the walls, bulletin boards, and blackboards explaining classroom rules, reviewing vocabulary, listing assignments, and describing daily schedules. Teachers can intentionally use words to enhance reading skills. Motivators to encourage reading follow.

Motivating Students to Read

1. Post daily quotations or questions to engage student interest in academic content.

2. Create "word walls" that display words in large letters for easy viewing. The words can be grouped according to categories such as high-frequency words, adjectives, content area vocabulary, commonly misspelled words, and active verbs. Five or more words can be added weekly and students can refer to the walls as needed. Typically, as time progresses, students' reliance on word walls diminishes.

3. Add names or labels to classroom posters, blackboards, and student papers.

4. Set up a message board or have a notebook on a podium to spark informal reading and writing. Students are curious about what their peers and teachers write, and will avidly read what's newly posted.

Other important reading resources in the classroom are the worksheets students use. As often as possible, teachers can prepare their own worksheets and exercises based on classroom experiences and vocabulary. Such materials are usually more relevant for students than impersonally written textbooks. Since students learn at varying rates and in different ways, textbooks and workbooks have to be adapted and extended regardless of their quality.

Many students suffer from poor reading skills. Fortunately, there are ways teachers can enhance the quantity and quality of reading in all content areas. Suggestions follow for ways to teach reading across the curriculum.

Reading Across the Curriculum

1. Model your own reading processes out loud to make such processes explicit for students.

2. Give students a clear purpose for reading a selection.

3. Ask what students may already know about the topic and apply that knowledge to the text to be read.

4. Identify and define new vocabulary words and phrases, and ask students to look for them when they read.

5. Explain text features such as headings, graphs, and pictures to help students predict the content. Ask students to make and test their predictions.

6. Chunk the content into sections that require five to ten minutes of reading. Ask students to read the section and note its key ideas individually, and then in pairs to check and revise their thinking.

7. Reflect on key ideas from assigned readings with the whole class.

8. Encourage recreational reading such as sports statistics for math or science fiction books for science.

Reading for Understanding

Gordon Cawelti (1999) in the *Handbook of Research on Improving Student Achievement* cites numerous studies that show reading a variety of materials both in and outside of school yields strong vocabulary and comprehension skills. Allocating blocks of classroom time to independent reading, teaching comprehension skills, and engaging students in sharing and discussing what they read are common practices that yield positive results. Below we list specific strategies teachers can use to boost comprehension skills.

Improving Reading Comprehension

1. Students can use three types of questions to improve their comprehension: questions that are asked before, during, and after reading a selection.

   Sample prereading questions include: "What do I already know about this topic?" "What should I learn?" "What predictions can I make about the content?"

   Questions to consider during reading include: "What are the most important facts or parts of the story?" "How does the structure of the text help me understand its ideas?" "How would I summarize what I have read so far?" "Did my earlier predictions come true?"

   Questions after reading include: "What information did I learn?" "What are some examples?" "What were the most important points?" "Did my predictions come true?" "Are there parts I should reread?"

2. Twice weekly, students can engage in sustained silent reading with self-selected materials. Some of this reading will occur in school and some outside the school day. Students can maintain weekly reading logs, read a set number of pages a month, and do culminating projects in which they reflect on themselves as readers.

3. Students can use reciprocal teaching techniques to work their way through reading assignments. These techniques include predicting, clarifying, questioning, and summarizing what is being read. To clarify what they have read, for example, students might reread portions of a selection, discuss the content in small groups, read further in the text to see if the meaning becomes clear, or connect the content with their lives.

4. Comprehension can be improved when students consider both content and process questions. Content questions ask "What is the key idea?" and process questions ask "How did you arrive at that answer?"

Writing

Writing cannot be segregated from other language acts. It is reinforced by speaking, listening, and reading. Fully incorporating language arts activities into all content areas helps students communicate more effectively and learn more thoroughly. As in speech, writing carries ideas from one person to another with distinct purposes and meanings. Students, through a variety of writing activities, can develop a sense of audience and perceive writing as a relevant act occurring between themselves, others, and society.

As with other areas of verbal-linguistic intelligence, it is essential for teachers to model effective writing skills, demonstrating pleasure in the writing process and efforts to refine their skills. Teachers interested in improving their writing ability can find support and inspiration in such sources as William Zinsser's *On Writing Well*, Natalie Goldberg's *Writing Down the Bones*, or Patricia O'Conner's *Words Fail Me*. A dictionary, thesaurus, and Strunk and White's *Elements of Style* ought to be accessible in any classroom.

Teachers can model specific writing skills for students whenever they think out loud about how to choose a topic, read samples of their own writing for students to critique (this takes courage), or write occasional lengthy comments on student papers with great care. They may wish to share with students a piece of their writing at various stages, pointing out the number of revisions and corrections on subsequent drafts.

Categories of Writing

James Britton, in his classic book *Language and Learning,* categorizes writing in a way that offers insight into the kinds of written work teachers assign. By reading the following descriptions of Britton's four categories, teachers can identify diverse writing approaches that may be appropriate for their lessons.

Britton's categories include the **mechanical** uses of writing such as multiple-choice exercises, fill-in-the blank, short-answer, math calculations, transcription from written or oral material, and translation.

The second category has to do with the **informational** uses of writing, such as notetaking, recording of experience (in a report or diary), summary, analysis, theory, or the persuasive uses of writing.

The third includes the **personal** uses of writing, such as diaries and journals, letters, and notes.

The last includes the **imaginative** uses of writing, such as in stories and poetry.

Although it is important that students write accurately and correctly on tasks related to the first and second categories, it is also important to focus on increasing the number of experiences in the other two categories since these hold the greatest promise for exercising and developing verbal-linguistic intelligence.

Writing Across the Curriculum

Many content-area teachers are hesitant to assume the role of language arts teachers when they have an abundance of content to teach in their disciplines. There are, however, ways to promote linguistic activities in all disciplines that deepen subject matter understanding. A brief survey of language-based activities is offered below.

History and Social Studies

1. Students can conduct local history projects and then create newspapers or news broadcasts of what they learn.

2. In some schools, students with special expertise in technology are doing research on computer networks for their state legislatures and senates. Letter writing about local social or political issues can also be e-mailed to prominent citizens or groups.

3. Correspondence among students in urban or rural schools can provide insight into the similarities and differences both groups encounter.

World Language and Bilingual Education

1. After listening to songs in another language, students can use new and familiar vocabulary to make their own word games by writing short definitions, antonyms, homonyms, or synonyms for some of the lyrics.

2. Students might take photographs of their school and local environments, bring the pictures to school, and then write about what the photos portray. At some schools, such activities have evolved into school guidebooks for newly arrived, non-English speaking students and their families.

3. Teachers can bring folklore, poems, riddles, and puzzles from various cultures into the classroom, read part way through a selection, and then ask the class to complete the piece. Student-suggested endings can be compared with the original literature.

Science and Mathematics

1. Journals or logs can serve as notebooks for students to record explanations and examples given in class, to list their questions, confusions, or criticisms, and to offer suggestions to improve classroom learning experiences.

2. Take-home writing projects for math and science might focus on local community issues. For example, students can research and write about local development and its environmental and economic affects.

3. Students can watch science fiction programs on television and write brief analyses of what is fact and what is fiction.

Language Arts

English teachers are often hesitant to include science or social studies content in their curriculum. However, there are many scientific and social issues that provide stimulating topics for students to consider. Possibilities include environmental, social, or political issues, the space program, genetic engineering, computers, video games, energy alternatives, and nutrition. In addition, some students would enjoy writing about popular culture or the current or future job market.

Writing Options for All Content Areas

In any subject area, students may be especially motivated to write after a field trip, seeing a demonstration or video, or listening to an interesting guest speaker. When debriefing such experiences, the teacher can record student comments on the board, and categorize them into separate topics. For example, after an early elementary grade's trip to the zoo, the teacher might ask what animals were seen, what their environments were like, and what students learned as they observed the habitats of different animals. Students can use the recorded vocabulary (which has already been correctly spelled) and add their own ideas to write in any one of several formats.

Other Stimuli

Students also enjoy writing to taped sound effects, or lively, dramatic, or mysterious music, as suggested in the musical chapter. Pantomime and creative dramatics activities, as described in the chapter on kinesthetic intelligence, lead to interesting writing options as well. Students of any age can generate possible topics by doing a "quick-write," starting with a "fuse" such as "On the first day of the year 2050, I . . ." "You will never believe this, but . . ." and writing for five or ten minutes as quickly as possible without attention to mechanics. These processes often access ideas lurking in the deep sources of creativity.

Teachers can suggest numerous alternatives for writing assignments. Instead of traditional procedures where every student completes the same assignment, students can make their own decisions about which options best suit their topics and their interests. All students should be held accountable to the outcomes the teacher seeks, such as the effective use of writing mechanics, the elaboration of key ideas with examples and evidence of individual student voice. However, the formats for writing may vary, as the following list suggests.

Student Writing Options

scripts for dramas, television, or radio productions

petitions

imaginary diaries

directions or "how to" manuals

autobiographical material

writing from another person's perspective

songs

bulletin boards

scrolls

advertisements

classroom newsletters

poems

folktales or myths

pamphlets or brochures

letters

dialogues

awards

posters

book jackets

prescriptions for help in a content area

freewriting samples

self-evaluations

checklists

sequels

interviews

booklets

editorial essays

Presenting one's written work to the class provides a powerful learning opportunity for the author as well as for fellow students to view the same topic through numerous linguistic lenses. Students can also practice their editorial skills by giving feedback to a classmate on pre-determined writing criteria.

Getting Started with Writing

Even though they may have interesting ideas for possible topics, writers of any age often have difficulty starting their work. Professional writers have suggestions for overcoming this obstacle. One author begins each session by turning on lively music and dancing out her ideas. Another makes "clusters" or mindmaps, filling pages as quickly as she can with free-flowing ideas. This author writes her books directly from mindmap to computer. Others like to write with certain kinds of paper and pencils or other special tools. Still others find it useful to change environments—by going into another room, exercising briefly, or working in a place that feels comfortable and inviting. One well-known writer spends ten or fifteen minutes reading one of his favorite authors before he begins writing. He says doing so gives him a running start for the day.

Other possibilities to jumpstart writing include foregoing the beginning by writing the middle of the piece, or writing the ending first, writing with or without music, jotting down notes with colored pens or pencils or on colored paper, quick writing on the computer, stream-of-consciousness writing, talking ideas over with a friend, talking into a tape-recorder, or brainstorming ideas with a classmate.

Another idea for writing is so unusual that it often produces startling results. Glossalalia is made-up language or gibberish. Students might attempt writing an entire paragraph in glossalalia (the weirder the words the better) and then translating it. It may be helpful to provide them with the following sentences to "translate" before writing their own:

> Weinsth guek einc ei! Ptionsiu dfetkj, atin et tetp slier ae ads etioj aseint. "Laeltij, iaeltij, iaelti," giaj Skloiae. "Lawei di Ieti?"

Possible to do in pen or pencil, this jumpstarter is even more fun on a computer and provides a unique warm-up for writers of all ages.

The Real Work of Writing

Many students have experienced the humiliation of receiving corrected papers covered with red marks. It may have appeared to them that correcting errors in grammar, spelling, or punctuation is the final step in writing a paper. Yet, as all of us know from our own efforts, writing is a process, with each draft warranting not only corrections but numerous revisions and refinements. It is important for students to realize that most professional writers spend a good deal of time rewriting, revising, deleting, adding, and changing words, phrases, and paragraphs, and polishing the entire piece before they submit their work to an editor. There are many ways to involve students in the process of writing. Some suggestions follow.

Nurturing an Appreciation for the Process of Writing

1. Teachers can review samples of professional writing with their students. They may wish, for example, to duplicate an article such as an 800 word newspaper column that is crisp and succinct and encourages the reader to read further. Students can analyze what makes the selection lively and suggest the choices the author may have made to create the well-written piece.

2. Local writers might provide earlier drafts of their published works and explain how and why they made the changes they did. Students might then analyze drafts of their own writing to determine ways to improve on their initial efforts.

3. Timely and frequent feedback is important as students practice their writing skills. Students may initially receive feedback from their peers or even write collaboratively, but individual appointments with the teacher at various stages of their work provide important opportunities for feedback and guidance.

4. Teachers may offer constructive suggestions on first drafts and withhold grading until final revisions are made. It is often in the process of discussing revisions and corrections that students are the most receptive to learning about the mechanics of language. Lessons in punctuation, parts of speech, and grammatical usage are not always retained when presented out of context. A quick lesson at a "teachable moment" when students are struggling with some problem may be the most relevant and lasting way for them to learn.

5. Students who use word processors can produce written work that looks deceptively polished when nicely formatted on a computer, yet most likely still requires reworking. Students will find it useful to print out the first draft double-spaced, then do the revising by hand. In this way, they will have a record of the change they make.

6. Keeping all drafts in sequence in a portfolio provides both students and teachers with comprehensive records of writing progress. Specific information about portfolios can be found in the assessment chapter.

Writing Groups

Most teachers do not have time to correct all the written work their students produce. Since there is no better way for students to learn to write than by writing, managing student feedback is an important challenge. One way to ensure that students receive feedback and develop editing skills is to use writing groups. Such groups typically consist of three to four students who work together for the duration of a project, quarter, or in some cases for longer periods of time. The group serves as a sounding board for ideas about a writing topic, gives feedback on rough drafts, listens to readings, makes suggestions for improvement, and sees the writing project through from beginning to end. Above all, the writing group offers support and encouragement for the difficult task of improving written work.

As writing groups are formed, it is important to discuss how students can offer constructive feedback to one another. Teachers can explain the negative effects of "rejection slip trauma" and how important it is to phrase suggestions in positive ways.

Together, the students and teacher may identify appropriate ways to respond to the writing of others. Some suggestions follow.

- Listen carefully and thoughtfully as the piece is being read.
- Note what is especially good about the writing, being as specific as possible in regard to content, mechanics, theme, tone, vocabulary, form, and general effect.
- Note ways in which the writing might be improved, once again making specific suggestions.
- Take turns reporting back to the author, always beginning with positive comments.
- As the author, listen carefully and take notes to guide later revisions.

Writing groups, like many other strategies suggested throughout this book, shift the role of the teacher to that of a "guide on the side." As students shoulder more responsibility for their academic work, they must organize, manage, and refine their learning as well as provide assistance to their peers. When given such responsibility, students usually rise to the occasion, much to their personal benefit and their teacher's delight.

Technology That Enhances Verbal-Linguistic Intelligence

Just as the printing press revolutionized learning and thinking in the fifteenth century, so has the computer created a similar revolution today. Through worldwide databases and computer networks students have direct access to current information. In every field of knowledge, educational systems are transforming as both teachers and students learn to use multimedia technology.

Because software changes so frequently, we avoid suggesting specific programs, but instead identify resources that offer continual recommendations and updates. For example, the International Society for Technology in Education (ISTE) at www.iste.org and Riverdeep's The Learning Company at www.riverdeep.com offer extensive resources for teachers.

Children who cannot yet read are writing stories on the computer with software that reads back to them what they have written. New programs allow children to write and insert graphics in rebus-like texts or make it possible to format writing projects in different shapes, write words in unusual forms and sizes, add accompanying sound effects, and wrap illustrations around the text. Such programs are highly motivating for both beginning and more accomplished writers.

Today's computer banks are filled with information on every conceivable subject, plus online experts including university professors, researchers, and scientists offer students an inexhaustible supply of information. Course content in any subject can be enriched and updated from such sources, and it is frequently the students themselves who access and share the information. Resources on verbal-linguistic intelligence abound on such sites as The Literacy Directory at www.literacydirectory.org; the National Council for Teachers of English, at www.ncte.org; the National Institute for Literacy with an electronic newsletter at www.nifl.gov/nifl/eliteracy; and the National Research Center on English Learning and Achievement at http://cela.albany.edu/.

Increasingly, user-friendly computer programs are making it possible to combine information in different forms, including words, images, and sounds. Students can store, sort, and cross-reference information, notes, bibliographies, and create multimedia reports to make an adventure of learning. Teachers are able to develop their own courseware, create databases linking documents, present preprogrammed slide presentations from videodiscs, and enrich their courses with a wealth of technology further described in the chapters on each of the other intelligences. Sites that include examples of teachers' projects include The George Lucas Educational Foundation at www.glef.org; New Horizons for Learning at www.newhorizons.org; and The Learning Space at www.learningspace.org.

The computer encourages students to revise and rewrite compositions and thus develop greater fluency and a more effective style. Recopying by hand or typewriter often inhibits ongoing correction and revision, but the computer facilitates these processes and gives students a greater sense of control over their writing. When students see their work in professional-looking formats they become more interested in studying and mastering the mechanics that will give it final polish.

Learning keyboarding in early elementary school today is as important as learning to write with a pencil, and learning to use a word processor is as important as learning to type. Children are encouraged to use these skills in communicating and collaborating with distant students on a variety of projects through an increasing number of electronic networks such as iEARN at www.iearn.org or the National Geographic Kids Network at www.nationalgeographic.com/kids. Telephones and modems essential to this process should be standard equipment in every classroom.

Electronic technology is also having an enormous impact on the development of speaking skills, as children find it possible to communicate with new friends around the country and world. Just as the computer has enhanced writing skills, so audiotape-recording, videotaping, and video conferencing are having positive effects on oral fluency. When students observe and hear themselves speaking they learn to express themselves more effectively.

Technology offers new communication and learning opportunities to students with multiple handicaps and "different abilities." For example, students who are able to move but cannot speak may write on computers that then "say" what they wrote. Students who are physically unable to move can talk into a computer that writes as they speak, or they can operate the computer with a pointing device, a mouth- or head-stick, or by simply focusing or blinking the eyes on specific keys. There are now keyboards adapted for single-hand users, expanded keyboards, or special input devices that replace mice. Some students with learning disabilities who find it difficult to read can be helped with enlarged character and voice synthesis devices, and Braille input devices are available for the blind.

Comprehensive resources for information on assistive technologies for those with special needs are available from such organizations as the University of Washington's DO-IT Program (Disabilities, Opportunities, Internetworking, and Technology) at www.washington.edu/doit, or from The Rehabilitation Engineering and Assistive Technology Society of North America at www.resna.org.

The development of linguistic skills for all populations can be catalyzed by remarkable new electronic tools for accessing and managing information and communicating, learning, and developing intelligence in unprecedented ways.

Summary
▪ ▪

How do we help students fall in love with words? A passion for language can lead students to savor the sound of words, to respect and use their power responsibly, to explore their subtle shades of meaning, and to draw upon them in endless ways to express love or sympathy, win an argument, explain a complex task, teach a child, or simply to enjoy communicating with others.

There are examples of students who have fallen in love with words in Multiple Intelligences classrooms. As the authors, Linda and Bruce Campbell, discovered in 1999 when writing their book *MI and Student Achievement,* students thrive in classrooms that emphasize rigor and multimodal learning approaches. In fact, disparity between white and minority student literacy achievement narrowed in significant ways when MI teaching was used at Russell Elementary School in Lexington, Kentucky, at EXPO for Excellence Elementary School in St. Paul, Minnesota, and at Key Learning Community in Indianapolis, Indiana, during the late 1990s.

At these three sites, teachers favored enrichment over remediation, student collaboration instead of competition, and high expectations for everyone. In some cases, students' reading and writing scores doubled after three years of MI instruction, and in others, students' literacy scores on standardized tests surpassed those of their peers at district and state levels. Teachers and students at these sites believed that everyone was talented in some areas and challenged in others. Such a belief meant that everyone had to work hard at some subjects. For those students who didn't readily excel at linguistic tasks, extra effort was needed and invested without stigma. At the same time, student strengths could be used to overcome weaknesses in writing or reading. As future chapters in this book show, using strategies such as visual outlines for writing and kinesthetic approaches for understanding literature allow some students to succeed academically when traditional approaches might prove futile.

In this chapter, we offered suggestions for engaging fundamental components of verbal-linguistic intelligence. Even these techniques with their singular focus are not relegated to one intelligence alone. The intelligences naturally combine and blend with others and, in the case of the linguistic strategies suggested here, most are dependent on interpersonal and kinesthetic engagement as well. Nevertheless, this chapter has highlighted four core components of linguistic intelligence: reading, writing, speaking, and listening. To help the reader summarize, reflect on, and synthesize the contents of this chapter, the following is offered.

APPLYING VERBAL-LINGUISTIC INTELLIGENCE

1. Important ideas or insights gleaned from this chapter:

_____

_____

_____

_____

_____

_____

_____

_____

2. Areas I'd like to learn more about:

_____

_____

_____

_____

_____

_____

_____

_____

_____

3. Ways I can use this information in my teaching. Please note that all of the strategies mentioned in this chapter are listed below with space provided to note how each strategy might be incorporated into classroom instruction:

VERBAL-LINGUISTIC STRATEGY	CLASSROOM APPLICATION
Establishing a Verbal-Linguistic Learning Environment	_____
Listening to Learn	_____
Keys to Effective Listening	_____
Listening to Stories and Reading Aloud	_____
Listening to Poetry	_____
Teachers as Storytellers	_____
Listening to Lectures	_____

VERBAL-LINGUISTIC STRATEGY	CLASSROOM APPLICATION

Speaking

Students as Storytellers   _____

Classroom Discussions   _____

Memorizing   _____

Reports   _____

Interviews   _____

Reading

Finding Materials   _____

Words in the Classroom   _____

Reading Across the Curriculum   _____

Reading for Understanding   _____

Writing

Categories of Writing   _____

Writing Across the Curriculum   _____

Writing Options for All Content Areas   _____

Getting Started with Writing   _____

The Real Work of Writing   _____

Writing Groups   _____

Technology That Enhances
Verbal-Linguistic Intelligence

_____

VERBAL-LINGUISTIC REFERENCES

Arends, R. (1994). *Learning to Teach*. New York: McGraw-Hill.

Britton, J. (1970). *Language and Learning*. Harmondsworth, England: Penguin.

Campbell, L., & Campbell, B. (1999). *Multiple Intelligences and Student Achievement: Success Stories from Six Schools*. Alexandria, VA: ASCD.

Cawelti, G. (1999, 2nd Ed.). *Handbook of Research on Improving Student Achievement*. Arlington, VA: Education Research Service.

Diamond, M., & Hopson, J. (1999). *Magic Trees of the Mind: How to Nurture Your Child's Intelligence, Creativity, and Healthy Emotions*. New York: Dutton.

Gardner, H. (1993; 1983). *Frames of Mind: The Theory of Multiple Intelligences*. New York: Basic Books.

Goldberg, N. (1986). *Writing Down the Bones: Freeing the Writer Within*. Boston: Shambhala Publications.

National Council of Teachers of English. (1996). *Standards for the English Language Arts*. Urbana, IL: Author. Also available online at www.ncte.org/standards/

O'Conner, P.T. (2000). *Words Fail Me: What Everyone Who Writes Needs to Know about Writing*. San Diego: Harvest Press.

Sandburg, C. (1950). *Complete Poems*. New York: Harcourt Brace.

Steil, L. (1983). *Effective Listening*. New York: McGraw-Hill.

Strunk, W., & White, E.B. (2000, 4th Edition). *The Elements of Style*. Boston: Allyn and Bacon.

Zinsser, W. (1998). *On Writing Well*. New York: Harper Reference Books.

2

The Calculating Mind
LOGICAL-MATHEMATICAL INTELLIGENCE

That vast book which stands forever open before our eyes, the universe, cannot be read until we have learned the language and become familiar with the character in which it is written. It is written in mathematical language, without which means it is humanly impossible to comprehend a single word.

—Galileo, 1663

FOR THE LOVE OF NUMBERS

When he was two years old, Daniel squealed with delight every time his mother uttered any random string of numbers such as 21, 47, 63, 150, 2679.

*N*ot only was the sound of numbers pleasing, but the abstract symbols themselves were mysteries to be solved. Pieces of cereal in a bowl had to be counted and numerically written. The same was true for rocks in the driveway and toys in the toy box. By the time Daniel was three, questions about time and sequence dominated his interest. To him, a half hour meant how long it took to watch a favorite television program or to drive to the grocery store. To the surprise of his parents, he opened a computer program after watching a series of steps performed once. Multiplication soon proved more compelling than random numbers since it allowed Daniel to manipulate predictable patterns. When he played toddler basketball, Daniel assigned each basket a number and practiced the times tables while

taking shots. His basketball scores mounted quickly, as did memorization of multiplication facts.

In first grade, Daniel was fascinated by the concept of negative numbers. His teacher accommodated his skills by challenging him with fourth grade math textbooks and asking him open-ended questions that engaged higher-level thinking skills. Throughout his elementary years, math was, expectedly, the boy's favorite subject. Outside of school, new interests emerged: computing sports statistics, classifying objects into similar categories, figuring out time differences across the globe, and posing questions about space.

FOR THE LOVE OF NUMBERS . . . continued

Today, as a middle schooler, Daniel's interest in math is evident not only in the advanced math classes he takes, but also in problem-solving real world issues. For fun, he asks his mother to "quiz him" with mathematical story problems and enjoys helping his family make decisions about household budget matters. At 13, Daniel has developed numerous short-cuts to mathematical problem-solving, easily beating adults and sometimes calculators at computational tasks. He often spends leisure hours sorting and pricing a sports card collection, measuring distances, and at school, scores among the highest in national math competitions. He is exacting about issues with time, scoffs at faulty reasoning, and still smiles at the sound of numbers whenever they appear in conversation. Whatever studies Daniel will pursue in high school and beyond, it is likely that math will figure prominently.

DEFINITION: Understanding Logical-Mathematical Intelligence

Gardner has suggested that Piaget's model of cognitive development, progressing from sensory-motor activities to formal operations, was, perhaps, a description of growth in one domain, that of logical-mathematical intelligence. Piaget described logical intelligence as beginning with a child's interactions with objects in the environment, to discovering numbers, to transitioning from using concrete objects to abstract symbols, to manipulating abstractions, and, finally, to considering hypothetical statements and their relationships and implications. Gardner doubts that Piaget's ideas of cognitive development apply equally well to other realms of human competence.

As is evident in the story about Daniel, logical-mathematical intelligence involves numerous components: mathematical calculations, logical thinking, problem-solving, deductive and inductive reasoning, and discerning patterns and relationships. At the core of mathematical thinking is the ability to recognize and solve problems. Although this intelligence has proven highly valuable in Western society and is often credited with guiding the course of human history, Gardner contends that logical-mathematical intelligence is not necessarily superior to other intelligences nor is it universally held in high esteem. There are diverse problem-solving processes inherent in each of the intelligences. Each possesses its own ordering mechanism, principles, core operations, and media that logical-mathematical intelligence cannot necessarily address.

CHECKLIST: Logical-Mathematical Intelligence Qualities

Gardner describes logical-mathematical intelligence as encompassing many kinds of thinking. He suggests that this intelligence encompasses three broad, but interrelated fields: mathematics, science, and logic. It is impossible in a single list to capture the range of mathematical expression in an individual, but some suggested descriptors follow. It is likely that a person with well-developed logical-mathematical intelligence:

1. Perceives objects and their functions in the environment.

2. Is familiar with the concepts of quantity, time, and cause and effect.

3. Uses abstract symbols to represent concrete objects and concepts.

4. Demonstrates skill at logical problem-solving.

5. Perceives patterns and relationships.

6. Poses and tests hypotheses.

7. Uses diverse mathematical skills such as estimating, calculating algorithms, interpreting statistics, and visually representing information in graphic form.

8. Enjoys complex operations such as calculus, physics, computer programming, or research methods.

9. Thinks mathematically by gathering evidence, making hypotheses, formulating models, developing counter-examples, and building strong arguments.

10. Uses technology to solve mathematical problems.

11. Expresses interest in careers such as accounting, computer technology, law, engineering, and chemistry.

12. Creates new models or perceives new insights in science or mathematics.

Logical-Mathematical Learning Processes

For the last two decades, numerous position papers generated by professionals and academic organizations have called for new forms of mathematics instruction. A series of reports from the National Council of Teachers of Mathematics recommend that mathematics curricula emphasize the awareness and appreciation of the role of mathematics in society, the ability to reason and communicate mathematically, to problem-solve, and to apply mathematics to students' everyday lives.

Similar recommendations are evident in science education. Many groups such as the National Science Teachers Association and the National Academy of Science, the organization that in 1995 created the National Science Education Standards, have identified principles, content, and pedagogy for science education. Some instructional suggestions include teaching the process skills of scientific inquiry, applying the basic concepts of science as appropriate, using science in everyday decision-making, and helping students recognize that science, technology, and society influence one another. Both science and math educators are calling for the development of higher-order thinking on the part of students as well as the teaching of problem-solving and decision-making skills.

This chapter does not address how to improve the instruction of mathematics or science. Nor does it assume that these subjects should forego being taught as discrete subject matter areas in their own right. Rather, it suggests instructional strategies to integrate mathematical and logical thinking into diverse subject areas. In so doing, logical intelligence may play a larger role in thinking and learning. Graphing, for example, can be used to present information in any classroom. Probability theory might predict the outcomes of physical exercise or current events. These and other strategies described in this chapter include:

Establishing a Logical-Mathematical Learning Environment

The Teaching of Logic
The Scientific Method
Thinking Scientifically Across the Curriculum

Deductive Logic
Syllogisms
Venn Diagrams

Inductive Logic
Analogies

Enhancing Thinking and Learning
Mediating Learning
Questioning Strategies

Mathematical Thinking Processes
Patterning
Graphs

Working with Numbers
Averages and Percentages
Measurement
Calculation
Probability
Geometry

Story Problems Across the Curriculum

Sequencing

Math Themes for All Subject Areas

Technology That Enhances Logical-Mathematical Intelligence

Establishing a Logical-Mathematical Learning Environment

In 2000, the National Council of Teachers of Mathematics released its most recent report, called *Principles and Standards for School Mathematics,* which describes a new vision for mathematics education. In addition to recommending principles and components of enriched curricula, the document portrays students as inherently mathematical. It notes:

> From a young age, children are interested in mathematical ideas. Through their experiences in everday life, they gradually develop a complex set of informal ideas about numbers, patterns, shapes, quantities, data, and size, and many of these ideas are correct and robust.

To build on prior knowledge and deepen students' understanding of mathematics, they must become active learners who engage in far more than the memorization and computation that dominated former approaches to mathematics instruction. Sample active learning processes that enhance logical thinking include:

- Using diverse questioning strategies
- Posing open-ended problems
- Applying math to real world situations
- Using concrete objects to demonstrate understanding
- Predicting and verifying logical outcomes
- Discerning patterns and connections in diverse phenomena
- Justifying or verifying statements or opinions
- Providing opportunities for observation and investigation

- Using technology to teach, learn, and extend student understanding

- Connecting mathematical concepts to other subject matter areas.

As the reader will find later in this chapter, certain math manipulatives can be used throughout all curriculum areas. By working with concrete objects, students become actively engaged in problem-solving. Teachers may find it valuable to have pattern blocks, games, puzzles, graph paper, rulers, compasses, protractors, calculators, computers, and a variety of computer software available in their classrooms. Since these items are not considered essential supplies in all subject matter areas, especially at the secondary level, such manipulatives can be borrowed from math teachers and made easily transportable. Placing the needed items in a plastic tub with an inventory list attached can tell teacher and students at a glance what is available as well as what might be missing. Student representatives might also be responsible for regularly inventorying the materials.

The learning processes that follow expand the concept of traditional mathematics education. Replacing the perception of math as a subject that develops only computational and algebraic skills, mathematics today includes problem-solving, reasoning, and making connections, skills that benefit any field of study. The following learning processes augment the work of math and science educators by assisting students in applying logical thinking more confidently in all of their learning opportunities.

The Teaching of Logic

Logic as an academic discipline was invented by Aristotle and is concerned with argument, validity, proof, definition, and consistency. Undoubtedly, before formal logic was recognized, people were reasoning in consistent and logical ways. Nevertheless, Aristotle was the first philosopher to identify and formalize rules for this branch of philosophy. During the Middle Ages, Arabic and European cultures contributed to the field and during the nineteenth and twentieth centuries, there were numerous developments in mathematical logic.

To introduce formal logic to students, it is useful to explain that logic examines how arguments are constructed. Logical arguments typically consist of two kinds of statements: premises that state evidence and conclusions that are drawn from the premises. Logic attempts to tell us what is true if the premises are true. By teaching logical reasoning processes, students are exposed to exacting mental discipline and can learn whether chains of reasoning are valid or invalid.

There are several kinds of logic, the most common of which are deductive and inductive. In deductive logic, the conclusion follows from the stated premises. In inductive logic, the conclusion is developed step-by-step from the particular to the general. The scientific method uses both types of logic; hypotheses are often developed through deductive reasoning and theories are built on inductive thinking.

The Scientific Method

The scientific method, a way of thinking about problems and solving them, involves extensive use of logic. Scientists have worked out the general process of the empirical scientific method, a series of five steps that seek to explain a problem and its solution in an orderly manner. The five steps of the scientific method are:

> STATING THE PROBLEM
>
> FORMING THE HYPOTHESIS OR EXPLANATION
>
> OBSERVING AND EXPERIMENTING
>
> INTERPRETING THE DATA
>
> DRAWING CONCLUSIONS

The scientific method endeavors to explain phenomena by examining cause and effect. An experiment typically involves manipulating one variable while holding all other variables constant, thus isolating the effects of the one manipulated variable. If, after repeated trials the results are predictable, then the scientific method allows scientists to answer the question: "What are the grounds for our beliefs?" Scientists attempt to design experiments with as few variables as possible because we consider our beliefs reliable when based on experiments that minimize the number of uncontrolled variables.

Thinking Scientifically Across the Curriculum

How can this kind of empirical thinking be incorporated into the classroom? Regardless of the subject area, information can be presented, hypotheses or explanations formed, examples found through research, experimentation, or observa-

tion, data examined, and relevant conclusions drawn. The following sample premises may be used to engage students in thinking scientifically across the curriculum. The students' tasks would consist of testing such premises to determine if their hypotheses are supported and to explain how they arrived at such decisions.

Premises to Be Researched Using the Scientific Method

(i.e., manipulating one variable and looking at the results in a responding variable)

- Putting an aspirin or a penny in a vase of flowers keeps them fresh longer.
- Cats always purr when you pet them.
- Aerobic exercise reduces resting heart rate.
- Blue lighting reduces tension.
- Mixing yellow with blue creates green.
- Bees are attracted to yellow.
- Smoking cigarettes makes people popular.
- Higher interest rates result in slower realty markets.
- Boys have faster reaction times than girls.

In addition to the empirical research method, there are numerous types of logic problems that question whether inferences are true. In using deductive logic, students can employ syllogisms and Venn diagrams to determine if premises are valid, while in using inductive logic, they might create analogies to reveal proportional relationships. These three logic problems, syllogisms, Venn diagrams, and analogies, can be applied to many subject areas. For example, analogies in science might assist students with concept development, and syllogisms or Venn diagrams in social studies might be used to compare or contrast different cultures or geographic regions.

Deductive Logic

Deductive reasoning begins with a general rule and attempts to prove that data are consistent with a generalization. Students frequently see such logic in action. If the principal announces that anyone throwing snowballs on the playground will suffer the consequences of his actions and Andy proceeds to throw snowballs, the results are predictable. Or, if directions in one's art class state that using too much glue will cause tissue paper to bleed, and Molly uses large amounts of glue, she should then not be surprised when she gets bright colored dye on her hands and shirt. This kind of reasoning represents syllogisms in action. Syllogisms are structured arguments composed of two premises and a conclusion, and are examples of deductive logic.

Syllogisms

Aristotle is the earliest known philosopher to use syllogisms as a form of logical problem-solving. He taught that the syllogism was the main instrument for reaching scientific conclusions. Aristotle determined that certain propositions could be inferred as true if their premises were true. For example:

> All men are mortal.
> Socrates is a man.
> Therefore, Socrates is mortal.

The structure of syllogisms is always consistent. The first line provides one piece of information or premise that describes the noun (men) as a member of a set (mortal). The second line provides an additional premise that describes a new noun (Socrates) in relation to the subset (man). The conclusion is the third statement in a syllogism which draws logical conclusions based on set/subset membership (since men are mortal and Socrates is a man, then

Socrates must be mortal). In this case, the conclusion is supported or proved by the premises, and the syllogism is considered valid.

Syllogisms are carefully worded. For example, premises begin with all, none, or some. The verbs used in premises consist of is, are, or are not. The conclusion begins with the word therefore. The challenge when working with syllogisms is to determine whether the conclusion is valid. Many syllogisms are invalid. For example,

> All weeds are plants.
> The tree is a plant.
> Therefore, all trees are weeds.

In the above syllogism, the conclusion is not supported by its premises and is considered invalid. Note that syllogisms are valid if the object of the second premise refers to the subject of the first premise. Students can diagram this to show increasingly small subsets based upon these premises.

Valid Premise

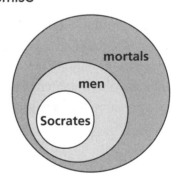

Invalid Premise

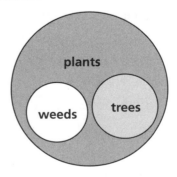

Syllogisms teach students about establishing premises and determining either logical or illogical conclusions. For example, teachers and students can apply syllogisms to different subjects. In a social studies unit on European geography, a teacher might pose the following problem:

All countries in Europe are north of the equator.

Spain, Italy, and Greece are in Europe.

Therefore _____.

Or in a life science or biology class:

All reptiles have cold blood.

_____ are reptiles.

Therefore, _____ have cold blood.

Solving syllogisms requires determining their validity or invalidity. The above examples are both valid, but when assessing students a teacher might provide them with a number of syllogisms, some valid, some invalid, to determine the effectiveness of their learning. The logic in a syllogism can be valid even though the content of the syllogism is invalid. Be careful to evaluate content knowledge and logical reasoning separately when using syllogisms.

Venn Diagrams

Venn diagrams are visual syllogisms. John Venn designed Venn diagrams using overlapping circles to compare or contrast sets of information. Generally, two intersecting circles are drawn resulting in three individual areas.

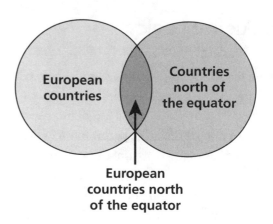

European countries north of the equator

In the above example, the circle on the left represents all European countries. The circle on the right represents all countries north of the equator. The area created by the overlap must represent countries that contain both attributes (European and north of the equator). Countries that are north of the equator and non-European would be placed outside of the diagram.

Venn diagrams are especially effective in helping students focus on attributes and compare similarities and differences. Students should gain experience fitting objects into precreated Venn diagrams and then they can be challenged to design Venn diagrams of their own. Some suggested attributes are:

characteristics of plants – characteristics of animals

short stories – novels

you – classmate

democracy – dictatorship

editorials – documentaries

words used as nouns – words used as verbs

rules for soccer – rules for rugby

In more complex Venn diagrams, three overlapping circles can be drawn resulting in seven individual areas. (Actually, the number of circles can extend indefinitely.) The following example asks students to place geometric figures into a more complex Venn diagram.

Place a trapezoid, square, rhombus, parallelogram, and rectangle in the right spot:

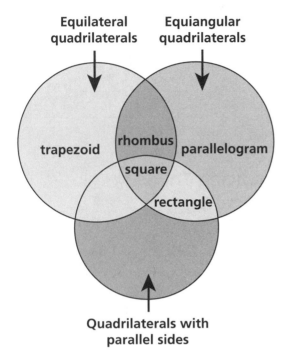

Students enjoy occasional challenges such as "What's My Rule?" Draw two large intersecting circles on the classroom floor. As students enter the classroom, sort them into secret categories (such as long-sleeved tops, tennis shoes, and both). Let them guess what attributes you are using to place them in the sections.

Inductive Logic

Aristotle, the father of logic, referred to inductive logic as "a passage from individuals to universals." Inductive logic involves reasoning from particular facts to a general conclusion. We use inductive logic whenever we try to solve a problem when no single answer exists. For example, inductive reasoning must be used in deciding where to go to college, the best time to harvest a crop, or how to introduce a new unit to students on Monday. When inductive thinking is used, pieces of information can be formed into a generalization.

One type of inductive reasoning is the analogy. An analogy reveals proportional relationships such as A is to B as C is to D. They compare one known item or circumstance to another. Analogies are commonly used to test reasoning on standardized tests, and they are effective classroom tools to engage logical thinking.

Analogies

Analogies are structured as two pairs or sets of words. The first pair reveals a relationship. The second set, when completed, reveals a similar relationship. The subjects of the two pairs may be different but the relationships are the same. To solve an analogy, look at the first pair of words to determine their relationship. Then look at the third word to determine how it relates to the first and what the missing word should be. When a word is identified to fill in the blank, it must reveal the same relationship as in the first set. For example: Car is to land as boat is to _____ [water]. An additional item to note in analogies is that the words in both sets must be in the same order.

In mathematics the symbol ":" represents "is to" and the symbol "::" represents "as." So: Bird : nest :: bee : _____ [hive].

Analogous thinking can be applied to various topics such as the following:

1. Churchill : England :: Stalin : _____ .

2. Electron : Nucleus :: Planet : _____ .

3. Bear : Mammal :: Rattlesnake : _____ .

4. Albany : New York :: Tallahassee : _____ .

5. Nick Bottom : *A Midsummer Night's Dream* :: Falstaff : _____ .

6. Monet : Impressionism :: Braque : _____ .

7. Hydrogen : Element :: Water : _____ .

8. *Moby Dick* : Herman Melville :: *Little House on the Prairie* : _____ .

9. Five : Ten :: Fifty : _____ .

10. Three : Triangle :: Five : _____ .

This same technique can be used with pictures instead of words or a combination of both. A student might picture an analogy in the following ways:

The analogies on standardized tests are usually closed-ended, multiple-choice options in which there is only one right answer. Both students and teachers can create more open-ended analogies to share in the classroom. Initially, it is often easier for students to begin by adding the second set rather than creating an entire analogy. For example,

Light is to dark as _____ is to _____ .

Minute is to hour as _____ is to _____ .

2/5 : 10/25 :: _____ : _____ .

Madagascar : Africa :: _____ : _____ .

Students can then progress to creating their own analogies simply by filling in the blanks as follows:

_____ is to _____ as _____ is to _____ .

_____ : _____ :: _____ : _____ .

Enhancing Thinking and Learning

Some students may find syllogisms, analogies, or other structured thinking processes difficult. In such cases, teachers may encounter challenges with how best to assist students who struggle with learning. The problem is further compounded when teachers cannot specify which cognitive skills require strengthening. Dr. Reuven Feuerstein, an Israeli clinical psychologist, has identified essential cognitive skills that underlie human thinking and learning. Feuerstein and others who have worked with his programs that teach the skills of intelligence, such as Instrumental Enrichment and the Learning Potential Assessment Device, claim that intentional mediation of fundamental intellectual processes results in great cognitive gains. In many cases, Feuerstein's methods appear to jumpstart learning when it has stalled. To improve the thinking of their students, educators around the world are looking to one of Feuerstein's cognitive programs called Mediated Learning.

Mediating Learning

Feuerstein initially developed his revolutionary Mediated Learning Experience (MLE) to address the educational needs of tens of thousands of traumatized refugee children who survived the Holocaust or impoverished conditions in North Africa. Finding their cognitive skills severely deficient as a result of their deprived environments and life experiences, Feuerstein created learning strategies to greatly enhance the logical thinking and learning abilities of these young people. During the last forty years, Feuerstein's methods have proved consistently effective with diverse populations and with those of all ages and ability levels.

Students with learning disabilities as well as those who are highly capable have made impressive academic gains with Mediated Learning. Feuerstein's system has been implemented in countries around the world and most states in the United States now include his methods in schools, districts, and corporate training programs. In 1990, Feuerstein was awarded the highest medal of honor bestowed by the president of France for retraining the work force of 250 French corporations. In 1991, he received the Humanitarian Award from the International Variety Clubs, for his work to improve learning at all ability levels. As recently as 1999, he received honorary doctorates, distinguished citizen awards, and commendations from American and European universities and professional organizations. What is this method that has received such wide acclaim?

Feuerstein describes Mediated Learning as "a quality of interaction . . . when I interpose myself between the learner, the child and the whole world, and I make the world accessible to the child." MLE occurs whenever an individual deliberately intervenes between stimuli and learner to transmit or mediate understanding.

Many parents, teachers, and trainers intuitively or explicitly mediate learning for others. Unfortu-nately, many do not, thus limiting the effective cognitive functioning of an individual. Feuerstein asserts that all people require the same basic intellectual skills to make sense of information and the world.

Feuerstein's theory is broad and complex. However, an American professor and researcher, Dr. Katherine Greenberg, has adapted the theory to make it accessible to parents and helping professionals. Greenberg's program, entitled COGNET (The Cognitive Enrichment Program), is based at the University of Tennessee in Knoxville and was approved by the federal government as a nationally validated program in 1995.

Greenberg notes that Feuerstein originally identified more than twenty-eight cognitive functions, the skills on which thought processes are based. In using Mediated Learning, the mediator evaluates the learner's cognitive competencies and seeks to develop any that are weak. Greenberg has condensed the number of cognitive competencies to ten, which she refers to as "Building Blocks of Thinking." One of the many ways in which the COGNET program applies the theory of Mediated Learning is through its emphasis on helping students understand and use the ten Building Blocks of Thinking.

Greenberg's Ten Building Blocks of Thinking

Approach to Task—refers to how one initiates, sustains, and completes a task. Gathering information, thinking about the situation, and expressing thoughts or actions about one's learning efforts are also components of approach to task.

Precision and Accuracy—refers to the ability to use language accurately, to imitate correctly when necessary, and to be exact and correct in understanding what constitutes the learning activity at hand.

Space and Time Concepts—refers to understanding basic spatial ideas about how things relate in size, shape, distance, and sequence. This building block also includes the ability to understand time and/or changes that occur over time.

Thought Integration—refers to pulling together and using multiple sources of information at the same time.

Selective Attention—refers to the ability to choose relevant pieces of information when considering thoughts or events, as well as the ability to ignore what is irrelevant.

Making Comparisons—refers to the ability to determine what is the same and what is different.

Connecting Events—refers to the ability to associate one activity with another and to use this association in a meaningful manner.

Working Memory—refers to the ability to encode and recall information from memory as well as to make connections among the information gathered.

Getting the Main Idea—refers to the ability to find a fundamental element that related pieces of information have in common.

Problem Identification—refers to the ability to experience and define within a given situation what is causing a feeling of imbalance.

Learners may experience difficulty with several of the Building Blocks, especially when they face a new or troublesome task. When frustration, anxiety, or a lack of motivation is present, such feelings frequently indicate that one or more of the blocks may be underdeveloped or misused. The following checklist created by the authors of this book identifies the Building Blocks of Thinking that students may struggle with or master. The teacher may use the checklist to observe a student in the process of learning, or the student may be asked to respond to the list independently. Interventions might be created to respond to any perceived cognitive weakness. Additional information on Greenberg's adaptation of Feuerstein's work is available in her book published in 2000 called *Cognitive Enrichment Advantage*.

The checklist on the facing page may reveal one or more cognitive functions that need strengthening. Frequently, teachers encounter children who are struggling with learning, but have found it difficult to identify what was wrong. The Building Blocks of Thinking help teachers and students recognize specific cognitive weaknesses and provide important clues for ameliorating learning difficulties. Mediated Learning can be integrated into classroom lessons on any subject; however, it requires fine-tuning many everyday classroom interactions.

Math and science teachers will probably recognize that Greenberg's Building Blocks of Thinking resemble the mathematical reasoning skills of the National Council of Teachers of Mathematics Standards and the process skills of science. The Building Blocks of Thinking reword those thinking processes in an interdisciplinary manner. Teachers can use the Building Blocks as ways to encourage the development of mathematical-logical intelligences regardless of the subject matter or theme of instruction.

Questioning Strategies

In the skillful use of the question, more than anything else lies the fine art of teaching; for in such use we have the guide to clear and vivid ideas, the quick spur to imagination, the stimulus to thought, the incentive to action.

—Charles DeGarmo, 1911

Long before Socrates, questioning served as one of teaching's most common practices. Questions commonly asked in classrooms vary greatly,

BUILDING BLOCKS OF THINKING

Name: _____

Assess whether each building block was used proficiently or inefficiently by checking the appropriate boxes below. The student demonstrated:

	Proficient	Inefficient
APPROACH TO TASK BY:		
Gathering information needed to complete the activity.	_____	_____
Making a plan to complete the task.	_____	_____
PRECISION AND ACCURACY BY:		
Asking for help if something was not clear or understood.	_____	_____
Expressing ideas clearly and accurately.	_____	_____
Meeting the goals of the task with precision and accuracy.	_____	_____
SPACE AND TIME CONCEPTS BY:		
Using size, shape, and distance adequately.	_____	_____
Sequencing appropriately.	_____	_____
Explaining how things change over time.	_____	_____
THOUGHT INTEGRATION BY:		
Clustering thoughts effectively.	_____	_____
Combining bits of information into a whole thought.	_____	_____
Retaining the relevant bits of information needed in a situation.	_____	_____
SELECTIVE ATTENTION BY:		
Identifying important information.	_____	_____
Ignoring unimportant information or stimuli.	_____	_____
MAKING COMPARISONS BY:		
Identifying similar items.	_____	_____
Identifying dissimilar items.	_____	_____
CONNECTING EVENTS BY:		
Connecting past, present, and future events.	_____	_____
Identifying cause and effect.	_____	_____
Perceiving that events are related.	_____	_____
WORKING MEMORY BY:		
Encoding information in memory.	_____	_____
Retrieving information from memory.	_____	_____
Making connections between parts of information.	_____	_____
GETTING THE MAIN IDEA BY:		
Identifying the fundamental element that relates pieces of information.	_____	_____
PROBLEM IDENTIFICATION BY:		
Articulating a problem.	_____	_____
Developing an approach to address the problem.	_____	_____

placing different demands on children and their thinking. Many questions can be answered by a single right answer: When did the Spanish-American War take place? What is the chemical symbol for hydrogen? What is the definition of a prepositional phrase? Since children's cognitive performance is linked to a teacher's pedagogical skill, it is important to find ways to challenge student thinking and responses. Questions that elicit factual recall are necessary since children must master basic information. However, to engage higher-level thinking processes, a variety of questioning strategies must be used.

Benjamin Bloom's taxonomy is a well-known resource that identifies and evaluates different kinds of thinking while also offering a framework for questioning. Bloom's taxonomy identifies six cognitive domains which include: recall, comprehension, application, analysis, synthesis, and evaluation. By reflecting on the quality of questioning to be used in classroom discussions or in students' assignments, teachers can elicit higher-level thinking by intentionally posing questions from each of Bloom's domains.

Certain follow-up strategies also improve the quality of classroom thinking. Teachers, on the average, wait less than three seconds after asking a question before asking another student to respond or answering the question themselves. If, however, a teacher waits ten seconds or longer, student responses improve as do teacher reactions. The benefits of wait time include enhanced participation in discussions, increased use of reasoning to justify answers, and more speculative responses. Similar benefits also occur when wait time is used before a teacher comments after a student response.

The quality of responses can also be enhanced by asking students to query each other in pairs before they respond in the whole group. This strategy makes it possible for more students to partici-

pate, allows students to "hear" their own thinking, and encourages them to listen to and understand other points of view.

When he worked with the Maryland State Department of Education, Jay McTighe and his colleagues developed a simple cueing device, a bookmark, for teachers to use during class discussion and question and answer sessions. One side of the bookmark features question starters based on the book *Dimensions of Thinking* by Bob Marzano. Discussion strategies are listed on the other side. The bookmark is included on the facing page. Copy and use it as a tool for easy referencing during class activities.

Mathematical Thinking Processes

Mathematics, a subject typically thought of as abstract and exacting, can actually serve as an exciting integrating focus of many lessons and curricular units. For students previously uninterested in math, activities such as patterning, graphing, and making and breaking codes may reawaken a curiosity about how things work and how problems are solved. Teachers can choose from among the numerous processes suggested below and adapt any that might encourage an appreciation of mathematical thinking processes.

Patterning

By observing and solving problems that involve patterns, students begin to notice underlying relationships that pervade logic, nature, and the universe. Patterns exist in everything from floor tiles to the shapes of galaxies, from beehives to modern paintings, from the cross-section of a tree to the

QUESTIONING FOR QUALITY THINKING

RECALLING
Who, what, when, where, how _____?

COMPARING
How is _____ similar to/different from _____?

IDENTIFYING ATTRIBUTES AND COMPONENTS
What are the characteristics/parts of _____?

CLASSIFYING
How might we organize _____ into categories?

ORDERING
Arrange _____ into sequence according to _____.

IDENTIFYING RELATIONSHIPS AND PATTERNS
Develop an outline/diagram/web of _____.

REPRESENTING
In what other ways might we show/ illustrate _____?

IDENTIFYING MAIN IDEAS
What is the key concept/issue in _____?
Retell the main idea of ____ in your own words.

IDENTIFYING ERRORS
What is wrong with _____?

INFERRING
What might we infer from _____?
What conclusions might be drawn from _____?

PREDICTING
What might happen if _____?

ELABORATING
What ideas/details can you add to _____?
Give an example of _____.

SUMMARIZING
Can you summarize _____?

ESTABLISHING CRITERIA
What criteria would you use to judge/ evaluate _____?

VERIFYING
What evidence supports _____?
How might we prove/confirm _____?

STRATEGIES TO EXTEND THINKING

REMEMBER "WAIT TIME I AND II"
Provide at least five seconds of thinking time after a question and after a response.

ASK "FOLLOW-UPS"
e.g., "Why? How do you know? Do you agree? Will you give an example? Can you tell me more?"

CUE RESPONSES TO "OPEN-ENDED" QUESTIONS
e.g., "There is not a single correct answer to this question. I want you to consider alternatives."

USE "THINK-PAIR-SHARE"
Allow individual thinking time, discussion with a partner, and follow with whole-group discussion.

CALL ON STUDENTS RANDOMLY
Avoid the pattern of only calling on those students with raised hands.

ASK STUDENTS TO "UNPACK THEIR THINKING"
e.g., "Describe how you arrived at your answer."

ASK FOR SUMMARY TO PROMOTE ACTIVE LISTENING
e.g., "Could you please summarize our discussion thus far?"

PLAY DEVIL'S ADVOCATE
Require students to defend their reasoning against different points of view.

SURVEY THE CLASS
e.g., "How many people agree with the author's point of view?" (thumbs up, thumbs down)

ALLOW FOR STUDENT CALLING
e.g., "Richard, will you please call on someone to respond?"

ENCOURAGE STUDENT QUESTIONING
Provide opportunities for students to generate their own questions.

Maryland State Department of Education

layout of the orchard, and from the eggs in a carton to atoms in a molecule. Mathematics is founded on patterns. The skill of recognizing and using patterns is a valuable problem-solving tool. Through working with patterns in any subject, students can explore, discover, and create a harmony of design while they deepen their appreciation for this vital mathematical concept.

Pattern Blocks

Pattern blocks, sets of wooden or plastic geometric shapes that fit together forming infinite configurations, are common manipulatives in elementary mathematics classes. Some pattern blocks serve as stamps or plastic stencils so that students can draw or "stamp" their designs on paper. Such manipulatives concretely represent abstract mathematical symbols, and are motivating to students who prefer to learn through touching, seeing, and experimenting.

Although generally used to introduce geometry or symmetry, pattern blocks are effective tools for numerous hands-on, problem-solving activities. For example, one creative chemistry teacher asked his students to replicate the atoms of elements in the periodic table with pattern blocks. Brightly colored blocks might also depict cubist art, covered wagons crossing the prairie, or electrons surrounding a nucleus. When students are confronted with open-ended problem-solving activities, they may use countless visual configurations to portray possible solutions. The following list suggests only a few of the possible ways to weave pattern blocks throughout the curriculum.

1. Demonstrate the configuration of different types of galaxies in space.
2. Show the internal geometry of a beehive.
3. Make a map of the continents.
4. Invent a musical notation system.
5. Design a building in which colors or shapes represent different rooms or stories.
6. Recreate what cells look like under a microscope.
7. Write a rebus story that includes pattern blocks.
8. Create a Venn diagram for sorting pattern blocks.
9. Represent a particular syllogism using pattern blocks.
10. Create analogies using pairs of pattern blocks.

If pattern blocks are available in the classroom, students will find ways to put them to use. For example, in one school, fifth grade students created a replica of the Mayflower, and eighth-graders used blocks to demonstrate an aquatic food chain. In another school, students enjoyed creating repetitive symmetrical patterns which prepared them for their future study of geometry.

Patterns in Data

From the recurrence of wars throughout history to changes in the stock market, from weather patterns to school enrollment, there are observable patterns in the institutions and phenomena around us. Students or teachers who wish to discover or analyze such patterns need look no further than the daily newspaper or readily available reference materials, or any group of students or teachers for that matter!

Many classrooms track the weather by noting temperature, rainfall, or the number of sunny days. Such data can be analyzed quantitatively to discern monthly or seasonal trends. In many locations, birds leave and return at predictable times which might help students observe patterns or cycles in their lives. Graphing data is one way to identify patterns.

Patterns are evident in all of the core disciplines. In the life sciences, there are patterns in the cross-section of a tree, the water cycle, and the arrangement of cells. In the arts, patterns are evident in modern paintings, the couplets of Victorian poetry, the structure of novels, and in musical compositions. There are patterns in architecture, quilts, clothing design, braille letters, and the treads on new tires. Regardless of the subject, teachers can identify or ask students to discover patterns evident in their studies. Students might create collages of patterns they observe, perhaps dedicating each collage to a different theme such as symmetry in nature or literature.

Codes

Some of the most valued members of the military during wartime are the code breakers. There are, however, other uses for codes besides those for military purposes. Governments may send memos to each other or to their consulates in foreign countries using codes. Businesses often use codes to prevent their rivals from accessing information on new products. Some retail stores code information on price tags so that fluctuating prices are retrievable during sales.

Codes can liven up learning in the classroom and involve students in active pattern-seeking. Students enjoy breaking codes and decoding messages that contain content information. A coded message sent from one revolutionary war general to another might provide students with important information about geography, battle strategies, or significant historical figures. Another coded message might provide information about the rules of grammar or spelling. The notes on a musical score could easily be turned into a code for music students to decipher a tune. Art students might create visual glyphs with which to communicate.

Teachers will find it easy to make codes with some of the sample formulas provided below.

- Alphabetic codes can be made so that each letter in the alphabet stands for the letter that comes before it, after it, or two letters before it.

- Numerical codes can have 1 represent A, 2 represent B, etc. Infinite variations are possible. The numbers might go backwards or count by 5's.

- Morse code, the traditional dot-dash language of the telegraph, can be used with sound, flashing light, or electronic pulses.

- Symbol codes feature icons or glyphs that represent letters or numbers. The optional symbol system on most computer keyboards and certain symbolized fonts in word processors make excellent codes.

Graphs

Graphs can make almost any information more easily understood. A graph generally consists of two variables on two coordinates. When information is plotted on the different axes, mathematical relationships become easier to understand. This process can be used by the teacher to present factual information or by the student to demonstrate information acquired through research or surveys. Samples of information that can be represented by either line or bar graphs follow.

- The number of students attending a particular school during the last ten years

- The national budget under each president during this century

- The quantities and kinds of animals native to one's locale

- The most common kinds of writing mistakes students make

- The growth of the use of pesticides during the last 25 years

Some graphs plot two or more curves over one time period. This is valuable for studying the relationship of the two curves. Two examples follow: one that plots population growth and one that demonstrates skill in shooting baskets.

- The population of major cities during each ten year census period over the past 20 years. Has one grown faster?

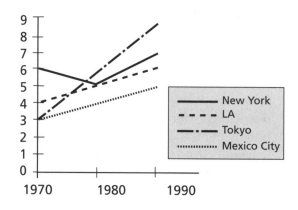

- The number of points made on a basketball court by two players can easily be plotted. Ten shots by each player could be attempted at increments of three feet from the basket. Does each have an optimal distance?

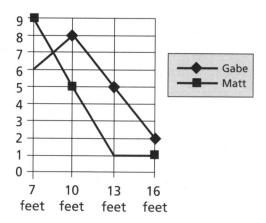

Some graphs are simply frequency charts that can be easily created by most students. Here are some examples that students might graph:

- Different activities and the number of hours students spend doing them in a week

- The number of times each letter of the alphabet shows up on the page of a storybook

- The number of days it rains each month

Bar graphs or pie charts can also represent such information. They may serve the same purposes as line graphs but are often used to represent categorical information (information that allows you to compare different categories). Instead of following a line across a graph, the viewer need only look at the relative lengths or sizes of the bars. For young children, bar graphs are the easiest kind of graph to understand and produce because of the ease of providing a developmentally sequenced experience from concrete graphs (putting the candy bars on a grid) to representational graphs (drawing the candy bars on a grid) to abstract graphs (such as the one listed below).

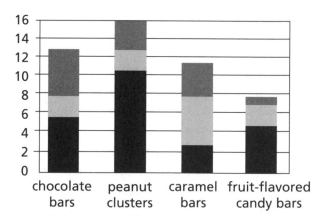

Working with Numbers

Because most school curricula are organized into discrete subject matter areas, students rarely encounter number problems unless they are studying math and working in their math textbooks. In reality, however, numbers and numerical thinking abound in all academic subjects. Since some students enjoy the precision involved in mathematics, they find it especially enjoyable to work with the numerical aspects of diverse subject areas. The following activities including averages and percentages, measurement, calculating across the curricula, probability, and story problems provide students with a numerical entry point into the humanities or other subjects not normally associated with the study of mathematics.

Averages and Percentages

Calculating averages and percentages are mathematical procedures that can be applied in many everyday situations. An artist can carefully compute the percentage of warm colors in relation to cool colors to achieve the desired effect in a painting. The young sports fan is often busy calculating batting averages, percentages of free throws made, the average number of shots stopped by a goalie during the season, or the percentage of first serves made in a tennis match. Some students find that a quantitative approach to information helps them readily grasp relationships and quantities. Averages or percentages can be calculated for the following and other content areas:

- The percentage of states in the United States that border oceans

- The average number of cells in a square millimeter of a leaf

- The percentage of spelling words spelled correctly each day of the week

- The percentage of walkers, bus riders, and car riders to school each day

- The percentage of paintings that are portraits, landscapes, or still lifes

- The average number of symphonies composed by great composers

- The percentage of specific instruments in the school band

- The percentage of democracies and dictatorships in the world

Measurement

Size, shape, weight, liquid measurement, distance, speed or motion, temperature, and time are some of the ways we measure or quantify the world around us. To develop students' measurement skills, ask them to determine which units are most appropriate to measure and how to convert between different types of units. It is also valuable for students to know when to measure accurately or when to estimate. Measurement and estimation can be extended into numerous subject areas:

1. Determine how to measure acceleration as marbles roll down a track in a physics lesson.

2. Measure the growth of bean plants on a daily basis.

3. Learn simple triangulation to measure the heights of trees.

4. Time laps walking, running, or bike-riding around the playground.

5. Measure the distances that different explorers traveled.

6. Record daily temperatures, wind speeds, or barometric pressure.

7. Weigh a clay sculpture before and after the clay dries.

8. Measure the lengths of shadows from a simple sundial on the playground.

9. Using a map, measure how far birds or whales migrate each year.

When conducting measurements, it is often helpful to record information on a table. Tables make it easy to compare and contrast information. Sample tables follow.

A Table for Recording Weights of Items before and after Drying to Determine Moisture Content

	Name of Object	Weight before Drying	Weight after Drying	Change in Weight	Percentage Moisture
1.					
2.					
3.					
4.					
5.					
6.					
7.					
8.					
9.					

A Table for Recording Laps and Times

	Student's Name	Number of Laps	Total Time
1.			
2.			
3.			
4.			
5.			
6.			
7.			
8.			
9.			

Calculation

Calculators can be easily integrated into class work, homework, and evaluation across all grade and subject areas. They are readily available tools that help students:

- concentrate on the problem-solving process rather than on the calculations associated with problems

- gain access to mathematics beyond computational skills

- explore, develop, and reinforce concepts including estimation, computation, approximation, and properties

- experiment with mathematical ideas and discover patterns

- perform tedious computations that arise when working with real data in problem-solving situations.

In the classroom, calculators can be used for problem-solving, the development of higher-level thinking, understanding mathematical operations, and learning estimation. They free students to exercise higher-order thinking skills, such as identifying number patterns or testing estimates and hypotheses. Teachers appreciate calculators because they allow them to focus on the processes of problem-solving rather than the rote application of computation methods. Calculators are capable of providing many possibilities for mathematical learning and can be used to:

1. Calculate averages and percentages.

2. Solve mathematical problems in subject areas. Simple examples follow.

   If there were two tons of tea thrown overboard during the Boston tea party, and 32 men were involved, how much tea did each man throw overboard if they all threw the same amount?

   If it takes 12 seconds for a skin cell to divide through the process of cell division, how many daughter cells will be formed from a single cell in 36 seconds? In one minute? In 3 minutes?

   If 56 Americans a day are infected with the HIV virus, how many will be infected in a year? If 42% are women, how many women will that be? If 23% of those women have babies who are infected, how many babies would have HIV?

If the sun is 93,000,000 miles from Earth, and light travels at 52,600 miles per second, how long does it take light from the sun to reach earth? If Neptune is 8,000,000,000 miles from the sun, how long will it take the sun's light to travel there?

3. Practice cumulative addition or subtraction. For example:

   Add the total number of minutes that students in the class spend reading after school and on weekends. As each student individually reports, other class members keep a running tally on the calculator. Or, after estimating a large number such as how many beans are in a jar, some students maintain a running tally as others count the beans.

4. Figure out grade-point averages.

5. Plan class or individual budgets.

6. Create numerical problems based on students' personal interests or experiences and use calculators to find solutions to their own or each others' work.

7. Play calculator games. For example:

   Elimination
   (A game for two players with one calculator)
   a. Players start by entering 15 into the calculator.
   b. Players take turns by subtracting 1, 2, or 3 and pressing "=."
   c. The player who causes the calculator to go to "0" or below (a negative number) loses.

8. Code and send messages, or write story problems for others with mathematical puzzles built into them. Students can answer each others' questions by decoding the problem. Try the following:

   After school yesterday, I hid $1.00 under a rock. The rock is in the front yard of a house on Maple Street. The address of the house is:

   $37,982 - 5514 + 80,174 - 96,225 + 1003 - 8502 = $ _____ Maple Street.

9. Undertake a personal challenge. Ask students to carry a small hand-held calculator with them for a week to explore how many real life uses they can find for such a tool.

Although knowing how to use a calculator is a valuable skill, it does not substitute for the mastery of math facts. This knowledge remains essential and throughout this book we suggest various ways to facilitate the learning of math facts.

Probability

Most of us take chances of one kind or another. Similarly, most of us have ideas about what might or might not happen. Taking chances and speculating upon the future have much to do with what mathematicians call probability, the likelihood of an event occurring. If you buy a lottery ticket, put the top down on your convertible, purchase insurance, or simply flip a coin, you are putting your own theory of probability into action.

Although probability involves guessing, the intention is to make good guesses or estimates that require logical thinking. Scientists rely on probability, as do army generals, politicians, artists, and composers. Teachers also depend on the probability that their lesson plans will be effective.

In the classroom, teachers can begin working with the intuitive probability of certain outcomes. Have students determine the likelihood of a particular outcome by using the following scale before working with mathematical models of probability:

Likelihood that something will occur:

0% 100%

Here are some sample questions that can help students to think in terms of intuitive probability:

- If two bar magnets face each other, will they attract or repel?
- What is the likelihood of the polar ice caps melting?
- Are nuclear power plants safe?
- Will the gray whales migrate past California in March this year?
- Will the next president be a Democrat, Republican, or Independent?

The mathematical probability of a certain outcome is represented as:

$$\text{probability} = \frac{\text{(the number of times the event can occur one way)}}{\text{(the total number of possible outcomes)}}.$$

For example, if you flip a coin once, the probability that it will be heads is 1/2 or 50% (one heads flip)/(two possible outcomes: heads or tails).

Sample questions to help students determine this simple one-stage event include:

- What is the likelihood that you will draw an ace from a deck of cards?
- What is the likelihood that the stop light will be green when you first see it?
- What is the likelihood that a new baby in your family will be a boy?

One-stage events can involve combinations of outcomes which make it necessary to look at all of the possible combinations before determining the probability. The following charts show all of the possible combinations of some simple events.

THROWING TWO COINS		
	Coin 1: HEADS	Coin 1: TAILS
Coin 2: HEADS	heads, heads	tails, heads
Coin 2: TAILS	heads, tails	tails, tails

Total possible outcomes:
heads, heads: 1 • heads, tails: 2 • tails, tails: 1
Probability that it will be two heads = 1/4 = 25%

ROLLING A PAIR OF DICE						
	1	**2**	**3**	**4**	**5**	**6**
1.	1, 1	1, 2	1, 3	1, 4	1, 5	1, 6
2.	2, 1	2, 2	2, 3	2, 4	2, 5	2, 6
3.	3, 1	3, 2	3, 3	3, 4	3, 5	3, 6
4.	4, 1	4, 2	4, 3	4, 4	4, 5	4, 6
5.	5, 1	5, 2	5, 3	5, 4	5, 5	5, 6
6.	6, 1	6, 2	6, 3	6, 4	6, 5	6, 6

Probability that it will be a 6 and a 3 = 2/36 = 5.5%

Two-stage events require a different mathematical model. If a coin is tossed once and lands as heads, what is the probability that heads will appear the second time? There is a 50% probability of getting heads the first as well as the second time. The two coin tosses are independent events. Other examples of independent events are whether it will rain each day or someone will find pearls in several oysters. However, the math changes if you ask the question "What is the probability that I will toss two heads in a row?" In this case, we multiply the probabilities of each event happening in a sequence:

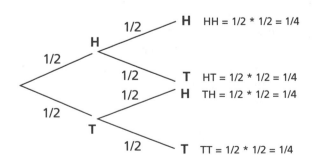

Using this logic we can address questions such as :

- If I win once, does that affect the probability that I will win again?
- What is the probability that three events will occur simultaneously such as clear sky, full moon, and Friday night?

Geometry

From cubism to cathedrals, from cells to skyscrapers, from the Parthenon to the pyramids, and from sand dunes to starfish, the principles of geometry are evident. Both the world of nature and that made by humans reflect symmetry, topology, points, lines, planes, curves, solids, and, of course, measurement and mathematics. In both, we find circles, hexagons, rectangles, spheres, triangles, cubes, cylinders, cones, pyramids, and prisms.

The word *geometry* comes from the Latin words meaning "earth" and "measure." Originally, geometry involved the measurement of farmland in places such as Egypt where the Nile flooded the valley each year and boundaries had to be reestablished. Even today, surveying is an extension of the earliest forms of geometry.

Architects, mechanics, fashion designers, engineers, builders, pilots, navigators, artists, and seamstresses all use geometry in their work. With the prevalence of geometry in our world, its applications throughout the school curriculum are extensive. Some suggestions are offered on how to incorporate geometric awareness into diverse subject matter areas.

1. Study the geometric designs on flags of the world and ask students to create their own flags using common geometric shapes.

2. Look at architectural structures throughout history (pyramids, temples, mosques, government buildings, cathedrals, domes, or skyscrapers) and compare styles and similar or varying geometric characteristics.

3. Use straight edges, compasses, and protractors to recreate designs in nature such as a forest of straight, tall trees, round rocks on the beach, rays of the setting sun on the horizon, jagged mountain peaks in the distance, the circular pattern of a sunflower, a close-up of an eye, the ripples formed by a pebble dropped on a smooth pond, snowflakes, rectangular rock outcroppings, reeds or blades of tall grass, the moon in different phases, the distant shore of a lake, the veins in a leaf, a tornado, a feather, a jellyfish, a spider web, or the cellular infrastructure of a rotten piece of wood.

4. Create symmetrical silhouettes of the profiles of famous historical figures.

5. Study the stylistic uses of geometry in cubism or other art forms incorporating explicit geometric shapes.

6. Write triangle poems with three lines, each leading into the next, e.g.:

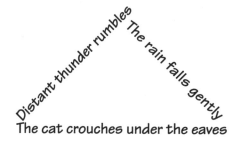

In triangle poems, there is no predetermined starting or ending point; any line can be the first or last. After students have attempted triangle poems, they can experiment with square, hexagonal, or pentagonal poems. In fact, some may want to determine how many sides would exist on a dodecagon poem!

7. Challenge students to find hidden geometric shapes. Using pictures from any subject area (Eli Whitney's cotton gin, the circulatory system of the human body, a tropical rain forest, the Spanish armada, the Great Wall of China, an Atlas booster rocket, London Bridge, or a city skyline) ask students to locate regular or irregular polygons or polyhedrons in the picture. For younger students, the teacher may want to draw hidden shapes into a nature scene, duplicate copies, and ask students to locate and label the hidden geometric shapes.

8. Ask students to make flash cards to learn vocabulary words, states and capitals, parts of speech, molecular compounds or any other information by putting the facts on geometrically shaped card stock. Rectangular cards are common, but how about hexagonal or oval cards? A variation could be normal rectangular flash cards with geometric shapes drawn onto them as visual cues serving as mnemonic devices.

9. Make a collage of geometrical shapes by cutting out circles, triangles, parallelograms, or rhombuses from different colors of construction paper, then pasting them into an artistic arrangement. The work of Mexican-American artist Carlos Merida could be presented as an example.

10. Study the history of geometry. It dates back to ancient times when the Babylonians and Egyptians used geometry to study the planets and stars, lay out cities, measure angles, and build large structures. Later, the Greeks used the principles of geometry to develop the reasoning and logic involved in proving mathematical statements that we still use today.

11. Cut out electrons, protons, and neutrons from various colors of paper to create different atoms with the shapes of the electrons' orbits sketched around the nucleus. The same could be done with atoms in various molecules or different planets orbiting the sun.

Story Problems
Across the Curriculum

The very name "story problem" strikes fear into the hearts and minds of many students. However, by making story problems interesting and meaningful, teachers can incorporate logical-mathematical thinking into almost any area of the curriculum. Here are a few examples.

- Tony Blair called George Bush on the telephone. It was 1:00 AM in London. Bush was in Washington, D.C. They talked for two hours. What time was it in Washington when Bush hung up?

- If it takes 22 days for a frog's egg to hatch into a tadpole, how many days does it take for 10 frogs' eggs to hatch into tadpoles?

- If Jeff has to diagram eight sentences every night for an entire week but his girlfriend, Melissa, does half of them for him and his sister does 14 for him, and he lost half of one daily assignment, how many sentences did Jeff diagram?

- If Monet, Gauguin, and Van Gogh began mixing paint together and Monet mixed the primary colors, Gauguin mixed the secondary colors, and they ended up with 23 containers of paint, then how many colors did Van Gogh mix?

- If the Pinta and the Nina left Spain on Tuesday and the Santa Maria left Spain one day later, and the Pinta sailed 500 miles by the following Monday and the Nina sailed 560 miles in the same time, then how far behind was the Santa Maria if she sailed at the same speed as the Nina?

- October 17 falls on a Saturday. List the dates of all Saturdays in April.

Sequencing

Putting things in logical order is a skill relevant to almost any undertaking. From making a tuna fish sandwich to planting a garden, it is important to follow the appropriate sequence. In school, we write in a certain logical order, we perform a play sequentially, we build things in order, we conduct experiments following a prescribed order, and we proceed through the school day in a predetermined manner. Following are several exercises for students to practice the skill of sequencing. Such activities can be made as simple or complex as the situation demands.

Writing a Business Letter
Put the following items in the correct order.

a. Type or write the date.

b. Type or write the closing.

c. Take an envelope from the desk.

d. Fold the letter and put it in the envelope.

e. Type the name and address of the person to whom the letter will go.

f. Seal the envelope.

g. Explain the purpose of your letter.

h. Mail the letter at the post office.

i. Put a postage stamp on the envelope.

j. Type or write the greeting.

k. Write the name and address on the envelope.

Your order: __ __ __ __ __ __ __
__ __ __ __

**How a Bill Becomes Law
in the United States**

Put the following items in the correct order.

a. The bill goes to the Senate.

b. The bill goes to the President.

c. Introduction of the bill to the House of Representatives.

d. The bill is printed by the Government Printing Office.

e. An idea for a new law is proposed.

f. A conference committee from both houses works out details.

g. The bill is sponsored by a member of the House or Senate.

h. The bill becomes law.

i. The Speaker of the House signs the bill.

Your order: ___ ___ ___ ___ ___ ___ ___
___ ___

**How Food Is Digested
in the Human Body**

Put the following items in the correct order.

a. Salivary glands make saliva.

b. Gallbladder stores bile made in liver.

c. Large intestine stores and finally disposes of waste.

d. Food passes to stomach through esophagus.

e. Duodenum receives bile and pancreatic juice.

f. Teeth chop food.

g. Small intestine completes digestion; sends food into blood stream.

h. Liver and pancreas make digestive juices for use in small intestine.

i. Stomach churns food and adds digestive juice.

Your order: ___ ___ ___ ___ ___ ___ ___
___ ___

Math Themes for All Subject Areas

Educators frequently discuss reading and writing across the curriculum, but it is less common to hear of mathematics across the curriculum. Mathematics is often isolated from other areas of study even though its central functions include thinking processes valuable to all disciplines such as identifying and representing patterns and relationships, problem-solving, and communicating precisely. One way to introduce logical thinking into any subject area is through rich themes drawn from mathematical concepts. Teachers might organize a curriculum unit around such themes or ask students to research them as they relate to classroom content:

Symmetry	Randomness
Perspective	Symbolization
Iteration	Multiplication
Modeling	Infinity
Space	Opposites
Balance	Progression
Growth	Chaos
Convergence	Division
Infinitesimal	Equality

By emphasizing such themes throughout the curriculum, students can see beyond their math and science textbooks into the real world of building and design, keeping records and allocating resources, playing sports and games, and exploring the physical universe.

Technology That Enhances Logical-Mathematical Intelligence

■ ■ ■ ■ ■ ■ ■ ■ ■ ■ ■ ■ ■ ■ ■ ■ ■

For many students, learning mathematics in abstract ways through numbers on a blackboard or on paper can be frustrating and defeating. Those same students, however, may find it possible to understand when they have opportunities to learn through model exploration or simulation toolkits in hypermedia environments. In fact, students at all ability levels may be helped to understand in greater depth. Challenging and innovative kinds of multimedia technology exercise and develop logical-mathematical intelligence. Students often learn more effectively through interesting software programs that offer immediate feedback and go far beyond drill and practice and "workbooks on computers." Many of these tools offer challenging opportunities to exercise and develop higher-order thinking skills that are essential in problem-solving. Software programs come and go, but we would like to suggest some that have a long track record and continue to be successful.

Edmark's "Millie's Mathhouse," now offered through Riverdeep's The Learning Company, is a delightful and successful computer program that introduces number and math concepts to preschool and early elementary children. It is alive with color, sounds, and graphics, and works with a touch screen.

Children are introduced to essential math concepts as they build animated bugs, operate a cookie machine, count wiggling critters, and make patterns with talking animals and shapes. As they explore and discover, children learn about numbers, shapes, sizes, patterns, and problem-solving.

Geometry Inventor, also through Riverdeep's The Learning Company, offers opportunities for students of ages 6 to 12 to build and manipulate geometric figures and analyze mathematical relationships. Such tools are especially helpful for youngsters who are not developmentally ready to grasp more advanced math concepts. This company is one of the foremost publishers of interactive K–12 curricula and incorporates resources from other major software companies, at www.riverdeep.com.

Videodiscovery publishes innovative multimedia products for science and math education, offering extensive visual databases and lesson plans as well as critical thinking and problem-solving simulations that use lively dramatized video. For example, their multimedia videodiscs, "The Physics of Sports," "The Physics of Flight," and "The Physics of Work" use real events to relate physics to practical applications. As students analyze real world events in scientific and mathematical terms, the principles of physics become more meaningful and relevant. The company also offers computerized assessment software that helps students and teachers to evaluate scientific inquiry skills. See www.videodiscovery.com.

"The Adventures of Jasper Woodbury," developed by Vanderbilt University's Cognition and Technology Group, provides additional rich contexts for developing mathematical thinking and problem-solving about real world situations through "anchored instruction." There are twelve dramatic episodes on videodisc that present complex mathematical challenges offering numerous opportunities for problem-finding, problem-solving, reasoning, communication, and making connections to other areas such as science, social studies, literature, and history.

One of the first adventures, "Rescue at Boone's Meadow," presents the task of transporting a critically wounded eagle to a veterinary 65 miles away as quickly as possible. Because of the difficult terrain, students must figure out optimal combinations of using a truck, ultralight aircraft, and hiking, taking into consideration fuel, payload, weight, and different starting points. The students use a combination of the random-access videodisc, maps, and computers to generate alternative solutions. Fifth grade students of average ability have been fascinated with the task, and have been motivated to solve it with solutions that require over fifteen steps. See the website at http://peabody. vanderbilt.edu/ltc/Research/jasper.overview. html.

In many of these new "authentic learning" projects, learners become contributors to the collaborative knowledge base of the community. In the Global Lab project organized by the Technical Education Research Centers (TERC), an international group of teachers, high school students, and global-change researchers are collaborating in studying local and world ecological change using instruments such as ozonometers, ion-selective probes for soil and water monitoring, and field data loggers. Students learn to collect, analyze, and report data that are used by the scientists. And in the MicroObservatory project at Harvard University, secondary school students are using remote computer-controlled optical telescopes to do their own research projects in astronomy. See www.terc.edu.

TERC and NASA are developing an interdisciplinary year-long course for middle and high school students using astrobiology as its unifying structure. Through NASA's Educator Resource Center Network the organization provides the means for educators to access and utilize science, mathematics, and technology instructional products aligned with national standards. See http://education.nasa.gov/ercn.

Stanley Pogrow's "HOTS" (Higher Order Thinking Skills) program combines Socratic thinking in small groups with activities utilizing computer technology. This program, focused on learning how to understand and problem-solve, demonstrates clearly that most students, including the "at risk" and "learning disabled" are capable not only of learning the basic skills, but of developing and applying higher-order thinking skills in the process. See the website at www.hots.org.

A number of recreational games also have much to offer in the way of new intellectual challenges. For example, Sierra's "Lost Mind of Dr. Brain" exercises all of the intelligences in challenging puzzles and problem-solving activities. Logical and mathematical skills, anticipatory thinking, quick decision-making, symbolic thinking, and effective reasoning are engaged as players meet a variety of unexpected challenges. As they unscramble inverted melodies, break codes, navigate mazes, use retrieval systems to find scrambled files, and manipulate and rotate mental images, players get a "total brain work-out." They have options of playing on several levels of difficulty, and can access helpful "scaffolding" hints from Dr. Brain's lab assistant. When used in classrooms, teachers may wish to follow with related activities to assure that transfer of skills will occur and persist.

The tools described above are consistent with current research on "situated cognition." The focus of this research is on demonstrating that learning and thinking are always situated in a context, that knowing and doing are strongly linked, and, as a result, that authentic learning activities and direct experience provide rich opportunities for successful learning.

The website of the National Council of Teachers of Mathematics at http://nctm.org/eresources offers standards-based research and commentary on the teaching and learning of mathematics at all levels. It includes activities, ideas and strategies, lessons, useful links, and reports on timely mathematics educational issues. Other useful websites for math and science resources include http://unr.edu/homepage/jcannon/ejse/ejse.html (Electronic Journal of Science Education), www.exploratorium.edu/IFI/index.html (Exploratorium Institute for Inquiry), and http://courses.washington.edu/tep521/mathlinks.html (on mathematics education at the University of Washington).

Summary

· · · · · · · · · · · · · · · · · · ·

This chapter suggests ways to integrate logical-mathematical thinking across the curriculum. We realize that the reverse is true for many math and science teachers. Some endeavor to integrate the multiple intelligences into their subject areas. As we found in our 1999 book, *Multiple Intelligences and Student Achievement,* secondary math and science students have made strong gains with MI-based instruction. For example, at an Edmonds, Washington, high school, a science teacher had her special education students undertake a "Biology through Caretaking" project. To learn fundamental concepts such as change, cause and effect, structure and function, systems and diversity, and to develop the skills of hypothesizing, data gathering, and synthesizing, students were required to select and care for a plant or an animal. This year-long assignment taught them how to begin and sustain a project, document and display data, develop and demonstrate expertise, and self-assess their learning. Through incorporating an array of intelligences in the science classroom, the students have scored well on district and state measures. Likewise, down the hallway, math students learn algebra kinesthetically. When studying how to graph equations, they head outdoors. There they identify X and Y coordinates in the lines of the large, square, cement blocks of pavement and plot themselves as points on the cement axes. The math teacher maintains that by physically "becoming" graphs, students learn more about equations in a single class session than in a month of textbook study. Math students at the school have outperformed their peers on state and national tests.

Not all teachers teach math and science, but all can tap the higher-order thinking skills of logical-mathematical intelligence. When students use deductive and inductive logic, study patterns, and use technology, their interests in math and science can increase. They may also decide to continue their studies of these disciplines and to prepare for careers where they can utilize what they have learned.

To summarize, reflect, and synthesize the content of this chapter, the following is offered:

· · · · · · · · · · · · · · · · · · ·

 APPLYING LOGICAL-MATHEMATICAL INTELLIGENCE

1. Important ideas or insights gleaned from this chapter:

_____

_____

_____

_____

_____

2. Areas I'd like to learn more about:

_____

_____

_____

_____

_____

_____

_____

_____

_____

_____

_____

3. Ways I can use this information in my teaching. Please note that all of the strategies mentioned in this chapter are listed below with space provided to note how each might be incorporated into classroom instruction:

LOGICAL-MATHEMATICAL STRATEGY	CLASSROOM APPLICATION
Establishing a Logical-Mathematical Learning Environment	_____
The Teaching of Logic	
The Scientific Method	_____
Thinking Scientifically Across the Curriculum	_____
Deductive Logic	
Syllogisms	_____
Venn Diagrams	_____
Inductive Logic	
Analogies	_____
Enhancing Thinking and Learning	
Mediating Learning	_____
Questioning Strategies	_____
Mathematical Thinking Processes	
Patterning	_____
Graphs	_____

LOGICAL-MATHEMATICAL STRATEGY   CLASSROOM APPLICATION

Working with Numbers

Averages and Percentages   _____

Measurement   _____

Calculation   _____

Probability   _____

Geometry   _____

Story Problems Across the Curriculum

_____

Sequencing

_____

Math Themes for All Subject Areas

_____

Technology That Enhances
Logical-Mathematical Intelligence

_____

LOGICAL-MATHEMATICAL REFERENCES

Bennett, A., & Foreman, L. (1991). *Visual Mathematics Course Guide, Volume I.* Portland, OR: Math Learning Center.

Burns, M. (May/June 1993). "Math Standards in Action." *Instructor*, Vol 102, No. 9.

Campbell, L., & Campbell, B. (1999). *Multiple Intelligences and Student Achievement: Success Stories from Six Schools.* Alexandria, VA: ASCD.

Feuerstein, R., Rand, Y., & Rynders, J. (1998). *Don't Accept Me as I Am: Helping Retarded People to Excel.* Arlington Heights, IL: Skylight Professional Development.

Feuerstein, R. (1980). *Instrumental Enrichment: An Intervention Program for Cognitive Modifiability.* Baltimore: University Park Press.

Gardner, H. (1993). *Frames of Mind: The Theory of Multiple Intelligences.* New York: Basic Books.

Greenberg, K. (1989). The Cognitive Enrichment Network *(COGNET).* The University of Tennessee Follow Through Sponsor Project.

Greenberg, K. (2000). *Cognitive Enrichment Advantage.* Arlington Heights, IL: Skylight Professional Development.

Kennedy, J.G. (1959). *A Philosopher Looks at Science.* New York: Van Nostrand.

Kleiman, G. (October, 1991). "Mathematics Across the Curriculum." *Education Leadership*, Vol. 49, No.2. Association for Supervision and Curriculum Development.

Liem, Tik. (1987). *Invitations to Science Inquiry.* Chino Hills, CA: Science Inquiry Enterprises.

Lovell, R. (1993). *Probability Activities for Problem Solving and Skills Reinforcement.* Berkeley, CA: Key Curriculum Press.

Marzano, R., Brandt, R., Hughes, C., Jones, B.F., Presseisen, B., Rankin, S., & Suhor, C. (1988). *Dimensions of Thinking: A Framework for Curriculum and Instruction.* Alexandria, VA: ASCD.

Merseth, K. (March 1993). "How Old Is the Shepherd? An Essay about Mathematics Education." *Kappan*, Vol. 74, No.7: Bloomington IN: Phi Delta Kappa.

National Academy of the Sciences. (1995). *National Science Education Standards.* Washington D.C.: National Academy of the Sciences. Available online at http://www.nap.edu/html/nses/html/

National Council of Teachers of Mathematics. Online at www.nctm.org

National Council of Teachers of Mathematics. (2000). *Standards and Principles of School Mathematics.* Reston, VA: National Council of Teachers of Mathematics. Also available online at http://standards.nctm.org/

National Council of Teachers of Mathematics. (1991). *Professional Standards for Teaching Mathematics.* Reston, VA: National Council of Teachers of Mathematics.

Zemelman, S., Daniels, H., & Hyde, H. (1998). *Best Practices: New Standards for Teaching and Learning in America's Schools.* Portsmouth, NH: Heinemann.

3

Moving to Learn
KINESTHETIC INTELLIGENCE

*Ah, if you could only dance all that you've just said,
then I would understand.*

—Nikos Kazantzakis, *Zorba the Greek*

PAULA'S DANCE

In first grade, Paula was assessed as learning disabled. For the next four years, she was placed in special education classrooms and experienced little if any academic success.

Paula consistently lagged two or more grade levels behind her peers in the basic skills. Her self-esteem decreased and, understandably, her dislike of school increased. By the end of the fifth grade, Paula hid under her bed in the morning to avoid going to school, and during the summer before her sixth grade year, she attempted suicide. Her parents, knowing it was necessary for her to have a successful sixth grade year, mainstreamed her into a classroom with an empathetic teacher.

Observing the girl for the first couple of days, the teacher noticed an exceptional physical grace. Paula moved with poise and dignity. Tall for her age, she walked and ran with ease, her long hair mirroring her movements. Watching Paula, the teacher saw a dancer, and one day asked the girl if indeed she had ever studied dance. Paula explained she had taken ballet lessons and loved them but discontinued them because of their cost. This information made the teacher wonder if Paula would learn more efficiently through movement.

PAULA'S DANCE . . . continued

Although in sixth grade, Paula's spelling skills approximated those of a second-grader. She refused to read, write, or practice spelling word lists. Following her hunch that the girl was kinesthetically talented, the teacher suggested that Paula create a movement alphabet using her body to form each of the twenty-six letters. For example, to demonstrate the letter "t," Paula could stand erect, with her legs together and her arms outstretched. Some letters would obviously be challenging to create, such as an *m, b,* or a *w,* but they'd be thought-provoking and interesting to tackle. Paula said she would think about the teacher's suggestion.

Before school the next day, Paula hurried to her classroom, telling the teacher she had something to show her. Paula began her demonstration, dancing the letters of the alphabet one at a time and then sequencing all twenty-six into a unified performance. The ballet, performed with confidence and skill, was accomplished in total silence. Paula was unabashedly pleased with her efforts and the teacher was awestruck. The girl was a dancer. The instructor asked Paula if she could dance her first name. The dance was done effortlessly, with Paula adding her last name as well. Next, she danced the words on the board, and that evening Paula practiced a list of spelling words at home and danced them for her classmates the following day.

Within a week Paula quickly moved from dancing to writing. First, she performed individual words, then wrote them. Then she danced entire sentences. Paula's spelling and writing scores began to increase as did her self-confidence in learning.

After four months, to everyone's chagrin, Paula no longer danced her writing. She remained seated and wrote her assignments along with the rest of the class. By the end of her sixth grade year, Paula was writing and reading at grade level.

Four months of kinesthetic learning, of learning through an inherent strength, transformed Paula's school experience and her self-image. For her seventh grade year, Paula attended the local junior high school where, mainstreamed in all classes, she earned above-average grades.

DEFINITION: Understanding Kinesthetic Intelligence

Paula is not alone in her need to experience physically what she learns. Many children and adults find visual and auditory modes insufficient sensory channels for understanding and remembering information. Such individuals rely on tactile or kinesthetic processes and must manipulate or experience what they learn to understand and retain information. Tactile students learn through touch and manipulation of objects, and kinesthetic learners involve their whole bodies in their activities or prefer to work with concrete, real life experiences. Both tactile and kinesthetic individuals learn through "doing" and through multisensory experiences.

Kinesthetic learning processes are frequently undervalued in school since other problem-solving approaches are held in higher esteem. In *Frames of Mind,* Gardner notes that a separation between mind and body has emerged in recent cultural traditions. He cites the loss of the Greek ideal of "... a harmony between mind and body, with the mind trained to use the body properly, and the body trained to respond to the expressive powers of the mind."

Bodily-kinesthetic intelligence includes the ability to unite body and mind to perfect physical performance. Beginning with control of automatic and voluntary movements, kinesthetic intelligence progresses to using our bodies in highly differentiated and skilled ways. All talented performances require an acute sense of timing and the transformation of intention into action. Highly developed kinesthetic intelligence is evident when observing actors, athletes, or dancers. It is also inherent in the work of inventors, jewelers, and mechanics who work skillfully with their hands or objects. Bodily-kinesthetic intelligence is the foundation of human knowing since it is through our sensorimotor experiences that we experience life.

Physical activities focus student attention in the classroom and aid memory by encoding learning throughout the body's neuromusculature. We all possess "muscle memory," which can be effectively applied to the learning of academic subjects.

Robert McKim (1972) in his book *Experiences in Visual Thinking* describes the power of kinesthetic thinking as follows:

Consider the sculptor who thinks in clay, the chemist who thinks by manipulating three-dimensional molecular models, or the designer who thinks by assembling and rearranging cardboard make-ups. Each is thinking by seeing, touching, and moving materials, by externalizing his mental processes in a physical object.

Externalized thinking has several advantages over internalized thought. First, direct sensory involvement with materials provides sensory nourishment—literally "food for thought." Second, thinking by manipulating an actual structure permits serendipity—the happy accident, the unexpected discovery. Third, thinking in the direct context of sight, touch, and motion engenders a sense of immediacy, actuality, and action.

Finally, the externalized thought structure provides an object for critical contemplation as well as a visible form that can be shared with a colleague or even mutually formulated.

Unfortunately, learning often becomes increasingly internalized as students move into higher grades. With fewer opportunities for active, participatory learning, many become apathetic due to passive and abstract instruction. Physical education—in the fullest sense—belongs in every classroom. The activities suggested in this chapter can make learning more stimulating, dynamic, and memorable.

According to Gardner, those who possess the ability to use their bodies or parts of their bodies, such as hands, to solve problems have well-developed kinesthetic intelligence. Athletes, dancers, choreographers, mimes, actors, surgeons, and craftspeople exhibit high degrees of this intelligence. It's important to remember that being skilled in one kinesthetic realm does not necessarily indicate talent in another. For example, an individual may be gifted in the art of mime and yet reveal little, if any, talent in sports or handicrafts.

The following list identifies potential characteristics of individuals with kinesthetic aptitude. Please note, however, that every learner will not exhibit all of the following characteristics. Some areas may be more developed than others. It is likely that a person with well-developed kinesthetic intelligence:

1. Explores the environment and objects through touch and movement. Prefers to touch, handle, or manipulate what is to be learned.

2. Develops coordination and a sense of timing.

3. Learns best by direct involvement and participation. Remembers most clearly what was done, rather than what was said or observed.

4. Enjoys concrete learning experiences such as field trips, model building, or participating in role play, games, assembling objects, or physical exercise.

5. Shows dexterity in working by means of small or gross motor movements.

6. Is sensitive and responsive to physical environments and physical systems.

7. Demonstrates skill in acting, athletics, dancing, sewing, carving, or keyboarding.

8. Demonstrates balance, grace, dexterity, and precision in physical tasks.

9. Has the ability to fine-tune and perfect physical performances through mind and body integration.

10. Understands and lives by healthy physical standards.

11. May express interest in careers such as those of an athlete, dancer, surgeon, or builder.

12. Invents new approaches to physical skills or creates new forms in dance, sports, or other physical endeavors.

All of us express some kinesthetic tendencies and needs; however, those who literally must hold ideas in their hands to learn rarely have opportunities to do so. Multisensory learning is sometimes overlooked in classrooms, since such processes are unfamiliar. As educators, we lack role models to emulate and have few resources to turn to. Yet it is kinesthetic learning that frequently offers the most potent, enjoyable, and memorable educational experience for *all* learners. John Goodlad, one of the nation's leading educational researchers, noted in his book *A Place Called School*:

Regardless of subject, students reported that they liked to do activities that involved them actively or in which they worked with others. These included going on field trips, making films, building or drawing things, making collections, interviewing people, acting things out, and carrying out projects.

Students want to be active participants in their learning, not passive recipients of information. The next section describes several processes that encourage learning by doing.

Tactile-Kinesthetic
Learning Processes

▪ ▪ ▪ ▪ ▪ ▪ ▪ ▪ ▪ ▪ ▪ ▪ ▪ ▪ ▪ ▪ ▪ ▪ ▪ ▪

There are a wide variety of tactile-kinesthetic activities that enhance instruction for students of all ages. In this chapter, we describe physical learning experiences from the following categories:

The Physical Environment
   Classroom Zones

Drama
   Formal Theatre
   Role Playing
   Creative Drama
   Simulations

Creative Movement
   Understanding Bodily-Knowing
   Introducing Creative Movement Activities
   Applying Creative Movement to
      the Basic Skills
   Creating Content-Specific Movement
      Activities

Dance
   Elements of Dance Warm-Ups
   A Sequence for Learning through Dance

Manipulatives
   Task Cards
   Task Card Puzzles
   Junk Drawer Manipulatives
   Stamps

Classroom Games
   Scavenger Hunts
   Large Floor Games
   Total Physical Response Games
   A Generic Review Game

Physical Education
   Characteristics of a Physically Educated
      Person
   Expeditionary Learning

Exercise Breaks
   Quick Energizers
   Ten Shin Go So
   The Eight Treasures
   Eye Exercises
   Waking Up
   Calming Down

Field Trips
   Field Trip Guidelines

**Technology That Enhances
Kinesthetic Intelligence**

This list is far from exhaustive. Instead, it introduces teachers to a variety of kinesthetic processes to incorporate into any academic area. Once teachers become familiar with such techniques, they often gain the confidence to add kinesthetic opportunities to a variety of classroom lessons.

Establishing the Physical
Learning Environment

▪ ▪ ▪ ▪ ▪ ▪ ▪ ▪ ▪ ▪ ▪ ▪ ▪ ▪ ▪ ▪ ▪ ▪ ▪ ▪

The environments we live and work in affect us physiologically and psychologically. Most of us pay a significant amount of attention to our home environments. We determine the neighborhood to live in, the colors of interior and exterior walls, the furniture, photographs, and art work in each room, the layout and design of the interior space as well as the yard. Such considerations are equally important for classrooms, and yet there is often little attention given to the design of school environments.

When it has been thoughtfully organized or designed, the four-walled, self-contained classroom has tremendous potential to contribute to the learning process. Anne Taylor, an architect specializing in learning environments at the University of New Mexico, maintains that a classroom can serve as "an active, three-dimensional textbook or teaching tool, rather than a passive space housing a disarray of things."

Classrooms can be transformed into learning-enhancing environments with thought, enthusiasm, and design planning. Taylor and other architects recommend establishing several "zones" or separate areas in each classroom to serve specific functions, and as a result these zones are visually and functionally distinct. By redesigning classrooms into specific zones, educators might better accommodate the tactile and movement needs of kinesthetically oriented children. Simply providing students with the opportunity to walk from one work space to the next satisfies the need to stretch, move, and be active. Potential zones appropriate for either elementary or secondary classrooms might ideally include the following.

Classroom Zones

Entry Zone Upon arrival at the classroom, students can be welcomed with an entry space that includes plants, hanging fabric, partitions filled with student art, or the day's schedule of events.

Work Zone To accommodate multimodal instruction, several work zones might be established around the classroom with spaces for private, small-group, and whole-group work. Learning centers or stations can be established if appropriate. For an aesthetic touch, decorating the room with carpeting, student art samples, fine art prints, or plants creates a comfortable, home-like atmosphere. Copies of art work, posters, photographs, or quotations that reinforce classroom lessons can be visually displayed. The humming, flickering neon bulbs in traditional light fixtures might be replaced with full-spectrum lighting. Teachers and students, if resources allow, can consider whether desks or tables are appropriate work spaces. If possible, equipment such as easels, large paper pads, lap boards, markers and paints, pencils, paper, and construction items should be readily accessible.

Storage Zones Storage systems can be delineated with individual desks, bins, or colorful, plastic stacking trays that serve as "classroom lockers." Rules about responsibility for maintaining the classroom environment will need to be clearly communicated and followed.

Display Zones To avoid visual overload, selected spaces can be dedicated to the display of art work, messages, or photographs. Display walls or partitions might even attain a museum-like quality by the way works are hung and through the use of negative space.

Library Zone Classroom reference materials, literature, video machines, typewriters, and computers can be well organized in this zone. This is often an appropriate place for independent or small group work.

Soft Zone Many students enjoy a classroom when it conveys a living-room atmosphere. In a soft zone, students can read, lounge, play quiet games, or participate in small group discussions or creative dramatics. Such a zone can accommodate the needs of students who like to stretch out on the floor or on a couch to read.

Movement Zone A space can be designated for performing role plays or skits or for quick energizing or calming exercises. In a movement zone, furniture should be moved easily to accommodate small or large group activities. Teachers may also want to reflect on the existing traffic patterns in the classroom and consider how students move from one place to another. With intentional planning, movement around the classroom can be made more efficient.

From these suggested zones, it is evident that classroom environments can better accommodate the physical, academic, and psychological needs of students and teachers alike. Educators may want to identify appropriate designs for their classrooms. Foregoing fixed rows of student desks by intentionally planning classroom space can transform schools into healthy, humane, and exciting places to learn. When provided the opportunity, students often are willing architects who enjoy creating environments tailor-made to suit their needs.

Drama

■ ■ ■ ■ ■ ■ ■ ■ ■ ■ ■ ■ ■ ■ ■

Drama has served as a method of learning and re-membering from the beginning of recorded his-tory. Pictures on cave walls depict the enactment of great hunts and heroic deeds. The plays of ancient Greece were written not only to entertain and pro-vide emotional catharsis, but to educate as well. The dramas performed on the steps of medieval churches and temples taught people the morality and history of their religion. Today's theatres and television are also powerful educational forces in society—for better or worse.

The authors, as classroom teachers, have often wondered how anything could be taught without drama! It provides students with opportunities to almost become what they are studying and is a powerful way to bring academic content to life. Learning through drama is valuable at any grade level, but most especially in the middle school years when hormonal, physical, and psychological changes make learning in abstract ways even more difficult.

Whether students present a formal play before an audience or participate in theatre games not in-tended for an audience, enhanced learning often results.

Formal Theatre

Formal theatre productions involve all of the intel-ligences in dynamically related ways. Reading the play, assuming roles, memorizing lines and actions, creating costumes and sets, practicing music and at times choreography, and, finally, performing be-fore an invited audience all result in memorable ex-periences, enhanced self-confidence and poise, and learning that lasts a lifetime.

Memorizing lines written by great playwrights can begin early. A second grade class recently performed with great gusto their own abridged version of Shakespeare's *A Midsummer Night's Dream*. Their parents were astonished to hear Shakespeare quoted at the dinner table. What a rich foundation for later studies of such plays in greater depth!

An eighth grade French class spent an entire quarter translating the songs of *Hansel and Gretel* into French, creating sets and costumes, choreo-graphing the dances, and memorizing the songs and dialogue. Their performance for the rest of the school revealed their unprecedented gains in vo-cabulary and fluency in the process.

Some teachers have used a single Shake-spearean play such as *Romeo and Juliet* or *King Lear* as the theme for a year-long interdisciplinary curriculum. In such classrooms, math assignments are integrated into set construction, history is based on Elizabethan times, science on what was then known about astronomy, anatomy, and biol-ogy, art on costume design, and health on conta-gious diseases of the period.

Teachers who are committed to incorporating traditional theatre into their classrooms explain that students learn far more than the script, stage presence, and integrated academic content. The mental, physical, and technical discipline required to succeed on stage is also needed to succeed in life. Additionally, important cognitive skills are de-veloped through rehearsing and performing, in-cluding the ability to organize thought, to perceive and analyze, to evaluate and reason, to discern the whole as well as the parts, to address complexity and ambiguity, and to collaborate with others to achieve a common goal. Theatre provides students with a rigorous educational experience that pre-pares them well for real world problem-solving.

Two useful sources of scripts can be found on-line. One is Samuel French at www.samuelfrench. com. A second is Baker's plays at http:// bakersplays.com.

Role Playing

Less formal than theatre, role playing gives teachers and students the freedom to create plays from topics studied in class. Unlike formal theatre, the process is more important than the product. Nearly any subject area can be transformed into role-plays, including mathematical story problems, scientific processes, the parts of speech, or historic events. Role-plays add action to language, are powerful tools for teaching information, and also develop interpersonal, intrapersonal, and problem-solving skills.

For teachers unfamiliar with the process, there are three main steps in preparing role-plays: planning, rehearsal and performance, and evaluation. Guidelines are provided below to assist teachers in their preparation.

Step 1: Planning

1. To ready students for a role-play, it is first necessary to determine the desired educational objectives. Specify the learning outcomes for students to attain.

2. After the objectives are determined, the teacher or students can outline the role-play. The situation, the problem, or the fundamental issue should be identified.

3. Next, develop the roles and a process for selecting performers.

4. Determine whether the actors will have set lines to memorize or make up their own scripts.

5. Specify the amount of preparation time needed.

6. If there are student observers of the role-play, explain the audience's role and appropriate behavior. Also identify what the audience should listen or watch for.

7. Arrange the physical environment as appropriate.

8. Secure necessary resources such as equipment, costumes, or props.

Step 2: Rehearsal and Performance

Once the scenes are designed and the class informed of the objectives and content, students are ready to rehearse. An adequate amount of time is needed for preparation. All nonperforming students should be reminded to be supportive audience members as well as constructive evaluators.

When the rehearsals are complete, specify a time, date, and place for the performances. Ask the actors if they would like to have other classes or parents observe. If not, honor their request to perform for their classmates only.

Occasionally, a teacher may want to intervene during a performance if an actor is in distress or the interaction is inappropriate. In such cases, the teacher can offer a brief reflection on what has occurred and then allow the group to resume its role-play with the noted adjustments or with additional rehearsal time.

Step 3: Evaluation

After the performances, have students debrief their experiences. Questions can address the academic content, performance skill, student reactions to their experiences, and the audience's reactions as well since student observers can highlight what was done well and what might be improved. The teacher may or may not choose to have a role in the evaluation.

Role-plays are easily devised for nearly any subject. Students can role play individuals addressing prejudice and its impact, scientists at a press conference after the discovery of a medical breakthrough, or a child having difficulty learning to regroup in subtraction with a helper explaining the process. Assuming the roles of diverse life forms and their dependence on the environment can be role played, as can individuals addressing social or behavioral issues. And current or historical events are easily enacted.

A secondary level example of a role-play that addresses diverse points of view is the confirmation of a political appointee. The class can research and discuss the appointment, its ramifications, and the fact that there are likely pros and cons to the individual's political agenda. Next, students identify the various characters involved in the confirmation process and "cast" the appropriate parts, ready the scene, including the confirmation panel, and determine whether the "audience" might actually serve as an interactive gallery in the process. The role-play can start with the appointee presenting herself and the panel members questioning or supporting her. After a few minutes the class could be asked whether they would approve the appointment and why.

A second example, at the elementary level, might address an unpopular rule for recess. Students might disagree with a rule that prohibits the use of hardballs such as baseballs during school hours. Roles could include those who support the rule, impartial students, the school nurse, administrators, parents, and neighbors. After the role-play, a discussion might follow with each participant explaining his point of view. It is often useful to have students represent an opinion different from the one they actually hold. Upon completion of the role-play, the class could write and send a recommendation to the school administration.

Creative Drama

Creative drama is less formal than role-plays since lines and actions are improvised as the play or scene develops. Reenacting a scene to incorporate suggestions for improvement is an important component of this kind of theatre experience. Working without an audience is often necessary to allow students to concentrate and perform without self-consciousness.

One easy way to begin working with creative drama in the classroom is to ask students to play "group characters." For example, a primary teacher might read a story with characters that include an old man, a little girl, and a giant. As a group the children can pantomime each of the characters, perhaps to appropriate music, and begin to develop confidence to play the part individually.

After the teacher reads the story, students can review the plot, discuss how to perform it, volunteer to play the different characters, plan the setting, and set the stage for action. A stage manager can be in charge of calling "Curtain" at the beginning and ending of the scenes. Following the performance, all students can critique what was successful and what needs improvement.

Once a class gains experience in such activities, they can begin to improvise and dramatize more open-ended situations such as the organization of state offices with appointed and elected officials, the causes and effects of extinction, magnets attracting or repelling each other, or predicting what will happen as the adult population ages in the United States.

One example of the power of creative drama emerged in a fourth grade science class when the teacher realized her students did not understand photosynthesis as described in their textbooks. Deciding to try a kinesthetic approach, the instructor asked volunteers to act out the five main "characters" involved in the process of photosynthesis: a plant, chloroplasts, water, carbon dioxide, and sunlight.

Simple signs made out of notecards were pinned onto each character. The teacher served as the narrator with the volunteer performers dramatizing chloroplasts resting on a leaf of a plant whose roots were drinking water from the ground. The water character sprinkled water on the ground and "feet" of the plant. Suddenly, sunlight shone on the leaf (portrayed with a flashlight) which caused the chloroplasts to absorb energy (flexed muscles). The chloroplasts, powered by sunlight, took the water and a gas from the air called carbon dioxide and twirled these two around to make sugar (candy bar), which then nurtured the entire plant.

This brief performance was repeated three times by different student volunteers, took five to six minutes of time, and greatly improved the students' understanding of the concept. After the performances, students drew the process of photosynthesis on a piece of notebook paper and verbally explained it to their partners. A week later, 90% of the students in the class accurately described photosynthesis on a written quiz.

As another example, a class of eleventh grade English students recently embarked on the study of Chaucer with less than enthusiastic attitudes until they brought Chaucer's *Canterbury Tales* to life through creative drama. Their teacher read the prologue aloud with feeling and humor and engaged the class in a discussion of the characteristics of these colorful people. Next, the teacher put student names in a medieval hat and let the students each draw one. The following day, after rereading the material, the students came into the classroom as the characters they had chosen. In groups of four, they planned a meeting at a likely place—on the road or at a wayside tavern—and improvised dialogue keeping in mind everything they knew about the characters they were playing. Within a few days, they requested help in speaking Middle English!

Simulations

Simulations are also powerful learning tools since they place students in an environment or situation where they must imitate or replicate real world scenarios. Simulations can be easily developed as appropriate for the content at hand. Examples of those used in classrooms follow.

- Visit a restaurant where students order food in a foreign language.
- Spend a class period "living" during a significant time in history such as the Renaissance, the Civil War, or under the rule of Stalin.
- Conduct a trial on the confiscation of land from Native Americans, new senate bills, or involvement in war efforts.
- Reenact the arrival of immigrants at Ellis Island.
- Establish a mini-classroom United Nations.
- Make decisions for school, medical, or environmental crises.
- Live in a lunar space colony with limited numbers of people and resources.

Designing Simulations

Teacher-generated or commercial simulations can be used or adapted to teach a variety of academic content. The following steps outline how to create simulations.

1. First, determine the learning goals as with role-plays.

2. Next, identify simulation rules so that the constraints inherent in the real life situation are replicated.

3. Gather and organize any resources or materials that will be needed.

4. Predetermine the logistics of the simulation such as dividing the class into small groups, assigning work spaces, and allotting time.

5. Schedule a discussion or writing session in which students debrief their completed simulation experiences.

Thoroughly prepared science and social studies simulations are commercially available with content areas appropriate for elementary, middle level, and high school students. One helpful resource is Interact, online at: http://www.interact-simulations.com/.

Whether working with formal theatre, role-plays, creative dramatics, or simulations, planning is essential to avoid classroom chaos. Freedom to create must exist within a clear structure guided by well-defined expectations. The main objective in using theatre-based strategies is to encourage students to enact information they are learning. For some, this will be the way they will truly absorb and understand the content. For most, it will be the way they will remember it.

Creative Movement

....

Movement theorists such as Rudolf Laban and Henri Bergson underscore the relationship between nonverbal movement experiences and abstract symbolic thought. Through movement we can both perceive and express the meaning in our experiences. By incorporating creative movement in the classroom, students are asked to problem-solve and analyze physically, while engaging their creative imagination in the process.

As Edward T. Hall, a noted anthropologist, states in his book, *Beyond Culture* ". . . Western man has created chaos by denying that part of his self that integrates while enshrining the parts that fragment experience." In order to integrate body and mind, it may be necessary to re-introduce ourselves to physical knowing.

Often teachers are uncomfortable using movement in the classroom. This may be because they do not perceive the value of physical activity, or they see themselves as physically limited, or they are simply unfamiliar with such processes. The following creative movement strategies introduce such concepts in ways that are comfortable and practical for teacher and student alike. The range of strategies includes reflecting on bodily knowing, initial creative movement activities, theatre games, and applying creative movement to basic skills instruction. We suggest you read through all strategies and then select the ones that appear most applicable.

Peggy Hackney, an author and a nationally recognized authority in Laban Movement Analysis, recommends that teachers and students address the following questions to heighten kinesthetic sensitivity and to increase body awareness.

Understanding Bodily-Knowing

1. On a piece of paper, jot down associations, images, sounds, feelings, thoughts, concepts, beliefs, and "shoulds" for the word "body."

2. Draw a picture of yourself. Indicate on the drawing where on your body different parts of your life are represented such as school, home, sports, family, friends, pets, hobbies, and work.

3. Next, consider unique forms of body knowing:

   Where in your body does sensation register when you and another person are in disagreement?

   Observe another person for a moment. What is his or her body communicating nonverbally?

   When you make a decision, where do you sense its right- or wrongness?

   When you are creating ideas for teaching or doing a school project, where do the ideas come from?

The above questions hint at dimensions of kinesthetic intelligence and the wisdom of bodily-knowing. When involved in any activity, it is often beneficial to reflect for a moment on how we are physically engaged, our sensations, and forms of physical insight. Knowledge is felt kinesthetically and can be accessed by listening to the body and by moving to learn.

In addition to getting in touch with physical knowing, it is also possible to use creative movement to learn. Hackney offers suggestions for introducing moving to learn in the classroom as follows.

Introducing Creative Movement Activities

1. Through individual or small group movement, physically represent an animal, cloud, tree, concept, or event. Such identification enables students to perceive relationships and deepens their knowing of the object or event being considered. Movement experiments can be linked directly to subject matter such as the water cycle, a historical event, a mathematical formula, or the structure of a short story.

2. Identify habitual movements in school and life situations. Learn to notice when your body is feeling physically tense, when your breathing stops, or when you avert your eyes. Such indicators signal discomfort and may compound physical stress. Conversely, notice situations that make you feel energized, eager, and comfortable. Reflect on what can be gleaned from such awareness to enhance other activities in life.

3. Imagine how ideas move. Catch an idea and encode it in physical movement. Provide students with five or so minutes during class to express through movement the concepts being learned. If students are initially hesitant, ask them to use only their arms and hands. Afterwards, ask them to explain what they learned about their topic by experiencing it kinesthetically.

It is important for the teacher to model physical activities as methods of enhancing learning and personal awareness. If the teacher feels uncomfortable doing so, mention such discomfort to students, enlist their suggestions and support, or bring a guest into the classroom to assist both the students and teacher with easing into such activities.

Applying Creative Movement to the Basic Skills

Creative movement activities are absorbing for many students. Teachers might initiate movement activities by asking questions such as, "How could movement reinforce this concept?" "How can classroom space be used to introduce today's math problems?" "How might you express what you have learned through movement?" As the teacher becomes accustomed to using movement as a tool for learning, answers will appear more readily.

To begin integrating creative movement into the teaching of basic skills, the following suggestions are provided for math and language arts.

Language Arts Students can study vocabulary through charades. They might role play parts of speech, proper outline form, the elements of literature, or characters and their motives. Individually they can develop finger or body alphabets or use macaroni, shaving cream, yarn, and glue for spelling-word practice. The whole class can silently pantomime stories as they are read. Students can physically punctuate written work by jumping out of their seats for exclamation marks, holding two fingers up on each hand for quotation marks, and arching an arm for a comma.

Mathematics Story problems can be enacted with small groups of students. Students can draw flow charts explaining subtraction, division, or algebraic problem-solving processes on carpeting or a cement floor. Once drawn, they can walk through the mathematical process in sequential steps. Geometry can be studied through kite-making, role playing theorems and axioms, and using one's arms to demonstrate right, obtuse, and acute angles. Area and perimeter can be learned by measuring distances within the classroom or on school grounds, and the metric system might be studied through paper airplane–building and –flying to scale.

For teachers who want to teach academic content with creative movement, responding to the following questions can help generate appropriate activities.

Creating Content-Specific Movement Activities

1. How can physical movement be added to this lesson? How can students use their bodies to "become" the topic under study?

2. What learning opportunities can be provided for students who need to move to learn while accommodating the needs of non-kinesthetic learners at the same time?

3. What kind of directions will clearly explain what is to be done kinesthetically?

4. How can students be encouraged to describe what they have learned after their kinesthetic experience?

5. How might students be involved in brainstorming their own kinesthetic opportunities to help themselves learn more efficiently?

6. What classroom management strategies will encourage appropriate participation?

Dance

∎ ∎ ∎ ∎ ∎ ∎ ∎ ∎ ∎ ∎ ∎ ∎ ∎ ∎ ∎ ∎ ∎ ∎

Another form of creative movement is dance. Through dance, students have the opportunity to learn, synthesize, and demonstrate their knowledge by means of choreography. For those interested in incorporating dance into the classroom, two excellent resources are *Teaching the Three R's through Movement* by Anne Green-Gilbert, published by MacMillan and *A Moving Experience: Dance for Lovers of Children and the Child Within* by Teresa Benzwie, published by Zephyr Press. Both books illustrate how teachers can help children discover qualities of space, time, numbers, and rhythm, while integrating cognitive learning with dance.

As with any form of creative movement, warm-ups are important before students explore dance. The following warm-ups not only help prepare students for kinesthetic activity, they also introduce the elements of dance. They are provided by Debbie Gilbert and Joanne Petroff , Co-Directors of the Whistlestop Dance Company.

Elements of Dance Warm-Ups

Time

1. To work with the element of time, ask students to walk at different speeds such as fast, medium, and slow. Suggest the use of other locomotive movements such as slide, jump, crawl, and leap. Select and play taped music with different speeds, play a drum at varying rates, or find a musician to accompany the movement.

2. From student work, select a "character" that is either a person, place, or thing. Ask students to move across the room as that character using motions that seem most fitting.

Space

1. Ask students to use their bodies to create and explore a small space, a large space, a high space, and a low space.

2. Suggest that students explore an imaginary cave with tiny passageways, large caverns, high ledges, and low tunnels. Musical instruments or voices can be used for sound effects.

Shape

1. While music is playing, ask students to move through the space in the room and freeze when it stops, noting the shapes of their frozen musical sculptures.

2. Together as a group, suggest that students make twenty-five shapes, changing with each beat of a drum or music.

3. In small groups, let students create shapes taken from classroom lessons, such as an isosceles triangle, a hydrogen molecule, quotation marks, or an historical date.

4. From students' academic studies, select a large, complex shape for students to create in groups such as a geometric theorem, a governmental system, a molecular structure, the parts of an essay, or the spread of a contagious disease.

Energy

1. As music plays or a drum beats, students move first with "swinging" energy, then with "shaking" energy, and finally with "smooth" energy, inventing sounds to go with each energy quality.

2. In a circle so that everyone can see one another, each student takes a turn as dance leader. The "leader" chooses an energy quality and demonstrates it, after which the others imitate this spontaneous choreography.

3. Select "actions" from class lessons such as dividing, borrowing, exploring, researching, or editing, and use any or all of the energy qualities to turn the actions into dance.

Once students have practiced the warm-ups, they can use the elements of dance to choreograph stories, poems, historical events, and mathematical formulas.

A Sequence for Learning through Dance

1. Select a story, event, or process to transform into a dance. Have musical selections or a drum available for student use.

2. Divide the selection into scenes or sections.

3. Assign a small group to each section.

4. Let the small groups explore ways to use the elements of dance and provide time for choreographing their sections.

5. As a whole group, have students create a beginning shape or entrance and an ending shape or exit.

6. Select a narrator to read or explain each section.

7. Put it all together. As the narrator explains the action, the students dance the information. The narrator may want to use a hand-held drum or play a musical selection to highlight the content, cue movements, set the mood, or inspire the dancers. Videotape the dance for later viewing and show the live or taped performance to an audience.

Many classrooms have discovered creative ways to incorporate dance into traditional curriculum areas. One third grade teacher, during a unit on space, created a dance of the planets. Students spun, imitating the rotation of the planets, while correctly moving counterclockwise in orbit. Students portraying the sun, moon, comets, and meteors all moved in appropriate relationship to each other.

A fifth grade teacher combined European folk dances with creative movement to teach spelling words. Students learned the basic steps and rhythms of traditional dances and then created their own variations. Additionally, they had to weave the spelling of their weekly words into the choreography.

A high school Spanish teacher asked students to write songs in Spanish and combine them with dancing. Vocabulary increased rapidly and test scores improved, particularly among many of the students who previously had difficulty with the new language.

Students of all ages love to move rhythmically. Reluctance to "dance" in front of one's peers can be overcome by beginning simply and using warm-ups and movement games. Above all, however, creative movement should begin with the teacher, his or her subject area, and a splash of creativity. There is no right way to move or dance. All of us can discover our own preferred ways to move, to dance, and to learn.

Manipulatives

In third grade, Jason loved to build with blocks, Legos, toothpicks, Popsicle sticks, anything that fit together. During a unit on ancient history, Jason built an object for every culture studied. He fashioned Babylonian ziggurats out of Legos, Egyptian pyramids with toothpicks and small marshmallows, the Great Wall of China from miniature clay bricks he made, the Greek Parthenon from styrofoam computer packing, Roman bridges out of Popsicle sticks and brads, and Mayan temples with molded plastic strips resurrected from an old science kit. Apathetic during most classroom activities, Jason was highly animated during his building projects. History came alive for him when he built the structures of each era and culture studied.

Piaget and others have noted the importance of experiential materials in the learning process. Frequently, the use of pattern blocks, plastic cubes, colored rods, geoboards, tangrams, and other manipulatives meet both tactile and developmental needs of students. Such manipulatives can be used to replicate anything from geometric shapes to Greek architecture to complex sugar molecules. What a student can see and manipulate in the environment ensures learning in ways that reading and lecture cannot.

Many ready-made materials exist to improve the teaching of math, spelling, science, reading, or geography. At times, however, teachers need materials for a particular unit that are not commercially available. The task cards and puzzles described below provide one option for making inexpensive classroom manipulatives.

Task Cards

Rita and Kenneth Dunn (1978), in their book *Teaching Students Through Their Individual Learning Styles*, recommend the creation of task cards as instructional aids. Task cards can augment the teaching of any subject and can introduce, reinforce, or review learning. Easy to make, these manipulatives satisfy the desire to see and touch at the same time.

Few materials are required to make task cards. Notecards (3'' × 5'' or 4'' × 6''), scissors, and a set of colored markers are the necessary supplies. Each card is cut into two pieces in a jigsaw fashion. A question can be written on one side of the card with the matching puzzle piece showing the answer. Or, one side might have a vocabulary word with the corresponding definition on the other similar to flash cards. Some samples follow.

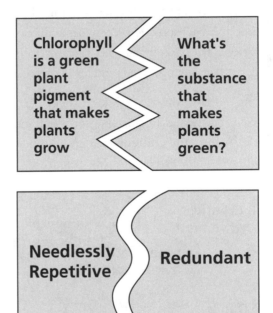

Once a set of cards is prepared, students can take turns in pairs or small groups fitting the puzzle pieces together and quizzing each other on the information. In addition to tactile experience, students should verbally explain each completed puzzle piece to reinforce learning. In some cases, students might put the cards in order while providing a verbal rationale.

After the first set of task cards is complete, ingenious ways of making future cards will become evident. Some sets might feature movable parts, color-coding, or self-correcting options. Students can volunteer to create their own sets to reinforce their learning or to use them to teach others. Sets can be stored in decorated or labeled boxes.

Task Card Puzzles

A variation of the task card is the task card puzzle, which requires a sheet of cardstock either 8″ × 11″ or larger. The topic is written in the center with subtopics or supporting details arranged around the central theme. The puzzle is cut into jigsaw pieces and scrambled. As a student fits the puzzle together, he or she has time to learn and reflect on the information at hand. Students can also be asked to embellish each puzzle piece with additional information, to paraphrase the information provided, or to create task card puzzles of their own.

One jigsaw puzzle of kinesthetic learning processes addressed in this chapter is offered as a sample. Again, any content area could quickly be introduced or reviewed with this strategy.

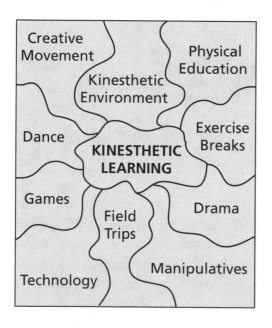

Junk Drawer Manipulatives

Other manipulatives can be found by scouring drawers at home. Maria Montessori found her classroom materials in the junk piles of Rome. But-

tons, beans, pebbles, and pennies are just a few of the items that can be used for math counters. Toothpicks connected by marshmallows or dried peas soaked overnight make wonderful building materials for geometric shapes, houses, or spaceships.

Colored electrical wire can be bent and twisted into diverse shapes for use in many subject areas. This easy-to-manipulate material can replicate the anatomy of plants, animals, or structures, enabling students to sculpt them according to scale. Old shoe boxes make fine backgrounds for dioramas of all sorts. Play dough or clay can also recreate scenes or characters from stories. With a little imagination, manipulatives can be found or made to add a tactile dimension to almost any lesson.

Stamps

Stamps and block print devices are readily available classroom manipulatives. They can be made from everyday materials such as vegetables, plants, sponges, styrofoam, egg cartons, plaster, linoleum, and cardboard. By gluing string onto a dowel, spool, roller, or rolling pin, a "running" stamp can be made. Even fingers make effective stamps.

Making Classroom Stamps and Block Prints

An inexpensive and easy way to make durable, long-lasting stamps is to use inner-tube rubber. They are free at any tire store.

1. Cut rubber into 2-inch squares with scissors and distribute the squares to students.

2. Cut small blocks of wood in two, one for each student. 1″ × 2″s from the lumber yard work well, as do thick sticks cut into 2″ lengths.

3. Students first draw a model stamp design or stencil on paper. When the stencil is complete, it can be cut out of the rubber with scissors.

4. Next, glue designs on blocks of wood. (Remember, like mirror reflections, they print in the reverse of what is seen.) Students may put a stamp on both ends. Most types of glue work well; however, adequate drying time is essential, preferably overnight.

5. For printing ink, stamp pads work effectively, requiring the least clean-up. Block printing ink is the most permanent and professional looking, while tempera paint is cheap but messy. Elementary students can use markers applied directly to the stamp to create simple prints.

From simple inner-tube stamps to commercial selections, endless possibilities exist for their uses. Once made, ask students to use their stamps in a variety of ways: in math, problems and solutions can be stamped; "signature" stamps can identify student work; patterns can be studied in art, music, or math; in science, stamps can create molecular chains, electrical circuits, cell parts; in language arts, stamps can be used for punctuation. Any art history or multicultural unit would be incomplete without stamps, since cultures throughout time have used them for everything from calligraphy in manuscripts to the decoration of wedding garments. Everyday designs like arrows, stars, hearts, and other symbols can serve as student logos or simply beautify classroom work.

Examples of stamp designs printed by third-graders follow. The first are Chinese characters. The second is a traditional design from Ghana, West Africa.

One class used storm, sun, and rain stamps on state and United States maps to track, analyze, and predict weather patterns. Another used stamps to create rebus stories for younger children. Although commercially made stamps are available in educational supply outlets, catalogs, and stationery stores, students usually enjoy the process of making them as much as using them.

Classroom Games

Game-based teaching has had numerous advocates. John Dewey (1990) claimed games were integral to schooling since they provided active and positive learning experiences. George Herbert Mead, a colleague of Dewey's, acknowledged their importance for the healthy socialization of children. Through games, children learn to imitate and assume diverse social roles. Likewise, Jean Piaget stressed the importance of game-playing in cognitive development.

Games involve students in imaginative and challenging situations that increase factual knowledge and decision-making and interpersonal skills. When learning through games, most students eagerly and enthusiastically pursue their studies.

Games exist in many forms and can be elaborate technological simulations or as simple as "Simon Says." There are many ready-made classroom games such as "Take Off" or "Yotta." Teachers, however, frequently want games that teach specific academic content. The ones described in the following section are easy to make and adaptable to any subject matter area. They include scavenger hunts, large floor games, total physical response games modeled after the foreign language learning method developed by James Asher, and a generic review game.

Scavenger Hunts

One game eagerly played by elementary and secondary students alike is a revised version of the scavenger hunt. Scavenger hunts serve as fun-filled research processes appropriate for gathering data on any topic. Guidelines for creating scavenger hunts follow.

Creating a Classroom Scavenger Hunt

To create a scavenger hunt, the teacher first identifies a topic the students are about to study. It is necessary to list ten to thirty essential concepts the unit will cover. This list, once compiled, serves as the basis of the scavenger hunt and directs student research. When the "hunt" is distributed, students are organized into small groups. Working in teams, each student is responsible for collecting two to six items on the list. Once all data have been gathered, the teams present what they have learned to the other groups in the class. Points may be assigned to each item to turn the activity into a class competition or omitted to emphasize collaboration.

One high school history teacher wanted students to study the fall of Rome and make generalizations about the cycle of civilizations. Some of the sample scavenger hunt items she created included:

1. Find three written resources that describe the decline of the Roman Empire. Compare and contrast their versions of what happened.

2. Identify and watch a film or videotape about the fall of Rome.

3. Identify and interview a knowledgeable adult about the reasons for the decline. Such adults may include other social studies teachers at the high school, community members, or history professors from the local university.

4. Gather data on Rome's monetary systems and its weaknesses.

5. Gather data on Rome's leaders and the military.

6. Gather data on the countries surrounding Rome and their increasing strength.

7. Pool all relevant information from the above items.

8. Make a chart that explains the potential causes and effects involved in Rome's downfall.

9. Make an educated guess as to the decline of Rome other than the reasons cited above and substantiate the claim.

10. Create a visual that explains your group's perception of the cycles of civilization.

11. Compare and contrast your group's theory of civilization with American culture today.

Scavenger hunts are an effective kinesthetic research process. Students may need two to three weeks to gather information and to prepare a group presentation for their classmates. Teachers will find it necessary to set aside classroom space on bulletin boards, desks, or tables for students to display their data.

Large Floor Games

Large floor games can reinforce any kind of academic content. Simple materials such as paper plates and colored markers are the only supplies needed to create the games described below.

Paper Plate Games

One effective physical learning format is a paper plate game. Teachers write facts on paper plates that are placed on the floor about two feet apart. For example, a science teacher might want to devise a game to review the names and symbols of the chemical elements. He would write C (for carbon) on three to four plates, Ca (for calcium), H (for hydrogen), and Mg (for magnesium) on several additional plates. It is necessary to write each symbol on three or four plates so that there are multiple copies. Next, the teacher picks a small group of approximately four to six student volunteers to play the game.

Two simple rules for game-playing must be explained: Students must not talk or touch anyone else while playing. They are to silently hop onto the answer they think is correct. When they are ready to begin, the teacher calls out the element and students jump onto the paper plate with the correct symbol. The audience verifies whether the game players have selected the correct answers.

Students enjoy playing this game, which can be readily adapted to science, math, language arts, world language, health, or art.

Kinesthetic Flow Charts

Numerous large floor games of all types can be created from simple flow chart formats. The best kind of academic content for this game is sequential as is found in plot structure, math formulas, recipes, scientific processes, or historical events. Teachers or students first design flow charts on notebook paper and then transfer them onto large sheets of butcher paper or vinyl. To begin creating a kinesthetic flow chart, first consider information to be placed into each of the boxes below.

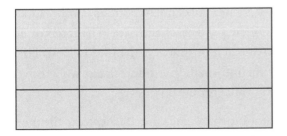

Cut out the boxes and arrange them in a logical sequence. Arrows can indicate the order of steps involved. Once satisfied with the mock-up of the

flow chart, transfer it to a large piece of vinyl or butcher sheet as follows:

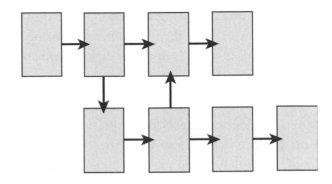

When the chart is ready, students actually walk or hop through it while explaining the information they step on. Such verbalization reinforces the kinesthetic learning of the academic content. For sample flow charts, refer to the visual-spatial chapter that follows later in this book.

Total Physical Response Games

Dr. James Asher is the originator of a second language learning method called Total Physical Response (TPR). This movement-based approach involves students in games and kinesthetic activities and mirrors the way infants acquire their first language. A teacher's verbal commands and corresponding gestures convey the meaning of her spoken words. Students replicate the instructor's movements and are encouraged to use words when they feel confident doing so. TPR is currently used extensively in this country and abroad with thousands of second-language learners. Those interested in learning more about TPR language instruction should read Asher's (2000) book, *Learning Another Language through Action*.

Because of its success, TPR components have been adapted for general teaching. Its game-like nature readily transfers to the teaching of all content areas. Some simple games for the basic skills follow.

Math Divide students into three groups such as decimals, fractions, and percents. Give each group approximately ten minutes to determine the benefits and purposes of being a fraction, percent, or decimal. Each group then attempts to convince the other two of the superiority of their mathematical process.

Students form a circle and a ball is tossed to one. A student or teacher calls out a math problem; students who know the answer raise their hands; the ball is tossed to one who must give the correct answer. Another question is asked. The student with the ball throws it to a classmate with a raised hand. The ball is tossed each time an additional question is asked and someone responds correctly. Those students who have difficulty generating correct answers can be assigned as the question givers before the game begins. The point of the game is to help everyone experience success in learning.

Science Groups of students can volunteer to portray elements that become different molecules. For example, one group might be methane (CH_4), another water (H_2O), another sulfur trioxide (SO_3). Each group must decide how many atoms of carbon and hydrogen to enact for the rest of the class. As the formulas of the molecules are demonstrated, the audience guesses the identity of each, and students quickly draw a picture of the formula as well.

Any Curriculum Area Draw a large hopscotch grid on a concrete floor or on a carpeted floor in chalk. Inside each square, write a vocabulary word students are learning. In groups, students proceed through the hopscotch, taking another turn only if they offer a correct definition for the vocabulary word in their square.

If asked, students will eagerly generate game ideas based on their studies. Teachers might occasionally include creating a classroom game as an optional assignment.

A Generic Review Game

To involve students in a kinesthetic review of academic material, gather a few simple resources and prepare the following game. The required materials include one notecard per student, colored markers, and one large ball of twine. On each notecard, students write one vocabulary word, fact, or name they recently learned from a classroom lesson. Each card ideally contains information distinct from every other card.

Once the cards have been prepared, the game is ready to begin. Gather and redistribute the cards, giving one to each person in class. Students then form a large circle. The teacher begins by throwing a ball of twine to a student in the circle. That student starts the game by stating what's written on her card and expanding on that information in some manner. If a student is stuck, she may ask for assistance from someone to her right or left. Once the information is shared, other students in the circle raise their hands if they can explain how their cards relate to what was just said. The student holding the ball wraps the twine around a finger and tosses the ball to a student with her hand raised. The second student explains how the information on her card relates to what was just shared and adds any other additional information as well. Other students then raise their hands to continue the game.

For the initial round, each student should have only one opportunity to contribute and catch the ball of twine. Subsequent rounds can be added if the students and teacher desire. The interconnecting twine demonstrates visually and kinesthetically how the information is interrelated while offering an enjoyable review process.

During the game, the teacher can change the level of questioning to engage higher-level thinking skills. After six or seven students have played, or during a second round, the teacher might request that students explain how their card differs from what was just stated, whether the preceding comments were correct, and/or create new responses that are unique and imaginative. After everyone has contributed and the game is over, assign a student at the end of the review to rewind the ball of twine for future use.

Physical Education

New definitions of physical education are emerging from sport and educational associations. Rather than viewing physical education as a class that takes place in the gym three or more times a week, many groups call for a broader perspective of the field. In 1995, the National Standards Association for Physical Education identified the characteristics of a "physically educated student." The standards emphasize an essential aspect of kinesthetic intelligence: the importance of knowing and participating in health-enhancing activities.

Characteristics of a Physically Educated Person

1. Competency in many movement forms and proficiency in a few

2. Informed approaches to learning and developing motor skills

3. A physically active lifestyle

4. The maintenance of a healthy level of physical fitness

5. Responsible personal and social behavior in physical activities

6. Respect for differences in physical abilities among others

7. Appreciation of the opportunities for enjoyment, challenge, self-expression, and social interaction available in physical activity

While the definition of physical education is expanding, important work has been done in refining performance in specific physical endeavors. Peak performance researchers have learned much about educating for and perfecting physical and academic skills. One outcome they emphasize in physical education is the necessary union of body and mind to enhance any physical skill. Some of this information is shared in the intrapersonal knowledge chapter.

Expeditionary Learning

Expeditionary Learning emerged from the Outward Bound program created by Kurt Hahn. It confronts students with academic and physical challenges to overcome. Just as in wilderness programs, students learn to work together in teams, are challenged to accomplish more than a single individual could, and use their efforts to benefit a local community.

Nearly 100 schools across the country have adopted Expeditionary Learning as a school redesign approach. In such schools, students participate in learning expeditions that are long-term, multidisciplinary explorations of a single theme such as Einstein's theory of relativity, the Civil Rights Movement, or the immigration and migration of humans, plants, and animals. Capitalizing on a sense of adventure and discovery, teachers design expeditions individually or in teams and align curricular content with state and district standards. Expeditions also feature projects, field work, service, and culminating performances. Community members become actively engaged by visiting schools to share their expertise. Such guests might include a transmitter of oral history, a zookeeper, or an author.

Core Practices

Schools that redesign themselves as Expeditionary Learning sites have five core practices to incorporate. The first of these is learning expeditions or long-term investigations of a topic that involves students in real world studies inside and outside of the classroom. The second core practice consists of establishing a culture of reflection, critique, revision, and collaboration. Examining and assessing the processes and content of learning enable teachers and students to engage in respectful and honest dialogue about learning.

The third core practice involves creating a schoolwide culture that encourages high expectations, respect, collaboration, and risk-taking to surpass self-imposed limits. The fourth practice involves reorganizing time, student grouping, and resources to support learning. For example, at many expeditionary programs, schedules are rearranged to accommodate blocks of time, and students may remain with the same teacher or teams of teachers for more than a year. Finally, the fifth core practice includes an annual cycle of reflecting on student achievement results, curriculum, and pedagogy, and developing action plans for continuous improvement.

Expeditionary Learning at the Elementary Level

At Table Mound Elementary School in Dubuque, Iowa, first grade students undertake an expedition called Books! Books! Books! to become readers and writers. They are immersed in literature and skills study and are required to write individual and class books and create and perform a class play. They take books home on a daily basis to read with family members, and they are required early in the school year to reflect on and critique their written work.

Fourth grade students at Clairemont Elementary School in Decatur, Georgia, participate in an expedition that integrates science, social studies, language arts, the arts, and research. Students conduct research on migration and immigration. They each study the migratory habits of an animal and write and illustrate a report as well as sculpt their animal. Collaboratively, the students study migration, creating murals to show how seeds travel.

They also study immigration to find out why and how American citizens traveled here and write and perform plays of immigration stories.

Expeditionary Learning in the Middle Grades

At the New York City School for the Physical City, students undertook landscape design for a local park. They conducted a needs assessment, considered the relationships of plants and environments, and developed a restoration plan for the park.

At Rafael Hernandez School in Boston, Massachusetts, eighth-graders studied journalism and Americans who have served as social activists. Through reading history textbooks, historical documents, and watching films, students considered the contexts and issues of various historical periods such as slavery and abolitionists. They practiced reading, writing, and interviewing skills and spent time applying those skills in meeting with local activists. For culminating projects, students compiled portraits of current and historical figures, sought critiques of their efforts, and revised their work before submitting letters to the editor of local newspapers and creating student-authored magazines.

Expeditionary Learning at the High School Level

At the Rocky Mountain School of Expeditionary Learning in Denver, Colorado, high school students study aspects of physics through considering life during Galileo's times. Students immerse themselves in the Italian Renaissance and consider the change in thinking during that period and the use of technology. Students construct a telescope like the one Galileo used, analyze how it works, note what they can see through it, and consider how our solar system works.

At the Tulalip Heritage School on the Tulalip Reservation in Marysville, Washington, secondary students plan for and participate in a canoe journey. Their preparation reinforces and extends basic skills while promoting traditional knowledge and cultural preservation of Coast Salish traditions.

Teachers who are interested in designing learning expeditions may find two books helpful in guiding their efforts. These include *Guide for Planning a Learning Expedition* by Campbell, Leibowitz, Mednick, and Rugen (1998), and *Literacy All Day Long* by Cousins, Mednick, and Campbell (2000). For additional information on Expeditionary Learning, schools that have embraced this method, and research on its effectiveness, readers are directed to the website at www.elob.org.

Exercise Breaks

Students often sit at desks for long periods of time in positions that prevent adequate, easy breathing. Shallow breathing is enough to sustain life, but not enough to keep the body relaxed and the mind alert! Brief exercise breaks with windows open— even for a few minutes—can bring new alertness and energy. They can also help refocus attention.

The kinesthetic activities that follow are not intended to mirror the content of academic lessons, although in some cases they might do so. Their goal is to energize the mind/body system and in so doing equip students for enhanced learning. It is recommended that teachers first select and practice the suggested exercises before sharing them with students.

Quick Energizers

When students appear to be lethargic such as at the beginning of the school day or after lunch, a minute or two of physical exercise can quickly refresh bodies and minds. Use any or all of the following familiar activities. Students can take turns leading their classmates through:

Hip rotations

Knee rotations

Neck rolls

Shoulder rolls

Picking apple stretches—reach one arm and hand up at a time, making a grasping motion; alternate with the other arm

Deep breathing—extend arms with open hands. Pushing with palms, inhale and reach way up. Exhale and reach down to the floor.

Ten Shin Go So

A simple, yet powerful physical and mental focusing activity is called Ten Shin Go So. This exercise was developed jointly by Tai Chi and Aikido masters. The physical movements tell a story of offering one's talents in service to others. Initially, the storyline can be recited. Doing so assists in memorizing the sequence of movements, but for those who prefer, it can be omitted. Ten Shin Go So gently energizes the body, calms and directs mental attention, and requires about three minutes of time.

Begin by standing with your feet and big toes touching. Clasp your left thumb in your right hand. Lower your head. Calm your mind and body. *Storyline: You assume the position of the unborn.*

Inhale and spread your feet to shoulder width. Circle your arms up and back with fingers open and outstretched. *Storyline: You greet life.*

Exhale and bring your arms down, drawing a mountain shape (or triangle) in the air in front of you. Relax your shoulders and bring your arms down until they are behind you. *Storyline: You view your mountain to climb in life.*

Inhale, pulling your arms forward. Bring your hands together. Link your index fingers and thumbs together as your hands move up, forming a triangle. Look through the triangle, while continuing to push your palms upwards. *Storyline: You see your path to walk in life.*

Bring your arms up and back. Exhale and spread your arms backward and downward, bending slightly forward as you gather energy until hands reach waist level. *Storyline: You prepare for your life's work.*

Inhale and bring your hands up and together at the wrists with open palms and fingers pointing down. Raise your outstretched arms to chest level with palms making an offering motion. *Storyline: You offer your talents in service to others.*

Exhale and relax. Return to the beginning position with head bent slightly, left thumb clasped in right hand, feet together, shoulders relaxed, and mind peaceful. *Storyline: You rest from your efforts.*

Some teachers use Ten Shin Go So at the beginning of a class session to focus student energies or during class to provide a needed stretch break. Telling the storyline the first couple of times as the sequence is learned helps commit the movements to memory. After the process is known, however, it is best done silently.

The Eight Treasures

Some ancient Tai Chi warm-up exercises, called The Eight Treasures, are described below. These exercises have been used by people of all ages in China for hundreds of years. They are useful with students at any grade level, early in the morning to wake up the mind and body, when attention of the group starts to wander, and after lunch when energy wanes.

1. *Touch the sky with two hands:* Begin by bending over with knees slightly bent. Fold fingers of both hands together like a basket and gradually begin straightening up the body, breathing in deeply. When the hands are at waist level, turn palms upward and continue raising arms until they are overhead with palms pressing upwards. When lungs are full, fill them fuller. Unclasp hands, lower arms, and repeat.

2. *Open the bow to the left and right:* With feet shoulder-width apart, bend knees and hold an imaginary bow in one hand. Place an imaginary arrow on it with the other, and draw across the chest, all the while breathing in deeply. Repeat on the other side.

3. *Raise the hands separately with one palm up and one palm down:* Raise one hand overhead with the palm facing upwards, and the other hand down at the side, with the palm facing the floor. Stretch while breathing deeply, then reverse hands and repeat.

4. *Looking backwards over both shoulders:* Slowly turn one's head to one side, stretching the eyes as though looking behind you. Breathe in slowly, and breathe out as one's head returns to the front. Repeat over other shoulder.

5. *Hold the fists tightly and gaze with angry eyes:* With feet shoulder-width apart, bend knees, and bring both fists into the chest. Extend one, breathing out, and widening the eyes. Breathe in as the fist comes back in towards the chest, and repeat with the other fist. (Make sure students are as far apart as possible on this one, and suggest that no one "gaze" at anyone else with the angry eyes!)

6. *Jump lightly:* Jump up and down on toes ten times, lightly. (Have students imagine they are jumping on clouds, and you'll be surprised by how quietly this can be done.)

7. *Shake the head and wave the body:* With feet shoulder-width apart, make a circular motion with the upper body, breathing out as you go down one side of the circle, then breathing in as you go up the other side. Repeat several times. Then reverse directions.

8. *Hold the toes with two hands:* Flop over and let the hands hang downwards. Bend the knees slightly, and try to touch your toes or go as far down as you can bend easily without straining the back. Breathe in deeply as you come up slowly.

These exercises may be done in sequence, or just a few at a time. They are simple tools to relax the body and refocus the mind.

Eye Exercises

Simple eye exercises are useful after extensive reading or computer work. 1) Cup the hands over the eyes and look into the blackness for a minute or two. Then open the eyes wide and circle in a clockwise direction without moving the head. Reverse directions. 2) Extend the arm in front with thumb up. Circumscribe a large circle and let the eyes follow the thumb, first clockwise, then counter-clockwise. Bring the hand to the nose. Slowly extend the arm and hand outwards, and follow with the eyes. Move in and out several times. 3) Alternate looking at distant and close objects. Such exercises relax the eyes, and help strengthen the eye-accommodation muscles involved with reading.

Waking Up

When students are sleepy or losing focus, try this brief exercise. Extend arms in front and shake hands vigorously. At the same time, say, "Zzzzzzzzzz," like a hive of bees, until the top of your head vibrates. Keep shaking your hands as you extend arms overhead, out to the side, down in front, one up and one down, the other up and other down, overhead again, and repeat the sequence. End with several deep breaths, extending arms overhead, and breathe out as arms come down.

Calming Down

There may be times when students are hyperactive, perhaps overstimulated by a field trip or other activity, and you may wish to quiet such energy. Slow, deep breathing and stretching exercises with eyes closed and quiet music playing in the background can be remarkably effective. Or, ask students to imagine swimming slowly with breaststrokes in warm water, while breathing in rhythm with the arm movements.

Field Trips

Well-planned field trips offer meaningful learning experiences for many students, particularly when the trips are integrated with areas studied in the classroom. From simple nature walks or guided museum tours to international exchange programs, field trips provide concrete, experiential learning opportunities. Camping and discovery trips to wilderness areas and field trips to businesses, cultural organizations, and research centers all vitalize learning. Students who are reluctant to work in the classroom are often highly motivated to gather information from a field trip to present later to others.

To be successful, learning goals must be well planned and communicated before the excursion. If unaware of learning goals, many students might view field trips as entertainment and not realize their value. By engaging in preparatory and follow-up activities, students can appreciate the value of hands-on, real world learning. Some guidelines for organizing effective field trips are offered below.

Field Trip Guidelines

1. Identify the purpose and expected outcomes of the experience.

2. Provide logistical information such as the location, time, appropriate clothing, and materials. Secure required signatures from students, parents, school district personnel, and the field trip agency if needed.

3. Organize student groups and specify their responsibilities. Establish behavior expectations.

4. Assign a task to complete or let students devise their own tasks. Distribute any materials the students might need on the field trip.

5. Debrief the event with the whole class, small group discussions, journal sharing, or art work.

6. Encourage sharing of the experience with other classes, administrators, parents, or community members.

Since many schools limit the number of field trips because of budgetary or transportation reasons, teachers often find creative ways to expand learning beyond the four walls of the classroom. One German language teacher led her students on weekly walks during which the class conversed in German, identified items in the environment, and even conjugated verbs to a marching beat as the class made its way down the street.

An elementary art teacher routinely takes her class outdoors to gather materials for class art projects: tall grasses for weaving, rocks for painting, sticks and other articles (including litter) for mobiles, and a variety of leaves, flowers, and bark for printing and textures.

An elementary music teacher has his students go outside after a big storm to gather fallen tree limbs to cut up or break up for rhythm sticks. Every student finds his own personal pair of sticks and uses them regularly as percussion for learning rhythms.

A high school American history teacher takes his class on walks to survey the community in its present form. Upon returning to class, students write about any changes they noticed in the community. Similar "walking field trips" are effective for literacy learning since students can write descriptions or stories about objects observed during their walks. Whether in the city, the suburbs, or the country, walking field trips as well as bus or car excursions offer a variety of opportunities for science, social studies, and language experiences.

Technology That Enhances Kinesthetic Intelligence

Learning through technology is a highly active and interactive process when used appropriately. As computers rely on hand–eye coordination for their operation, this kinesthetic activity in itself can reinforce learning and facilitate students becoming active participants in the learning process. Christopher Dede, the Timothy E. Wirth Professor in Learning Technologies at Harvard University, notes that many new technologies also facilitate the development of kinesthetic intelligence in shared virtual environments, multisensory immersion, computer-supported collaborative learning, and knowledge networking as students access each other through barriers of space and time. He is also researching the connection between certain kinds of computer games and learning. See Dede's website at www.gse.harvard.edu/~dedech.

Since most computer games involve the total engagement of the player and skillful physical response to challenges, there may be interesting implications for education. For example, "Tetris," which was designed by Russian mathematician Alexey Pazhitnov, demands fast decision-making and hand–eye coordination, along with quick testing of hypotheses. Undoubtedly, it is these action-packed challenges that engage students who might otherwise be bored in conventional math classes even though they call for the same kind of spatial and logical thinking. See http://vadim.www.media.mit.edu/Tetris.htm.

Programs such as "Lego Logo" offer ways to connect the computer to external manipulatives, such as Lego blocks with gears, wheels, and motors. Starting with these, students can invent innumerable kinds of machines to control through computer programs they develop themselves. An outgrowth of these tools is StarLogo, a powerful tool that fits well into progressive constructionist practices. It was developed at MIT's Media lab, and it may be downloaded free at www.media.mit.edu/starlogo.

StarLogo was recently used by a group of Seattle middle school students who were involved in a Salmon Summit with peers from around North America. The students worked in teams building an interactive model in which salmon would hatch, travel, return, spawn, and die. Along the way, the salmon would meet dangerous obstacles just as they would in the real world. It is important to note that the students built this system with a series of very simple rules using math that they already knew or that they had a great incentive to learn for the project.

Another kind of program that combines kinesthetic activity with the development of analytical thinking is Broderbund's "Personal Science Lab" that makes use of probes including Source Ranger, Photogate, and probes for rotary motion, pH, temperature, and light. Through these tools, students can create physical or scientific experiments, the results of which are analyzed and displayed on a computer screen. We are seeing just the beginning of a whole new series of computer programs that enable students to experience events seldom encountered in everyday life.

Electronic field trips through the Jason Project may not involve the physical body, yet students feel as if they are actually exploring the depths of the sea or the inside of a volcano as they accompany researchers in areas where very few can go. Students in classrooms, linked electronically to explorers investigating the tectonic plates in the depths of the Mediterranean, have been able to communicate with the scientists, ask questions, or request the viewing of areas or objects more closely. The project is tied to a rich classroom curriculum as well as an online science content course for teachers. Learn more about the Jason Project at www.jasonproject.org.

The Neptune Project, based at the University of Washington's School of Oceanography, was formed to establish a network of underwater observatories in the northeastern Pacific Ocean. The project's 3000 kilometers of fiber-optic/power cable provide communications and power to scientific instruments. For the first time, researchers, as well as shore-based learners of all ages, participate in detailed studies and experiments on a wide area of seafloor. Each year, the Neptune Project takes groups of teachers to sea, where they explore the depths and participate in research with the scientists aboard and link back to students in their classrooms. The project is also linked to a special curriculum. See www.neptune.washington.edu.

At a time when technology makes it very easy to become a passive observer or only a recipient of information, it is not only possible but essential for students to become actively engaged in learning, as these foregoing examples demonstrate.

Summary

This chapter highlights a variety of hands-on strategies that can be incorporated into individual lessons or used to transform entire curricular programs. We realize that initially some teachers and students may be self-conscious about adding kinesthetic components into the classroom. In such cases, it is often beneficial to discuss such hesitation with students and to identify the potential benefits of new classroom activities. More likely than not, some students will eagerly volunteer to participate in or to lead others in movement activities, role-plays, or hands-on games. One of the likely outcomes is that students who underachieve with conventional methods will have opportunities to succeed through kinesthetic means. Additionally, learning becomes highly memorable when drama, challenge, and real world interaction are integrated into classroom work.

All too often adventure and excitement are missing from school. When these ingredients are added into the classroom, students are motivated to excel. As research on the Expeditionary Learning schools has shown, student academic and behavioral gains are realized when their minds, bodies, and hearts are encouraged to reach new heights.

To reflect on kinesthetic strategies and to identify ones that may be appropriate for an individual educator's classroom, we offer the following inventory.

APPLYING KINESTHETIC INTELLIGENCE

1. Important ideas or insights gleaned from this chapter:

_____

_____

_____

_____

_____

2. Areas I'd like to learn more about:

_____

_____

_____

_____

_____

3. Ways I can use this information in my teaching. Please note that all of the strategies described in this chapter are listed below with space provided to note how each might be incorporated into classroom instruction:

KINESTHETIC STRATEGY	CLASSROOM APPLICATION
The Physical Environment	
Classroom Zones	_____
Drama	
Formal Theatre	_____
Role Playing	_____
Creative Drama	_____
Simulations	_____

KINESTHETIC STRATEGY	CLASSROOM APPLICATION

Creative Movement

Understanding Bodily-Knowing _____

Introducing Creative Movement Activities _____

Applying Creative Movement to the Basic Skills _____

Creating Content-Specific Movement Activities _____

Dance

Elements of Dance Warm-Ups _____

A Sequence for Learning through Dance _____

Manipulatives

Task Cards _____

Task Card Puzzles _____

Junk Drawer Manipulatives _____

Stamps _____

Classroom Games

Scavenger Hunts _____

Large Floor Games _____

Total Physical Response Games _____

A Generic Review Game _____

Physical Education

Characteristics of a Physically Educated Person _____

Expeditionary Learning _____

Exercise Breaks

Quick Energizers _____

Ten Shin Go So _____

The Eight Treasures _____

Eye Exercises _____

Waking Up _____

Calming Down _____

Field Trips

Field Trip Guidelines _____

**Technology That Enhances
Kinesthetic Intelligence** _____

KINESTHETIC REFERENCES

American Alliance for Health, Physical Education, Recreation and Dance (AAHPERD). (1995). *A Guide to Content and Standards.* Reston, VA: AAHPERD. Also available online at www.aahperd.org

Asher, J. (2000). *Learning Another Language through Action.* Los Gatos, CA: Sky Oaks Productions.

Benzwie, T. (1988). *A Moving Experience: Dance for Lovers of Children and the Child Within.* Tucson: Zephyr Press.

Campbell, M., Leibowitz, M., Mednick, A., & Rugen, L. (1998). *Guide for Planning a Learning Expedition.* Dubuque, IA: Kendall-Hunt.

Cousins, E., Mednick, A., & Campbell, M. (2000) *Literacy All Day Long.* Dubuque, IA: Kendall-Hunt.

Dewey, J. (1900). *The School and Society.* Chicago: University of Chicago Press.

Dunn, R., & Dunn, K. (1978). *Teaching Students through Their Individual Learning Styles.* Reston, VA: Reston Publishing Co.

Gilbert, A. G. (1989). *Teaching the Three R's through Movement.* New York: MacMillan.

Gilbert, A. G. (1992). *Creative Dance for All Ages.* Reston, VA: AAHPERD.

Goodlad, J. (1984). *A Place Called School: Prospects for the Future.* New York: McGraw-Hill.

Hackney, P. (1988). "Moving Wisdom" in *In Context Quarterly.* No. 18, Bainbridge Is., WA: In Context.

Hackney, P. (1998). *Making Connections: Total Body Integration through Bartenieff Fundamentals.* New York: Taylor & Francis Group.

McKim, R. (1972). *Experiences in Visual Thinking.* Monterey, CA: Brooks Cole.

Spolin, V. (1963). *Improvisation for the Theater.* Evanston, IL: Northwestern University Press.

Spolin, V. (1986). *Theater Games for the Classroom.* Evanston, IL: Northwestern University Press.

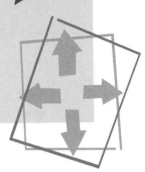

Everyone Is an Artist

VISUAL-SPATIAL INTELLIGENCE

I found that I could say things with color and shapes that I had no words for.

—Georgia O'Keeffe

SARAH'S STORY

Sarah appeared unmotivated, lacking pride in her school work and turning in papers that were not indicative of her true capabilities.

*T*he one area where she excelled was drawing, yet such skills were rarely needed for most classroom tasks. Sarah was usually obligated to draw on the sly, adorning the margins of her papers with artistic flourishes or filling blank sheets of paper with complex imagery. Teachers often requested that Sarah refrain from doing art work so that she could better pay attention.

Throughout her early elementary years, Sarah was described as restless and disruptive; moreover, she seldom recalled information from a day's study. By the time she was in fifth grade, her teacher noticed that when Sarah was allowed to draw during a lesson, she was not only quiet, but also appeared attentive to class material. Her hand went up occasionally to answer questions and her recall was sharp.

One day as the teacher was speaking with Sarah about a science unit on the structure of the earth, Sarah excitedly showed her a drawing of the morning's lecture. There, in a visual language developed and understood by the girl, were images that represented the earth's core, the mantle, and crust with appropriate features and proportions displayed in an artistic code. Sarah's drawings captured the essence of the subject matter itself.

Whenever Sarah could draw, chart, or visually symbolize information, learning came to life for her. She possessed diverse cognitive skills that enabled her to visualize information and synthesize data and concepts into visual metaphors. Such abilities indicate some of the components of visual-spatial intelligence.

DEFINITION: Understanding Visual-Spatial Intelligence

Visual imagery is a means of knowing the world that is older than linguistic symbolism. Fossil records indicate that long before the human mechanisms for speech had evolved, the organs of vision were highly developed, serving as important tools of knowledge for early human beings. It was visual-spatial intelligence that inspired the earliest record of human drawings. During the Ice Age, between 60,000 to 10,000 B.C., cave dwellers in France, Spain, Africa, and Scandinavia painted drawings of animals and scenes from their own experience. Such pictorial imagery eventually led to the development of writing and mathematics. Language evolved from images to pictographs to symbolic codes, becoming increasingly abstract. Today, most educational programs stress the importance of abstract symbols in reading, writing, and arithmetic.

Visual-spatial intelligence includes an aggregate of related skills that encompasses visual discrimination, recognition, projection, mental imagery, spatial reasoning, image manipulation, and the duplication of inner or external imagery. Any or all of such skills may be expressed by a single person. In individuals such as Leonardo da Vinci, visual-spatial intelligence manifests itself in great works of art. In others, such as Newton, who visualized the universe as a machine-like collection of interrelated parts, it is evident in subtle inner imagery.

Although visualization is central to spatial intelligence, it is not directly related to sight, and in fact, can be highly developed in those who are blind. In this chapter, we refer to this intelligence as both visual and spatial since people perceive and process information through both modalities.

In elementary and secondary classrooms, many visually oriented learners respond well to movies, television, slides, posters, charts, diagrams, computers, and color-coded materials. Learning can also be enhanced with visual tools such as computers, telescopes, cameras, stencils, signs, artistic media, and building and drafting supplies. Some visually capable learners arrive at unique, unconventional solutions to artistic problems that express their unique vision.

Classroom environments can be made inviting when visual humor is part of the setting. Cartoons, posters, or photographs related to the subject matter can convey pleasant messages about learning. Visual-spatial intelligence can also be tapped when students are encouraged to perceive, process, and demonstrate their learning with mindmaps, graphs, or colorful images.

CHECKLIST: Visual-Spatial Qualities

Robert McKim (1980) in his classic book, *Experiences in Visual Thinking*, suggests that visual thinking pervades all human activity. It is not solely the domain of artists but also of surgeons, engineers, businesspeople, architects, mathematicians, carpenters, mechanics, and football coaches. It is used when we plan what to wear for the day or when we daydream.

Visual-spatial thinking underlies moving figures in a chess game, organizing one's schedule for the day, moving furniture within a room, or reading maps on a trip. Not all visually capable learners exhibit the same skills. Some may be talented in painting, others at building three-dimensional models, and still others at critiquing fine art. It is likely that a person with well-developed visual-spatial intelligence:

1. Learns by seeing and observing. Recognizes faces, objects, shapes, colors, details, and scenes.

2. Navigates self and objects effectively through space. This includes moving one's body through apertures, finding the way through a forest without a trail, moving a car through traffic, or paddling a canoe on a river.

3. Perceives and produces mental imagery, thinks in pictures, and visualizes detail. Uses visual images as an aid in recalling information.

4. Decodes graphs, charts, maps, and diagrams. Learns with graphic representation or through visual media.

5. Enjoys doodling, drawing, painting, sculpting, or otherwise reproducing objects in visible forms.

6. Enjoys constructing three-dimensional products, such as origami objects, mock bridges, houses, or containers. Is capable of mentally changing the form of an object—such as folding a piece of paper into a complex shape and visualizing its new form, or mentally moving objects to determine how they interact with other items, such as gears turning parts of a piece of machinery.

7. Sees things in different ways or from "new perspectives" such as the negative space around a form as well as the form itself, or detects one shape "hidden" in another.

8. Perceives both obvious and subtle patterns.

9. Creates concrete or visual representations of information.

10. Is proficient at representational or abstract design.

11. Expresses interest or skill in being an artist, photographer, engineer, videographer, architect, designer, art critic, pilot, or in other visually oriented careers.

12. Creates new forms of visual-spatial media or original works of art.

These are only a few of the possible expressions of visual-spatial intelligence. It is important to acknowledge that spatial intelligence cannot adequately be confined to a single list of qualities or characteristics.

Visual-Spatial Learning Processes

In academic settings, visual intelligence is often relegated to the domain of the visual arts. As such, many students forego opportunities to develop perceptual, imaging, and aesthetic skills. In McKim's book, *Experiences in Visual Thinking*, the author identifies three broad components of visual imagery: external imagery we perceive, internal imagery we dream or imagine, and the kind of imagery we create through doodling, drawing, or painting. According to McKim, visual thinking consists of what we see, imagine, or draw. The instructional strategies in this chapter suggest activities for each of these three capacities and include:

Establishing a Visual Learning Environment
- Visual Tools
- Intentional Display Areas
- Peripheral Stimuli
- Changing Perspective through Rotating Seating
- Nonverbal Communication

Pictorial Representation
- Flow Charts
- Visual Outlines
- Unit Charts
- Visual Chart Starters

Visual Notetaking and Brainstorming Tools
- Concept mapping
- Mindmapping
- Clustering
- Mindscaping

Visualization
- Classroom Imagery
- Visual Memory Techniques

Visual Variety in Learning Materials
- Highlighting with Color
- Varying Shapes
- Visual Accompaniment for Lectures, Discussions, or Readings

Board and Card Games
- Guidelines for Making Board Games
- Card Games

Architecture
- Learning to Think Like an Architect
- Getting Started with Architecture in the Classroom

The Visual Arts
- Art as an Instructional Tool
- Blending the Visual and Language Arts
- Integrating Art and Math
- Integrating the Arts at the High School Level
- Art Across the Curriculum

Technology That Enhances Visual-Spatial Intelligence

Establishing a Visual Learning Environment

With a little forethought, effort, and assistance from the students themselves, classrooms can be transformed into aesthetically pleasing environments. Lighting might be improved with full-spectrum bulbs and a floor lamp or two. Crescent or circular seating patterns are often preferable to rows of desks, since students can more readily see and interact with one another. Pieces of inviting furniture such as a comfortable couch, chairs, or pillows can be welcome classroom additions. Colorful fabric or floor covering, bright and nicely displayed art work, posters or charts, and cut flowers or a plant or two establish a positive ambiance that greets students with visual vitality. With time, effort, and respect devoted to the visual environment, teachers might effectively engage the classroom as a powerful learning tool. Some suggestions follow for enhancing the visual dimension of the classroom.

Visual Tools

A variety of tools including paper, chalk, pencils, markers, paints, cameras, computers, videos, and overhead projectors should be readily available for students' and teachers' use. Organized storage is a necessity for maintaining supplies and limiting distracting clutter.

Intentional Display Areas

To avoid visual overload, selected spaces can be identified for the display of art work, messages, or photographs. Walls, bulletin boards, or partitions selected for display can attain a museum-like quality by the way in which works are hung.

Peripheral Stimuli

Accelerated learning theory suggests that the rate and quantity of learning can be greatly increased. One accelerated strategy taps human peripheral perception both to instruct and to facilitate long-term memory. Dr. Georgi Lozanov, the creator of accelerated learning methods, claims that peripheral visual material is subconsciously registered in the mind and can be recalled readily when activated later in a lesson. In Bulgarian studies of adult foreign language learning classes as well as elementary reading and math classes, students were able to recall increased quantities of information when peripheral stimuli were present in the room, even though their attention was not directed to such visuals. The use of peripherals in accelerated learning is considered an important visual component in immersing students in subject matter.

Teachers who are interested in experimenting with peripheral stimuli will need to collect and then display copies of art work, posters, photographs, charts, maps, or quotations that reinforce the topics taught. It should be realized, however, that once displayed, visual information quickly loses its interest and impact. In order to remain intriguing, such visuals need to be either changed or transformed in some manner once a week. This task can be time-consuming unless it is shared by students or other teachers. At many schools teachers have weekly meetings during which they swap visuals and other instructional materials they have developed.

Changing Perspective through Rotating Seating

It is common for many students to sit or work in the same part of the classroom. By asking students to change seating placements, their visual and social perspectives also shift. The room can assume a new appearance, and group dynamics may transform when students interact with a variety of classmates. Teacher/student relationships may improve with new seating arrangements. Perspectives can also be affected by reconfiguring classroom furniture with circles, U shapes, or with tables or chairs arranged in small groups.

Nonverbal Communication

A teacher's demeanor and gestures project countless messages as students silently interpret what is being said through body language. This is especially true for English language learners. Consistency between gestures and words can positively affect learning and communication. When teachers are enthusiastic, their gestures reflect such feelings and encourage similar ones among students. Conversely, when teachers are tired or stressed, their body language tends to reflect such feelings and evoke similar reactions among students.

Often people are unaware of the body language they "speak." Students daily observe a teacher's facial expression, gestures, body posture, body space requirements, eye contact, voice tone and inflection, rate of speaking, habitual mannerisms, laughter or other utterances, all of which communicate attitudes and feelings. To determine whether appropriate nonverbal messages are conveyed, teachers might videotape themselves. Doing so can reveal what students observe every day. Teachers may discern ways to make nonverbal communication more purposeful for enhanced teaching and learning.

Pictorial Representation

By supporting written or spoken language with charts, diagrams, or photographs, learning can be facilitated and retention reinforced. The phrase "One picture is worth a thousand words" certainly has application in classrooms. Graphic representations serve valuable educational functions: they present, define, interpret, manipulate, synthesize, and demonstrate data. Visuals can clarify concepts and give students another sensory means to understand and communicate what they have learned. Many teachers and students, however, are hesitant to use pictorial representation because of their unfamiliarity with graphic techniques and the incorrect assumption that such images must be artfully done. Rather than emphasizing polished aesthetic displays, both students and teachers should use such tools with the goal of probing the subject matter at hand.

There are many forms of pictorial representation that can be used effectively in the classroom. The ones described in this section include flow charts, visual outlines, unit charts, visual chart stencils, and noting strategies.

Flow Charts

Flow charts describe the structure of concepts and symbolize the direction of flow between ideas. Any "cause-effect" phenomenon, whether in math, history, science, health, literature, or instructions, can be illustrated easily in flow chart formats. Some students will more readily grasp concepts when they are illustrated in this form.

Flow charts, whether simple or complex, can be of any size and shape. A large flow chart drawn on butcher paper, a shower curtain, or other fabric might be placed on the floor for students to experience kinesthetically as they walk through its steps. A geometric or freeform shape including rectangles, circles, triangles, or clouds can also be used to

"chart" the flow of the concept being explained. Additionally, rather than a flow chart leading only from one step to the next, there can be dual or multiple extensions from any one component of the chart, as demonstrated below. The first chart describes the procedure for the addition of numbers larger than one digit, and the second offers a simplified explanation of the causes leading up to the Civil War.

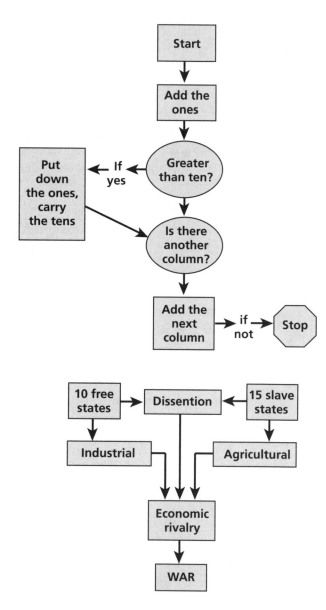

Teachers can put information they plan to teach into flow charts, or students can use them to demonstrate any conceptual sequence. Making a flow chart is a simple process. Begin with a rectangle or square divided into smaller boxes. Decide on a concept to display visually. The facts of the concept should be identified and then written one at a time in each of the boxes. Once all the facts are noted, the boxes can be cut out and arranged sequentially, adding arrows or other symbols to indicate the flow of ideas.

Visual Outlines

Another approach to charting is to ask students to "fill in the boxes" of a paragraph, report, or essay in preparation for writing. Such visual outlines identify the necessary components of writing assignments. They also clarify what students are expected to write.

Two outlines are offered below. The first shows parts of a paragraph, and the second shows components of a three-paragraph composition. Teachers should feel free, however, to develop outlines that suit their needs.

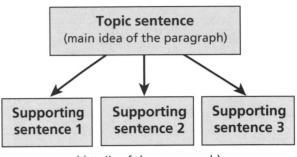

(details of the paragraph)

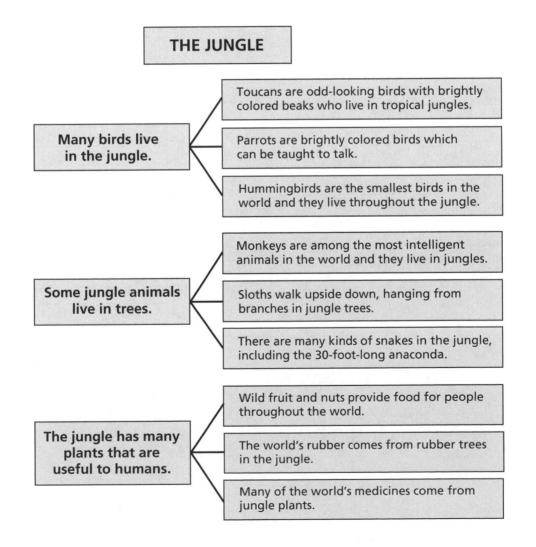

As an example, elementary students who are studying the jungle might enter "jungle" in the title box at the top. Under topic sentences, their entries could include birds, animals living in the trees, and plants that are useful to humans. Supporting sentences next might be added as demonstrated. Later, an introduction and conclusion can be included and the entire chart transferred to conventional writing formats. Many students, initially daunted by writing assignments, are less threatened when they organize their thoughts in a visual format as a rough draft and then rewrite the draft into a standard written report. Using such visual processes, students not only clarify their understanding of a writing assignment and the teacher's expectations, they also learn visual ways to organize their thinking.

Students who are capable of extended writing may find the following outline helpful for organizing a written report or essay.

A REPORT OR ESSAY TITLE

Introduction: _____

_____

SUPPORTING SENTENCES   **SUPPORTING DETAILS**

TOPIC SENTENCES

Conclusion: _____

_____

Unit Charts

Visual charts can be displayed on the blackboard, bulletin board, or in student notebooks to track progress through a unit of study. As a new unit is introduced, a chart can identify the main topics students will cover. This is especially helpful for students who struggle with identifying main ideas. To begin, list the topic and its major concepts in a flow chart or visual outline format. As studies progress, students can fill in additional information as appropriate. With such a learning tool, students can tell at a glance where their studies are going, what has been covered, and what remains to be learned. An example of a unit chart follows.

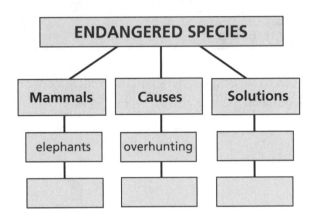

Visual Chart Starters

There are countless ways of representing information graphically. By learning several chart "stencils," teachers and students readily expand their options for manipulating and communicating information.

Numerous simple-to-use stencils or "thinking frames" were developed by Beau Fly Jones, author and former program director of the North Central Regional Educational Laboratory. They are useful tools for improving comprehension of academic material. Jones points out that graphic organizers must appropriately reflect the structure of the text being studied. For example, with ordinary chapter assignments, students should first skim the material to determine its structure. Questions can be asked about whether the information is presented as a hierarchy, a comparison or contrast, or as a timeline. Once the appropriate graphic structure is determined, the material can be read with the visual format in mind. Next, students can create the visual image on paper, compare their graphic structure with others, and finally summarize or critique it in an oral or written report.

On the following pages are a number of graphic organizers that teachers and students can adapt to academic material. Such graphic starters provide both students and teachers with options to visualize written information; however, after gaining familiarity with these strategies, it is important to generate original charts and diagrams. Designing one's own representations requires a synthesis and expression of information in a format that best suits individual needs. Also, when teachers review student-made visuals, they can identify incomplete or incorrect thinking and offer suggestions for improvement. For some lessons, teachers may also find it helpful to request that students create both a graphic representation of information as well as a "white paper" that explains in written form the information contained in the pictorial.

An additional resource for graphic organizers is *Visual Tools for Constructing Knowledge*, by David Hyerle (1996). Hyerle's book explains how to develop and use visual tools across the curriculum and grades and for a variety of purposes. He also gently coaches the reader into creating graphic forms to brainstorm, process, and remember information.

Graphic representations are visual illustrations of verbal statements. **Frames** are sets of questions or categories that are fundamental to understanding a given topic. Following are nine "generic" graphic forms with their corresponding frames.

Spider Map

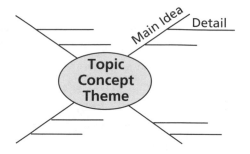

Used to describe a central idea: a thing (a geographic region), processes (meiosis), concept (altruism), or proposition with support (experimental drugs should be available to AIDS victims).

Key frame questions: What is the central idea? What are its attributes? What are its functions?

Series of Events Chain

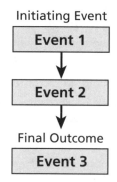

Used to describe the stages of something (the life cycle of a primate); the steps in a linear procedure (how to neutralize an acid); a sequence of events (how feudalism led to the formation of nation states); or the goals, actions, and outcomes of a historical figure or character in a novel (the rise and fall of Napoleon).

Key frame questions: What is the object, procedure, or initiating event? What are the stages or steps? How do they lead to one another? What is the final outcome?

Continuum/Scale

Used for timelines showing historical events or ages (grade levels in school), degrees of something (weight), shades of meaning (Likert scales), or ratings scales (achievement in school).

Key frame questions: What is being scaled? What are the end points?

Compare/Contrast Matrix

	Name 1	Name 2
Attribute 1		
Attribute 2		
Attribute 3		

Used to show similarities and differences between two things (people, places, events, ideas, etc.).

Key frame questions: What things are being compared? How are they similar? How are they different?

Problem/Solution Outline

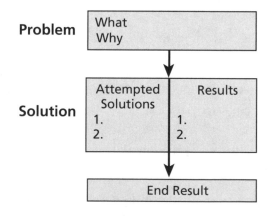

Used to represent a problem, attempted solutions, and results (the national debt).

Key frame questions: What was the problem? Who had the problem? Why was it a problem? What attempts were made to solve the problem? Did those attempts succeed?

Series of Events Chain

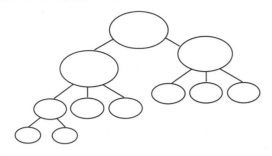

Used to show the stages or subcategories of a single event or concept (the impact of the Great Depression).

Key frame questions: What is the concept or triggering event? What were the stages or consequences of the event? What are the subcategories of the concept? How does the original event or concept lead to those that follow? How many stages or steps are evident? What outcomes are evident?

Series of Events Chart

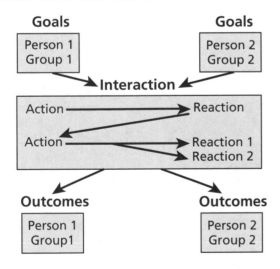

Used to show the nature of an interaction between persons or groups (European settlers and American Indians).

Key frame questions: Who are the persons or groups? What were their goals? Did they conflict or cooperate? What was the outcome for each person or group?

Fishbone Map

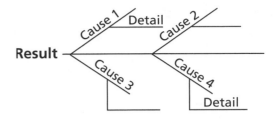

Used to show the causal interaction of a complex event (an election, a nuclear explosion) or complex phenomenon (juvenile delinquency, learning disabilities).

Key frame questions: What are the factors that cause X? How do they interrelate? Are the factors that cause X the same as those that cause X to persist?

Cycle

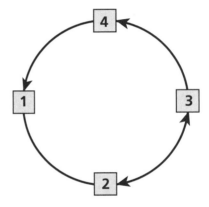

Used to show how a series of events interact to produce a set of results again and again (weather phenomena, cycles of achievement and failure, the life cycle).

Key frame questions: What are the critical events in the cycle? How are they related? In what ways are they self-reinforcing?

Visual Notetaking and Brainstorming Tools

Most people find that notetaking ensures better recall of information. One researcher, Michael Howe, at Exeter University, conducted a study of students and notetaking. He found that noted material was six times more likely to be remembered than unnoted material. Notetaking, as opposed to verbatim copying, can serve several valuable functions including storing information, encoding and organizing data, encouraging associations, inferences, and interpretations, and focusing attention on what is important.

Conventional noting that consists of grammatically correct phrases and sentences is often cumbersome and inefficient when compared with key word methods. *Key words* are nouns and verbs that stand out more readily in written or spoken material. Notes consisting of key words generate stronger images and are frequently remembered for longer periods of time. If one reflects on how a young child begins to speak, the importance of key words is apparent. For example, a two-year-old may state, "Dan, ball" uttering only the essential words to communicate his desire. Later, the same child will fill in his request with non-key words such as, "I want to play with the ball."

Some claim that key words constitute only five to ten percent of language. Students who rely on conventional notes may be at a disadvantage since they waste time and energy, lose information, and clutter the key words.

Visual forms of notetaking offer many advantages over conventional formats. They capitalize on several factors that enhance recall. Essential key words are noted, associations and relationships are highlighted, conscious involvement is required, and subjective visual organization is imposed. Four visual noting techniques are described in the following sections including mindmapping, clustering, and mindscaping.

Concept Mapping

Joseph Novak and Bob Gowin (1984) in their book, *Learning How to Learn*, suggest the use of a graphic organizer they call "concept mapping." Novak, a professor of biology at Cornell, uses this visual technique to teach scientific processes to his students and to indicate the sequence and relationships in the concepts. Novak also uses concept maps as an assessment device since they reveal whether there is clear understanding of a biological process. Originally developed for the sciences, this strategy is useful in other subjects as well. Two sample concept maps are included below. One was written by a team of seventh grade science students and the other by a history student. Note the use of verbs and key words in both.

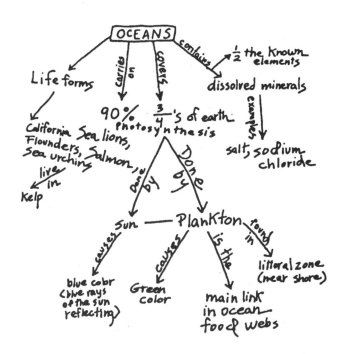

Mindmapping

One effective visual notetaking strategy is mind-mapping. This spatial, nonlinear notetaking approach taps the mind's ability to work in an integrated, interlinked, complex manner. Similar to concept maps, mindmaps feature tree-like branches of information that display key concepts and their relationships. Differing from more linear concept maps, however, mindmaps are global in their approach. Beginning with a central idea, students quickly create a "big picture" of their topic.

Mindmaps are useful for several purposes. They can help in organizing and remembering written or verbal information, preparing to write essay questions, planning and evaluating projects or events, or making a visual record of a meeting in progress. In meetings, they can record discussions, keep the meeting on track, eliminate redundancy, and encourage everyone to "piggy-back" on others' ideas. Both students and teachers will find many uses for this strategy. Mindmaps can be enhanced by adding color and graphics to make the information memorable.

Many visually talented students enjoy mind-mapping and will create symbols or images to illustrate their concepts as well as beautify their work. For all students, however, mindmapping can be appealing, since the details are organized in categories, and a visual pattern unifies the separate parts into a whole.

To create a mindmap for notetaking or brainstorming purposes, a central concept should be placed in the middle of a page. Working outward from the center in all directions, key words or images can be quickly recorded and color-coded if

To create concept maps, students can skim a text or listen to a lecture and identify the key concepts presented. Next, they compile a list of the major concepts, ranking them from the most general, all-inclusive concept to the most specific. Rank-ordering concepts requires students to seek meaning in what they are listening to or reading.

Concept maps have tree-like shapes, with the broadest, most inclusive concept featured at the top. Two to five sub-categories are connected by lines to the first concept. Verbs are added to the lines to describe the relationships. A third level of the hierarchy can be added so that all important ideas are included and key relationships identified. Additional cross-linking may be included to show relationships between one section of the concept map and another. Both teachers and students will find concept maps useful for constructing meaning from a variety of academic resources.

desired. The words in a mindmap should be printed, since this heightens visual recall, and placed on the connecting lines. Colors, images, and codes can serve as mnemonic devices, for individual expression, and for transforming and synthesizing information in visual ways. An example of a mindmap by teacher and artist Sarah Welsh follows. It reviews the contents of this chapter.

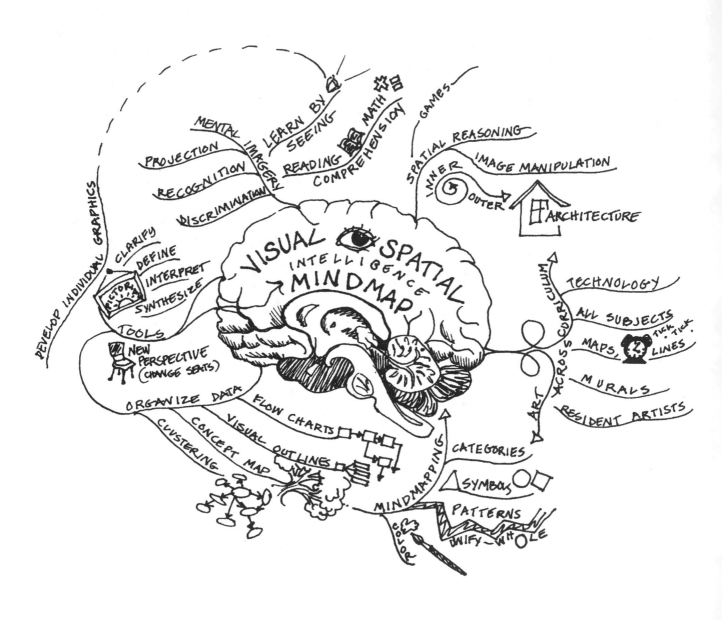

Clustering

Clustering, as developed by Gabriele Rico (1999) in her book, *Writing the Natural Way*, is an open-ended process for generating creative ideas. As an effective preliminary to almost any form of writing, clustering can be used to jump-start thinking for creative writing projects, articles, reports, term papers, even books. Rico writes her own books by creating clusters and then writing directly from them on a word processor.

To use clustering for creative writing, place the main concept in the center of the page, then draw a circle around it. Using this topic as a springboard, freely and quickly associate as many ideas as possible, circling each and connecting it to the central concept. As in any brainstorming process, it is important to put down everything that comes to mind, even though it may seem irrelevant. Often irrelevant ideas later trigger useful ones. When the page has been filled—neatness is not important here!—a theme may emerge. Rico calls this a "felt shift." At that point, move to writing a few lines below the cluster. For many, the clustering process is an enormously valuable approach to creative writing, which is often unusually rich in metaphors and insights. A student cluster with its resultant writing sample follows.

Runner

He is still,
Frozen by the photographer's lens
As he is about to break through the tape.
Look more closely;
Look at his expression,
His face contorted
In agony.
Look at his body,
His muscles tight
As steel bars,
His flesh soaked
in sweat,
His arms dangling with indifference.
Look at his stride,
The small stride of a tired runner.
He is almost at the end
Of his strength,
Almost,
But not quite.
He is still,
Frozen by the photographer's lens.

—Steve Sano

Mindscaping

A method of recording abstract information from lectures or books in the form of images with few words has been developed by Nancy Margulies (2002). Her book entitled *Mapping Inner Space* teaches nonartists how to create visual images that transform information from a verbal to a visual format. Margulies, herself, often "mindscapes" conferences, with her easel beside the podium, creating visual records of each presentation. These colorful creations are posted around the room and offer a graphic review of each presentation as the conference unfolds.

Mindscaping not only enhances learning and memory, it also can be used to map out the day, plan individual lessons, create interesting resumes, or promote new ideas. Margulies offers the following visual symbols that are easily reproduced by most people who want to begin working with graphic imagery.

Each graphic approach—visual outlines, spatial organizers, concept maps, mindmaps, clusters, or mindscapes—is clearly useful for different purposes and preferences. Some of the processes are more linear in nature and lend themselves to analytic tasks, whereas others are more global, and are useful for creative purposes. None is difficult to teach or to learn, and they all offer both teachers and students an array of tools for the variety of tasks involved in the learning process.

Visualization

....

Visualization is the ability to mentally construct or to recall visual imagery. Many great discoveries begin with an insight, a clear image, or a vision. For example, Einstein first conceived his general theory of relativity "daydreaming" on a sunny day, imagining riding on a beam of light through space. The German chemist Friedrich August Kekule solved another scientific problem one evening as he gazed into the fireplace and imagined a ring of snakes, each with its tail in the mouth of another. This image revealed the molecular structure of benzene. Leonardo da Vinci imagined and drew such technological wonders as the helicopter hundreds of years before it was invented. Diverse fields of human endeavor have been advanced through insights gleaned from inner imagery. By intentionally working with visualization in the classroom, students may gain tools for learning, knowing, and discovering. Encouraging students to produce their own mental imagery also ensures their ability to do so as the world grows increasingly visual with the imagery of others on television, movie, computer, and video screens.

Classroom Imagery

Simple visualizations can be employed spontaneously in most learning situations. At any point in a lesson, students can be asked to generate and manipulate images. For example, in a French class, students might imagine the Cathedral of Notre Dame from different angles; in a science class, the anatomy of a bird; in math, an isosceles triangle; and in reading, pictures of key words. Such moments provide students with the opportunity to visually experience and assimilate the information at hand.

Significant gains have been reported in reading comprehension when students create mental images of what they have read. One study conducted by Marjorie Pressley in Escondido, California, taught children how to identify key words in reading and create mental images of such words. Even though the program ran for only nine weeks, reading test scores made dramatic gains. Reading comprehension nearly tripled gains from previous years, speed and accuracy doubled, and recall was twelve times greater.

In math, combining visualization with rote memory also offers powerful learning opportunities. One fifth grade student had not yet mastered her multiplication tables and her progress in math was seriously hindered. Knowing that Suni was a talented visual artist, her teacher assumed that if the multiplication facts were learned artistically, Suni would experience success. Following a hunch, the teacher asked the girl to close her eyes and visualize what 81 or 9×9 looked like artistically. Suni readily explained that 81 looked like turquoise, pink and purple lines going in different directions. The teacher asked Suni to draw what she visualized on a notecard. The design was quickly reproduced and the teacher requested that 9×9 be written on top of the design with the answer 81 on the back of the notecard. Suni's visualization of 81 is shown at right.

Encouraged with her first math visualization, Suni went on to picture other multiplication facts and their images. At the end of the two weeks, Suni had completed a set of beautiful math art cards, each with its own unique visual symbol.

In the process, she easily memorized the multiplication tables.

Many other students, inspired by Suni's example, have since made their own sets of art flash cards for a variety of subject areas. By creating both internal and external images, these students are not only learning academic content, they are also creating and expressing their own visual and symbolic language systems.

Visual Memory Techniques

The ancient Greeks explained the phenomenon of human memory in the myth of the great goddess Mnemosyne. The myth recounts that in the beginning of time, the Elder Gods reigned supreme in the universe and were of enormous size and enormous ability. Mnemosyne, one of the original goddesses, possessed a special gift: memory that was as long as her hair. As the goddess of memory, Mnemosyne knew each event that had taken place from the beginning of time. One day, deciding she must share her knowledge, Mnemosyne gathered her daughters, the nine Muses, about her and told them the stories of the universe. She explained the creation of the earth, the stars, and the moon. She talked of the glorious gods and the brave heroes and heroines on earth. The nine Muses, cherishing what their mother taught them, desired to preserve these wondrous stories. To do so, the Muses turned Mnemosyne's tales into poems, stories, and songs to ensure they would never be forgotten. Through such means, the Muses were able to share their knowledge with mortals so that humankind could know and remember all that was important.

From this explanation of memory, the Greeks created techniques using stories and associations to improve memory and to achieve what appeared to be superhuman feats of memorization. The ancient orators could remember hundreds of items such as decks of cards placed in any order, backwards, forwards, or randomly, dates and numbers, and, indeed, entire domains of knowledge. Such skills were possible because of the use of mnemonics, from the Greek word, *mneme*, meaning memory. Mnemonics are techniques that facilitate retention and recall of information by exercising visual-spatial intelligence. These processes also facilitate the ability to work with mental images that is often a characteristic of great creative thinkers.

The success of the ancient memory systems was based on one common principle, association. Association consists of taking one idea or image and linking it to another. By using memory techniques that stress interconnections, studies demonstrate the capability to store and recall far more information than we generally expect. An excellent book explaining memory systems is *The Memory Book* (1996) by Harry Lorayne and Jerry Lucas.

In the classroom, associative techniques can be used when committing to memory the names of the fifty states, the dynasties of China, the Dewey Decimal System, the Articles of the Bill of Rights, or lists of spelling or vocabulary words. To begin teaching students a memory device, take a list and together generate a class "story" for memorizing the items using clear and distinct images.

For example, students might be asked to memorize the Dewey Decimal System. This classifying system divides books into ten main groups:

000–099	Generalities (encyclopedias, periodicals, journalism)
100–199	Philosophy
200–299	Religion
300–399	Social Sciences
400–499	Language
500–599	Sciences
600–699	Technology
700–799	The Arts
800–899	Literature
900–999	Geography and History

To memorize the above, the following story-line comprised of association and imagery was quickly created:

I went to the general (Generalities) store to buy up to 99 items. The first person I saw was Phil (Philosophy), the owner of the store, who showed me two hundred religious books, (Religion). I said what I needed was three boxes of SOS (Social Science) pads. When I walked down the fourth aisle, I noticed all sorts of people speaking different languages (Language) and bought five science kits (Science). In the sixth aisle, I saw computers (Technology) but decided to buy seven paintings (The Arts) instead. There were eight wads of litter (Literature) on the floor. When I picked them up, I saw nine world maps (Geography) painted on the floor. Then left to return another day.

Such a story, when generated by students, can serve as a powerful memory booster. The images might be discussed to bring them into greater clarity, and the storyline rehearsed once or twice. Later, the students should find it relatively easy to silently recall the story while accurately writing the Dewey Decimal System including both the numbers and classification categories.

Associating items with parts of one's home or room is another effective associative device from an ancient Greek memory system. By associating each item of a list with an object in one's room, a mental tour of the room can aid recall. For example, one teacher assigned students a few extra credit words from a short story:

trapeze

juggler

equestrian

acrobat

grease paint

Students were asked to memorize the above list of words by imagining their bedrooms containing these items. The trapeze might be suspended from the ceiling, the juggler on the bed, the equestrian coming out of the closet, the acrobat in front of the dresser, and the grease paint on top of a night stand. When asked to recall the words, the students mentally walked through their rooms noting the location of the extra items and writing the respective words on a piece of paper.

Ultimately, such techniques are most effective when students individually create their own imagery. As the above example demonstrates, once students have mastered the technique, the classroom teacher should cease providing lists for quizzes or exams, requiring that students produce such lists from memory instead. For example, on Fridays in classrooms around the country, students take spelling tests. Usually, the teacher reads the words to be spelled. When students have learned the association memory techniques, they can assume responsibility for recalling the list as well as for the accurate spelling of their words. Students can be instructed to get their papers out for the spelling test, silently recall their memory story, and then list and accurately spell the words. In this way, students are tested on both their memory and spelling skills.

Since students frequently find that such memory stories are retained for long periods of time, some have wondered whether their minds will become too cluttered with silly storylines. They can be assured that there is no such possibility. Some researchers claim that if human brains were fed ten new bits of information every second of our lives, we would still have memory room to spare. Associative techniques do not begin to tax our memory skills; they only strengthen them.

Memory techniques, effective for recalling and storing facts, are particularly valuable when students must learn the multiplication tables, spelling and vocabulary words, principles, and formulas. Although drill and practice are useful for memorizing certain facts and skills, they can minimize the importance of meaning and understanding. It is important to teach facts, skills and concepts as part of rich multisensory and interactive experiences. Memory techniques can be embedded in such study and should not, themselves, comprise the sole agent of instruction. Complex, experiential learning opportunities engage the vast realms of human memory while making learning fascinating and meaningful.

Visual Variety in Learning Materials

Interest and excitement in learning materials can be generated by the visual alteration of color, shape, and imagery. Color is an important component of visual thinking. It distinguishes ideas, guides attention, and enhances recall. Color can highlight information on dittos, student packets, lecture overheads, chalkboard visuals, bulletin boards, class notes, and assignments.

Highlighting with Color

Color can also serve as an important instructional tool. Steps in solving mathematical problems can be clarified through the use of color. For example, the first step in long division can be written in red, the second in blue, and the third in green.

Spelling mistakes can also be corrected through the use of color. The letters of the word that were written correctly appear in one color with the corrections in red or orange to highlight what must be remembered. While it is important for teachers to model color usage in the classroom, students will often establish personal visual language systems when they are free to choose the colors and approaches with which to work.

The steps of open-ended, creative problem-solving can also be highlighted with color as follows:

1. Black—The first step of creative problem-solving is determining the who, what, when, and where of a situation. Such data can be written in black ink.

2. Red—The second step is defining the major problem(s), which can be written in red.

3. Green—Numerous solutions can be generated in green.

4. Blue—The best solution is selected and circled in blue.

5. Orange—An orange-colored action plan is developed.

Similar sequential color procedures can be used in following directions, notetaking, or memorizing sequences in any content area. When working with color in these sequential ways, teachers can tell at a glance where students are stuck in a problem-solving process.

Varying Shapes

The computer provides another convenient way to add visual variety to classroom lessons. It is a simple process to add graphics, font variations, larger and smaller letters, boxes, signs, and banners to learning materials. For example, to remedy a student's misspelling of certain words, misspelled letters can be enlarged to visually "grab" attention and improve recall.

rec**e**ive **a**isle conven**ie**nce

It is also easy to help students focus on key words, concepts, or spelling practice by suggesting they visualize such words and their shapes. The shapes or configurations of the words can be highlighted as follows:

Students can draw the outer configurations of words and later have others fill in what is missing. They might also create sentences or math theorems of configurations which they "read" and give to others to read as well.

Visual Accompaniment for Lectures, Discussions, or Readings

Although many teachers are uncomfortable with their own drawing skills, some students will volunteer to "illustrate" what is being learned and create classroom posters for display. Occasionally, a teacher may identify a student who can quickly draw images of spoken information. Such a student might be encouraged to volunteer to sketch at the blackboard, capturing the words of a speaker during a lecture or discussion.

Students can also be encouraged to embellish their own written work with color, doodles, symbols, and varying shapes. Before a reading assignment begins, suggest that students preview the photos and graphs in written materials since visual scanning creates mental "hooks" for written information and increases understanding. Once students begin reading, suggest that they transform key words or events into their own personal "mind movies" to improve later recall.

Board and Card Games

One of the oldest known pastimes is playing board games. About 2500 B.C., Egyptian carvings on tombs depicted board games in process. A wall painting on the tomb of Nefertari shows the queen playing a board game with movable pieces. The ancient Babylonians, Chinese, Romans, and Aztecs all played games that were often instructional and required logical thinking skills. Some games were spatial, teaching the way around the city or the ways to stalk an animal. Since board games are as popular today as they were in ancient times, they can often ignite students' enthusiasm for learning.

Games with movable pieces often challenge a player's foresight and imagination as well as exercise memory skill and visual-spatial intelligence. Chess is an ancient game that originated in Asia, spread to Persia in the fifth century A.D., then into the Middle East, Spain, and throughout the rest of Europe. Today, while chess is well known as a favorite pastime, some educators are perceiving its value as a tool to enhance students' thinking and learning abilities. Studies in Venezuela have shown that students seven years of age and older who frequently played chess at school experienced IQ gains on traditional measures of intelligence. Perhaps such gains were due to the exercising of a variety of higher-order skills demanded in chess, which include critical thinking, decision-making, spatial reasoning, and strategizing.

While there are many prepared games for classroom use, teachers frequently require curriculum-specific ones not readily available in stores. Fortunately, board games can easily be made for any subject area.

For those interested in creating their own classroom games, the easiest kind to design is a Monopoly-style game in which players travel along a path encountering obstacles or boons relating to the subject matter in question. Simple statements, such as "Meet British soldiers, go back 5 spaces," or "Name the square root of 169 and take an extra turn," or "Huck Finn and Jim are recognized. Lose your next turn," or "Copernicus makes an important discovery. Draw a bonus card," all teach important facts or reinforce learning. To demonstrate how such games are constructed an example follows.

The game on the next page was made by an elementary teacher whose students were studying the continent of Africa. For teachers interested in designing their own games to introduce a topic, to teach subject matter, or to review student learning, see the guidelines that follow.

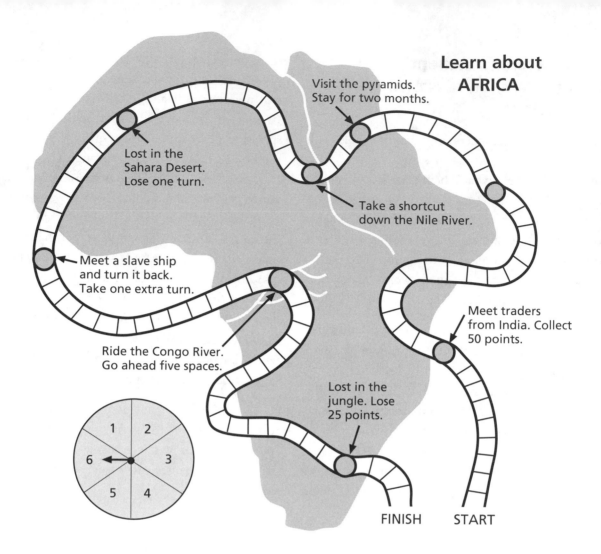

Learn about **AFRICA**

Visit the pyramids. Stay for two months.

Lost in the Sahara Desert. Lose one turn.

Take a shortcut down the Nile River.

Meet a slave ship and turn it back. Take one extra turn.

Meet traders from India. Collect 50 points.

Ride the Congo River. Go ahead five spaces.

Lost in the jungle. Lose 25 points.

FINISH   START

Guidelines for Making Board Games

1. Determine the learning objectives and purpose of the game. Is it to acquaint students with new information, review old information, evaluate a unit, or all of these?

2. Consider how the information and skills might be taught. Commercial games can inspire the structure and format of many classroom games such as Concentration, 20 Questions, and Scrabble. Is there a commercially available game that, with modification, would provide a workable structure? Is there an original format that is more appropriate?

3. To make the board game, draw a rough draft on large paper, creating a path or design to fit the needs of the topic. Game boards can assume the shape of a world map, a DNA molecule, the solar system, a town or city, or a simple path.

4. Once the path or design is made, determine how the game will end. Will it be the first player to complete the path, the first to accumulate a quantity of points or objects, or the first to visit a certain number of locations on the board by correctly answering questions?

5. Players will need a way to move around the game board. This is often done with spinners that are easily constructed as circles divided into numbered, pie-shaped sections. Fasten the spinner directly to the game board with a brad and draw an arrow on the board. Students spin the wheel and the arrow indicates the number of steps to move. Movement around the board can be accomplished by dice or cards with directions on them, or directions on the board itself.

6. If movement around the game board with dice is preferred, students can make their own dice out of cubes of wood. With sandpaper and markers, number dice can be easily fashioned as can special-purpose pieces that best meet the needs of a particular game. For example, dice might feature different kinds of animals on each side, countries, presidents, punctuation marks, or symbols such as the letters for chemical elements.

7. If needed, cut cards from cardstock for questions, bonuses, or penalties.

8. The final step is to transfer the rough draft of the game to large cardstock, cardboard, plywood, or another more permanent surface.

Teachers can benefit by sharing games with colleagues, and students will often enthusiastically create games based on material they are studying. When student games are created, ask students to share them with classmates so that the opportunities for playing to learn are increased.

Card Games

Card games also serve as effective visual learning tools. The game "Authors" has helped many children and adults learn literary figures and the titles of their written works. In "Authors," players attempt to collect sets of four cards for each author, each card having the name of a different piece of literature as well as a picture of the writer. The player with the most sets at the end wins. Similar games are available for inventors, composers, and explorers.

The same type of card game can be adapted for most subject areas. Instead of different authors, an algebra game might have quadratic equations or polynomial expansions. Players would have to collect sets of four of each. Another example for a simple card game could be parts of speech. Players would have to collect four verbs, four adjectives, four nouns, and four adverbs. Students might decorate their own cards for additional visual appeal and laminate the finished decks for durability. When time is an obstacle, commercial educational card games for a wide range of topics, including endangered species, math facts, and vocabulary words are available for numerous subjects and can be found in educational supply catalogs.

Architecture

On a field trip one day, Alec stopped as his schoolmates were halfway across the parking lot on their way to the museum. He was gazing at a high span bridge arching over a nearby waterway. The teacher went to retrieve the boy who excitedly explained without technical terminology, how the configuration of the steel beams distributed the load and carried the enormous weight of the structure. Alec's fascination with bridges did not quickly subside. During the subsequent two months, he drew a series of complex bridges. Alec's interest piqued the teacher's, and one day she asked her students to think about what makes it possible for buildings and bridges to stand up. This launched a search for explanations that included the exploring of math and physics principles seldom discussed in most fifth grade classrooms.

The goals of architecture in school curriculums extend beyond training future architects or enhancing aesthetic awareness. Some educators claim that architecture provides an effective means for students to learn and apply mathematics, physics, critical and creative thinking skills, spatial reasoning, problem-solving, and collaboration— all through hands-on projects. For many students, architecture offers entry points into content that previously was abstract or unrewarding. For example, students learning the calculation of area and volume find that such concepts are meaningful when viewed in architectural models.

The study of architecture can be integrated into numerous subjects and made appropriate for all grade levels. Linkages to architecture can be discovered when teachers consider how the built environment is involved in various instructional units. Additionally, by viewing humankind as part of the environment, architecture becomes integral to all of life's activities, and is no longer perceived as a separate subject.

Numerous architecture-in-the-schools programs have emerged, all teaching students how to acquire an architect's spatial thinking skills while applying and demonstrating their learning through real world applications. Anne Taylor, Professor of Architecture at the University of New Mexico, has created an innovative curriculum entitled *Architecture and Children*. This program uses architecture, design, and creative problem-solving to teach basic skills and subject matter content through the built, natural, and cultural environment. Interweaving math, science, and art, students creatively problem-solve while building design activities for the physical environment.

Learning to Think Like an Architect

Taylor's (1991) *Architecture and Children* curriculum guides students through a series of problems that teach the steps of the design process. This cognitive apprenticeship approach to learning does not train students to be architects, but instead uses real life projects so that students experience how experts solve problems. Some of the initial "think like an architect" activities ask students to visualize structures that contain a Ping-Pong ball, a fast-food restaurant, or a theatre for children. Students also symbolically draw what happens to a bubble as it emerges, floats, and pops. While the teacher blows ten or more bubbles, students scrutinize their form and function. Told not to draw the bubble itself, students attempt to schematically represent what happens during its "life cycle." A

similar task, "The Great Balloon Race," involves catapulting four balloons in diverse directions around the classroom while students draw arrows and lines depicting them moving in space as well as their spatial relationships.

To increase spatial reasoning, students learn how to develop a plan for an architectural structure that they later build as a model. The first task is to draw bubble diagrams of the areas of a house. Next, students extend the bubble diagram into a plan view for their structure. This is next turned into an elevation view to visualize what the building might look like if it were standing. Next, students draw a two-point perspective sketch to capture the illusion of space and depth. After this is accomplished, students take their plan views and make three-dimensional models of their structures. If resources permit, some students can draw their plans using computer-aided design software. Once students complete their models, they present them to the class. This step of the design process encourages peer feedback, student self-assessment, and ultimately yields a visual portfolio.

Many educational architectural programs involve students in redesigning their classroom space. One fifth grade teacher in White Plains, New York, gave his students free reign in altering their classroom environment. To carry out this project, students had to measure, make scale drawings and three-dimensional models, develop a budget, and implement their plans. Before their foray into architecture, students were below grade level in math. After their classroom redesign efforts, average math scores on both teacher-made and standardized tests increased. Such scores, however, don't begin to measure the positive attitudes or motivation the students exhibited towards learning.

Another approach to environmental design consists of students commemorating landmark structures. For instance, they can study a public building and document its history, architectural and interior design, construction materials, and landscape elements. Such projects can culminate in producing a book that includes student drawings, interviews, and observations. Some students go so far as to bake cakes resembling the building's floor plans!

Doreen Nelson, a former classroom teacher, created the well-researched City Building Education program. This program immerses students in designing efficient classroom traffic patterns or places where people might live, work, and shop. Called Backward Thinking, students begin with an invention, and continuously change and rearrange variables to ensure positive results. For example, in art, students might be asked to invent a still life of flowers never seen before. In science, students studying erosion could suggest ways to use piles of earth or rock that would limit further damage to a hillside. Elementary and middle schools who have adopted City Building Education for a year's time have realized dramatic assessment results. Sixty-five percent of sixth grade students were admitted to higher-level math classes and third grade ESL students gained two or more years of basic skill growth.

Getting Started with Architecture in the Classroom

Teachers interested in integrating architecture into their classrooms will find several resources to support their efforts. By getting in touch with local chapters of the American Institute of Architects, teachers may identify architects who are willing to work in the schools or offer technical assistance. Some states' arts councils fund architect-in-the-schools residency programs. Diverse training programs in architecture and design for educators are also available. Some of these include the Salvadori Center for the Built Environment at New York's City College, Architecture and Children with Anne Taylor at the University of New Mexico, and City Building Education workshops. Other useful

resources for teachers include the books *Architecture Is Elementary: Visual Thinking Through Architectural Concepts* by Nathan Winters, and *Design as a Catalyst for Learning* that documents 30 years of K–12 City Building Education.

The Visual Arts

Some schools across the country are reconsidering the value of arts programs. With the push for national standards in the early 1990s, the arts have had an opportunity to describe their preferred academic content and pedagogy. In 1994, the consortium of National Arts Education Associations mapped out literacy in four disciplines: music, dance, theatre, and the visual arts. This standards-based document defends the arts in public education and their role in enhancing society.

Many schools approach the arts in two ways: by teaching them as disciplines in their own right, and by using them as pedagogical tools to improve teaching and learning. Thus, the visual arts of drawing, painting, sculpting, designing, and collage are often integrated into elementary classrooms. As students grow older, however, such activities are typically omitted from their studies and are offered as separate classes usually attended by adolescents brave enough to claim some artistic talent.

Art as an Instructional Tool

A New York City program called *Learning through an Expanded Arts and Academic Program* (LEAP) has found that hands-on art experiences help K–12 students learn academic content. In fact, 97% of LEAP participants develop a more positive attitude toward school and take greater pride in their work.

LEAP is a nonprofit educational organization based in New York City with a mission to improve the quality of kindergarten through twelfth grade education for all students, including urban minority, economically disadvantaged, and middle-class suburban students. LEAP has worked with 450 schools and agencies in the Northeast. It serves over 200,000 students annually through its 200 experts who work directly with teachers and their classes. LEAP projects are geared to improve student achievement in language arts, math, science, and social studies through arts-based activities. Examples of LEAP lessons for both elementary and secondary students follow.

Blending the Visual and Language Arts

To improve literacy among elementary students, literature, puppetry, and mural painting are used to actively engage children in reading, writing, speaking, and performing. One arts-based LEAP project begins with teacher and students reading a story aloud together. Students then volunteer to work in one of two groups: some elect to make puppets, while others become mural painters.

All the students are taught how to draw quick figures and make storyboards that visually capture the main idea of each scene. The story is next reread slowly, with pauses inserted at the end of each scene. While listening, students create their storyboards scene by scene and then proceed to retell the whole story sequentially. Once able to recall the sequence of the story, students are next asked to identify the main ideas of each scene. If this task proves difficult, students are referred to their storyboards for potential answers. The instructor also suggests that when asked about the main idea of a scene or story, students might consider how they would draw it as a single picture. Next, they select the single, most important event in the story and defend that choice.

Additional lessons for the puppet makers include rereading the story, making puppets, or drawing the main characters to reflect personality traits as well as physical characteristics. Students are asked to imagine how the story might change if the personality of the main character changed, or to assume points of view of various characters. Such activities enhance both reading and higher-level thinking skills. Some students who desire to do so write dialogue for different scenes in the story using appropriate vocabulary. Others may read the story aloud and use puppets to enact it.

The mural painters, meanwhile, identify the scenes of the story, listing the adjectives for the time, place, and descriptions of each location. Small groups of students select scenes to paint and begin sketching the background with colored chalk on large pieces of butcher paper. The background is then painted or filled in with tissue paper collage.

The story's characters are next presented much in the same way as for the puppet group. The mural painters make paper cutouts of the characters for each scene and glue them to the prepared backgrounds. Once the preliminary murals are done, the story is reread to reveal additional details to be included in each scene. Students identify which details should be included and why, and these are then drawn, cut out, and glued onto the scenes. The scenes are joined together, and as the story is read, the students point out the main ideas and details in each scene. Storytelling is rehearsed and, finally, other classes are invited to hear the storytelling and see the puppet shows and mural.

Integrating Art and Math

An especially effective approach to integrating math and art is evident in the LEAP fractions quilt project. To introduce the concept of fractions, intermediate students are provided with scissors, a pencil, and four squares of construction paper. Rather than being given pre-cut paper, students must cut the pieces themselves to comprehend the concept of fractions. The first fraction taught is one half. The students are directed to fold one piece of construction paper in half, cutting it down the middle. They next draw a line across the middle of each half of the paper as the teacher explains that this line indicates they are no longer dealing with a whole but now rather with a part. The students are asked to identify how many parts they have and write the number two as the denominator, which indicates into how many pieces they have divided the paper. Holding one piece of paper, the students write one as the numerator on it to help them learn that numerators indicate the number of the whole they represent. To see how many halves make a whole, students place both halves on top of a whole piece of construction paper. This process of folding, cutting, writing, and placing parts onto wholes is repeated for quarters and eighths and sometimes extended into other fractions as well.

With a basic understanding of fractions, students are now ready to construct a quilt. On a large square of construction paper, they mount different-sized pieces of paper into various "quilt" patterns. All the fraction patterns are next mounted on a classroom wall to look like a quilt. Space is left between each of the fraction patterns so that students can write equations beneath each pattern. They then solve the equations, reducing them to the lowest common denominators.

For teachers interested in learning more about the LEAP approach, including lesson plans, programs, and training tapes, contact LEAP online at http://leapnyc.org/.

Integrating the Arts at the High School Level

The LEAP programs are by no means for elementary students only. They offer secondary level math, physics, and science curriculums as well. For example, one lesson teaches students about plate tectonics. Students are organized into small groups, are given four blocks of colored plastecine clay and photocopied information of plate tectonics, and proceed to make model plates. Students mold and flatten the clay into small strips that are placed on each other in four layers: one represents the floor of a valley, another lava from the eruption of a mountain, the third sea residue, and the fourth layer is volcanic lava. The students, through both verbal and visual instructions, go on to make mountains, islands, and faults and experiment with the shifting of plates. As they learn how the earth's surface moves, they can consider prehistoric Pangea and are asked to draw what the earth might look like 50 million years from now.

One program called Partners: Artists and Schools for Students (PASS) specifically targets students in grades 9–12 for integrated arts experiences. By 2000, this collaborative effort among high school teachers and arts organizations had involved 5000 students, 30 arts organizations, and 16 high schools in St. Paul and Minneapolis. PASS seeks to demonstrate the profound effect of the arts on teaching, learning, and living. As of 2000, research on the program revealed that PASS students exhibited increased achievement, problem-solving skills, multicultural understanding, and engagement with school. The students also had reduced drop out and absenteeism rates. Additionally, the high schools have experienced increased parental involvement.

Still other high school teachers in New York City have used the arts to improve math and reading achievement. Examples of their efforts follow.

Underachieving readers meet once daily in a studio with an art teacher who works with a reading specialist to develop lessons. The lessons, based on art experiences, address four specific reading skills: word identification, comprehension, study skills, and scanning. One comprehension unit includes making comparisons. Students read about Picasso and talk about the transformations in his artistic style. They make comparisons between figurative and nonfigurative paintings in written form while painting an abstract still life themselves.

Daily class sessions in the art studio begin with vocabulary and written instructions posted on an easel. In their personal journals, students record the day's vocabulary lesson, write plans for their projects, and list books they select from the studio's reading corner. Once a week, students write a paper based on their notes, plans, and readings. These papers are maintained in a writing portfolio and an art portfolio contains records of their visual projects. To highlight reading improvement, each project culminates with two sets of records.

Similarly, math and arts teachers have experimented with integrating math and art. During two-hour daily blocks, the students spend the first period learning about mathematical concepts that enable them to build models. During the second period, an art teacher supervises the construction of mathematical designs. In this approach, students learn about and then construct products that demonstrate their knowledge of prime numbers, modular arithmetic, geometric forms, and theorems. Learning is also collaborative and shared, with students turning to each other as resources for ideas and feedback. Throughout their construction activities, students are required to use and master basic computational and conceptual skills.

As the preceding examples demonstrate, stimulating arts-based lessons result when content area teachers and arts specialists team teach or co-plan. Not only do students learn well; they also benefit from the fundamental artistic processes of problem-solving, self-expression, and invention. If, however, teachers are unable to team with arts specialists, opportunities for students to learn and demonstrate their knowledge through the visual arts might still be offered. Some suggestions follow.

Art Across the Curriculum

1. Each classroom can feature an art center complete with markers, paints, colored paper of varying sizes and textures, cloth, natural and human-made objects. Supplies should be frequently refurbished and students encouraged to use them.

2. Classroom projects that involve drawing, construction, photographic essays, videography, and model building enliven learning in any content area. At least one art option can be suggested for each unit of study.

3. Collages provide opportunities for visual interpretation of ideas and can illustrate classroom lessons. Old magazines and journals appropriate for diverse subject matter areas can be collected, stored, and made available for student use.

4. Timelines, maps, and charts embellished by students with color, imagery, and fanciful backgrounds will spark attention and memory.

5. Classroom friezes can bring important facts to life. One junior high school teacher encircled her room with a frieze of Greek and Latin word parts. Each student contributed one or more visual images to represent the meaning of his or her words. Colorful friezes can be constructed and displayed for nearly any content area.

6. Wall-size murals personalize a classroom and make it possible for students to see the concepts they are learning. Those students with artistic skills can draw the murals for their classmates to paint or label.

7. Large or small scrolls, made out of butcher paper and doweling, make excellent graphic displays of quantities of information. One seventh grade class created a visual history of ancient civilizations on 200 feet of four-foot-wide butcher paper. Scenes focused on lifestyles, customs, and major historical events of four early civilizations, and their contributions that remain with us today. Students also wrote poems on the topics and included these on the scroll. Different roles emerged among the students as the project unfolded, including planners, sketchers, painters, writers, and even mechanics to design and construct the scroll.

8. Replicas of famous art, maps, or other visuals can be reproduced by students through jigsaw or grid techniques. For example, one class made two twelve-foot-square maps of the eastern and western hemispheres. After sketching the continents onto large paper, they drew jigsaw puzzle lines on the back, dividing each map into twenty-five pieces, the number of students in the class. After the pieces were cut out, each student took one. They next had to determine where the pieces fit onto the map, what constituted land, water, and continents, and how to coordinate adjacent pieces. In another school, a giant mural of Van Gogh's *Starry Night* was created as a school project. Filling one entire wall of the middle school's library, the mural was made from dozens of paper squares, each corresponding to a smaller one from a grid of the original painting. Each student painted an enlarged version of what appeared on the numbered square of her grid. Again, coordination was necessary, particularly when a star, house, or tree crossed from one square on the grid to another.

9. Prints, posters, and photographs that relate to the subject matter can decorate the classroom while providing springboards for discussions and inspiration for student art work. Holt, Reinhart and Winston, Inc. have a package called *Art Works* featuring a wide variety of gender-balanced art from many cultures. By writing art museums to request their catalogs, teachers will find a wealth of resources. From postcards to full-sized prints, artists' works can be brought directly into the classroom. Local galleries and framing shops often have good selections of prints as well.

10. Computer software that facilitates drawing, timelines, and graphing can add a visual dimension to classroom assignments and displays.

11. At the secondary level, students who are particularly artistic may be able to design an arts-based classroom activity and teach it to their peers.

12. Teachers might create a list of local community artists or arts agencies who upon invitation are willing to share their expertise with schools.

13. Teachers can take advantage of numerous resource books such as *Doing Art Together* by Muriel Silberstein-Storfer and Mablen Jones; *Art from Many Hands* by Jo Miles Schuman; *Making Things: The Handbook of Creative Discovery* by Anne Wiseman; and *Cultural Journeys: 84 Art and Social Science Experiences from Around the World* by Margaret Ryan. They can also tap some of the arts resources on the Internet that are described in the pages that follow.

Of course, some teachers and students may want to develop their own visual skills. Mona Brookes, author of *Drawing with Children* and *Drawing with Older Children and Teens* and founder of Monart Visual Arts Schools, believes everyone is an artist. Her own drawing method consists of five basic shapes easily learned and applied by anyone from preschoolers through senior citizens. Brookes recommends, however, that budding artists take advantage of diverse drawing methods. To nurture children's artistic skills, teachers might encourage early childhood symbolic stick and figure drawing. At around age four, or with beginners of any age, instructors may want to use Brookes' books to nurture the artist in us all.

Enrichment activities at this time might consist of cartooning from Mark Kistlers' *Draw Squad*. For the development of art history awareness and art appreciation, educators may want to turn to the Los Angeles Getty Center for Education in the Arts' Discipline-Based Art Education programs. The DBAE programs are dedicated to improving the quality of arts education by including studio art, art history, criticism, and aesthetics in school programs. When older students are ready to tackle live model drawing and fine art styles, they may want to work with an art classic such as Nicholaides' *The Natural Way to Draw*.

Technology That Enhances Visual-Spatial Intelligence

The world was already becoming increasingly visual with the advent of slides, movies, television, videos, and video walls, but the development of digital technologies has taken it to a whole new level. For example, we now have interactive digital television that makes it possible for the user to watch programs and simultaneously access supportive information by clicking on website links, thus creating "teleputers." In many classrooms slide shows have been replaced with PowerPoint presentations, and many students now have portable laptop computers and even smaller hand-held devices that can be used anywhere. Mobile wireless devices make it possible for people to access the Internet throughout the world, even in locations without electricity or phone lines.

CD-ROMs and DVDs make it possible to access selections at any point, allowing for discussions to take place without completing the entire program. Frequent opportunities to discuss what students have already seen and what they are about to see next make possible the anticipatory and participatory learning that are critical to the educational process. Many students now use camcorders to film events, download the recording on a computer, and edit it online to create their own iMovies. High definition TV and IMAX huge screen videos create a new sense of reality for the viewer, and educational games are now being played in virtual environments.

"Magic books," created in Japan, are being explored and developed further at the University of Washington's Human Interface Technology Laboratory (the HIT Lab). These new products look like real books, but are read using special goggles hooked up to a computer. The reader can watch a story come to life as the objects seem to jump right off the page. They can be examined from any angle, and the characters move, cry real tears, and play hide-and-seek in the woods. These virtual reality tools hold great promise for the teaching and learning of such subjects as the sciences, math, architecture, and medicine.

In another project at the HIT Lab, at-risk students learned how to create virtual reality games and produced a game that pitted the immune system against the HIV virus. The game included challenges in the form of drugs, behavior, and environment. For many of the students this was one of the rare times when they were engaged and successful in the learning process.

A research group, the Senses Bureau, at the University of California/San Diego, has created a science-based virtual reality adventure called Virtual Explorer that has been made available at no cost to schools, museums, and researchers. This educational game, now also on CD-ROM, is an interactive simulation of a voyage through the human immune system, during which students can interact in real time with concepts being studied. The student pilots a microscopic "nanobot" ship through his or her own blood stream and lymph system. After choosing which cellular character to play, the user performs functions such as cellular navigation, white blood cell recognition, and molecular docking. This virtual environment has colorful animation and four-channel spatialized sound. For further information see http://www.wilson.ucsd.edu/ve.

For rich classroom resources, The National Geographic Kids Network is a telecommunications system that links students throughout the world. Students share information with each other about geography and experiments in science using computer-generated maps and charts. See www2.edc.org/NCIP/library/telecom/Geo.htm. Also, Geographic Television (GTV) continues to be useful in many classrooms. Developed by the National Geographic Society in association with Lucasfilm Ltd., it combines the interactive capabilities of the computer with instant access of the videodisc composed of National Geographic pictures.

Another excellent source of high-quality classroom materials is being provided through educational television stations in partnership with UnitedStreaming.com to provide the long-awaited video-on-demand. The programs can run on either a Mac or PC and include teachers' guides and blackline masters. Over 1200 titles are segmented into 12,000 content-specific video clips that can be searched by keyword, subject area, grade, and/or academic learning requirements.

Students with special needs can also be helped in new ways through visual media. For example, those with speech difficulties can actually see their speaking patterns through IBM's SpeechViewer; from this visual feedback, they learn to make appropriate changes. Students who cannot move may talk into the computer and it will print out what they say; others who can move but cannot speak may work with computers that say back what they have written on the screen. Children with delayed speech may be helped by using a "Wolf" board with overlays of pictures or words that "say" what they are when touched.

Computers allow visually oriented students to learn through their strengths as they interact with the technology. They can take advantage of opportunities to see and manipulate the material they are accessing or creating in many different forms before they make final copies of a written project. Such publications as Stanley's *Exploring Graphic Design: A Short Course in Desktop Publishing* offer helpful information on the essential principles of design and how to apply them to the preparation of publications.

Since increasing numbers of schools are using demonstrations of student work as a means of assessment, multimedia reports provide an excellent alternative or adjunct to traditional tests. Reports may include film clips, slides, photographs, and other illustrations or be in the form of an iMovie. These multimedia productions make learning a fascinating process, letting students work with knowledge in many forms. Scholastic HyperScreen is one example of a software program that contains built-in fonts, clip art, and drawing tools. Each screen can contain up to fifteen "hotspots," or buttons, that make it possible for users to interact with the lesson or report. Students can design their own screens using clip art, backgrounds, borders, fonts, music, and sound effects from this program.

An increasing number of graphics programs, such as Adobe Photoshop or Adobe Photoshop Elements, Serif Draw, Adobe Illustrator, Corel Draw, and Macromedia Freehand offer a wide range of experiences that can enhance artistic creativity and fluency by facilitating the technical processes involved in graphic design. Students can create their own works of art or modify existing ones as they explore such compositional devices such as perspective, balance, and color.

As an interesting experiment to see what the Internet offers in regard to understanding and appreciating the arts, use any of the many high-powered search engines and type in "Guernica." You will find numerous websites that examine Picasso's famous painting, and give information about the artist and his time, about the Spanish Civil War, and the historical and mythological sources of the subject matter. The same can be done with other famous artists perhaps for art appreciation classes.

For additional excellent resources related to the visual arts see the following websites:

Americans for the Arts, at www.artsusa.org/issues/artsed, offers resources to make a case for the arts in school and after. It includes research, tool kits, exemplary programs, an audio-video library, and an e-newsletter.

The Getty's Educational website is a magnificent example of colorful, interactive, and fascinating ways to explore and expand on their exhibits. It includes teaching tools, lesson plans, and curriculum ideas on such topics as the history of science and artists as scientists. Seewww.artsed.net.getty.edu.

The Kennedy Center supports the place of arts education at the center of the curriculum through the creative and appropriate uses of technology at artsedge.Kennedy-center.org.

The Perpich Center for Arts Education is a state agency, charged by the Minnesota legislature to bring the arts into K–12 education. It includes, on a 30-acre campus in the suburbs of Minneapolis, a public Arts High School, a Professional Development Institute, and a Research, Assessment, and Curriculum Division. To learn more about this program and its resources see www.pcae.k12.mn.us.

The Association for the Advancement of Arts Education teaches teachers how to use the arts to teach social studies, science, math, and language arts, and how to incorporate them into the curriculum. See www.aaae.org.

Although visual-spatial tools are not essential for the learning process, they do offer exciting and motivating ways to engage the learner through exercising visual-spatial intelligence and make any subject more accessible to a variety of students. They will surely be of major value to students with physical disabilities or other special needs, and will often provide strong motivation to learn for at-risk students. The arts will, in fact, move what might otherwise, for many, remain meaningless abstractions into understandable, visible, and memorable reality.

Summary

Although not all of visual-spatial intelligence is associated with the arts, many of its facets are. As mentioned throughout this chapter, creating and manipulating visual images are powerful allies in K–12 learning. In 2002, a compendium of arts education research called Critical Links explored the role of the arts in enhancing cognitive capacities. Nearly 3000 studies showed that spatial skills influenced our capacity to understand spoken and written language. As we come to better understand the role of drawing, designing, building models, and other art forms in learning, it is likely they will become embedded in K–12 curriculum and classroom practice.

The visual-spatial techniques included in this chapter are listed below so that readers can summarize and identify those that may be appropriate for their classroom use.

 APPLYING VISUAL-SPATIAL INTELLIGENCE

1. Important ideas or insights gleaned from this chapter:

   _____

   _____

   _____

2. Areas I'd like to learn more about:

   _____

   _____

3. Ways I can use this information in my teaching. Please note that all of the strategies mentioned in this chapter are listed below with space provided to note how each strategy might be incorporated into classroom instruction:

VISUAL-SPATIAL STRATEGY	CLASSROOM APPLICATION

Establishing a Visual Learning Environment _____

    Visual Tools _____

    Intentional Display Areas _____

    Peripheral Stimuli _____

    Changing Perspective through Rotating Seating _____

    Nonverbal Communication _____

Pictorial Representation

    Flow Charts _____

    Visual Outlines _____

    Unit Charts _____

    Visual Chart Starters _____

Visual Notetaking and Brainstorming Tools

    Concept Mapping _____

    Mindmapping _____

    Clustering _____

    Mindscaping _____

Visualization

    Classroom Imagery _____

    Visual Memory Techniques _____

    Visual Variety in Learning Materials _____

    Highlighting with Color _____

    Varying Shapes _____

    Visual Accompaniment for Lectures, _____
    Discussions, or Readings

Board and Card Games

    Guidelines for Making Board Games _____

    Card Games _____

Architecture

    Learning to Think Like an Architect _____

    Getting Started with Architecture _____

The Visual Arts

    Art as an Instructional Tool _____

    Blending the Visual and Language Arts _____

    Integrating Art and Math _____

    Integrating the Arts at the High School Level _____

    Art Across the Curriculum _____

Technology That Enhances Visual-Spatial _____
Intelligence

VISUAL-SPATIAL REFERENCES

Arts Education Partnership. (2002). *Critical Links: Learning in the Arts and Student Academic and Social Development.* Available online at: http://aep~arts.org/CLT.

Brookes, M. (1986). *Drawing with Children.* Los Angeles: Tarcher.

Brookes, M. (1992). *Drawing for Older Children and Teens: A Creative Method for Adult Beginners, Too.* Los Angeles: Tarcher.

Consortium of National Arts Educational Associations. (1994). *National Standards for Arts Education. What Every American Should Know and Be Able to Do in the Arts.* Reston, VA: Music Educators National Conference.

Davis, M., Hawley, P., & Spilka, G. (1998). *Design as a Catalyst for Learning.* Alexandria, VA: ASCD.

Gardner. H. (1993, 1983). *Frames of Mind: The Theory of Multiple Intelligences.* New York: Basic Books.

Hyerle, D. (1996). *Visual Tools for Constructing Knowledge.* Alexandria, VA: ASCD.

Jones, B. F. (1988). *Graphic Forms with Corresponding Text Frames.* Aurora, CO: North Central Regional Educational Laboratory.

Lorayne, H., & Lucas, J. (1996). *The Memory Book.* New York: Ballantine Books.

Margulies, N. (2002). *Mapping Inner Space.* Tucson, AZ: Zephyr Press.

McKim, R. (1980 2nd Ed.). *Experiences in Visual Thinking.* Monterey, CA: Brooks/Cole Publishing.

Novak, J., & Gowin, B. (1984). *Learning How to Learn.* New York: Cambridge University Press.

Rico, G. (1983). *Writing the Natural Way.* Los Angeles: Tarcher.

Rico, G. (1999). *Writing the Natural Way.* New York: Putnam.

Taylor, A. (1991). *Architecture and Children.* Albuquerque, NM: American Institute of Architects.

Tuning In
MUSICAL INTELLIGENCE

Music is the manifestation of the human spirit, similar to language. Its greatest practitioners have conveyed to mankind things not possible to say in any other language. If we do not want these things to remain dead treasures, we must do our utmost to make the greatest possible number of people understand their idiom.

—Zoltan Kodaly, *A Zanei Iras-Olvasas Modszertana*

DANNY'S SONG

The American singer and composer Danny Deardorff was struck by polio when he was an infant. The disease left his body crooked and crippled, but from the earliest years, his strong spirit has revealed itself through song.

*A*s a child, Danny made up songs about the mailman walking down the street and about the screen door keeping bugs out and letting cool air in. Whatever he saw was translated into lyrics and music.

Today Danny is an internationally recognized composer, performer, producer, and inspirational speaker. He has received numerous national awards and believes that music is a powerful form of communication, one that reaches the mind through the heart. Danny's music teaches important social messages, some of which include learning to love more fully, caring for the environment, and appreciating the differences among individuals.

One song Danny wrote and recorded with Lorraine Bayes is entitled "Everyone is Differently Abled." The lyrics replaced the term "disabled" with "differently abled," which Danny asserts applies to everyone and emphasizes what we can do, instead of what we can't do.

DANNY'S SONG . . . continued

The song echoes Howard Gardner's Theory of Multiple Intelligences by affirming:

Everyone is Differently Abled.

Everyone has abilities.

Everyone is Differently Abled

Making their lives work differently.

You might use a chair with wheels to get around.

Or, you might use your hands to speak without a sound,

'Cause there are a million ways to do most anything.

Some people love to dance.

Some people prefer to sing.

Now you can use a working dog to help you see.

Or use your mouth or feet to paint and write poetry.

There are a million different ways that you can be.

It's true that all of us live interdependently.

I will not be defined by my limitations,

But rather by my possibilities.

We can respond to the needs of those around us.

The best ability is response-ability.

Everyone is Differently Abled.

Everyone has abilities.

Everyone is Differently Abled

Making their lives work differently.

This song is part of an album entitled, *Let's Be Friends*, by the award-winning children's performing group Tickle Tune Typhoon.

DEFINITION: Understanding Musical Intelligence

Music is undoubtedly one of the oldest art forms, utilizing the human voice and body as natural instruments and means of self-expression. It is an art that accompanies each of us into the world. We listened to our mother's heartbeat for nine months while in utero. We live with the rhythms of our own heartbeat and respiration and the more subtle rhythms of metabolic and brain wave activity. We are all inherently musical and can develop this capacity in ourselves and in others.

The early childhood years are crucial to musical growth. Between the ages of four to six we experience a heightened sensitivity to sound and pitch. During that time, a rich musical environment can provide the basis for later musical ability. In

Bloom's *Developing Talent in Young Children*, he points out that among the gifted pianists he studied, many were not from musical families. They all had parents, however, who were supportive of their children's musical interests. In addition, the musicians' first teachers were consistently warm, caring, and supportive. Taskmasters came later in their careers.

Musical intelligence involves its own rules and thinking structures, not necessarily linked to other kinds of intelligence. Stravinsky once commented that "Music expresses itself," underscoring the uniqueness of this form of human competence. Music is an aural language and consists of three basic components: pitch, rhythm, and timbre or the quality of a sound. The countless combinations of these three elements have given rise to the remarkable variety of music found throughout the world. It also has its own with unique notational system.

Howard Gardner asserts in *Frames of Mind* that any normal individual who has had frequent exposure to music can manipulate pitch, rhythm, and timbre to participate with some skill in musical activities, including composing, singing, or playing instruments. The foundations for such interests can be laid at an early age in the home, and musical experiences can be integrated throughout a school's curriculum.

Such experiences might include exploring sound through singing, moving, listening, and playing instruments. Music literature in a curriculum might feature folk songs, classical music, and music from a variety of cultures, styles, and time periods.

Because of strong ties to emotions, music in the classroom can promote a positive environment that is conducive to learning. It can intentionally be used to heighten the suspense, sadness, tragedy, or joy of stories from great literature and history. Music can even be used for humorous purposes. Musical puns such as those by P.D.Q. Bach are interesting tools for sharpening listening and concentration skills.

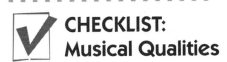

CHECKLIST: Musical Qualities

Many ancient philosophers included music as an important part of education. Plato claimed that "Rhythm and harmony sink deep into the recesses of the soul and take the strongest hold there, bringing the grace of body and mind which is only to be found in one brought up in the right way." Aristotle was also an early proponent of extensive music education believing that "We become of a certain quality in our characters on account of it."

Confucius thought music was influential both personally and politically: "The superior man tries to promote music as a means to the perfection of human culture. When such music prevails, and people are led toward ideals and aspirations, we may see the appearance of a great nation." During the Middle Ages and Renaissance, music was considered one of the four pillars of learning, along with geometry, astronomy, and arithmetic.

In our time, however, music often suffers as one of the first subjects to be cut from school programs when budget reductions are made. Standards and accountability systems cause many administrators to devote more time to reading, math, and science. Ironically, music may be one of the important means of developing those very skills so desired in American students. For example, an extensive compendium of arts education research studies called *Critical Links* was released in 2002. Published by Arts Education Partnership, the document showed that music instruction, including training in keyboard skills, develops spatial reasoning and spatial-temporal skills that are key in understanding and using mathematical ideas and concepts.

Activities such as constructing and playing instruments, taking lessons to improve performance skills, playing or singing in ensembles, dancing, and attending concerts can be positive challenges for students when it is a standard part of their education. At the St. Augustine School of the Arts in the Bronx, New York, all students have such opportunities. The children who attend this school are mostly from poor, undereducated families, yet the school ranks among the highest academically in the United States. The school was the subject of the 1994 Sundance Film Festival award-winning documentary *Something Within Me*.

There are those students who have greater musical ability than others, and their gift may appear early in life. As Howard Gardner notes, musical talent emerges inexplicably earlier than giftedness in other areas of human intelligence. These unique children are compelled to make music, and it is essential they have opportunities both to experience and create music. As noted earlier, however, virtually everyone, including hard-of-hearing and deaf students, has the potential to develop his or her musical abilities.

Many, if not most, children and adults enjoy rhythm and melody and like to listen to or participate in musical activities. Individuals without prior exposure often enjoy learning through musical methods or appreciate music in the classroom as they work on nonverbal tasks.

It is a complex matter to identify students who have musical aptitude or well-developed musical intelligence. A broad range of musical abilities exists and it is unlikely any one individual embodies them all. For example, there are many well-known cases of musicians who were successful at some musical endeavors and failed with others. It is rumored that Tchaikovsky nearly ruined the premiere of his Sixth Symphony because of his poor conducting. Chopin was a gifted composer for the piano but appeared uninterested in writing for any other instrument. Some individuals may fail music theory classes but demonstrate giftedness in singing. Others such as Louis Armstrong may have an outstanding ability to improvise in certain styles of music without the training to read musical notation. Thus, it is impossible to determine musical intelligence by using a checklist that captures only a few of the dimensions of this complex intelligence. However, a list such as the following may help to identify some of the characteristics of musically endowed learners. It is likely that a person with well-developed musical intelligence:

1. Listens and responds with interest to a variety of sounds, including the human voice, environmental sounds, and music, and organizes such sounds into meaningful patterns.

2. Enjoys and seeks out opportunities to hear music or environmental sounds in the learning environment. Is eager to be around and learn from music and musicians.

3. Responds to music kinesthetically by conducting, performing, creating, or dancing; emotionally by responding to the moods and tempos of music; intellectually by discussing and analyzing music; and/or aesthetically by evaluating and exploring the content and meaning of music.

4. Recognizes and discusses different musical styles, genres, and cultural variations. Demonstrates interest in the role music has and continues to play in human lives.

5. Collects music and information about music in various forms, both recorded and printed, and may collect and play instruments, including synthesizers.

6. Develops the ability to sing and/or play an instrument alone or with others.

7. Uses the vocabulary and notations of music.

8. Develops a personal frame of reference for listening to music.

9. Enjoys improvising and playing with sounds, and when given a phrase of music, can complete a musical statement in a way that makes sense.

10. Offers interpretations of what a composer is communicating through music. May also analyze and critique musical selections.

11. Expresses interest in careers involving music such as being a singer, instrumentalist, sound engineer, producer, critic, instrument maker, teacher, or conductor.

12. May create original compositions and/or musical instruments.

Musical Learning Processes

The activities suggested in this chapter are not intended to provide a comprehensive or sequential course in music education or to substitute for such programs taught in the schools by trained music educators. Children and young people can develop their musical abilities through programs designed to achieve a balance of skills in performing, listening, and creating as well as reflecting on music. There are many fine music programs at all levels in schools throughout the nation. Standards for such programs are available from the National Association for Music Education accessible online at ww.menc.org.

Instead, the following musical activities are meant to facilitate the learning of other academic content. Many educators shun musical teaching strategies because of their own lack of musical experience. No training, however, is necessary to incorporate these activities into lessons. The strategies offered here provide successful ways for students and teachers alike to foster positive attitudes toward music and to recognize its relationship to other kinds of learning. When teachers incorporate music in classroom lessons, an additional benefit may ultimately emerge: musical appreciation and skill may develop in formerly nonmusical teachers and students!

The strategies described in this chapter include:

Establishing a Musical Learning Environment
Introducing Music into the Classroom

Listening to Music
Songs in the Content Areas

Music for Skill Building
Musical Spelling
Music and Learning Skills
Teaching Reading Musically
Improving Language Skills with Music
Music Across the Curriculum

Warming Up to Singing
Nonsense Sounds
Choral Reading

Musical Notation
Introducing the Concept of Musical Notation

Creating Curriculum Songs

Jump-Starting Creativity with Music

Making Musical Instruments in the Classroom
Using Instruments Creatively

Technology That Enhances Musical Intelligence

Establishing a Musical Learning Environment

▪ ▪ ▪ ▪ ▪ ▪ ▪ ▪ ▪ ▪ ▪ ▪ ▪ ▪ ▪ ▪ ▪ ▪

Music can become an important part of any educational setting. It provides a welcoming atmosphere as students enter; it offers a calming effect after periods of physical activity; it smoothes classroom transitions; it reawakens energy on gray days; and it reduces stress that commonly accompanies examinations or other academic pressures.

One principal, noticing the calming and quieting effect of background music in some teachers' classrooms, decided to play music in the school's hallways where numerous behavior problems frequently erupted. As an experiment, the principal played Steven Halpern's "Spectrum Suite" and other quiet selections in the school's passageways and lunchroom. Student behavior dramatically improved and music became an essential component of the total school environment.

When used softly in the background as students enter a classroom, music has the ability to focus student attention and to enhance physical energy levels. Students typically enter class with a variety of individual concerns, feelings, and preoccupations. Music can create a positive atmosphere that will help them focus to learn.

Introducing Music into the Classroom

Teachers interested in playing background music to enhance classroom ambiance may first want to increase student awareness of the ways music can enhance everyday living. We are surrounded with the sounds of radios, video games, CDs, laser discs, television, and music as accompaniments to many of our daily activities. To heighten awareness of music and its influence in our lives, the teacher may want to engage the class in a discussion of how and when students listen to music. It can be suggested that since students often listen to popular culture selections for entertainment, they may want to expand their awareness of other kinds of music to discover how a variety of musical styles can enhance the quality of life.

There are several things a teacher might consider before making music a part of the classroom. These include sound equipment, types of music to play, and times when cultural considerations of its use is appropriate. For teachers who want to create a musical classroom environment, some guidelines follow.

Guidelines for Using Background Music in the Classroom

1. Musical equipment, ideally of good quality, should be located and installed in the classroom. Music played through a sound system with two separate speakers in different locations of the classroom provides the most effective sound. When speakers are placed at a distance from each other, it is easier for all students to hear well.

2. Although high-quality sound systems are rarely present in most schools, it is important to realize that the sound of poor-quality equipment can be distracting and frustrating. By identifying a school or household's available equipment, teachers may discover a variety of options.

3. Since many homes do not have recordings of different kinds of music, teachers will want to share with their students a broad representation of selections including contemporary, romantic, baroque, and classical pieces played by orchestras, chamber groups, or soloists. Excellent recordings of world music should also be included. Some selections are suggested later in the chapter.

4. It is important to determine when and how background music is to be played in the classroom. Frequently, it is effective as students enter the room, and during quiet reading, individual work sessions, study periods, tests, and transitions. Ultimately, teachers and students will want to experiment with timing such as at the beginning, middle, or end of a day or class period to determine what is most effective for each group. Selections may be chosen to quiet active or restless groups or energize students who are tired or sleepy.

5. Some research indicates that music may interfere with verbal tasks, and that some students may be distracted by music during any kind of academic work. In general, it is recommended that background music be played only occasionally. Just a few minutes of appropriate music can be useful in bridging between subjects or activities. Such a minimal amount of time allows students who enjoy a musical environment to have access to rhythmical stimulation without causing discomfort for those who find it distracting.

6. If the teacher plans to speak while the music is playing, the volume should be set at a level that does not compete with his or her voice.

7. Students often provide valuable feedback about their reactions to music in the classroom. Class discussions might address preferred selections, volume, and timing, as well as the type and the location of the sound system. Thus, students and teachers together can establish a positive musical learning environment.

Once students and teachers have experimented with a melodic background in the classroom, additional purposes for the use of music can be explored. The research of psychiatrist and educator Dr. Georgi Lozanov in Sophia, Bulgaria, suggests that music strongly influences our ability to relax, rejuvenate, and concentrate. Lozanov's work also suggests that music integrates the emotional, physical, and cognitive dimensions of the learner, and accelerates the quantity of information learned and retained.

In addition to creating a pleasant classroom ambiance, music can be used for specific purposes. Many teachers have intentionally used music in four ways: to relax, invigorate, focus student attention, or ease transitions. For example, when students appear overly stimulated, certain selections such as *Water Music Suite* by Handel or *Concerto for Three Violins and Orchestra* by Telemann often help them relax. After lunch when lethargy sets in, other pieces may prove invigorating such as *Divertimento* by Mozart or *Flight of the Bumble Bee* by Rimsky-Korsakov. When well-focused attention is necessary, some compositions such as *Four Seasons* by Vivaldi or *Piano Concert in C Major* by Mozart may enhance student concentration. If teachers are interested in working with music for such purposes, they might want to review their personal collections, sorting their albums or cassettes into the four categories of relaxation, focusing attention, invigoration, and transitions, or locate music elsewhere that may be appropriate for such purposes.

Some suggestions are offered below that diversify classroom listening experiences with both contemporary and classical selections.

A Variety of Musical Selections

For Relaxation

The Four Seasons	Vivaldi
Inner Rhythms	Randy Crafton
Water Music	Handel
Afternoon of a Faun	Debussy
Deep Breakfast	Ray Lynch
Fantasia on Greensleeves	Vaughan Williams

For Focusing Attention

Flute Concertos	Vivaldi
Concerto Grossi #4, 10–12	Corelli
"Silver Cloud"	Kitaro
"Music for Accelerated Learning"	Steven Halpern
Piano Concerto in C Major	Mozart
"Snowflakes Are Dancing"	Tomita

For Invigoration

Alexander's Feast	Handel
"Dances for a Sleep Walker"	Don Campbell
Well Tempered Klavier	J. S. Bach
Divertimento	Mozart
The Sting	Movie soundtrack
"Saving the Wildlife"	Mannheim Steamroller

For Transitions

Music for the Royal Fireworks	Handel
Apurimac	Cusco
"The Norwegian Bridal Procession" from *Peer Gynt Suite*	Grieg
"Breezin'"	George Benson
Nouveau Flamenco	Ottmar Liebert

The compositions suggested above all rely on a musical theme and are structured with patterns and symmetry that are capable of influencing body rhythms and mental alertness. When well used, music can serve teachers and students as a powerful ally in the classroom.

Listening to Music

Sharing a variety of musical styles and compositions in the classroom can lay the groundwork for the development of musical taste and appreciation. It is important to offer opportunities for all children to hear, sing, and dance to the folk songs of their own and other countries. They should also be exposed to fine music by soloists, and small and large ensembles playing both classical and modern music. Students' musical interests may be piqued by studying the role of music in world cultures and the lives of various composers and performers. Teachers can create a composer-of-the-month learning center in which recordings, biographies, pictures, and literature are available for independent exploration and research.

For students to benefit from a musical learning environment, they must do more than listen passively to many musical selections. They should also learn to listen actively, focusing on the music itself. To shift from hearing background music to active, structured listening, teachers can engage students in a discussion about a musical composition, its qualities, and the impact it has on them as individuals. To assist students with structured listening, select a musical piece to play once or twice, and preview the following questions so that students can prepare for their listening experience.

Listening Discussion Questions

What did this music make you think of? Did it suggest colors, images, patterns, or scenes?

What feelings did this selection evoke?

What instruments or singing did you hear?

Were there any repetitive sound patterns the composer used? Can you sing or tap them?

What portions of the music did you especially enjoy? What made them appealing?

Can you think of a situation when this music would be especially appropriate to play?

Does this music remind you of another selection? What is similar to it?

Can you imagine movement or dance to accompany this music? If so, can you move or dance in that way?

If you could, would you change this music in any way? How?

What do you think the composer was trying to communicate when he wrote this composition? Might the listener hear something quite different?

The questions listed above are not meant to develop a sophisticated understanding of music. They are intended, however, to help students listen actively and critically. Teachers can add other questions according to their interest and expertise. Students might also respond to music in nonverbal ways. While listening to a composition and using music as a source of inspiration, students might draw or paint, build with clay or wire, or move and dance.

Whenever possible, students should have opportunities to attend performances to listen to accomplished musicians. Some students may perceive the powerful, inspirational quality of music as did 12-year-old Josef Knecht in Herman Hesse's *Magister Ludi*:

The boy looked at the player's clever white fingers, saw the course of the development faintly mirrored in his concentrated expression while his eyes remained quiet under half-closed lids. Josef's heart swelled with veneration, with love for the master, his ear drank in the fugue. It seemed to him that he was hearing music for the first time in his life. Behind the music being created in his presence, he sensed the world of mind, the joy-giving harmony of law, and freedom of service and rule. He surrendered himself, and vowed to serve that world, and this master. In those few moments he saw himself and his life; saw the whole cosmos, guided, ordered and interpreted by the spirit of music.

Songs in the Content Areas

Song lyrics containing curriculum information are invaluable instructional tools. Most students find it easy to memorize the lyrics to songs, and will find it just as easy to memorize academic content set to music. We recently met a trainer of European real estate sales people. He was challenged by the difficulty of his task, since each country had a different set of real estate laws and it was difficult to remember which laws were legislated by which country. The trainer tackled this problem by setting the laws of each country to representative music of that nation. For example, the laws of Spain were set to a Spanish tango, the laws of Italy to an Italian street song, the laws of Germany to a Lederhosen song, and the laws of France to a romantic ballad. He greatly reduced the required training time and retention of key information increased.

Resources for Songs That Teach Curriculum

Singing songs not only helps many students remember important information, it also enlivens classroom learning. A challenge for educators is to locate tapes or records that include concepts to be taught. School supply catalogs list recordings, and music teachers are an additional resource. Music series texts with recordings are often available in schools or from textbook companies. Media centers of most school districts also lend cassettes, videos, and records that frequently contain curriculum-based songs. Students and colleagues may have other suggestions that could lead to the development of a library to share throughout the school.

Recorded Songs for a Variety of Curricular Areas

Some delightful resources are currently available to help teach common curricular topics. A popular book titled *Rise Up Singing* by Amy Patterson and Peter Blood (1992) is an outstanding resource of 1200 songs. The songs are indexed according to curricular topics such as cities, freedom, food, war, and physical disabilities. Even more comprehensive in scope is Jeff Green's book, *The Green Book of Songs by Subject: The Thematic Guide to Popular Music.* The fifth edition of the book, published in 2002, features 35,000 songs in 1800 categories and covers an impressive array of themes. All genres of music are featured and the index makes it easy to find songs to complement any curriculum area at any grade level.

Other resources include a book written by Rosella Wallace (1992). Her *Rappin' and Rhymin': Raps, Songs, Cheers, and Smartrope Jingles for Active Learning, Grades K–8* uses songs, cheers, and raps to teach the names of continents, oceans, and planets, as well as vocabulary words and math facts.

An additional source of content-rich songs appropriate for elementary classrooms is available from the children's performing group, Tickle Tune Typhoon. Winner of seven awards for their highly professional, socially relevant, and always entertaining music, Tickle Tune has produced several CDs, videos, cassettes, and albums offering a wealth of songs to enrich many instructional units. An online resource is also available. M.U.S.I.C, Musicians United for Songs in the Classroom, at www.wpe.com/-musici/ offers a song directory and classroom strategies.

Songs for the Sciences

Excellent subject-specific resources for common curricular topics are also available. Some for science follow. One is entitled *Sing a Song of Science*, by Kathleen Carroll (1998), and features nineteen songs, raps, and stories about the physical and life sciences. One of the selections is called "Advantages and Disadvantages of Energy Sources." Its lyrics include:

Wind,
Wind can be a terrific source of energy.
It's very, very cheap you know
But then sometimes it doesn't blow.

We need a source of energy,
For heat, transportation, and electricity.

Water,
Water can be a terrific source of energy.
It turns things here, it turns things there.
But you can't find water everywhere.

We need a source of energy,
For heat, transportation, and electricity.

Coal,
Coal can be a terrific source of energy.
It's easy as can be to store,
But it pollutes our air that's for sure . . .

The songs on the cassette are catchy, enjoyable tunes sung by the students of the Duke Ellington School of the Arts. They effectively reinforce K–6 science concepts and may motivate students to write lyrics for their science lessons. Similar inspiration may be found in Tickle Tune Typhoon's *Singing Science.* In 2001, this award-winning CD was recognized for its outstanding production and educational merit.

Secondary students will appreciate the humor and complexity of songs exploring aspects of earth and space science, life science, and physical science. Many products and resources including entertaining lyrics are online at www.tranquilitynet-scimusic/resources/html. This site features songs written by teachers, scientists, and musicians. Some of the titles are "Ain't Nothing But a Groundhog," "The Ballad of Sir Isaac Newton and the Three Laws of Motion," "50 Ways to Love Your Liver," and "Physics Pholk Songs." The CDs, cassettes, and lesson plans available at this site ensure enjoyable and memorable learning.

Songs for Math

Fortunately, musically talented individuals have created resources for math instruction. At the secondary level, high school teacher Bob Greenlee has compiled a CD with hundreds of math songs. It can be accessed online at www.wwshs.org/academics/mathfiles/greenleefiles/ictmcd.php.

There are many resources available for K–6 math instruction. Some are: *15 Fun to Sing Collaborative Math Learning Songs and Activities* by Mitzi Fehl and Bobbie Williams; *Times Tunes: 12 Super-Fun Songs and Hands-On Activities That Teach Multiplication Facts* by Marcia Miller and Martin Lee; *Sing Along and Learn Marvelous Math: 12 Delightful Learning Songs* by Ken Sheldon.

Nearly all students will appreciate replacing repetitive drill and practice with musically motivating learning. Music adds more than fun to learning, however. It is a powerful ally in improving memory skills. Songs help make information "stick," as many radio and television advertisements remind us daily.

Music for Skill Building

Most people are aware of music's remarkably effective ability to enhance various physical skills such as typing, swimming, or aerobic exercises. The rhythm and flow of music can result in increased coordination, regularity, and speed of the activity in enjoyable ways. For young children, skipping, marching, running, or dancing to music develops rhythm and grace. For older children and adults, musical accompaniment can make tedious exercises and daily routines pleasurable. It is also useful in developing a sense of timing, whether it is getting ready to "1-2-3-go!" in sports, or learning how to deliver the punchline of a story. However, music's influence with skill building extends beyond the kinesthetic realm into the academic.

Musical Spelling

Learning to spell new words to music is not only fun, it also accelerates learning. For example, two eighth grade girls who had difficulty spelling both enjoyed playing the piano. One of the authors asked the girls to label the piano keys with the letters of the alphabet, so that the girls could "play" the words on their keyboards. Later, on spelling tests, the students were asked to recall the tones and sounds of each word and write its corresponding letters. Not only did spelling scores improve, but the two pianists began thinking of other "sound" texts to set to music. Soon, they performed each classmate's name and transcribed entire sentences. Much to everyone's delight, the pianists and their classmates experienced the powerful bridging of language and music. Words can also be spelled by chanting in rhythm while accenting certain letters that are frequently missed or confused.

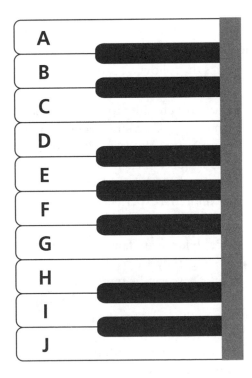

Music and Learning Skills

Two studies suggest that background music may enhance learning skills. Research conducted by Hall in 1952 showed that reading comprehension of junior high school students increased when background music was played during their study halls. A more recent study in 1997 by Cockerton, Moore, and Norman, showed that college students realized gains in thinking and cognitive skills when music was played. Similar gains were not apparent when students worked in silence. Although much more research is needed, teachers and students may want to consider whether background music enhances learning or studying skills.

Teaching Reading Musically

Although many teachers are not musicians, there are easy ways to use music as instructional strategies. Sheila Fitzgerald at Michigan State University has developed a musical approach for teaching reading that does not require formal musical instruction. For teachers interested in developing reading skills through rhythm and music, Fitzgerald suggests the following procedures:

1. Encourage children to sing on a daily basis. Elementary classroom teachers might identify songs that children will enjoy and teach these as a part of each day's activities. Songs that are selected should ideally be a part of the children's experience or environment or ones that the students compose.

2. Once children are familiar with the words of a song, they are ready to see the lyrics in print. These can be transcribed onto the blackboard or a large chart. Usually, when reading the lyrics for the first time, there is great excitement among the students. Their musical familiarity with the words eases the transition to reading.

3. Students may next progress to reading individual words from a song chart. Students might volunteer to point out individual words written on the blackboard or they might locate words that appear more than once in the song. Additionally, teachers might provide students with words or phrases written on pieces of tagboard which are the same size as the words on the chart. The children might then match their cards with the chart by actually placing their piece of tagboard on the appropriate spots.

4. Students might be given a song booklet to help them learn the lyrics. To enhance sight reading skills, students can point to words they are singing, read (or sing) the lyrics with a friend, read (or sing) them to someone who doesn't know the song, or point out the words as they listen to someone else sing the song. Using their song books as references, students might also become word detectives locating words in the song in other printed texts.

5. When children have sung and read a favorite song many times, they may be able to write from memory at least part of the lyrics. Nursery rhymes work well for this activity. Students should be encouraged to problem-solve, such as use invented spellings, and the teacher and classmates should accept and value all efforts at initial songwriting without undue attention to correctness or completeness.

Improving Language Skills with Music

Songs can serve as an excellent tool in helping English Language learners strengthen their oral and written language skills. In 1992, educator Tim Murphey analyzed the lyrics of many pop songs and found that their features were beneficial for those studying English. Most pop songs use a conversational language with repeated vocabulary and grammatical structures. The words are usually sung at a slower rate than spoken English, the meanings of the lyrics are open for interpretation. Such qualities make some songs good tools for language skills practice.

There are a variety of listening, speaking, writing, and reading strategies that can be based on songs. Students can listen to a song and give a brief summary of its storyline and theme. They might work in groups to dictate the lyrics of a song and practice reading them aloud. Students might also contrast the cultural assumptions in the songs with those from their cultures.

For reading purposes, lyrics can be cut into strips for students to organize sequentially. For this activity, many lyrics can be retrieved from the Internet or from lyric sheets included with recordings. Lyrics also often provide a rich source of vocabulary words that can enrich comprehension. Samples of songs that are appropriate for language skill study include "Yesterday" by the Beatles, "It's Too Late" by Carole King, and "Where Have All the Flowers Gone?" by Pete Seeger.

Music Across the Curriculum

Don Schiltz, a songwriter, provided testimony to the National Commission on Music Education in Nashville, Tennessee, in 1990. He described how important music was for him as a secondary student:

I'll tell you about a class I had . . . music appreciation. I didn't really think of it as a class. I thought of it as the period where we went and sang songs. We were learning that English precisely presents a writer's thoughts and feelings, that songs are a form of communication. We were learning history through the songs of the nation. It was better than any other history class in my life. We were learning math, discovering the relationships between parts, and that

composition followed mathematical rules. And, we were learning to listen; if you don't listen you can't learn. This music appreciation connected my entire studies.

As Don Schiltz explains above, music enhances learning throughout the curriculum. For example, since music is an integral component of any historical era, it provides an effective approach for identifying issues, attitudes, events, and values of a specific time period. Students might learn about political and social issues by listening to songs, operas, or musical comedies. For example, students might sing the late 1600s song "Come to North Americay" and discuss the reasons why people left Britain to come to the New World, or after listening to the quiet spiritual "Steal Away," they could talk about the song's hidden messages for enslaved people.

As a language spoken in all cultures, music offers a stimulating way to learn about multiculturalism. One wonderful resource is *Worlds of Music: An Introduction to the Music of the World's Peoples* by Titon, Fujie, and Locke (1996). This book and its accompanying CDs present diverse insights into musical creations and their evolution and roles in a wide variety of cultures. The book suggests music-making activities for students so that they can experience rich ethnomusical traditions.

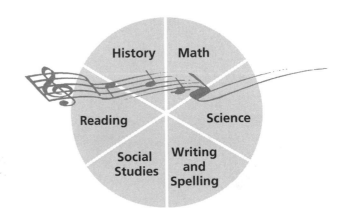

Mathematics can be taught through music, and for some students what would otherwise be a puzzling abstraction becomes clearly understood. For example, in learning to understand fractions, students can work with a simple song such as "Twinkle, Twinkle Little Star." While singing the song, one group claps on every syllable, in quarter notes. Another group claps on just the first beat of each measure, another on every other beat, and a fourth group claps eight times for each measure. Students can then compare whole, half, quarter, and eighth notes and relate them to cutting up a circle in the same proportions. To learn math facts, students can chant or sing addition, subtraction, multiplication, or division problems to familiar tunes. Older students may set geometric or algebraic formulas to music.

One resource that will help integrate music throughout the curriculum is Sporborg's (1998) *Music in Every Classroom: A Resource Guide for Integrating Music Across the Curriculum, Grades K–8*. This book not only suggests ideas for enriching all major disciplines with musical additions, it also highlights themes that are frequently addressed. Samples include immigration, women's history, careers, the Civil Rights Movement, and technology.

Warming Up to Singing

Students and teachers are often shy about singing. When a teacher introduces singing in the classroom, it should be emphasized that the goal is not to turn students into accomplished singers but rather to enliven the learning process. At the same time, people learn to sing by singing. Teachers can increase singing accuracy by establishing the starting pitch of a song by singing or playing it (most children are comfortable singing in the range of middle C to the C above). The meter and flow of the song can be established by counting "1, 2, rea-dy sing" for a song in 2 or 4, and "1 rea-dy sing" for a song in 3. Students should be encouraged to sing with energy rather than to sing loudly and to blend with the voices of their classmates.

To alleviate concerns about the sound of one's voice, students and teachers might approach singing by initially chanting nonsense sounds. Such activities emphasize the playfulness of sound-making and reduce fears about singing in perfect pitch or sounding accomplished like well-known vocalists. Over time, the teacher can progress from chanting, to exaggerating the words in a sort of "heightened speech," and then into singing. It is important to encourage children to hear the differences between their "speaking voices" and their "singing voices."

Nonsense Sounds

The following song incorporates nonsense sounds, and can be successfully used with students of varying ages.

Divide the class into four groups of equal size. Number the groups from one to four. The first group chants:

*RAT-A-TAT-TAT   RAT-A-TAT-TAT
RAT-A-TAT-TAT...*

Once the first group has its part going, the second group joins in with:

BOOM-DA   BOOM-DA   BOOM-DA BOOM-DA . . .

With the first two groups continuing, the third sings:

FIZZLE-WIZZLE   FIZZLE-WIZZLE FIZZLE-WIZZLE . . .

The fourth group now begins singing the A-B-C song to the tune of "Twinkle, Twinkle, Little Star." After the students practice their four part songs two or three times, the teacher might want to record their singing. Frequently, this song sounds better than anyone would have anticipated, with the tape recording providing an important confidence boost.

Although at the outset this particular song involves singing the alphabet, once the technique is mastered, more sophisticated subject matter can be tackled, replacing the A, B, C's with the fifty states, the steps in conflict resolution processes, Spanish vocabulary words, or the periodic elements. Another nonsense syllable approach to singing consists of creating a refrain that reluctant singers might easily imitate. For example, adding sounds like oo-ee-oo-ah-ah-ting-tang-walla-walla-bing-bang provides interesting sound effects for passages read aloud. Young children can learn their addresses and telephone numbers to a tune. The music thus becomes a string to unify and memorize abstractions, much like beads strung into a necklace.

Choral Reading

Once students have experienced success with nonsense syllable sound-making, they might progress to choral reading. Finding short poems, literary passages, or famous quotations that require vocal variations in rhythm, pitch, emotion, or dialect encourages students to use their voices in new ways while adding fluency, confidence, and expression in reading aloud. Poems such as de la Mare's "The Highwayman," Langston Hughes's "Homesick Blues," Poe's "The Raven," or Frost's "Mending Wall" are some examples of poetic selections that lend themselves to interesting choral interpretations.

Original writing integrated with a lesson's content can be used for choral reading activities. The following excerpt was written by a teacher for a class studying the Stone Age:

Get ready for a party
Time to set the stage
It happened long ago
In the Old Stone Age.

GATHER ROUND THE FIRE
GRAB A BIG STONE
BEAT IT TO THE RHYTHM
WITH AN OLD LEG BONE.

Here come the women
Bringing tasty roots
They gathered fresh berries
And other wild fruits.

GATHER ROUND THE FIRE
GRAB A BIG STONE
BEAT IT TO THE RHYTHM
WITH AN OLD LEG BONE.

Such a selection can be performed in a variety of ways. The choral reading might be staged with the class divided in parts, forming girls' and boys' parts, adding loud and quiet sections, and varying the pace. The important point in using either nonsense sounds or choral reading is to acquaint students with using their voices with greater expression, vocal range, and skill. Such preliminary warm-ups ready students for the joy of singing with confidence.

Musical Notation

Music is . . . like mathematics, very nearly a world by itself; it contains a whole gamut of experience, from sensuous elements to ultimate intellectual harmonies.

—George Santayana

Unless students take formal music courses, they rarely learn to read musical notation. The abstract musical symbol system may remain an unfamiliar foreign language throughout their lives because of a lack of exposure. To decrease the mystery of musical notation, students can initially create their own symbol systems and then more readily grasp standardized musical notation. Research by Rena Upitis (1999) suggests that developing personal notational systems for music enhances the development of musical thinking. Her books, *This Too Is Music* and *Can I Play You My Song?* are useful tools for explaining personalized notation and give many practical ideas for classroom application.

Introducing the Concept of Musical Notation

To introduce students to the concept that different shapes represent different sounds, Don Kaplan's book, *See with Your Ears*, suggests a variety of ways to draw the sound "Aah" to demonstrate the holding of a note. Teachers and students may want to experiment with pitch, timbre, volume, and duration with the following "aahs":

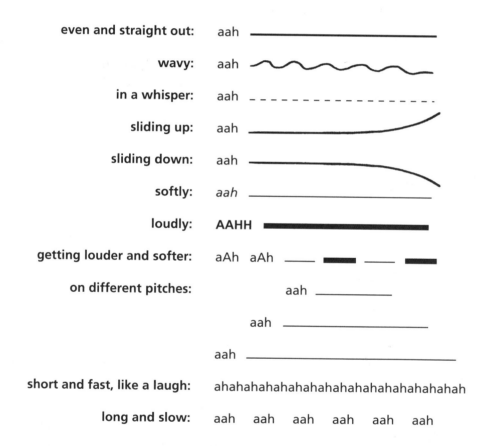

Once students sing and learn these sounds and their corresponding "notations," they could each be given a notecard with one of the above notations drawn on the card. Divided into small groups of five or six, each group can read and practice their notations, composing a melody to perform for the rest of the class.

The following approach moves students to graphic representation of musical notation. The teacher can demonstrate that a simple bar system represents the length of time each note is held in a song. For example, "Mary had a little lamb . . ." might look like this:

To extend this system to standard notation, the same bars can be put on a staff.

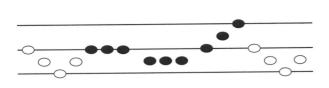

Students can create their own graphic symbols to transcribe simple songs such as "Twinkle, Twinkle Little Star," "Row, Row Your Boat," or "Hickory, Dickory, Dock."

Another simple and enjoyable approach to musical notation combining music and art follows:

After selecting a provocative piece of instrumental music, explain to students that they will listen to a musical selection and while listening, they will be asked to draw simple symbols of what they hear. Blank paper and colored markers or crayons should be distributed to all students. As they prepare to listen, ask them to imagine lines, shapes, and colors suggested by the music itself. Inform them that they will listen to the music a second time and will then "draw" what they heard.

Students may want to pay particular attention to repeated musical patterns, using the same visual symbols for these portions of the composition. Or, they might focus on representing the beats, meters, or rhythmic patterns. If dynamic change (loud and soft) is particularly dominant, students may wish to draw those changes. Some works of music such as

Pachelbel's *Canon* will suggest melodic lines or layers of melodies. The unique features of each musical composition will be perceived by attentive students. To effectively notice and represent what is happening in the music, students may need to listen to the selection several times.

After students have listened to and drawn the music, engage them in brief discussions about "translating" their drawings by noting which symbol or color represents which sound. Students may also volunteer to sing a portion of their musical notation. A sample sixth-grader's musical notation drawing follows.

Although student-generated musical systems may appear abstract and unreadable to others, they often provide valid ways for learners to begin "reading" music.

Yet another approach to musical notation helps students learn keyboarding. By bringing a small synthesizer or keyboard into the classroom, the teacher can number the keys on a scale, one through eight. Many simple melodies can then be played. For example, the song "Mary Had a Little Lamb" would read:

3-2-1-2-3-3-3

2-2-2

3-5-5

3-2-1-2-3-3—3

3-2-2-3-2-1

The number 1 would represent middle C on the scale, 2 would be D, and so on. By using this simple system, students can proficiently play a variety of melodies as well as create their own number systems to accompany class songs.

Whether students are working with numbers, squiggly lines, or other symbols for musical notation, such approaches can ease the transition into reading standard notation. Students often gain confidence about working with abstract symbol systems when they have first created their own.

Creating Curriculum Songs

Since recorded songs are not always available for each curriculum unit, students and teachers can compose songs that are appropriate for any content area. Little musical talent is required to begin creating original songs by writing words to a simple, well-known melody. For example, one teacher wrote the following song about the water cycle to the tune of "Row, Row, Row Your Boat."

> *Drip, drip, drip from the sky*
> *Into a little stream,*
> *Down the mountains, through the plains,*
> *And out into the sea.*
>
> *Up, up, up it goes*
> *Up into the sky,*
> *Over the mountains it blows again,*
> *Then watch the snowflakes fly.*

Depending on the age level and maturity of the students, longer songs can be written and memorized. Teachers and students may want to brainstorm familiar musical selections, using them to provide the rhythm and melody for the original, curricular-appropriate lyrics the students will add. Of course, original music can also be composed to accompany the words, adding yet another dimension to the project; however, teachers and students may want to use tunes they know to provide the

rhythm and melody for their lyrics. A few selections are listed next that are familiar to many.

Familiar Musical Selections
"You Are My Sunshine"
"Twinkle, Twinkle, Little Star"
"Jingle Bells"
"Kumbaya"
"When Johnny Comes Marching Home Again"
"Oh, Susanna!"
"Yankee Doodle"
"She'll be Comin' Around the Mountain"
"When the Saints Go Marching In"

One example of a curriculum song written by elementary students to the tune of "When Johnny Comes Marching Home Again" follows. The song represents the culmination of a social studies unit on multicultural art. Small groups each contributed a verse about the art of different cultures to create the song, "Art Around the World."

> *Sumeria, Egypt, China, Oo, Hooray, Hooray*
> *Africa and America too, Hooray, Hooray*
> *Japan and Greece have much to see*
> *On and on through history*
> *And they all had art that we have learned about.*
> *(Refrain, repeat after each verse:)*
>
> *In China they made paper and they printed*
>   *on it too.*
> *They also built pagodas and made kites that*
>   *really flew.*
> *They painted dragons in the air,*
> *They played their music everywhere,*
> *And they all had art that we have learned about.*
>
> *In Africa, they kept the beat, Hooray, Hooray.*
> *They played their drums and danced their feet,*
> *Hooray, Hooray.*
> *They dyed their cloth with patterns bright*
> *And sculpted metal to catch the light.*
> *And they all had art that we have learned about.*

*Long ago in America they worked with yarn,
     it's true.
The Mayans and the Aztecs and the Inca people
     too.
With temples like the pyramids,
Big clay pots with perfect lids,
And they all had art that we have learned about.*

*In Japan they wrote Haiku, Hooray, Hooray.
They folded colored paper too, Hooray, Hooray.
Their gardens they made perfectly,
And did the same when they drank tea,
And they all had art that we have learned about.*

Teachers may assign the content that curriculum songs are to cover. For example, if students have studied current world conflicts, or read literature that explores conflicts between individuals or groups, the teacher may ask for a song about conflict resolution strategies. Specific guidelines for such a song might be to:

1. Identify the actions taken by those involved in the conflict.

2. Provide reasons for the actions and feelings of those directly involved.

3. Suggest alternative solutions and brainstorm possible consequences.

4. Select the best solution.

5. Consider similar situations and what happened to resolve or exacerbate the conflict.

6. Determine if there are lessons to be learned from efforts to resolve previous conflicts.

7. Modify one's proposed solution if appropriate.

8. Generalize one's assumptions about conflict and how it might best be resolved.

Students can work in groups to write their curriculum songs. To adhere to the above requirements, they may create a stanza for each step or two of the conflict resolution process. For example, in reflecting on the conflict over rights for all South Africans, one group of high school juniors began their song with:

*When all South Africans lacked rights and
     free expression,
The whites in power were accused of racial
     oppression.
The blacks rose up to gain self-determination.
The whites wanted to maintain their lofty
     position.*

Most students enjoy this approach to singing and songwriting. When an entire class sings curriculum songs, not only is subject matter learned and creativity expressed, but the affective atmosphere of the class also improves. An intangible bond is often created among those singing the same song for fun and learning. And not surprisingly, many students claim at the end of the school year that they still remember the curriculum songs composed months earlier.

Jump-Starting Creativity with Music

■ ■ ■ ■ ■ ■ ■ ■ ■ ■ ■ ■ ■ ■ ■ ■ ■

Schools are supposed to be able to help us express ourselves. Without knowledge of music, we are being deprived of a unique form of communication.

—Kenny Byrd, student who testified
at the Nashville Commission on
Music Education in 1990

Frequently, when asked to write a story or poem, students complain they don't know where or how to begin. Music can serve as a source of inspiration, stimulating images and feelings and igniting storylines to pursue. When children are writing to music in the classroom, creative energies can be released, enabling them to write more prolifically and with greater pleasure, ease, and depth.

The following sample activities can spark creative writing in classrooms.

1. To introduce students to the potential flow of images and ideas generated by music, ask them to pretend they are film producers who must create a storyline appropriate to any portion of the following compositions: Prokofiev's *Peter and the Wolf,* Moussorgsky's *Pictures at an Exhibition,* Debussy's *Clouds, Fireworks,* or *Golliwog's Cakewalk,* or more abstract selections such as a Chopin prelude, a Strauss waltz or a Bach fugue. After listening, students might discuss the images and movie scripts they imagined, and next generate poems or descriptive paragraphs based on this brainstorming process.

2. Short stories might also be developed from recordings played in a sequence. Beginning by playing either music or an environmental recording such as "Tropical Thunderstorm," "Dawn in an English Meadow," or "Slow Ocean," teachers may ask students to mindmap or write a description of the setting. Next, play a recording that suggests the first character. This could be any colorful selection, even a piece of popular music. Students then may mindmap or write a description of the character they "see" in the music. (Be careful to introduce the character without using "he" or "she" or even suggesting it is a person. Students might see animals, or wind, or imaginary objects in the music.)

Next, play a sharply contrasting piece of music and go through the same procedure for the second character. Finally, go back to the original "setting" sound or music as students "see" the plot unfolding around the characters they have created. Similar processes may be used to stimulate the writing of poetry to music. Such writing exercises will springboard most students into expressing themselves in remarkably creative ways.

3. Have students generate word banks of descriptive words in response to recorded music, then use such terms to write poetry describing the music. The poems might include the title of the music and the name of the composer.

In addition to writing activities, students may also explore other ways to shake off lethargy and ignite creativity with music. Music can be played while students are preparing class projects, doing silent reading, working in cooperative groups, taking tests, memorizing facts or scripts, or working on computers. By tuning into their own inner rhythms and needs, students can begin to identify the times when music might optimize their learning.

Making Musical Instruments in the Classroom

When given the opportunity to make instruments, students not only enjoy the hands-on activity, they also increase their understanding of music itself. Simple instruments can be made from common everyday items. Pan lids, sandpaper, coffee cans, nails, boxes, fishing line, bamboo, conduit, hard wood, rawhide, and carpet tubes all have musical potential. If notified, parents often gladly contribute throwaways, white elephants, and junk drawer treasures, most of which can become important parts of musical instruments.

Some teachers approach instrument-making by appointing a day when collected items from home and school are made accessible to students with one stipulation—that each student invents an instrument capable of producing sound. Instruments can be made from directions found in one of many instrument construction books. Two excellent resources on simple-to-make instruments include *Cool Cardboard Instruments to Make & Play* by Dennis Waring (2000) and *Making Musical Instruments* by Jay Havighurst (1998). Folk instruments can be constructed based on ideas from *Great Folk Instruments to Make and Play* by Dennis Waring. Folk instruments can be decorated to represent the designs of the cultures from which they come.

Once the instruments are made, they can be played individually, listened to, and discussed. Music terminology such as loud/soft, high/low, bright/dull, hollow, ringing, raspy, and rattling can be used to describe their sounds. Small ensembles or an entire classroom orchestra might emerge next.

Teachers might suggest that students make musical instruments representative of the four instrumental groups found in symphonic orchestras: strings, woodwinds, brass, and percussion. Another possibility is to group instruments into categories commonly used by ethnomusicologists to describe instruments from around the world: membranophones (vibrating membrane); chordophones (vibrating strings); idiophones (vibrating surface); aerophones (vibrating column of air); and electranophone (vibrating electrical current).

Using Instruments Creatively

With access to instruments in the classroom, students and teachers can experiment with creating original compositions, adding musical accompaniment to songs, or performing instrumental works. Students might work in small groups to compose short, aural plans for musical pieces. They might work with solo instruments, then combine sounds. To begin the composition process, students can start with a favorite work of children's literature or a video they have recently watched at school. They might improvise their own opera for the dialogue and add instruments for color and rhythmic motion. Many other ideas for involving students in classroom musical composition can be found in the book *Sound and Silence* by John Paynter (1970) and in an online article by Gail Burnaford-Farrell at www.ncrel.org/mands/docs/3-12.htm.

Students can also work with familiar songs such as "She'll Be Comin' around the Mountain." For example, one musical arrangement might consist of students adding different sounds to each verse. They could play some sounds with the beat or alternate beats and some with the rhythm of the words. The sounds should be carefully selected to fit the quality and character of the music and should not overwhelm the song itself. It is also not necessary that every student play constantly. Often the arrangement will be more musical if just a few instruments are added.

Orchestral arrangements can be explored. Teachers can divide the students into two groups to create echoes, omitting certain instruments and bringing them in later during the song or gradually omitting instruments until only one remains playing softly. Additionally, students' curiosity may be piqued about how an orchestra is physically structured: Which instruments are placed where? A visit to a high school music classroom or a field trip to the nearest symphonic orchestra may be better appreciated after classroom hands-on experiences.

Technology That Enhances Musical Intelligence

Music is an essential part of every culture, building on the human need for rhythmic sound and movement and adding beauty to the world. The development of musical intelligence can be enhanced by technology in the same way that verbal fluency is enhanced by word processors. Fledgling composers can hum a tune into synthesizers such as those made by Ensoniq or Casio, for example, and have it sound like one of many instruments, fully accompanied by an electronic rhythm section. The Musical Instrument Digital Interface, or MIDI, makes it possible to compose for and orchestrate many different instruments through the computer.

"Band-in-a-Box" by PG Software lets students improvise backups to familiar jazz, pop, rock, and folk music. It also features editing capability so that students can create their own musical styles. Their improvisations and compositions can be saved on a MIDI file and sent to a music printing program such as "Nightingale" by Musicware which creates musical scores for other instruments.

One might wonder if such "artificial" music removes the need to understand and learn harmony, notation, scoring, and reading music. In fact, many students are so motivated by what they create through musical technology that they are stimulated to learn more about each of these areas. Their success becomes a driving force for further learning.

It is being discovered that digital technology, which combines digital audio with visual input, makes it possible for many students to learn about elements of music that are often too complicated for beginners to understand. One example is the Voyager Company's interactive multimedia compact disc of Beethoven's *Ninth Symphony,* which enables the listener to understand the piece musically, historically, culturally, and politically. Stravinsky's *Rite of Spring* is even more extensive, progressing from simple to complex concepts; it can be accessed at any knowledge level. Such programs are exciting ways of learning about and creating music. Warner's "Music Exploratorium" CD-ROM explores various aspects of the orchestra through Benjamin Britten's *Young Person's Guide to the Orchestra*. It presents, in a combination of video and audio, information about the composer and conductor, the players, the instruments, and the structure of the composition. Such interactive videodiscs on music make it possible to "break out" and hear individual instruments, see the score while the music is playing, or identify the source of a particular theme or melody. The information on these discs is "random access," making it possible for the learner to follow a particular line of interest in a self-directed manner, at any ability level.

The Association for Technology in Music Instruction (ATMI) annually publishes a directory that lists and summarizes existing computer programs, videodiscs, films, CD-ROMs, and other music technology on the market. See the website at http://bauer.edu/technology.html.

Numerous websites are now available for music educators and other teachers who wish to include music in their curriculum. These resources include:

M.U.S.I.C, Musicians United for Songs in the Classroom, at www.wpe.com/~musici. This non-profit organization promotes the interdisciplinary use of popular music in education, and the site includes a song directory, classroom strategies and links, and a gallery of students' writing and visual arts inspired by music.

The National Association for Music Educators website at www.menc.org includes information on music curriculum and assessment for all ages. Its publications explain and interpret the National Standards for Music Education.

The Music Madness Site has lesson plans, software reviews, news, and Kids Korner musical games. See www.music-madness.net.

The American Music Conference promotes the benefits of music, music making, and music education. It includes tools for teachers at www.amc-music.com.

See Technology Directions in Music Learning at http://music.utsa.edu/tdml that offers "cutting edge" music technology.

Such a technological support system for the learning of music and music appreciation leads not only to proficiency, but also to in-depth understanding. The development of musical thinking and creativity—musical intelligence itself—can thus be enriched and expanded.

Summary

Each year, second and third grade students at Russell Elementary School in Lexington, Kentucky, produce operas. Their company, Russell Elementary Small-People-Doing-Big-Deeds Opera Company, lives up to its name. The students write scripts, compose songs, send out press releases and invitations, win awards for their performances, and raise their academic achievement (Campbell & Campbell, 1999).

In 1995, the inner-city school received a grant from the Metropolitan Opera Guild for students to add opera to its curriculum. Prior to the grant, Russell had become a multiple intelligences school with a strong music component of general music classes and piano labs. Opera was a natural extension of the school's musical emphasis.

Once annually, Russell students produce operas based on their life experiences. One entitled *Responsibility in Deed* described how a boy named Chuck cared for his sick father after school while his mother worked two jobs to pay the medical bills. Chuck couldn't play after school, and his friends missed him. They decided to help Chuck's family by raising money. The boys worked a variety of odd jobs and saved what they earned. One day, one of Chuck's friends was spotted with a large stack of dollars in his hand. The bystander assumed the money was stolen. The rest of the opera addresses the social implications of Chuck and his friends' experiences.

Another opera focused on fire safety after a classmate tragically died in an apartment fire. The students sang fire safety songs, read and performed diaries of fire survivors, and made escape plans for schools, apartment buildings, and homes. The opera won awards and has been used as a teaching tool to assist others with fire safety.

The rich musical experiences at Russell have proved magnetic for parents. Family participation has increased since students showcase their talents and entertain and teach the community about relevant issues.

This chapter includes listening, singing, memory-enhancing, creativity-inspiring, and music-making techniques to introduce students and teachers alike to the joy of musical learning. To summarize, reflect on, and synthesize the content of this chapter, the following is offered:

APPLYING MUSICAL INTELLIGENCE

1. Important ideas or insights gleaned from this chapter:

_____
_____
_____
_____
_____
_____
_____
_____
_____

2. Areas I'd like to learn more about:

_____
_____
_____
_____
_____
_____
_____
_____
_____
_____

3. Ways I can use this information in my teaching. Please note that all of the strategies mentioned in this chapter are listed below with space provided to note how each might be incorporated into classroom instruction:

MUSICAL STRATEGY	CLASSROOM APPLICATION

Establishing a Musical Learning Environment _____

    Introducing Music into the Classroom _____

Listening to Music _____

    Songs in the Content Areas _____

Music for Skill Building

    Musical Spelling _____

    Music and Learning Skills _____

    Teaching Reading through Music _____

    Improving Language Skills with Music _____

    Music Across the Curriculum _____

Warming Up to Singing

    Nonsense Sounds _____

    Choral Reading _____

Musical Notation

    Introducing the Concept of Musical Notation _____

Creating Curriculum Songs _____

Jump-Starting Creativity with Music _____

Making Musical Instruments in the Classroom _____

    Using Instruments Creatively _____

Technology That Enhances Musical Intelligence _____

MUSICAL REFERENCES

Arts Education Partnership. (2002). *Critical Links: Learning in the Arts and Student Academic and Social Development*. Washington DC: Author. Available online at http://aep-arts.org

Burnaford-Farrell, G. (2002). *Integrating Music Across the Curriculum: Opportunities for Classroom Teachers*. Available online at www.ncrel.org/mands/docs/3-12.htm

Campbell, L., & Campbell, B. (1999). *Multiple Intelligences and Student Achievement: Success Stories from Six Schools*. Alexandria, VA: ASCD.

Carroll, K. (1998). *Sing a Song of Science*. Tucson, AZ: Zephyr Press.

Cockerton, T., Moore, S., & Norma, D. (1997). Cognitive test performance and background music. *Perceptual and Motor Skills, 85,* 1435–1438.

Gardner, H. (1983). *Frames of Mind: The Theory of Multiple Intelligences*. NY: Basic Books.

Green, J. (Ed.) (2002). *The Green Book of Songs by Subject: The Thematic Guide to Popular Music*. Nashville, TN: Professional Desk References.

Hall, J. (1952, February). The effect of background music on the reading comprehension of 278 eighth and ninth graders. *Early Child Development and Care, 66,* 85–91.

Havinghurst, J. (1998). *Making Musical Instruments by Hand*. Gloucester, MA: Rockport Publishing.

Murphey, T. (1992). The discourse of pop songs. *TESOL Quarterly, 26*(4), 770–774.

National Association for Music Education. Available online at www.menc.org.

National Standards for Arts Education. (1994). *Dance, Music, Theatre, Visual Arts: What Every Young American Should Know and Be Able to Do in the Arts*. Reston, VA: Music Educators National Conference.

Patterson, A., & Blood, P. (1992). *Rise Up Singing*. Bethlehem, PA: Sing Out! Publications.

Paynter, J. (1970). *Sound and Silence: Classroom Projects in Creative Music*. New York: Cambridge University Press.

Sporborg, J. (1998). *Music in Every Classroom: A Resource Guide for Integrating Music Across the Curriculum, Grades K–8*. Westport, CT: Libraries Unlimited.

Tickle Tune Typhoon. *Let's Be Friends*. Available online at http://tickletunetyphoon.com

Titon, T., Fujie, L., & Locke, D. (1996) *Worlds of Music: An Introduction to the Music of the World's Peoples*. New York: Macmillan.

Upitis, R. (1992). *Can I Play You My Song?* Portsmouth, NH: Heinemann.

Upitis, R. (1999). *This Too Is Music*. Portsmouth, NH: Heinemann.

Wallace, R. (1992). *Rappin' and Rhymin': Raps, Songs, Cheers, and Smartrope Jingles for Active Learning, Grades K–8*. Tucson, AZ: Zephyr Press.

Waring, D. (1999). *Great Folk Instruments to Make and Play*. New York: Sterling.

Waring, D. (2000). *Cool Cardboard Instruments to Make and Play*. New York: Tamos.

6

Understanding One Another

INTERPERSONAL INTELLIGENCE

If civilization is to survive, we must cultivate the science of human relationships—the ability of all peoples, of all kinds, to live together, in the same world, at peace.

—Franklin Delano Roosevelt

WORKING TOGETHER TO ACCOMPLISH THE IMPOSSIBLE

The Flying Karamazov Brothers are a world-famous juggling/comedy team of four individuals who believe that "people working together can accomplish the impossible."

In watching these skilled and humorous performers, one might assume that juggling and comedy come easily for this foursome. Part of their skill seems to derive from their years of working together. As they juggle in complex patterns while carrying on witty repartee, the Karamazovs appear connected to each other's thoughts and action. They say they concentrate "exactly enough and no more." According to these performers, it is this intense "nonconcentration" that enables their seemingly impossible juggling feats.

Paul Magid and Howard Patterson met in college over two decades ago, and began juggling at college functions. A few years later Sam Williams and Timothy Furst joined them. The four believe that humor provides the "connecting wires" in their performances. Humor permeates their performances and inspires their work together. Each individual not only works according to plan but also improvises in response to unanticipated comments from one another or from unexpected events. They refer to such moments as "surfing," and their audiences respond with delight. At each appearance, The Flying Karamazov Brothers find ways to interact with the audience. They are adept at encouraging people to sing, make

- music, provide juggling objects, and tell jokes.
- Their interpersonal skills also extend to other performers. Recently, the Karamazovs have identified several fledgling performing artists whom they invite to tour with them. This increases the visibility of the younger artists while also helping the Karamazov Brothers to create a contemporary vaudeville show with a diverse troupe of performers and active audience participation.

What do the Karamazovs say about the development of their interpersonal intelligence? As children, the individual performers were loners, all of whom were bored with school routines. Their interpersonal skills flourished as they began working together. Perhaps they might have found school more interesting and challenging if they had had opportunities to exercise interpersonal intelligence through group projects of the kind described in this chapter.

DEFINITION: Understanding Interpersonal Intelligence

Interpersonal intelligence enables us to understand and communicate with others and note differences in moods, temperaments, motivations, and skills. It includes the ability to form and maintain relationships and to assume various roles within groups such as group members or leaders. This intelligence is evident in people with polished social skills such as political or religious leaders, skilled parents, teachers, therapists, or counselors. Individuals who demonstrate a genuine commitment to and skill in bettering the lives of others exhibit positively developed interpersonal intelligence.

Interpersonally skilled students enjoy interacting with others of similar or diverse ages. With a capacity to influence their peers, they often excel at group work, team efforts, and collaborative projects. Some are sensitive to the feelings of others, curious about multicultural variations in lifestyles, or interested in the social relevance of classroom studies. Some are able to entertain diverse perspectives on any social or political issue and can often help others appreciate differing values and opinions.

Interpersonal intelligence is also exhibited through humor whenever students make their friends and teachers laugh, when they create amusing skits, or analyze videos of old comedy teams such as the Marx Brothers or Laurel and Hardy, which offer caricatures of different interpersonal skills.

✔ CHECKLIST: Interpersonal Qualities

One British psychologist N.K. Humphrey claimed that social intelligence is the most important feature of the human intellect. Humphrey stated that the greatest creative use of the human mind is to maintain human society effectively. Because of social foresight and understanding, many people are able to consider the consequences of their own actions, anticipate the behavior of others, determine potential benefits and losses, and successfully cope with interpersonal issues locally and beyond. Successful living is often largely dependent on interpersonal intelligence.

It is likely that a person with well-developed interpersonal intelligence:

1. Bonds with parents and interacts with others.

2. Forms and maintains social relationships.

3. Recognizes and uses a variety of ways to relate to others.

4. Acknowledges the feelings, thoughts, motivations, behaviors, and lifestyles of others.

5. Participates in collaborative efforts and assumes various roles as appropriate, from follower to leader, in group endeavors.

6. Influences the opinions or actions of others.

7. Understands and communicates effectively in both verbal and nonverbal ways.

8. Adapts behavior to different environments or groups and from feedback from others.

9. Considers diverse perspectives in any social or political issue.

10. Develops skills in mediation, organizing others for a common cause, or working with others of diverse ages or backgrounds.

11. Expresses an interest in interpersonally oriented careers such as teaching, social work, counseling, management, or politics.

12. Develops new social processes or models.

Interpersonal Learning Processes

Most educators claim they couldn't teach without pairing or grouping students. This chapter describes collaborative learning processes currently in use in many classrooms, as well as numerous other categories of interpersonal learning activities:

Establishing a Positive Interpersonal Environment
Criteria for Effective Groups
Determining Class Values and Rules
Determining Schoolwide Values
Class Meetings

Collaborative Learning
Collaborative Grouping Considerations
Student Roles
Social Skills
Cooperative Learning Activities

Conflict Management
Common Causes of Conflict

Learning through Service
Incorporating Service into a School Program
Reflecting on Service Learning
Service Resources

Appreciating Differences
Teaching Students about Learning Styles

Establishing a Positive Interpersonal Environment

▪ ▪ ▪ ▪ ▪ ▪ ▪ ▪ ▪ ▪ ▪ ▪ ▪ ▪ ▪ ▪ ▪ ▪

In today's rapidly changing society, many students are deprived of close, stable relationships with caring adults. As a result, some children bring unmet needs into the classroom. Besieged with numerous demands, schools might prefer to overlook students' social and emotional needs, yet ultimately, our educational institutions must compensate by evolving into supportive, caring communities.

Although students spend their school careers in groups, the potential benefits of group life are seldom realized. When the focus is primarily on achieving competitive and individualistic goals, students are isolated and their affective and social needs are often neglected. Much recent research indicates, however, that learning is more productive and enjoyable when students feel a sense of belonging and the classroom functions as a caring community. How can such an environment be established? The starting point is to transform the numerous individuals in a classroom into an effective and cohesive group. Some suggestions follow.

Criteria for Effective Groups

In researching effective groups, consistent qualities have emerged. The following criteria, while not exhaustive, nevertheless do enable teachers to assess their current classroom environments. After reviewing the list below, teachers can identify the qualities currently present in their classrooms and strive to include any missing components.

1. The classroom's environment is warm and accepting. Extensive, positive interaction among students and teacher is evident and a sense of "school as family" is promoted.

2. Classroom rules, mutually established by students and teacher, define appropriate codes of conduct and are based on human values such as helpfulness and fairness. Together, the students and teacher develop solutions to behavior problems.

3. An emphasis on collaborative learning removes the win/lose pattern prevalent in many classrooms. Conventional, independent, competitive learning is frequently replaced with interdependent processes that require the participation and contribution of all students.

4. Learning is the well-articulated mission of the classroom. The teacher and students acknowledge that their chief purpose is to learn from the curriculum, one another, and life experiences.

5. Leadership functions are equally distributed. Responsibility for classroom and small group tasks is evenly shared so that students view themselves as valued members of the classroom community.

6. The learning activities are enjoyable. A variety of instructional and evaluation methods are used. Students occasionally make choices about what and how to learn and a sense of playfulness and humor are present.

7. Opportunities are available for students to develop social, affective, and ethical skills in addition to academic ones.

An interesting perspective of an important group, that of the family, has been offered by Dr. Mihaly Csikszentmihaly (1991), professor of behavioral sciences at the University of Chicago. Dr. Csikszentmihaly has researched the family background of high achievers. He found that the highest achieving and happiest students came from "complex" environments in which clear rules and high expectations were communicated, but which were warm, positive, and nurturing and offered many opportunities for choice. Classrooms can be "complex" environments as well.

Determining Class Values and Rules

It is important for each classroom to establish explicit codes of conduct based on important human values. When students know what is expected of them and their peers, positive relationships can develop more easily. Often the most effective rules are those initiated by the students themselves. By using democratic processes to determine classroom values and appropriate conduct, students can assume responsibility for their behavior and for successful participation as members of their group.

Many teachers involve their students in determining classroom values and rules at the beginning of the school year or a new term. One simple approach consists of asking students to identify the behaviors that are conducive to learning. How should students behave so that a positive classroom environment is established and maintained? Which social values such as justice, compassion, or helpfulness do they want to embrace as a group?

Students can respond individually to such questions by writing their ideas for classroom values and conduct. Responses can then be discussed in small groups of three to five. Each small group makes a chart of ideas for classroom values and behaviors. These charts, when shared with the whole class, can be pared down to the values or behaviors most students support. Teachers can emphasize

that successful group life requires balancing one's individual needs with the needs of others. A list of rules and values, developed collaboratively, can be displayed prominently in the classroom.

Recently, one fifth grade classroom decided to guide their behavior with the following rules:

1. Everyone in this room has the right to learn.
2. We will be creative and original.
3. We will think and learn in many ways.
4. We will have fun while learning.
5. We will cooperate with group members.
6. We will be respectful of one another.
7. We will make friends with each other.

These fifth graders were not only committed to creative learning opportunities, but they also hoped to have many social and emotional needs met in the classroom.

After rules are established and classroom activities undertaken, explicit discussions of group values and behavior can be initiated to reinforce important social skills. The students and teacher may want to meet periodically to develop solutions to discipline problems. In some classrooms, elected or appointed councils oversee classroom operations. Rotating councils of approximately five or six students make recommendations to the class and teacher about social concerns.

In such a governance system, each person in the class, including the teacher, has a single vote and the council implements the decisions voted on by class members. As the school year progresses, it is important that all students have the opportunity to serve as council members. Many teachers claim that such activities help students internalize classroom rules and assume responsibility for the successful operation of their class. By contributing to the well-being of the classroom, many students willingly abide by the norms and values their school community deems important.

Determining Schoolwide Values

In addition to efforts by individual classrooms to identify codes of conduct, some schools embrace shared values schoolwide. For example, EXPO for Excellence Elementary School in St. Paul, Minnesota, has created a Behavior Curriculum that teaches the personal intelligences (Campbell & Campbell, 1999). This curriculum is based in part on Susan Kovalik's (1994) LIFESKILLS model. Kovalik has suggested that students can attain their "personal best" through caring, problem-solving, being flexible, collaborating, persevering, and other skills. EXPO students and teachers define such qualities, role play model, and assess them.

Another example of schoolwide values in action is evident at Russell Elementary School in Lexington, Kentucky. Each fall, Russell students receive Character Education Handbooks listing skills that will be taught during the year. Each week, one new skill is introduced and applied. Sample skills include asking for help, using self-control, completing assignments, acknowledging others' feelings, responding productively to failure, and being honest. These and other schools with articulated values teach that academics and healthy attitudes, positive self-regard, and follow-through are essential qualities.

Class Meetings

Once classroom rules and values are in place, student relationships can be strengthened. Often this can be accomplished by conducting class meetings once daily or weekly. Such meetings usually have an open-ended agenda for students to discuss differences, resolve personal or academic problems, and learn to listen to and support one another. Class meetings can foster affective, social, and ethical development of all students in the class.

At the elementary level, many teachers set aside a few minutes at the beginning of each day for students to greet one another, discuss important issues, and focus attention on the day's learning tasks. At the secondary level, some teachers devote twenty minutes during a class period once weekly for a "family" meeting. An agenda sheet is posted throughout the week and students are free to list issues they want to discuss.

To ensure successful and positive class meetings, it is important to establish ground rules. Some guidelines follow.

Guidelines for Conducting Class Meetings

1. Identify a regular schedule for class meetings and the approximate length of the meetings.

2. Ask students to move chairs or desks in a circle so everyone is included equally.

3. Select a meeting facilitator. With younger children, this is most frequently the teacher or a parent. Older students, however, may assume the facilitator role.

4. Explain that the purpose of the meetings is to improve the atmosphere in the classroom and give students a chance to address their interests and concerns.

5. Provide everyone with an opportunity to talk. When one student is speaking, others cannot interrupt. Some teachers structure the taking of turns with a Native American tradition of the "talking stick," a decorated, small branch or piece of driftwood. The talking stick is handed to those who wish to speak. When a student has the talking stick, he must speak briefly, truthfully, and from the heart. He then passes it to the next person who desires a turn.

6. Explain that all students must feel free to express their feelings and opinions at the meetings, so negative comments about one another are not tolerated.

7. Request that everyone bring an open mind and heart to the meetings. Efforts should be made to consider the diverse perspectives shared by class members.

8. Bring closure to each meeting by thanking everyone for participating, reviewing the main issues discussed, or identifying unresolved concerns that should be raised at the next session.

Family meetings nurture a sense of interconnectedness and enable supportive relationships to flourish between children and teachers alike. A positive sense of group identity emerges from listening to and showing respect for one another. Such meetings can help transform classrooms into personal, humane, and caring communities.

Collaborative Learning

Collaborative learning is one of the most thoroughly researched instructional techniques in the United States. There are numerous models, theorists, and resources with various perspectives on cooperative learning. Some of the better known books include David and Roger Johnson's (1994) *Cooperative Learning in the Classroom*; Robert Slavin's (1994) *Cooperative Learning: Research, Theory, and Practice*; and Elizabeth Cohen and John Goodlad's (1994) *Designing Groupwork: Strategies for the Heterogeneous Classroom*. In reviewing the research on cooperative learning, wide agreement exists that such methods enhance student achievement, accelerate learning, improve retention and recall, and result in positive attitudes toward learning. The Johnson brothers have identified two essential components of any successful collaborative learning approach, which include:

Individual Accountability A group's success is based on each member's ability to demonstrate that he or she has learned the required material.

Student achievement has been shown to increase when group success depends on the combined score of all group members' quiz grades or when individual group members are assessed on contributions to a team project. Achievement gains are less when a single worksheet or project is given to a group of students without assigning individual tasks and responsibilities.

Positive Interdependence The success of the group depends on its ability to work together to achieve desired results such as recognition, grades, rewards, or free time. Merely asking students to collaborate does not ensure that social skills will be learned. Such skills must be taught intentionally.

Collaborative Grouping Considerations

When students are beginning to learn to collaborate, group sizes should remain small, ranging from two to four members. As skills are developed, students are capable of working in larger groups. It is also important to consider the length of time a group will work together. Groups meeting regularly over an extended period of time tend to be more successful than those that work together only occasionally.

Students can be grouped in different ways for different purposes. Some researchers distinguish between achievement groups and work groups. Achievement groups are homogeneous clusters formed according to achievement levels to organize instruction to match student needs. Work groups are more heterogeneous and are organized to promote social interaction as well as academic outcomes. Both rely on cooperation.

Some teachers experiment with grouping according to gender, but mixed groups have proved to be more successful. Cross-age grouping can also be effective, as is mixed-ability grouping. It appears that low-achieving students increase their performance in heterogeneous groups whereas gifted students benefit from working at least part of the time with other high achievers. Teachers may want to experiment with a variety of groups to determine which is most appropriate for a variety of activities in their classrooms.

Student Roles

When students are assigned individual roles in groups, they become active participants in the learning process and personally accountable for their tasks. Roles can take the form of specific jobs such as illustrator, recorder, resource person, facilitator, direction-giver, time-keeper, summarizer, and reporter. Sometimes, students can be assigned individual numbers so that a teacher can call on a number "3," for example, who is accountable for information generated by the whole group. Roles can be assigned according to where students sit, by drawing task cards, by teacher assignment, or by group consensus.

Social Skills

It is essential that social skills be taught as part of any collaborative experience. Students do not have inherent interpersonal skills nor do such skills automatically emerge by placing students in groups. It is necessary to intentionally learn their importance. Common social skills that can be taught include: organizing effective groups, demonstrating appropriate behavior, using effective learning skills, and critiquing and evaluating ideas collaboratively. All require reflection, practice, and refinement and are appropriate for classroom use with preschool through adult learners. Before any task is undertaken, teachers might identify a social skill for groups to incorporate in their activities. Once such skills become internalized, they enable students to work effectively with others while improving academic achievement and chances for success as adults.

Cooperative Learning Activities

One of Roger and David Johnson's many books is *Structuring Cooperative Learning: Lesson Plans for Teachers* (1987). The three following activities adapted from the book can be implemented into most classrooms. They are The Jigsaw, Out-Loud Problem-Solving, and Cooperative Discussions of Literature.

The Jigsaw

The Jigsaw is an effective technique that nurtures positive interdependence among group members. It is appropriate for studying portions of textbooks or other written materials in any content area. The steps for a jigsaw activity are as follows.

1. Select a social skill students should practice, such as management skills, paraphrasing, or summarizing one another's input. Provide the students with a rationale for practicing the specific skill.

2. Organize students into small groups of three to five.

3. Distribute a set of materials to each group. The set needs to be divisible into the number of members of the group. Give each member one part of the set of materials.

4. Assign students the task of meeting with someone else in the class who is a member of another learning group and who has the same set of materials. These pairs should then learn their material together and plan how to teach the material to the members of their original groups.

5. Send students back to their original groups where they take turns teaching their areas of expertise to group members.

6. Ask each group member to quiz the others until he or she is satisfied that everyone knows the information.

7. Evaluate each student's mastery of the information and the selected social skill in an appropriate manner.

Cooperative Out-Loud Problem-Solving

This activity teaches explicit problem-solving and social skills simultaneously.

1. Identify a social skill to develop as well as a rationale for doing so.

2. Assign small groups of approximately four students and provide each group with a worksheet. Ask group members to divide the problems among themselves equally.

3. Model out-loud problem-solving with one problem from the worksheet. Determine that all groups understand the correct problem-solving procedures.

4. Ask the groups to begin with each member taking a turn to problem-solve out loud. The other students check for accuracy of the strategy and its answer and suggest any changes in the problem-solving process. Each group member should also make an effort to encourage the other students.

5. Additionally, advise the groups that for any individual to be successful, everyone in the group must know all information on the worksheet. Each group must determine that its members have mastered the material.

6. For accountability, the teacher might give students another worksheet with similar problems. This time, the students can answer the questions individually and receive grades on the basis of their individual scores. Additionally, the teacher may reward groups whose members reach predetermined criteria of excellence. In assessing performance, attention should also be given to the social skill that was practiced.

Cooperative Group Discussion of Literature

At the secondary level, students can practice advanced social skills. In the following activity, they learn to participate in discussions while critiquing others' ideas.

1. Assign a piece of literature for students to read.

2. Prepare "talking" and "critiquing" chips. The talking chips should consist of enough red squares of paper or pieces of plastic so that each student has three chips. The critiquing chips can be made out of blue paper or plastic, allowing five per student.

3. Prepare discussion questions that encourage individual interpretation of characters, themes, and events in the story. Divide students into small groups and provide each group with a set of discussion questions.

4. Explain to the groups that a red chip goes to the center of the table each time a student answers one of the questions. A blue chip is added for each critique. Emphasize that student critiques should be based on the ideas shared and are not to be derogatory or directed at individuals. Each student must answer each question, and every time someone talks she must put a chip on the table. Since everyone is limited by the number of assigned chips, no one can dominate the conversation.

5. The teacher will most likely want to monitor the groups during their discussions to determine that ideas and not individuals are being critiqued and that all students are contributing equally.

6. Evaluation can be conducted of individuals, groups, or both.

The above activities merely hint at the countless possibilities for cooperative learning in the classroom. Because of the effectiveness of cooperative techniques in teaching social skills and improving academic achievement, some researchers recommend it as the dominant mode of instruction, comprising 60% of classroom time. Whether or not educators devote a significant portion of their teaching efforts to this method, collaboration makes school pleasant and enhances success for students and teachers alike. Since students are usually eager to work with their peers, enthusiasm for such activities makes teaching more enjoyable.

Student Collaboration in the Multilingual Classroom

Another approach to groupwork, developed by Elizabeth Cohen at Stanford University, addresses linguistic, ethnic, and skill differences in heterogeneous classrooms. Cohen's (1994) model called "Complex Instruction" fosters interracial and interethnic trust as students learn to use each other as linguistic and academic resources. The term "Complex Instruction" refers to different groups of children working at different learning stations in the classroom at the same time. Each center has an activity card for the group, plus individual work sheets. The group cannot move to another center until each member of the group is finished with the task. The tasks are multimodal in nature and emphasize learning by doing. The questions asked or the problems to be solved are open-ended, without a single right answer.

Each group member is assigned a role to ensure accountability. One person in each group also serves as the facilitator and makes certain that everyone receives the help she requires. Roles are rotated to share leadership. Students are taught to use each other as resources, and classroom rules include the right to ask anyone in the group for help and to take the responsibility for assisting anyone who requests guidance.

Teachers introduce the daily tasks by describing the different skills each requires. Students are informed that no one will be good at every task, but that each group member will probably excel in at least one. Teachers also make a special effort to acknowledge the skills of those children who typically lack status or prestige in the classroom. Once work begins at the centers, authority is delegated to the students, a situation that encourages reliance on peers and not on the teacher. Ten years of research at Stanford University indicates that Complex Instruction yields significant achievement gains and reduces status problems for culturally different students. Linguistic, ethnic, and skill differences in the classroom need not be viewed as liabilities, but rather as assets that provide a rich environment in which students learn from one another.

Conflict Management

During early childhood, our sense of self takes shape and our approaches to addressing frustration and conflict are developed. Since schools are second only to families in influencing children's attitudes and values, they can play important roles in teaching ways to manage conflict. Conflict, as an inevitable part of life, can be viewed as a challenge that teaches positive and constructive ways to address disagreements.

One way to introduce conflict management is to identify the common causes of conflict. Teachers might ask their students to list as many underlying causes of conflict as they can find. Once the students have made their lists, they can be compared with the following list.

Common Causes of Conflict

1. Individual needs are not being met.
2. Power is inequitably distributed.
3. Communication is ineffective or nonexistent.
4. Values or priorities differ.
5. Perception of a situation varies.
6. Learning approaches or personalities differ.

After discussion, further causes may be added to the lists. Personal, school, local, or world events can be analyzed to discern the underlying causes of conflict. By articulating the source of a conflict, students often find it easier to seek positive resolutions.

Another interesting aspect of conflict is how individuals respond to it. There are various styles of handling conflict that people exhibit, including the following:

Competing   Collaborating
Avoiding   Accommodating
Compromising

After a discussion of the above responses, it may prove interesting for students to note which style they use most frequently in conflict situations. Discussions might also include alternative styles that students may want to intentionally develop.

There are many approaches to conflict management. Teaching students simple conflict resolution processes can empower them to resolve their disagreements peacefully and without adult intervention. The following six-step process adapted from Dr. Thomas Gordon's (2000) book, *Parent Effectiveness Training*, has been used extensively with children and adults alike. It can be put to good use in the classroom when conflicts erupt.

Gordon's Conflict Management Process

Step 1: Identify and define the conflict.

Step 2: Brainstorm possible solutions.

Step 3: Discuss the potential solutions.

Step 4: Select the best solution.

Step 5: Develop a plan to implement the solution.

Step 6: Implement, then review and modify the solution.

To introduce students to the above process, the teacher can ask the class to name a problem they frequently observe at school such as skipping class or interrupting others. Volunteers can role play fictitious individuals such as a student who has skipped class and a teacher who is concerned with her absenteeism. The role-play should incorporate Gordon's six-step process with the class observing the procedure. Next, the teacher can divide students into small groups, asking each to select a different conflict and resolve it with the same six-step procedure. Practice with structured conflict management prepares students to handle disruptions in and out of school. Those who learn this process can be encouraged to apply it in a variety of situations; in fact, many students will apply it spontaneously.

As a junior high teacher, one of the authors encountered two seventh-graders who had chronic and serious differences of opinion. At least once weekly, their conflicts resulted in fighting. The teacher taught the above six-step process to the entire class, hoping it would be used to resolve the differences between the two boys. A couple of days later, the teacher overheard the boys arguing outside her classroom door. Assuming she would have to intervene once again, she was surprised as she heard the boys working through Gordon's six steps. Fighting was avoided and the teacher realized that the boys had not only learned a strategy but were able to apply it effectively.

Several resources exist for teaching students effective conflict management skills. A classic book for older students is *Getting to Yes* by Roger Fisher, William Ury, and Bruce Patton (1991). A conflict management book geared for elementary students is entitled *Learning the Skills of Peacemaking* (1995) by Naomi Drew. Other resources for preschool through sixth grade students is *I Can Problem Solve: An Interpersonal Cognitive Problem Solving Program* by Myrna Shure (2001). This award-winning program teaches children nonviolent ways to resolve everyday problems. The "I can problem-solve" (ICPS) program teaches children to consider the impact of their behavior upon others and diverse approaches to solving problems. Its 25 years of research shows that ICPS reduces impatient, aggressive, and social withdrawal behaviors. These are risk indicators for later problems such as violence, substance abuse, and dropping out of school. In its use with thousands of children in both low- and middle-income groups in cities around the country, ICPS has consistently enhanced positive peer relations, concern for others, ability and willingness to share, cooperation, and helping others in distress. This program results in long-term benefits that prevent adolescent social and emotional problems from occurring.

Learning through Service

Youth Service America, a national clearinghouse for community service programs, reported that between 1984 and 1997 the number of K–12 students who participated in community service jumped from 2 to 25 percent. A study of over 400,000 freshmen entering 700 universities in the fall of 2001 showed that 83 percent reported having done volunteer work. Some claim that student altruism is one of the most underreported stories of our time.

These are numerous important effects of service on students. Students benefit by making significant contributions to their community, learning about responsible citizenship first-hand, applying academic studies to real life situations, exercising individual initiative, and experiencing a positive transition into adulthood. Recent studies also suggest that service improves academic learning, increases social competence, and bolsters self-confidence.

Incorporating Service into a School Program

Many teachers and administrators are finding creative ways of incorporating service as part of their school programs. In some schools, community service is an integrated and required part of a school's curriculum. In others it is offered as an option for student volunteerism. Teachers interested in service learning may want to implement one or more of the following models currently in practice.

Volunteer Information Center Some schools approach service learning by establishing a central place in the school that identifies volunteer opportunities. When students find a suitable opportunity posted at the center, they call the agency, and, if interested, sign a contract to carry out the service. Follow-up and review may be done by whoever operates the center—frequently teachers, community volunteers, or the students themselves.

Club or Co-Curricular Activity Frequently, students perform community service through after-school clubs or co-curricular organizations. Some programs such as the Key Club identify volunteerism as its central mission, and others such as the Honor Society frequently include service as one responsibility of all members. In this model, a teacher acts as an advisor and students receive neither credit nor release from school for their service efforts.

Community Service Credit Many schools not only encourage learning through service, they also offer credit to students who volunteer according to school guidelines. In some programs, students pursue a community service elective for a preestablished number of hours of work. In others, students are required to perform a specified number of hours of volunteer service to graduate. To earn the community service credit, students usually write a proposal specifying the activities, the timeframe, the purpose, and the product or goal to be achieved. A faculty adviser or program coordinator reviews student proposals and also evaluates the project at its completion. The students conduct their service projects outside of the school day as an independent activity.

Service as Authentic Applications of an Existing Course In this model, students perform service as a way to gather, test, and apply the information for an existing school course. For example, students in a world language course might tutor immigrants who speak the language they are studying. Social studies students might work with homeless families to learn directly about this complex political and economic issue. Industrial arts students can design and build furniture for persons with special needs. Such volunteer efforts may be a onetime project or an ongoing commitment and be treated either as extra credit or as a class requirement.

Community Service Class Some schools offer a community service course, frequently a one-semester social studies class. Many service classes are two hours in length to enable students adequate time for their projects. These longer courses offer two credits and count as two classes for the teacher in charge. Frequently, four days a week are spent in the field, with one day back in class to reflect on the experiences, skills, information, and principles that make service activities successful.

Community Service as a Schoolwide Commitment In some schools and districts, community service is not an isolated activity but an integral part of the total school program. For example, each department in the school identifies ways to apply the knowledge and skills of its disciplines to improve the local community's quality of life. Thus, computer students provide services to nonprofit organizations, English students write letters for the elderly or disabled, science students collect water samples from a nearby river for a governmental agency, and art students design posters to advertise community events. Service at the school site may be offered by integrating cross-age tutoring into the school program. As of 2002, 200 middle and high schools have been identified as models of exemplary service learning. For information on their programs go to www.leaderschools.org.

Reflecting on Service Learning

Teachers who implement some form of service learning will want to encourage students to reflect regularly on their experiences. Such reflection assists in real life problem-solving, in articulating concerns students may have, identifying positive approaches, and discerning the benefits of their experiences. Many students will readily practice reading, writing, and speaking skills in the context of their service activities. Such reflection can be promoted in a variety of ways: through weekly class meetings, individual conferences with teachers and/or community members, and journal writing. Guidelines can help students structure their reflection and writing more carefully. Some possible questions include:

- What is the most satisfying thing about your service project?
- What is the hardest thing about your service project?
- What personal qualities does it take to do your job successfully?
- What are you learning about yourself, the community, and others from your work?
- What is the most unexpected thing you've encountered in your project?
- Are you changing as a person from the work you have done? If so, in what ways?
- If you were in charge at your work, what would you change to improve the services or program?

Service Resources

Several resources exist to assist educators in establishing effective learning through service in their classrooms or schools. Organizations and websites to turn to for information on service learning include:

Corporation for National and
  Community Service
1201 New York Avenue NW
Washington D.C. 20525
(202) 606-5000
www.nationalservices.org

KIDS (Kids Involved Doing Service)
215 Ubson Street, Suite 12
Lewiston, ME 04240
(207) 784-0956
www.kidsconsortium.org

National Youth Leadership Council
1667 Snelling Avenue North
St. Paul, MN 55108
(651) 631-3672
www.nylc.org

Youth Service America
1101 15th Street, Suite 200
Washington D.C. 20005
(202) 296-2992
www.ysa.org

Learning through service fosters an ethic of caring and community within a school. It also establishes positive partnerships between schools and their communities. Students learn that education is more than assimilation of information: it is a

means to improving the lives of others. Many students also gain profound insights from their service experiences. This is perhaps best reflected in excerpts from their written reflections. One student who worked at a homeless shelter claimed:

> For me, this experience was eye-opening, stereotype-breaking, and attitude changing. I really grew attached to some of the kids at the shelter, and found myself wanting to return to see them again. I am a person who was initially opposed to the whole service learning thing . . . but I changed my attitude almost completely (which is not something I do very often.) You can be told about poverty until you think you've heard all there is to know about it. Until you witness poverty and homelessness first-hand, however, it will not have an impact. It does not take much exposure to a human need to get personally involved and begin to care about a situation. I am convinced that just a little time required in community service will yield a lifetime of dedication to help.

Another student who worked in a teen runaway shelter wrote:

> The way in which I personally benefited the most was by what I realized by the end of that Saturday night. I was feeling good about myself and was, in fact, on a small ego trip. After all, just look at what I had done—I must have spent thirteen hours collecting clothes and five hours slaving over an oven baking and eating peanut butter cookies. I essentially gave up my whole Saturday to feed the hungry. But after watching these teenagers, who had so little material wealth compared to myself and who could be satisfied with what I considered garbage, I began to see the truth. A very uncomfortable notion crept into my mind— the idea that these kids were, if anything, superior to myself. Not in what they had, but in who they were.

Appreciating Differences

Henry David Thoreau once said, "If a man does not keep pace with his companions, perhaps it is because he hears a different drummer. Let him step to the music which he hears, however measured or far away." The diversity that Thoreau refers to has fascinated psychologists for centuries. Hippocrates delineated melancholic, sanguine, choleric, and phlegmatic personality types. At the beginning of the twentieth century, the psychologist Carl Jung described varying preferences among individuals for perceiving the world through "sensing" or "intuiting" and making decisions based on "feeling" or "thinking."

Terms for understanding human differences in learning have been variously described as psychological types, personality types, cognitive styles, and learning styles. Since the 1970s, educators have been interested in the classroom applications of learning styles. *Learning styles* refers to individual differences in the way information is perceived, processed, and communicated.

To help students develop the ability to appreciate differences, it is important both to model the behaviors and to use strategies that articulate learning style concepts. While discerning individual differences, it is also crucial to emphasize to students the neutrality of variations in style. One's habits or traits are not better than anyone else's; they are simply different. Some ideas follow about introducing students to style concepts.

Teaching Students about Learning Styles

- There are a variety of perceptual activities and puzzles that help students understand differences in style. One is simple word association. The teacher says words like "orange," "shell," "play," or "table." Students jot down a word or phrase that comes to mind, and then compare their responses with those around them. Students quickly notice the differences, and a discussion can ensue about individual perceptions.

- There are many optical illusions and visual perception tasks that illustrate the same point, such as the familiar design with the vases and the faces which can be found in many books of optical illusions. There are also sentences written with an extra word, such as "Paris in the the springtime." When this is read quickly, the extra "the" is usually ignored.

- Students can be offered a puzzle to solve or a logic problem that is brief and developmentally appropriate. Ask students to observe the process they use to problem-solve rather than focusing on a single correct response. By comparing their problem-solving strategies, students can recognize significant differences in how people address the same task.

- Students might discuss issues that are pertinent to their own lives such as favorite music, learning to ride a bicycle, playing video games, or other pastimes. When asked to tell why certain activities are enjoyable, students come to realize that individual preferences are unique, rather than right or wrong.

- When students finish a project, it is useful to discuss how they went about doing the assignment. Questions might include "How did you begin?" "How did you make that decision?" "What did you do when you ran into the challenge?" "If you were doing this again, would you do anything differently?" "Which parts were hard?" "Which were easy?" Discussing such questions in small groups can emphasize that people learn in different ways.

- There are also opportunities to capture the "teachable moment" when a child describes how he accomplishes a task. For example, one student may learn to ride a bicycle with training wheels, raising them gradually until he is no longer dependent on the wheels. Another might learn to ride a bike by spending all day Saturday practicing on the street in front of her home, with many falls and scrapes on her knees, until success is achieved. Students who play musical instruments will find, when they discuss how they practice, a variety of individual differences and yet, the final quality of their work may not vary significantly.

- Many teachers administer inventories and tests so that students can identify patterns in their own learning as well as formal activities which describe the applications of those patterns.

Perhaps most importantly, teachers must model an appreciation for individual differences in their behaviors throughout the school day. Every student can be expected to develop the same skills and gain the same competence—learning to read, for example, knowing how to multiply fractions, spelling words correctly, or understanding the historical significance of events, yet teachers must be responsive to the fact that not all students learn and develop competencies in the same way. Educators who model that distinction, who maintain high expectations for all students while appreciating and celebrating the diversity of ways students learn, will teach more through their behavior than through strategies.

Developing Multiple Perspectives

■ ■ ■ ■ ■ ■ ■ ■ ■ ■ ■ ■ ■ ■ ■ ■ ■

Our perceptions of others and of different situations stem from our life experiences, value systems, assumptions, and expectations. Although it is easy enough to state that everyone perceives the world differently, such a concept is difficult to internalize. Repeated and ongoing effort is needed to see the world through the eyes of others and to understand situations from diverse points of view. In an increasingly complex world, students may need to develop what Steven Lamy, a foremost American global educator, calls "intellectual pluralism." Intellectual pluralism is the capacity to analyze or evaluate different or opposing perspectives.

The preceding section, Appreciating Differences, introduces students to the concept that people approach learning differently. The following activities ask students to consider multiple perspectives in their interactions with others. The strategies include acknowledging perceptions of others, understanding diverse points of view, reflecting on current events from several perspectives, considering global implications, and learning to think systemically by considering the impact of human action on natural and human-made systems. The first strategy focuses on students and their perceptions of each other.

Who Are We?

Students are usually surprised to learn that others often perceive us differently from the way we perceive ourselves. The following activity introduces children to the concept of multiple perspectives by exploring the discrepancies between self-perception and the perceptions of fellow classmates.

Collage Portraits

Students can be asked to create "Collage Portraits" at home, omitting any identifying name or picture. When these are brought to class and displayed, classmates guess which collage belongs to whom. A discussion then follows about how well students know each other.

To initiate the activity, ask students to collect items at home for their collages. The teacher should provide poster boards and discarded magazines for those who would like to use such materials. Once supplies are gathered, each student should make a collage at home that features favorite pastimes, baby or early childhood photos, travel experiences, heroes or heroines, or personal opinions on important issues. The collages must be anonymous and not reveal names, pictures, or identifying symbols in the art work.

On an assigned day, students bring their collages to class hidden in a grocery bag or other cover. While students are out of the room, the teacher displays the collages and places an envelope directly underneath each. On their return to the classroom, students observe the "portraits" and attempt to guess the artists. The guesses are written on slips of paper and placed in the appropriate envelope. When everyone has viewed all collages, debriefing begins. Possible group discussion questions include:

- Was it easy or difficult to identify classmates by their collages?

- Which students were easily identified as the artists of their collages? Why?

- What did you learn about others that was new or surprising?

- How well do you think you know your classmates?

- Is it possible to find one unique thing about each collage and person?

- Can you now perceive each student in a new light? If so, how?

Students might end the discussion by reflecting on the problems that arise when assumptions are made about others without truly knowing such individuals.

Understanding Diverse Points of View

One way to introduce elementary students to the concept of multiple perspectives is to study stories from diverse points of view. One delightful resource is *The True Story of the Three Little Pigs* by Jon Scieszka (1995). This book explains the wolf's perspective in the story "The Three Little Pigs." Rather than being the mean, meat-eating wolf as portrayed in the original version of the story, Mr. A. Wolf explains he was merely suffering from allergies, causing him to huff and puff. Young children enjoy reading both stories and discussing the opposing perspectives. Older students may want to compare and contrast the account of historical events from their social studies textbooks such as the arrival of Columbus in the Americas with portions of Howard Zinn's (2000) *A People's History of the United States*.

Another way to help students explore points of view is to encourage them to share their reactions to a variety of situations. It will first be necessary to develop a list of events such as attending a football game or being assigned a mystery to read as homework. Read each event one at a time to the class with students volunteering their reactions to the situations. Encourage the sharing of a variety of opinions. After several students have reacted to the events, select one student to read silently and form an opinion about the next event on the list. The class then attempts to guess the selected student's reaction. Continue this process as long as the students enjoy comparing and contrasting one another's reactions.

List of Events

1. You win a trip to Egypt.
2. You are invited to a basketball game.
3. You are selected to write a feature story for the school newspaper.
4. Your mother buys you a piano.
5. A relative suggests that you study to become a doctor.
6. You are asked to take a lead role in a school play.
7. Your teacher assigns a book of your choice to read outside of class.
8. A birthday gift you wish you could receive is . . .

To bring this activity to closure, ask students to discuss whether the predictions of their classmates' responses were accurate. If not, why not? It is also important to discuss whether students acknowledge the validity of others' perspectives.

After grasping the concept of points of view, students might be asked to reflect on events from their own lives. For example, what might a school bus driver think about children who are talking loudly on the bus? How would students perceive their actions? What would be their reasons for talking loudly? Why would the bus driver want them to talk softly?

Role Playing Current Events from Diverse Perspectives

Older students can develop an appreciation for multiple perspectives through role playing current local or world events. One simple activity is to ask students to bring newspaper articles to class that address controversial or conflict-ridden issues. Assign students to groups with each person briefly describing an article. The groups then select one article to pursue in greater depth by working through the following steps:

1. One student volunteers to read the article to the group.

2. The group identifies the conflict in the article and the diverse perspectives of the conflict.

3. Students determine potential roles represented by those involved in the conflict.

4. Each member of the group assumes a role.

5. The group role plays the diverse perspectives.

6. Each group discusses the role-play, reflecting on the roles assumed, the validity of the diverse perspectives expressed, and any insights they gained.

7. The groups next consider how the conflict might be resolved by using win/win approaches.

8. The small groups share their experiences with the whole class.

Global Perspectives in the Curriculum

Another approach to seeing through the eyes, minds, and hearts of others is to infuse global perspectives into all curriculum areas, including the arts and sciences, literature, and extracurricular activities. As the world becomes more interdependent and students have increased opportunities to communicate with those from other cultures, it is important that cultural differences not simply be judged as right or wrong.

Educators can consider whether they encourage students to perceive the complexity of cultural plurality. To infuse global perspectives throughout the curriculum, teachers can begin by responding to the following questions:

- When do students have opportunities to consider numerous world views?

- Are they knowledgeable about global issues and events? If not, how might world events be included in the curriculum?

- How can students understand that humans are diverse in terms of attributes, cultures, and experiences and yet share common human needs and goals?

- Where in class lessons do students acknowledge the interdependence of numerous world systems?

- What strategies might students be taught to participate in local, national, and international issues and settings?

- How are students acquiring the skills of decision-making, information analysis, and citizenship participation?

By using resources available in most communities, students can explore cultural differences and similarities through the literature, music, games, or arts of diverse countries. Artists, guest lecturers, exchange students, discussion leaders, and resource materials can enrich any subject matter. One excellent resource that offers short stories written by living authors from around the world is called *The Art of the Story: An International Anthology of Contemporary Short Stories* by Daniel Halpern (2000). The book features seventy-eight authors from thirty-five countries recounting their personal, social, and political views of the world.

Systems Wheel

Another way of gaining perspective is to consider the consequences of one's actions. For example, the last few years have witnessed increasing concerns about the long-term impact of human behavior on natural and human-made systems. Many contemporary issues reveal the interconnectedness of cultural, ecological, economic, political, and technological systems. To extend students' thinking beyond short-term solutions they can identify multiple factors and potential consequences involved in any one issue. The following five-step exercise called a "systems wheel" is a helpful tool for forecasting potential consequences.

1. Ask students to identify an issue or make a forecast that is pertinent to class content. When one issue or forecast is selected, ask students to draw a circle in the center of a blank piece of paper and write the name of the issue in the circle. For example, assume that students in a science class identify increasing air pollution as the issue they want to address.

2. Next, students should brainstorm the global systems that will be affected by increased air pollution. Examples might include the natural environment, international relations, technology, world economies, or political systems. Once global systems are identified, students draw the appropriate number of spokes from the first circle and at the end of each spoke draw another circle. Inside each new circle, a global system affected by air pollution is noted:

3. A third set of spokes and circles is drawn from the second to indicate potential consequences of air pollution. The third ring of circles forecasts the likely impact of air pollution on the global systems identified in the second ring.

4. Students continue extending their rings of consequences as far as they can forecast. They may also want to predict the number of years before such effects are noted.

5. Students next identify circles that have relationships to each other by coloring all related circles in the same color or by drawing interconnecting lines.

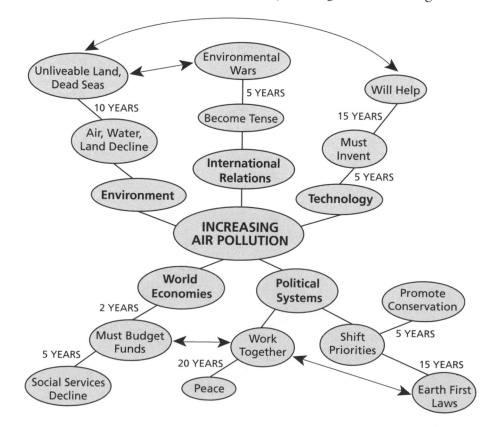

To bring closure to the activity, students might share their systems wheels in small groups, noting similarities and differences with classmates' forecasts. Research and class discussions can follow, with students synthesizing and revising their forecasts and identifying appropriate courses of action.

Local and Global Problem-Solving

Students are usually eager to tackle real life problems. When provided with information about current local or global problems and when taught problem-solving processes, children and youth often surprise adults with ingenuous approaches to addressing pressing needs. For example, during the 1980s a group of Russian and American students worked together to advocate limiting the proliferation of nuclear arms. To publicize their cause, they created jewelry made from dismantled rockets to sell as world peace jewelry. They also created a flag with powerful visual symbolism: half of the flag was the former Soviet Union's and half was the American flag. The two halves were blended together with a large heart framing the borders. The students' visual imagery and jewelry grabbed the attention of local citizenry as well as national radio and television.

Students can be taught problem-solving processes to address local and global concerns and perhaps, most importantly, they can take action to implement their own creative solutions. The problem-solving strategies suggested below are taken from a global education series entitled *Our Only Earth*, published by Zephyr Press. These strategies, which are part of a process called a Youth Summit, have been used in individual classrooms, entire schools, and with students in countries around the world to address real life problems. The process begins with individual students or small groups researching a local or global issue.

After the research phase, the following problem-solving steps can be initiated:

Step 1: In small groups, encourage students to share what they learned about the problem they researched and the feelings such content evoked. Such discussions enable group members to get to know each other and to share affective reactions to the problem at hand.

Step 2: Next, ask the groups to review what is known about the issue and to categorize key ideas generated by the group. Students may want to make a copy of the data retrieval chart below on a large sheet of butcher paper to synthesize their knowledge.

DATA RETRIEVAL CHART

Name	Who	When	Where	Why

The chart can be completed in one of two ways:

a. Each student summarizes and adds information in the appropriate categories by placing his name in the name column and completing one horizontal section of the chart. After group members have individually made their contributions, the completed chart displays information that is readily available for easy reference.

b. Another use of the data retrieval chart is to consider the issue from diverse perspectives. Students brainstorm individuals, organizations, or countries concerned about the problem and consider it from diverse perspectives. Each student writes the name of the group or nation under the name column and then completes the horizontal questions from that perspective. Discussion follows based on the diverse perspectives represented on the chart.

Once the chart is completed, the following problem-solving steps can be undertaken:

Step 3: Students identify a specific problem they want to tackle. Initially, topics might be too vague or unwieldy. For example, students might state they want to help resolve the problem of air pollution, but such a notion is too large to be manageable. However, if students narrow their focus to air pollution's connection to human respiratory ailments, or industrial pollutants crossing national borders, the greater specificity will make their projects more successful.

To narrow their topics, ask students to consider the problem from several angles. How do people, animals, plants, businesses, or nations view this problem? What sub-problems become evident when the issue is considered from many points of view? Students should brainstorm the sub-problems related to the original issue. Next, ask that they review their lists to identify which sub-problems appear most interesting to pursue as a group.

Once a sub-problem has been selected, students need to refine the issue further. This is often best done in the form of questions rather than statements. For example, if students are addressing the topic of air pollution, they can pose questions such as "How can we cut down on our families' use of cars?" Or, "How can we inform our community about the dangers of CFC's?" Ask students to experiment with the use of different verbs as they generate their questions since the verbs will suggest actions to take.

Once students have generated their questions, they may discover the need for additional research. If so, groups should plan a strategy for information gathering and allot time to do the work.

Step 4: In their small groups, students brainstorm multiple solutions to the questions generated in Step 3.

Step 5: From their solution lists, suggest that students select the top two they could actually implement. Using the chart below, each group should

SOLUTIONS: Rank in order your top 2 solutions and list	POSITIVE OUTCOMES: List 3 positive outcomes for each solution	NEGATIVE OUTCOMES: List 3 negative outcomes for each solution	POSSIBLE SHORT- AND LONG-TERM CONSEQUENCES List the consequences that might result from the implementation of your solutions in 1-, 5-, 10- and 20-year timeframes. Put a + or – by each consequence to signify whether it is positive or negative.			
			1 YEAR	5 YEARS	10 YEARS	20 YEARS
SOLUTION #1:						
SOLUTION #2:						

YOUTH SUMMIT SOLUTION EVALUATION PROCESS

evaluate the pros and cons of their solutions. Such analysis demonstrates that well-intentioned ideas frequently yield some negative consequences. It is therefore important to consider short- and long-term consequences before implementing solutions.

Once the analysis of potential outcomes and consequences is completed, students should select the best solution. Each group then discusses its final solutions and makes any modifications necessary to minimize potential negative effects.

Step 6: Students plan how to carry out their solution. This step, while requiring much forethought, empowers students to take action by implementing their solutions in the broader community. To organize their action planning, students may use the group action plan and individual commitment forms that follow.

Step 7: Each group prepares a presentation for the class and/or school, families, and community members on the selected problems and plans of action.

YOUTH SUMMIT GROUP ACTION PLAN FORM

Group Topic: _____
_____

Group Members: (Please list first and last names.)

_____
_____
_____
_____
_____
_____

Describe the specific problem your group decided to solve:

_____
_____
_____

Describe your best solution:

_____
_____
_____
_____

List the specific steps your group will take to carry out the solution, beginning with what you will do first, second, third, and so on. Also list the name of the group member who will be responsible for doing each step:

_____
_____
_____
_____
_____

Create a timeline stating dates of completion for the steps listed above:

_____
_____
_____
_____

Describe the end result of your efforts. What exactly will you have accomplished?

_____
_____
_____

YOUTH SUMMIT STATEMENT OF INDIVIDUAL COMMITMENT TO WORK ON AN AREA OF GLOBAL CONCERN

Name: _____

Area of global concern: _____

_____

_____

_____

List the commitments you made to your group at the Summit:

_____

_____

_____

_____

Please describe below any additional commitments you would like to pursue independently:

_____

_____

_____

_____

Signature: _____   Date: _____

Thank you for your efforts to make the world a better place!

Step 8: Projects should be carried out and celebrations planned to acknowledge student efforts.

Student participants in the Youth Summit problem-solving process have generated numerous approaches to local and global issues. Some of their action plans have included a game about the effects of plastics on the environment; presentations to the United Nations, schools, community groups, and churches about the importance of international youth exchanges to promote world peace; booths at local fairs to educate others about ocean pollution; the implementation of school-wide self-esteem programs to combat drug abuse; and the creation of a film about wildlife's struggle to survive. Such projects help students acquire skills to address complex, real life issues. As Jason Schmidt, age 9, noted after participating in a Youth Summit,

I learned to be more caring for the world. I see that we can be world changers.

Multicultural Education

The changing nature of demographics is one of the strongest rationales for multicultural education in the United States. The Census Bureau has predicted that while the Caucasian population will increase by 25% between 1990 and 2030, the African American population will increase by 68%, the Asian American, Pacific Island American, and American Indian populations by 79%, and the Hispanic American population by 187%. The Population Reference Bureau forecasts that by the year 2080, 24% of U.S. citizens will be Hispanic, 15% African American, 12% Asian American, and a little over 50% Caucasian. As the former University of Chicago President, Robert Maynard Hutchins, once said, "The best education for the best is the best education for all." It appears imperative then that the best education requires the inclusion of multicultural education for every student of all racial, ethnic, social, academic, and language groups, since each will participate in an increasingly multiethnic future.

Many teachers view multicultural education as content limited to ethnic, racial, or cultural groups and irrelevant to many academic disciplines; however, just the opposite is true. Ideally, multicultural education should be an ongoing, integrated, multidisciplinary process for all students. James Banks, one of the country's foremost experts, and author of numerous books in the field says that multicultural education requires changes in teaching approaches and school environments. To infuse diverse cultural perspectives into their teaching, Banks recommends adjusting the content one teaches, helping students identify biases in how knowledge is constructed, ensuring the academic achievement of all students, and creating a total school climate that respects and values diversity. Bank's suggestions for infusing multicultural education throughout the curriculum follow. Adapted from James A. Banks, *Multiethnic Education: Theory and Practice*. Third Edition. Boston: Allyn and Bacon, 1994, pp. 3–15.

Teaching with a Multicultural Perspective

Integrating Multicultural Information into Content Areas

To successfully integrate multicultural education throughout the curriculum, teachers will find it necessary to use examples and content from a variety of cultures in all discipline areas. Before it is possible to do so, educators must first become informed about multicultural contributions and ask their students to provide additional examples from their cultural/ethnic heritages. Numerous resources exist for teachers in nearly all subject areas. Simply get online and use keywords for one's particular interests.

Reflecting on the Construction of Knowledge

Teachers can help students identify how cultural assumptions and biases influence the way knowledge is constructed within a discipline. Concepts, events, and issues taught in the classroom can be considered from the perspectives and experiences of a range of racial, ethnic, and cultural groups. For example, during a unit on the discovery of America, students might read portions of Fred Olson's *On the Trail of the Arawacks* and parts of Christopher Columbus's diary to discern how European and Indian views of this event differed. Through such comparisons, students develop critical thinking skills and actively construct their knowledge instead of passively consuming textbooks.

Offering an Equity Pedagogy

An equity pedagogy refers to adjusting teaching methods to ensure the academic achievement of all students from diverse racial, cultural, gender, and social class groups. By using cooperative learning, multimodal instruction, and personalized, self-directed options, students have more opportunities for success.

Research shows that the academic achievement of many students is increased when collaborative rather than competitive models of instruction are used. It is also important to give overviews at the outset of units about what will be covered and why. Some students learn best by having "big picture" concepts in mind since such concepts show how smaller chunks of information or content fit into the overall whole.

Creating an Empowering School Culture Teachers can create positive school climates by preventing or discontinuing unfair tracking, labeling, or disproportionality in special programs. This is also helpful to the positive interaction of staff and students across ethnic and racial lines both inside and outside of class times.

One urban high school wanted to visually acknowledge the diversity of its student body. A large map of the world was painted in the mail hallway of the school. Colorful note cards identified the countries students emigrated from, and once monthly, holidays and world events were highlighted on the map to raise awareness of multiculturalism within and outside of school.

An important goal of multicultural education is for students to acquire the knowledge and skill to take personal, social, and civic action that promotes democracy and democratic living. When students learn content about their country and world from the diverse perspectives of those who have shaped local and international cultures, they are being prepared to serve effectively as citizens in a pluralistic nation and world.

Understanding Cultural Diversity through the Arts

Many sociologists and anthropologists claim that art emerges from a cultural context. A culture's customs, tastes, ideologies, and philosophies have profound influences on artistic expression. When examining cultural artifacts, it is necessary to consider the social forces affecting their creation. Conversely, by analyzing a culture's art, one can gain insight into the mores that shaped the art.

A Canadian educator, E. Margaret Andrews, intrigued with the cultural impact on art, has developed a multicultural education program that introduces children to diversity through the arts. By becoming "anthropologists" or "cultural detectives," students consider another culture through its art. The procedures for this process consist of six steps described below.

1. Students become "anthropologists" or "cultural detectives" and assume the task of investigating another culture through the collection, organization, and interpretation of artistic data. To begin, the teacher and students identify a theme such as Chinese Culture and Art to explore. Once the theme is agreed upon, individual learning goals are specified for each student.

2. Students begin by collecting visual samples such as photographs, posters, magazine pictures, book pictures, and objects. Stories, legends, songs, and dances can also be gathered. They can secure such artifacts through books, magazines, the Internet, or individuals they may know.

3. Once the artifacts are brought into the classroom, the students examine and discuss the collection. They are asked to observe, describe, analyze, and interpret the meanings of the collected data. Discussions can focus on the:

   - types of art represented, such as fine art, folk art, utilitarian art, tourist art, or indigenous art
   - functions of the art, such as whether it was for use as apparel or personal adornment, everyday purposes (furniture, containers), play and leisure, ritual and celebration, or promotion of political, economic, or commercial pursuits
   - history associated with the cultural art forms, the motivation behind the creation of such art, and the values and beliefs reflected in the art
   - cross-cultural comparisons that analyze the similarities and differences in styles, symbols, or materials
   - the materials and techniques used in the artifacts

4. During discussion of the artifacts and their cultural implications, teachers might provide art projects for students to undertake. Classroom visitors who have special artistic expertise are invaluable resources at this stage.

5. For evaluation, students can be assessed on their group participation and through logs that track the most significant things they learned. Such logs can include personal insights, cultural awareness, and the attainment of individual and group goals.

6. Periodic sharing of cultural themes through school presentations such as puppet shows or culture-related events can augment student learning. Multicultural arts festivals for other classes, parents, or community members can exhibit the results of the cultural investigations.

Andrews' inquiry-based approach to multicultural education familiarizes students with diverse cultural perspectives and practices. Children also gain important learning and thinking skills as they begin to recognize and celebrate cultural diversity.

Culturgrams

Another approach to exploring cultural diversity is offered by Brigham Young University's David M. Kennedy Center for International Studies. The Center's research process called Culturgrams develops profiles of diverse cultural groups with the goal of fostering intercultural understanding. The Center has noted that there are approximately 20,000 cultures in the world, and it has created Culturgrams for over 170 countries, which are updated frequently. Since the task of understanding such an array of human cultures is immense, the Culturgram was developed as one means of organizing and understanding different cultures and their characteristics.

A Culturgram is a research effort to gather information on many dimensions of a single culture. After the research is conducted and compiled, it is validated through personal experience and/or interviews with individuals of the culture under study. Since one person's interpretation of cultural behavior can differ from another's, updating and validation are important parts of the research process.

There are twenty-four broad areas of study in a Culturgram. Teachers who are interested in having their students begin work on such cultural profiles may ask students to select one or more of the research areas rather than attempting to compile an entire Culturgram. Research can be gleaned from library materials, embassies, foreign service, cultural support organizations, and interviews. The twenty-four categories of Culturgrams are included below with permission from Brigham Young University's David M. Kennedy Center for International Studies:

1. Greetings
2. Visiting
3. Talks or speeches
4. Meetings
5. Role relationships
6. Gestures
7. Personal appearance
8. Expressions of general attitudes by age, sex, position
9. Languages
10. Religion and philosophy
11. Special holidays and holy days
12. Family
13. Dating, courtship, and marriage
14. Social and economic levels
15. Group distribution
16. Work
17. Diet and food customs
18. Recreation, leisure, sports, arts
19. History and government
20. Education
21. Transportation and communication systems
22. Health, sanitation, and medical facilities
23. Land and climate
24. Other distinctive customs, courtesies, conditions

After students have collected their data, they may want to identify a native of that culture to verify their research. The information should then be compiled and shared in a written or visual format and saved for others who may want to learn about that culture as well. Researching any or all of the components of a Culturgram introduces students to many key aspects of a culture. Culturgrams, especially when validated by those indigenous to the culture being studied, promote increased understanding of and communication with others.

Culturgrams by the David M. Kennedy Center for International Studies is available in a two-volume set that can be ordered through bookstores or online.

Technology That Enhances Interpersonal Intelligence

Today's new electronic technologies are making it possible for people to connect in seemingly unlimited numbers of ways, therefore expanding possibilities for developing their interpersonal intelligence. These new means of communication can never replace meeting face-to-face but they are important ways to develop relationships with others far away, continue and extend human contact between meetings, and provide opportunities for collaboration. They provide revolutionary ways for people to connect across time and space and are useful tools for both educators and students.

Among growing options for developing interpersonal skills through electronic technology are cell phones, Internet-based e-mail, chat rooms, message boards, newsgroups, multi-user virtual environments (MUVEs), online conferences, and distance learning that is moving beyond online lectures. An excellent MUVE for teachers is Tapped In at http://tappedin.org.

Making use of the Internet, the Japanese government has sponsored a program bringing together teachers from Spearfish, South Dakota, and Sakaide, Japan. The program is aimed at increasing understanding between students and educators in Japan and the United States through online activities and by visiting each other's websites. This is one of a number of such programs sponsored by the Fulbright Memorial Fund's Master Teacher Program. See www.glocomnet.or.jp/fmf/master_teacher_program.html.

Another example of interpersonal communication through the Internet is the International Education and Resource Network's (iEARN) First People's Project. In this project students from five continents learn about each other and their respective cultures by sharing their stories, poems, photographs, and art work on the Internet as well as sending packages through the mail. iEARN, a nonprofit organization made up of over 4000 schools in nearly 100 countries, offers over 100 projects designed and facilitated by teachers and students. See the iEARN website at www.iearn.org.about/index.html.

There are also other excellent safe services for setting up online pen-pal programs such as ePals at www.epals.com, Keypals Club at www.teaching.com/keypals, and the Flat Stanley Project at www.enoreo,on.ca/lflatstanley/index.htm. The latter is an intriguing international literacy and communication activity based on the books by Jeff Brown.

Walter Mackenzie, author of *Multiple Intelligences and Instructional Technology*, has developed a colorful, multimedia website that is filled with interesting, collaborative student projects. See his Surfaquarium at http://surfaquarium.com/projects.htm.

There are many ways that technology such as camcorders can be used in the classroom to enhance interpersonal skills. For example, students can be videotaped as they give presentations or performances. They can then observe their facial expressions and body movements to see whether these enhance or detract from what they wish to communicate. Groups of students can discuss their observations of each other, understanding that they should begin and end with a positive observation and that criticism is only to be offered in a constructive manner.

While one of the foremost goals of a strong educational program is to produce successful learners, it is also critical that they develop into well-balanced human beings who can function successfully in the adult world. The development of interpersonal intelligence is an important asset both in personal and professional life. As new technologies such as those described above become standard in classrooms and virtual settings, it is more important than ever to remember the importance of combining them with plenty of physical human interaction in real settings.

Summary

Howard Gardner asserts that the positive development of the personal intelligences determines whether individuals will lead successful and fulfilling adult lives. Interpersonal intelligence is called on to live and work with others in our immediate environments, in our communities, nations, and world. Learning to live collaboratively and manage conflict effectively are necessary skills for both individuals and nations.

Albert Einstein once said:

The general level of world information is high but usually biased, influenced by national prejudices serving to make us citizens of our nation but not of our world.

Student perspectives of local and global issues can be broadened so that they assume citizenship not only of one country but also of the world. While anchored firmly in one's cultural roots, it is possible to stretch beyond national borders to work with others in addressing the complex issues facing humankind.

This chapter has surveyed numerous interpersonal approaches important for an increasingly interdependent world. These processes include: 1) establishing effective groups, 2) collaborative learning, 3) conflict management, 4) learning through service, 5) appreciating differences by learning about learning styles, 6) developing multiple perspectives, 7) local and global problem-solving, 8) multicultural education, and 9) interpersonal uses of technology. In order to summarize, reflect on, and synthesize the content of this chapter, the following is offered:

APPLYING INTERPERSONAL INTELLIGENCE

1. Important ideas or insights gleaned from this chapter:

_____

_____

_____

_____

_____

_____

2. Areas I'd like to learn more about:

_____

_____

_____

_____

_____

_____

3. Ways I can use this information in my teaching. Please note that all of the strategies mentioned in this chapter are listed below with space provided to note how each strategy might be incorporated into classroom instruction:

INTERPERSONAL STRATEGY	CLASSROOM APPLICATION
Establishing a Positive Interpersonal Environment	_____
Criteria for Effective Groups	_____
Determining Class Values and Rules	_____
Determining Schoolwide Values	_____
Class Meetings	_____

INTERPERSONAL STRATEGY	CLASSROOM APPLICATION

Collaborative Learning

Collaborative Grouping Considerations _____

Student Roles _____

Social Skills _____

Cooperative Learning Activities _____

Conflict Management

Common Causes of Conflict _____

Learning through Service

Incorporating Service into a School Program _____

Reflecting on Service Learning _____

Service Resources _____

Appreciating Differences

Teaching Students about Learning Styles _____

Developing Multiple Perspectives

Who Are We? _____

Understanding Diverse Points of View _____

Role Playing Current Events from
Diverse Perspectives _____

Global Perspectives in the Curriculum _____

Systems Wheel _____

Local and Global Problem-Solving

Multicultural Education

Teaching with a Multicultural Perspective _____

Understanding Cultural Diversity through the Arts _____

Culturgrams _____

**Technology That Enhances
Interpersonal Intelligence** _____

INTERPERSONAL REFERENCES

Andrews, M. E. (1983). *The Innovation Process of Culturally-Based Art Education: A Qualitative Analysis of the In-Service Programming and Implementation Processes of an Innovative Multicultural Art Curriculum in Canada.* Unpublished doctoral dissertation. University of Bradford, Yorkshire, England.

Andrews, M. E. (1981). The Study of Art in Cultural Context. *The Annual Journal Canadian Society of Education Through Art.*

Banks, J. A. (1991). The Need for a Broad Definition of Multicultural Education. *Multicultural Leader, Vol. 4.* No. 1 Winter/Spring. Educational Materials and Services Center, 144 Railroad Ave. Suite 107, Edmonds, WA 98020.

Campbell, L., & Campbell, B. (1999). *Multiple Intelligences and Student Achievement: Success Stories from Six Schools.* Alexandria, VA: ASCD.

Campbell, L., & McKisson, M. (1998). *Our Only Earth: A Global Problem-Solving Series.* Tucson, AZ: Zephyr Press.

Cohen, E., & Goodlad, J. (1994). *Designing Group Work: Strategies for the Heterogeneous Classroom.* New York: Teachers College Press, Columbia University.

Csikszentmihaly, M. (1991). *Flow: The Psychology of Optimal Experience.* New York: Harper Rowe.

David M. Kennedy Center for International Studies. (2000). *Culturgrams: The Nations around Us.* Chicago, IL: Ferguson Press.

Drew, N. (1995). *Learning the Skills of Peacemaking: An Activity Guide for Elementary-Age Children on Communicating, Cooperating, and Resolving Conflict.* Rolling Hills Estates, CA: Jalmar Press.

Fisher, R., Ury, W., & Patton, B. (1991). *Getting to Yes: Negotiating Agreement Without Giving In.* New York: Penguin.

Gardner, H. (1993). *Frames of Mind: The Theory of Multiple Intelligences.* New York: Basic Books.

Gordon, T. (2000). *Parent Effectiveness Training.* Three Rivers, MI: Three Rivers Press.

Halpern, D. (Ed.) (2000). *The Art of Story: An International Anthology of Contemporary Short Stories.* New York: Penguin.

Humphrey, N. (1976). The Social Function of the Intellect. In P. G. Bateson & R. A. Hinds (Eds.). *Growing Points in Ethology.* Cambridge, England: Cambridge University Press.

Johnson, D. W., & Johnson, R.T. (1994). *Cooperative Learning in the Classroom.* Alexandria, VA: ASCD.

Kovalik, S. (1994). *Integrated Thematic Instruction: The Model.* Kent, WA: Susan Kovalik & Associates.

Scieszlca, J. (1995). *The True Story of the Three Little Pigs by A. Wolf.* New York: Dutton.

Shure, M.B. (2001). *I Can Problem-Solve (ICPS): An Interpersonal Cognitive Problem-Solving Program.* Champaign, IL: Research Press.

Slavin, R. (1994). *Cooperative Learning: Research, Theory, and Practice.* Boston, MA: Allyn & Bacon.

Zinn, H. (2001). *A People's History of the United States.* New York: HarperPerennial.

7

The World Within
INTRAPERSONAL INTELLIGENCE

*What lies behind us and what lies before us are tiny matters
compared to what lies within us.*

—Oliver Wendell Holmes

BILL'S INNER WORLD

When Bill was a young child, his mother found
him difficult to handle. He was slow to learn,
had frequent seizures, and suffered from
behavior disorders.

*W*ith two babies at home, a broken
marriage, and the necessity of returning to
work, Bill's mother felt overwhelmed with the
care her son required. Immediately after his
ninth birthday, Bill was sent to live in a state
institution for the mentally retarded, where he
spent the next twelve years of his life.

After entering the institution, Bill ceased to
share in the usual experiences of childhood. He
was isolated from his family, friends, and the
small town he lived in. Bill's isolation also
included illiteracy. Considered "ineducable"
with an IQ under 50, Bill was never taught to
read or write. His days in the institution were
spent doing menial chores.

Upon release from the state facility, Bill
lived with the support of a community agency
dedicated to assisting formerly institutional-
ized adults to achieve fuller and more independent lives. The agency required Bill to
pursue yearly personal goals to integrate into
his local community. When Bill turned 31, he
identified a new goal to pursue: learning to
read and write.

BILL'S INNER WORLD . . . continued

His service provider located a reading teacher who used a multimodal approach to reading instruction. Bill immediately expressed his desire to write a letter to his estranged mother. He carefully dictated his thoughts to his tutor, and then practiced reading portions of the letter. During the course of several weeks, Bill and his teacher worked with a reading series called *Ball, Stick, Bird* by Renee Fuller. They also read cigarette packs, cereal boxes, road signs, food and medicine labels, and newspaper headings. Bill practiced writing words and sentences first with colored markers and next with a typewriter given to him by his teacher.

Bill worked avidly on his own, filling notebooks with sentences to proudly show during his next tutoring session. Writing about reading material of his own choice and setting and achieving personal goals yielded positive results. Both Bill's skills and confidence increased greatly. After only a month of learning to read and write, Bill set a new goal: writing a book.

When Bill informed his teacher of his desire, she hesitated, wondering if the idea was realistic. As if to respond to these unspoken doubts, Bill told her that he also knew what the book should be titled. It would be called *The Inside World* and would describe his life in the institution. Six months later, Bill completed his book. The following excerpts are taken from Bill Knake's (1989) *The Inside World*:

I would like to be able to teach other people to learn to read. I'd be a good teacher. I could teach them what I know, and help them find the words they want to know. I am good at working with people. I do understand people and their problems. I'd like to see if I can help or not. I know a lot of people who do not know how to read. I would like to start a school to teach them how. Reading is fun. You're never too old to read. I'd like to take people who are illiterate and turn them around so they can read.

Since I learned to read I feel better about myself. I always wanted to read. I feel proud of myself. I want to keep getting better at reading and writing, and I want to write some more books. I'm done with the institution for now. I want to write about other things, good things like how we can get along much better. I feel good about myself and I feel good about my life.

Bill Knake's perseverance and compassion, two aspects of intrapersonal intelligence, have served to inspire countless others to set and achieve goals formerly assumed impossible. Today, Bill lives and works in Mt. Vernon, Washington.

DEFINITION: Understanding Intrapersonal Intelligence

At the heart of our inner world are the strengths we rely on to understand ourselves and other people, to imagine, plan, and solve problems. There as well lie qualities such as motivation, determination, ethics, integrity, empathy, and altruism. Without these inner resources, it is difficult to live a productive life in the fullest sense.

Most researchers believe that as soon as we are born, the personal intelligences begin to develop from a combination of heredity, environment, and experience. The infant's bonding with one or more adults establishes emotional security. Continued nurturing instills a healthy sense of identity and promotes positive social relationships. Thus, from the beginning, intrapersonal and interpersonal intelligence are interdependent.

Parents or other care-givers and teachers serve critical functions in modeling these intelligences for the developing child, and the positive, nurturing, stimulating environments they establish the foundations for healthy intellectual, emotional, and physical growth.

Intrapersonal intelligence includes our thoughts and feelings. The more we can bring them into consciousness, the better we can relate our inner world to the outer world of experience. Occasionally, when we find ourselves doing something automatically, it is useful to interrupt this pattern and begin again what we were doing, carefully and thoughtfully observing our own behavior. Such critical self-observation is one way to become more conscious of our inner world, an awareness as important for teachers as it is for students.

In this chapter, we explore ways to better understand ourselves, our desires and goals, and our emotional natures. Such intrapersonal awareness is crucially important to developing learners who may grow increasingly ethical, productive, and creative while simultaneously exhibiting positive independence and interdependence.

Intrapersonal intelligence is not necessarily a solemn quality. In fact, the ability to understand ourselves by being able to laugh at our foibles or mistakes is a nonthreatening way of enhancing self-understanding. Students will be well served by realizing that making an honest mistake should not automatically lead to self-depreciation, shame, or anger. Instead, when we laugh at ourselves, we are often able to start a task over again. When teachers model a light-hearted self-regard, they model a basic survival skill.

CHECKLIST: Intrapersonal Qualities

Young children are often curious about their inner experiences and can benefit from a variety of intrapersonal activities. Such activities include self-directed, independent learning approaches, opportunities to imagine, and quiet times and private places in which to work and reflect. In addition, students can benefit by learning strategies for processing their feelings, setting and achieving goals, and gaining self-knowledge and self-esteem. Posing questions about life and personal ambitions and seeking answers to such mysteries is rewarding for children and adults alike.

When attempting to describe characteristics of those with developed intrapersonal intelligence, it is important to note that individuals may not demonstrate all aspects of this intelligence. For example, a person may have an accurate inner image of himself but lack positive self-esteem. Another may exhibit self-contentment but not strive for self-actualization. The following list suggests some indicators of this complex intelligence. It is likely that a person with well-developed intrapersonal intelligence may be one who:

1. Is aware of a range of emotions.

2. Finds approaches and outlets to express feelings and thoughts.

3. Develops an accurate sense of self.

4. Is motivated to identify and pursue goals.

5. Establishes and lives by an ethical value system.

6. Works independently.

7. Is curious about the "big questions" in life: meaning, relevance, and purpose.

8. Manages ongoing learning and personal growth.

9. Attempts to seek out and understand inner experiences.

10. Gains insights into the complexities of self and the human condition.

11. Strives for self-actualization.

12. Empowers others.

Intrapersonal Learning Processes

The learning processes in this chapter fit into several broad categories: self-esteem, goal-setting, emotional processing skills, journal writing, clarification of values and purpose, the curricular model of self-directed learning, and intrapersonal forms of technology. These instructional approaches begin to nurture intrapersonal intelligence, but it should be noted that deep self-knowledge requires a lifetime of living and learning. The specific strategies described in this chapter include:

Establishing an Environment to Nurture the Sense of Self
Characteristics of Schools That Nurture Self-Esteem

Self-Esteem Enhancers: Learning to Love Oneself
Compliment Circles
Individual Acknowledgment
Peer Support
Guidelines for Enhancing Self-Esteem

Setting and Achieving Goals
Challenging Students to Learn
Olympian Goal-Setting

Thinking Skills
Metacognition

Emotionally Intelligent Education
Engaging Feelings in the Classroom
Establishing an Environment That Permits Emotional Expression
Identifying Feelings
Expressing Emotions
Educating for Human Values

Journal Writing
Suggestions for Classroom Journal Writing
Journals for Personal Insight

Establishing an Environment to Nurture the Sense of Self

Many educational programs attempt to enhance student self-esteem. Although there is no single agreed upon definition, self-esteem is generally viewed as the sum of people's attitudes about themselves, including their sense of self-respect and self-worth. To have high self-esteem, people must perceive themselves as worthwhile, lovable, competent, and capable of contributing to others in meaningful ways. Students with high self-regard believe in themselves and their abilities. They participate in school and other activities, learn from their mistakes, and are comfortable with not being "perfect."

School environments can be organized to enhance the self-esteem of all students. By creating a warm and caring atmosphere, adhering to democratic procedures, nurturing human dignity, and promoting cultural diversity, schools can make students feel welcome and accepted. Schools that successfully nurture self-esteem reveal common features. They are briefly described next.

Characteristics of Schools That Nurture Self-Esteem

Equity A schoolwide belief system exists that acknowledges that all students can learn and that makes sure that all are offered high-quality educational opportunities.

Community Students, school personnel, and family and community members share a common goal of making school positive, relevant, and meaningful.

Participation Students are actively involved in school governance, curriculum planning, and evaluation.

Collaborative Grouping At times, students are grouped heterogeneously so that they can value interdependence and cultural diversity.

Active Learning Processes Hands-on, problem-centered or project-based curriculums emphasize the personal and social relevance of what is being learned.

School conditions that undermine self-esteem include ambiguity about academic and behavioral expectations, disrespect among students and teachers, high levels of competition, and negative or low expectations. Practices such as tracking, authoritarian decision-making, competition, and a monocultural curriculum limit students' sense of self-worth. Enhancing the self-image of teachers so that they feel positive, affirmed, and encouraged is also an important aspect of any schoolwide effort. Teachers who respect and care for themselves find it easier to offer care, respect, and acceptance to others, thus modeling and encouraging greater self-acceptance among students.

The Apollo High School in Simi Valley, California, is dedicated to enhancing the self-esteem of its 300+ at-risk students. The school offers an alternative for students who have not succeeded in traditional secondary environments. To nurture students' sense of self-worth, the Apollo teachers base their programs on the four A's: Attention, Acceptance, Appreciation, and Affection.

Apollo students help establish and enforce school rules and have input into their learning experiences. At teacher-student meetings, which are held frequently, students discuss their opinions about school. The staff, valuing and respecting their ideas and suggestions, often make curricular adjustments to incorporate such suggestions.

The Apollo model is based on William Glasser's Control Theory which suggests that human behavior is motivated by five needs: survival, belonging, power, freedom, and fun. Brad Greene, the former principal of Apollo High School, and consultant with Glasser's Institute, helped teachers and administrators structure the school's environment to address these five needs. Discipline is not handled in traditional ways at Apollo but rather through problem-solving approaches with students' input. A number of common high school problems were resolved with the following procedures:

- Graffiti on school walls disappeared after students painted murals.

- Alcohol and drug abusers are not suspended but receive credit for attending support groups that help them discontinue drug use.

- Nonproductive students are motivated by lessons geared to their learning styles and interests.

The Apollo approach has proven effective. That is why William Glasser (1998) dedicated his book *The Quality School* to Apollo High School.

Self-Esteem Enhancers: Learning to Love Oneself

In addition to schoolwide endeavors, there is much teachers can do to enhance their students' self-concepts. This section highlights a variety of classroom approaches to bolster student self-esteem. It is important to recognize, however, that because of individual and cultural differences, some students thrive with group acknowledgment and others prefer individual feedback and interaction. All students benefit, however, from peer support and feedback.

Compliment Circles

One of the authors first participated in this activity at a faculty meeting. The principal placed the teachers in small groups of six to eight, carefully including those who seldom interacted with each other in this large suburban high school. The teachers were instructed to take turns giving and receiving compliments from everyone in the small group. Some of the heartfelt comments are still remembered and appreciated to this day!

Before conducting a compliment circle with a classroom of students, important ground rules must be considered. Each student should be the compliment recipient at least once during the school year. With a class of twenty-five to thirty students, a circle will require approximately a half hour, so time factors must be considered. Some teachers hold a circle for birthdays to spread them out over the year. Others plan them towards the end of the school year, and some teachers host them on an "as needed" basis such as when certain students might benefit from positive acknowledgment.

To begin, arrange chairs in a circle and identify the compliment receiver to sit in the center. Make sure students understand the following procedures: As the compliments are given, the receiver can only smile or say, "Thank you." Those who are sitting in the circle must each think of something to say that is honest and sincere. No "passes" or duplications are allowed. Some teachers like to create a written record of the compliments by assigning two students to copy what is said. The written version is then presented to the recipient. Such documents usually become lifelong, cherished items.

Another approach to conducting compliment circles is to tape-record classmates' messages. A tape recorder can be set up in a corner of the room for students to record compliments for an individual throughout the school day. At the end of the day, the teacher can send the tape home with the recipient.

For some students, compliment circles can serve as morale boosters and self-image transformers. For example, an eighth grade boy named Dave had been in several fights and had few friends at school. One of his teachers planned a compliment circle for Dave. He was visibly shaken by listening to the twenty-eight compliments from his peers. He later commented to the teacher, "I didn't know anybody thought of me like this!" Dave's behavior and demeanor softened after seeing himself through the eyes of his classmates and discovering new qualities to appreciate within himself.

Individual Acknowledgment

Some students prefer not to receive public acclaim, and others desire recognition both publicly and privately. A teacher can boost a student's self-esteem by individually communicating concern and support. As all teachers know, spending a few extra minutes with a student often provides important opportunities to recognize and affirm the value of the child. Success in an academic, social, or real world event can be acknowledged and suggestions given for transferring such skills or qualities into classroom applications.

During such encounters, student concerns can also be expressed. By using active listening, teachers can try to understand students' deep concerns and can rephrase the conversation to verify its message. It is important for teachers to avoid adding their own messages including advice, opinions, judgments, questions, or solutions. In active listening, the teacher expresses as accurately as possible what the student says and often a positive, personal relationship may be created. As a result, many students may decide to participate more fully in school.

During individual or whole-group discussions, it is important to communicate high expectations for student achievement. Even though some students may face difficult personal or academic challenges, teachers can express confidence that everyone is capable of accomplishing learning goals. By individually suggesting ways for students to jump-start their learning, many can find ways to meet such expectations.

After students have participated effectively in class activities, private and authentic recognition often encourages ongoing involvement; on the other hand, inappropriate types of praise should be avoided. Some students interpret praise or concern as indicators of low expectations. It is necessary then, that praise, when given, be sincere, appropriate for the task accomplished, and specifically descriptive of what the child did. As with many aspects of teaching, self-esteem is complex, and teachers must proceed with sensitivity in meeting the needs of their students.

Peer Support

Some students, who have difficulty with their grade-level work, often find success tutoring younger children. Many schools have formalized cross-age tutoring programs between high school and elementary school students or between various grade levels within the same school. Typically, leadership opportunities are reserved for high-achieving students, making it difficult for those with low self-esteem to participate in a variety of student relationships. Cross-age tutoring multiplies the opportunities for students to experience the satisfaction of helping others while boosting self-esteem in the process.

Some teachers have experimented with establishing peer support networks combining students who lack self-confidence with those who enjoy social interaction. Such networks offer a group approach to improving self-esteem, academic achievement, and the opportunity to develop friendships. Guidelines for establishing positive youth networks follow.

Peer Networks

1. Identify an even-numbered group of students who agree to meet once weekly, perhaps after school, during lunch, or before school. The students must be willing to make one phone call to their partner each evening. Participation in the peer support group should extend for at least one month.

2. At the first session, ask students to list academic and social strengths on sheets of paper. Such pages can be copied and distributed as resources to others in the group. Explain that students can call any person in the resource pool for assistance.

3. Additionally, during the first session, ask each student to reflect on academic or social challenges they would like to address so that their school experiences can be improved.

4. Assign each student to a peer partner to work with for a month or longer. Partners should make lists of all assignments or social efforts they will collaboratively undertake. The partners are responsible for phoning one another each evening to troubleshoot problems and to determine whether progress is being made.

5. At weekly meetings attended by both peer networkers and the classroom teacher, students can discuss and refine their support network. Evidence of progress can be celebrated and as goals are achieved, students may leave the network if they wish.

Support networks can assist students in acknowledging and using skills that are valuable to others. Through positive interdependence, students not only enhance self-esteem but improve their academic and social skills as well.

Guidelines for Enhancing Self-Esteem

Since classroom approaches to enhancing self-esteem are limitless, some brief suggestions are offered to address this important part of classroom learning.

1. Each day, acknowledge every student in the classroom either verbally or nonverbally.

2. Maintain and communicate high expectations for each student.

3. Seek student input on ways to make classroom learning more relevant and meaningful.

4. Involve students in establishing classroom rules, lessons, and assessment approaches.

5. Provide hands-on, multimodal learning experiences.

6. Use a variety of group processes, including pairs and small and large group options.

7. Assist students in identifying their strengths.

8. Acknowledge students' positive qualities and contributions in ways that are appropriate for each.

9. Help students understand that setbacks are a part of the learning process and that they often indicate ways to succeed in the future.

10. Model positive self-esteem for oneself.

Many educators' efforts to enhance student self-worth reach far beyond the classroom. In some elementary and secondary schools, students who would benefit from extra time and attention are identified. Their teachers volunteer to mentor one or more such students on an ongoing basis. Mentoring responsibilities include any or all of the following: meeting with the students during the teacher's regularly scheduled preparation time, occasional phone calls or visits at home, attending extracurricular activities the students are involved in, providing tutoring assistance, serving as advocates for the students at school, connecting students and their families with appropriate community agencies, and other activities that seem appropriate. Such gifts of time, attention, and love help students to discover that they are worthy and lovable. Their resultant positive identities will benefit them both inside and outside of school.

Setting and Achieving Goals

Students can discover aspects of their inner selves by identifying their interests, strengths, and preferred forms of recognition. Noting such information benefits students by making such attributes explicit and provides teachers with data for individualizing instruction. The following survey (see page 194) asks students to reflect on their interests, concerns, and preferred forms of praise. The survey can be used in numerous ways: as an ice breaker when new groups have formed, as a data-gathering source of confidential information, or as a small group discussion tool. Before administering the survey, it is advisable to ask students to specify any items they want to remain confidential.

Once students have completed the survey, they can discuss items they are willing to share with one other person, with a small group, or with the teacher. Ask students to reflect on what they learned about themselves from the activity, what they learned about others, what similarities and differences among themselves and their peers they discovered, and what might account for the contrasts. The data gathered from the student interest survey can assist teachers in planning curriculum and personalized projects that appeal to individual students.

Once interests and challenges are identified, students can move into identifying goals they want to pursue. Goal-setting is an important process because it offers concrete and tangible standards for identifying and monitoring progress. Also, when students determine individual goals, their attitude towards learning is frequently enhanced, resulting in improved academic performance.

STUDENT INTEREST SURVEY

Student Name: _____

1. Three words that describe me are _____
   _____

2. Things I like to do when I'm not at school are _____
   _____

3. The subject I do best at in school is _____

4. I would like to learn more about _____

5. Someday I would like to _____

6. Learning is fun when _____

7. If I could do anything I wanted at school, it would be _____

8. I like to get praise for _____

9. At school, when I've done something well, I like to be acknowledged by _____

10. I wonder a lot about _____

11. I like people who _____

12. Sometimes I worry about _____

13. I learn best when _____

14. One thing that really bothers me is _____

15. Something that really challenges me is _____

16. One thing I know about myself is _____

For student-determined goals to be effective, they must meet several criteria: they should be specific rather than general, short-term rather than long-term, harder rather than easier, realistic and not idealistic, and action-oriented rather than passive. The following form can be used to help students identify and meet their personal goals.

INDIVIDUAL STUDENT GOAL SHEET

Student Name: _____   Date: _____

My specific goal for today (this week) (this project) is _____
_____
_____

The skills I need to accomplish this goal are _____
_____
_____

The reason I think I can attain this goal is _____
_____
_____

Possible challenges I might encounter are _____
_____
_____

Resources and people I can go to for help are _____
_____
_____

(Please respond to the following at the end of the activity)

I met or did not meet my goal because _____
_____

From this experience, I learned _____
_____

My level of satisfaction with what I accomplished is _____
_____

What I feel about this project is _____
_____
_____

Goal-setting can be used at any grade level with any content. In addition to academic topics, goals can be identified for social skills such as courtesy, sharing, or collaborative problem-solving, or for behavior issues such as raising hands before speaking, completing assignments on time, or attending class regularly.

When students have met their goals, it is important to point out that successful outcomes resulted from their personal effort. It is also helpful to identify the techniques students used that led to their success. Conversely, when students are unsuccessful, explain that the failure was due to a lack of appropriate strategies rather than lack of intelligence or potential. Because many students do not understand why they fail, it is vital for them to gain insight into ways to improve their performance in the future.

Challenging Students to Learn

Occasionally, students may pursue goals at an inappropriate challenge level. When students succeed at easy classroom activities, they often attribute their success to the ease of the task. When they succeed at extremely difficult endeavors, they often credit luck. Neither type of success enhances a sense of self-worth. Feelings of pride and accomplishment result from succeeding at activities that are at the edge of one's ability level, or in the Soviet psychologist's Lev Vygotsky's terminology, "in the zone of proximal development." Students need opportunities to learn what is just beyond their grasp.

When developing challenging classroom procedures, teachers and students can discuss how to set stimulating goals. Ask students whether their goals are just beyond reach. The following questions can help students learn to identify appropriate challenges.

1. What ability level is challenging for me?
2. How might games, simulations, or practice sessions help me learn?
3. What would I pursue in depth if I had the opportunity?
4. What kinds of learning opportunities are most meaningful to me?
5. What motivates me to do my best?
6. What learning processes am I using?
7. Are there other learning processes that might be more effective?
8. How can I learn from my mistakes?
9. What kind of feedback is helpful? From whom?
10. How do I want to be assessed?

Teachers who are successful at challenging their students offer feedback that sustains self-confidence and encourages students to take control of their learning. By nurturing risk-taking and celebrating successes, teachers can instill a love of learning in their students that helps them face the world with confidence and curiosity.

Olympian Goal-Setting

Marilyn King, a former Olympic athlete, has investigated what gives peak performers their competitive edge. Marilyn herself was a member of the U.S. Olympics team in 1972 and 1976 and competed in the pentathlon. While preparing for the 1980 Olympics, Marilyn suffered a back injury that resulted in her being bedridden for four months. During that time, while unable to practice physically, she watched films of successful pentathletes, visualizing and mentally rehearsing herself doing the same events. Despite her lack of physical preparation, Marilyn placed second in the trials, and believes her success was the result of her well-prepared psychological state.

After her years of training and competing in the Olympics, Marilyn began wondering why she was able to accomplish so much physically when her athletic skills were, in reality, only slightly above average. To answer this question, she decided to interview other Olympians about their experiences with superior performance. Marilyn hoped to identify any commonalties the peak performers shared.

During their discussions, three consistent elements were identified by the athletes. Peak performance appeared to be based on passion, vision, and action. Passion was defined as "knowing what really matters on a gut level." The Olympians asserted that what appeared to be willpower and discipline to others was actually inner passion and emotional commitment. Being passionate about something, they claimed, unlocked the energy and creativity necessary to achieve one's goal.

The second component of peak performance was identified as vision. This referred to envisioning one's achievement in detail as well as the "how to" images of attaining the goal. The athletes stated that it was important to understand the influence of self-fulfilling prophecies and to learn how to control one's inner imagery.

The third component, action, underscored the importance of taking action on a daily basis according to a plan that moves toward goal accomplishment. Such plans included short, intermediate, and long-term goals as well as a daily challenge. While physical skills were important to the Olympian athletes, they determined that superior physical skills were not the primary factor in peak performance. Far more important were passion, vision, and the dedication to daily work at attaining one's goal.

Another interesting aspect of peak performance consists of social support. The Olympic athletes stated that their families did not push them into their activities, but rather helped them believe in their ability to succeed at their goals. Sometimes instead of their families, it was a coach or a friend who believed in the individual and was there to cheer him on. The Olympians concluded that high performers are not gifted with unique talents. Instead, they have innate abilities common to all of us if we choose to develop them.

Marilyn King now teaches others how to apply the skills of peak performance in any endeavor. She has worked with numerous schools and districts helping students excel academically. To unite body, mind, and spirit in achieving goals, Marilyn recommends that students pursue the following guidelines and push the upper limits of their ability in any endeavor.

Peak Performance Guidelines

1. Identify what you truly care about, want to do, or want to be.

2. Determine the skills, traits, and characteristics needed to achieve the desired goal.

3. Identify the qualities you already possess and those that need to be developed.

4. Select the traits you want to acquire.

5. Identify a knowledgeable mentor who would be willing to help you develop the new skills.

6. Find another person who is also reaching for success and wants to be your training partner.

7. Identify any obstacles that must be overcome, and develop action plans to address them.

8. Create some form of measuring stick or award to acknowledge success along the way.

9. Make a short-term contract to achieve your goal.

10. Affirm on a daily basis that you are already whatever it is you want to be.

This process for achieving peak performance has been used successfully beyond the classroom with Olympic athletes, astronauts, and corporate executives. It has also been successful with inner-city youth who, against numerous odds, have succeeded in earning their high school diplomas. Successful people share the qualities of passion, vision, and action. Ordinary people are capable of extraordinary accomplishments when they incorporate the same three qualities King has identified into their behavior.

Thinking Skills

Many educators, philosophers, and psychologists agree that an important goal of education is the teaching of thinking. Today's society demands creative, critical thinkers. Yet educational methods that focus on single right or wrong answers do not produce this kind of thinking. Students must be prepared to face a world of rapid change, seemingly unanswerable questions, and complex personal decisions.

The teaching of thinking meets individual and societal needs and benefits both. The success of our institutions, private enterprise, and the democratic system are all based on a population's ability to analyze problems, make thoughtful decisions, and create workable solutions. Ethical, altruistic, creative, and long-range thinking are desirable and needed attributes of an educated person at the dawn of the twenty-first century. By acquiring effective thinking processes, students can probe their own inner natures, learn to self-monitor and adjust, and discern who and what they are and can be, both in their personal and professional lives.

Thinking skills programs have been developed and implemented in schools around the country. Arthur Costa's (2001) book *Developing Minds* contains an overview of thirty such programs. Costa and others caution against teaching thinking as a separate topic, recommending instead that thinking skills be taught in conjunction with regular classroom content. They suggest that educators teach rich and interesting content, as well as an array of cognitive skills so students can meaningfully use information, academically, socially, and personally. It is helpful if teachers model the ongoing development of their own thinking skills such as intellectual curiosity, flexibility, goal-setting, and problem-solving to encourage similar efforts in their students.

There are many types of thinking skills. Some of the terms commonly used include higher-order thinking skills, learning-to-learn skills, questioning strategies, decision-making, problem-solving, and metacognition. Although it is beyond the scope of this book to explore the spectrum of thinking skills, the next section introduces classroom activities that engage metacognitive processes.

Metacognition

One way that human beings are distinct from other forms of life is our ability to reflect upon our own thinking. The term *metacognition* literally means "thinking about one's thinking." Through reflecting on how they learn at school, students can gain metacognitive insight about their individual thinking processes. There are several aspects to metacognition. Some include awareness of preferred modes of learning, persistence with tasks, goal-setting, attitudes about education, risk-taking, and paying attention. To assist students in gaining metacognitive awareness, teachers can hold class discussions or create questionnaires asking students to reflect on their perceptions of themselves as learners. Such processes give insight into individual characteristics and attitudes that can be beneficial or detrimental to their thinking.

Through self-observation, students can glimpse the control they possess in academic and nonacademic situations. Ultimately, responsibility for commitment, attitude, attention, and persistence rests with them. This metacognitive awareness can encourage students to make positive choices for effectively refining their behavior.

Taking Control of the Learning Process

Another aspect of metacognition entails giving students the tools to control their own learning experiences. At the outset of an assignment, give students an overview of what is expected of them and how best to proceed. Ideally, they should be informed of the facts and concepts they must master, and which strategies or procedures are necessary for success. Frequently, asking students to consider what should happen before, during, and after a task provides them with information to effectively manage their learning. For example, if students were asked to illustrate the process of photosynthesis, they might initially ask if they knew enough to complete the task, if they needed additional information, and if so, where and how would they find it. While drawing a photosynthesis model, students could decide whether they had adequate information, whether their model was accurate, and if not, how to revise it. After their drawing was completed, they could reflect on what they learned and what else they might like to know.

To teach students how to manage their assignments, the following form (see page 200) asks questions to organize learning tasks.

Until recent decades, little recognition was given to the fact that thinking skills could be taught and learned. The above information suggests only a few key components of thinking to integrate into instruction. When applied to classroom instruction, students can learn more effectively, enhance their intellectual processes, and gain valuable insight into their nature as learners.

ASSIGNMENT PLANNING AND REFLECTING FORM

Student Name: _____

Before you begin this assignment, answer the following:

Brief description of the assignment: _____
_____

What I already know about this topic: _____
_____

Facts or concepts I must know or learn to complete this assignment: _____
_____

Resources I have to turn to for assistance: _____
_____

Activities that will help me succeed at this assignment include: _____
_____

What I should do before beginning this assignment: _____
_____

After you have completed this assignment, answer the following:

What I did to complete this assignment: _____
_____

On completing this assignment, I found I learned the following facts and concepts: _____
_____

On completing this assignment, I learned the following about myself as a student: _____
_____

I am now curious about: _____
_____

My feelings about this task were: _____
_____

Emotionally Intelligent Education

Research in the neurosciences suggests that emotions and cognition, long considered separate and distinct from each other, are clearly linked. Dr. Paul MacLean (1990), a former researcher at the National Institute of Mental Health, claimed that information is processed not only by the neocortex, which controls higher-order thinking processes, but also by the limbic system, which is the emotional center of the brain.

MacLean asserted that positive emotions such as love and humor facilitate the neocortex's higher-order thought processes, while negative feelings such as tension, fear, anger, or distrust inhibit learning and higher order thinking. Whether a student learns is at least partially dependent on emotions that affect all thought processes. Emotions are also a key component of intrapersonal intelligence. Teachers can assist students in positive affective ways to express their emotions in the classroom. In so doing, they enhance learning.

Engaging Feelings in the Classroom

Emotional issues are overlooked in some classrooms, but it is frequently this facet of intrapersonal intelligence that determines academic and lifetime opportunities for success. As Daniel Goleman (1995) has noted, emotional intelligence enables us to recognize our feelings, make positive decisions, manage distressing moods, and feel hopeful and optimistic toward life. For teachers interested in nurturing this aspect of intrapersonal intelligence, there are ways to foster healthy emotional interaction in educational settings. Some approaches include establishing a positive classroom environment, teaching emotional awareness and

appropriate methods of emotional expression, and offering feedback on emotional behavior. Some suggestions follow for addressing the affective domain of human experience in the classroom.

Establishing an Environment That Permits Emotional Expression

The classroom environment can facilitate emotional expression of both students and teachers. To determine whether a classroom adequately encompasses the affective domain, teachers can reflect on their facilitation of emotional expression. Consider the following questions:

Are lessons taught with emotional expression?

What kinds of feelings are encouraged in the classroom? From whom?

What behaviors or feelings are discouraged? Why?

How are emotions expressed—verbally, physically, or visually?

What tools do students possess to express their feelings? What tools might they need?

When are feelings expressed—at lunch or recess, during math?

How might appropriate expression of emotion be encouraged in the classroom?

Responses to such questions help teachers gain insight into their classrooms' emotional climate and their own facility with emotional expression in the school setting.

To create an enhanced affective atmosphere in the classroom, teachers can intentionally increase the emotional impact of their instruction. Students respond both to content that is taught and how it is taught. When planning lessons, it's possible to highlight the potential feelings associated with different subjects or topics. Is there humor, pathos, courage, or intrigue to emphasize so that the minds and hearts of students become engaged in their learning?

One high school algebra teacher tired of the negative reaction his students had whenever story problems were assigned. Deciding to relieve student anxiety, he donned a monster mask one day during math class and announced that he was the story problem monster. In a fearsome, booming voice he stomped around the room, bemoaning the ghoulish nature of story problems, and howling the students' typical complaints about such assignments. Delighted with their teacher's display of humor and fun, the students eagerly attacked the day's assignment and laughed through similar assignments in the weeks that followed.

In addition to teaching with feeling, educators can teach students about emotional expression through appropriate role modeling. By identifying and expressing their own feelings, students learn that classrooms can accommodate this dimension of human experience. A teacher might want to reflect on current emotional issues or events that are relevant for the students and then risk speaking from his heart. Chances are the students will respond in kind.

Asking students to share their emotional reactions to coursework involves them in expressing feelings in a low-risk way. Such discussions often reveal unexpected insights about class lessons and give students the opportunity to reflect on their affective experience of school work. By encouraging honest answers, teachers can monitor and adjust assignments to reduce anxiety or boredom. Conversations might follow about the importance of positive emotion for enhancing learning, and teachers and students can work together to make the classroom and its activities as positive as possible.

Time might also be set aside on a weekly, monthly, or as-needed basis for class meetings when students and teachers openly discuss issues of concern to the group. By allotting time for emotionally charged topics, the teacher demonstrates that such discussions are valuable learning opportunities. Spontaneous emotional events that erupt in the classroom also provide rich opportunities for reflection.

By modeling appropriate emotional expression and initiating conversations about affective issues, teachers can create classrooms that nurture students holistically. When students tap their emotional nature, they connect with a wellspring of energy to apply to learning and remembering.

Identifying Feelings

By acknowledging and experiencing a variety of feelings, students develop a strong emotional foundation that enriches their lives. Frequently, however, many children lack the vocabulary to identify their emotions and can only indicate a limited range of feelings such as "happy" or "sad." Creating an emotional vocabulary helps students name and understand inner experiences. Some ideas follow to expand affective vocabulary.

Ask students to name diverse feelings. One way to do so is to identify one or more emotions for each letter of the alphabet. Another is to create broad categories of feelings such as happy, sad, mad, confused, strong, weak, and fearful. To work with feeling categories, have students brainstorm at least ten words synonymous with each category. For example, under "confused," students might add "addled, anxious, baffled, bewildered, bothered, confounded, disoriented, embarrassed, foggy, flustered, mixed-up, muddled, panicky, and uncertain."

After several emotions have been identified, ask students to consider how many of the listed feelings they have personally experienced, how such feelings affected them physically and intellectually, when they experienced them, and how and why their feelings shifted.

Teachers can display emotions alphabets or categories of feelings so that such information is available to tap for discussions or in written work. Such displays also serve to remind students of the range of emotional experiences commonly encountered within.

Expressing Emotions

Students need opportunities to express their feelings and to channel them into constructive outlets. Once students can articulate their affective experiences, it may be appropriate to provide options for self-expression. To assess current emotional behaviors, teachers may ask students to respond to the following inventory.

Once students have completed the inventory, ask them to review it and add the name of someone with whom they can be happy, worried, or excited.

FEELINGS INVENTORY

Most people experience and express feelings in a variety of ways. List below how you typically respond to different emotions:

1. When I am happy, I often _____

2. When I am worried, I _____

3. When I am confident, I _____

4. When I am nervous, I often _____

5. When I am bored, I often _____

6. When I am excited, I _____

7. When I am scared, I might _____

8. When I am confused, I _____

9. When I am upset, I sometimes _____

10. When I am feeling content, I _____

Next, organize students into small groups to discuss how they currently express emotions, sharing two or more feelings they are willing to address with classmates. (They should not be expected to share the names of individuals they have listed.) Also, ask students to consider how their emotional reactions affect others. Next, the groups can generate alternative responses to each inventory item. Once completed, everyone's responses can be shared to generate multiple options for expressing common feelings. One group of eighth grade students who had been discussing their responses to different life events created the following list to display in their classroom:

When You Feel Upset, You Can . . .

1. Have a discussion with someone you trust.

2. Go for a walk, run, or do some kind of physical activity.

3. Listen to music that you enjoy.

4. Do some art work of your choice.

5. Write in a journal.

6. Take a shower.

7. Cry!

8. Go shopping.

9. Brainstorm all the possible ways to react to the situation and choose one.

10. Play an instrument.

11. Talk it out with a pet.

12. Play a game.

13. Seek advice.

14. Watch a video or go to a movie.

15. Know that your feelings will shift and change, so be patient with yourself.

Expressing Feelings through the Arts

Intentional instruction in emotional behavior can nurture significant intrapersonal development. There are many creative approaches to educating the emotions in the classroom. The arts, including the visual arts, drama, movement, or music help students access their feelings while simultaneously relieving stress, hurt, or excessive excitement. When teachers sense that emotional issues raised in the classroom should be processed, they can review the following suggestions to identify which might be beneficial:

Visual Art Suggest that students draw their feelings using color, abstract shapes, or images to represent the issues they are controlling. Students might also watch films or videos that address their concerns.

Music When some students could benefit from relaxing, ask them to listen to soothing background music. Students could try their hand at composing music or writing lyrics to express feelings. Some may even want to choreograph a dance to familiar or original music. Certain musical selections can be played to evoke specific feelings such as Tchaikovsky's *Nutcracker Suite* for happiness, Dvorak's *Symphony No. 5 in E Minor* for sadness, and Edvard Grieg's *Peer Gynt Suite* for fear.

Role-Play Hypothetical, impromptu situations can be performed to highlight emotional issues. Mini-dramas might deal with fictitious characters but real events.

Creative Writing Students can create clusters or mindmaps, beginning with their feelings as central concepts. Their associations can be synthesized into poems or paragraphs. Stream-of-consciousness journal writing or story writing also serves as an appropriate outlet for some students.

Sculpting Students can use clay to sculpt in abstract or representative forms the emotions they are experiencing such as "angry" or "happy" shapes.

Although the arts offer languages for feelings, some students require other forms of emotional expression. For those who become especially aggressive or angry, time-out options such as running laps or hitting a punching bag in the gym can release excessive tension. (It is especially important with such students to teach the conflict management techniques described in the interpersonal chapter.) Some students benefit by processing their feelings through talking with a classmate in a quiet part of the room or out in the hallway.

Literature containing emotionally charged issues, in fiction or nonfiction stories, books, or articles, offers a springboard for discussing and expressing feelings. Once a selection for sharing is identified, prepare the students for the context of the material, read it, and then begin a class discussion. Some excellent resources that address the feeling life of students through literature include *Helping Children Cope* by Joan Fassler (2001), *Helping Children Cope with Separation and Loss* by Claudia Jewett Jarratt (1994), and *The Read-Aloud Handbook* (2001) and *Read All About It: Great Read Aloud Stories, Poems, and Newspaper Pieces for Preteens and Teens* (1993) by Jim Trelease.

Occasionally, a student's emotional needs may require the help of a school counselor, intervention or at-risk specialist, psychologist, or psychiatrist. Both teachers and students should know whom to turn for help from available community resources. Teachers can also ask students to identify individuals they trust in times of need. The following form may prove helpful for identifying such resources.

RESOURCES FOR PERSONAL SUPPORT

Consider those whom you trust, and list their phone numbers:

Friend: _____

No. _____

Teacher: _____

No. _____

Neighbor: _____

No. _____

Relative: _____

No. _____

Counselor: _____

No. _____

Other: _____

No. _____

Identify by name and phone number the following community resources available, should you or a friend need their services:

Emergency (911) _____

Crisis Line _____

Children's Protective Services _____

Youth Suicide Prevention _____

Mental Health Center _____

Runaway Hot Line _____

Hospital _____

Alcohol/Drug Help Line _____

Youth Services _____

Family Services _____

Community Information Line _____

Public Health _____

Other _____

To better meet specific emotional needs, some schools are integrating human services into their programs, cutting across the traditional boundaries of education, mental health, and welfare. Such schools are frequently called "full service schools." They offer mental health programs, drug and alcohol dependency services, career counseling, and family welfare services.

When schools intentionally teach forms of affective expression, students can experience positive emotional growth. So far the activities above address creating a healthy classroom environment, enhancing affective awareness, seeking support from others, and learning positive ways to self-express. There are, however, other dimensions of intrapersonal intelligence that have not yet been considered. Students also need opportunities to understand values and ultimately develop their own value systems. The next section begins to address these needs.

Educating for Human Values

The word value is derived from the Latin word, *valere*, meaning to be worth, to be strong. Values refer to the ideals that are significant in our lives. They are established by family, school, society, religion, and our personal belief systems. Some values may be maintained throughout one's entire life, and others may change as a result of experience and maturity.

While debate exists about whether schools should teach values, students are confronted with a variety of daily distractions. It appears that willingly or not, schools must address some form of ethical education. One approach is to teach commonly accepted values that underlie both traditional religious and secular principles such as integrity, altruism, justice, honesty, human dignity, and diligence. All students need opportunities to identify their ethical perspectives, to find inner purpose and direction from their value systems,

and then translate that commitment into their daily behavior.

Many school subjects are replete with ethical issues. Teachers can facilitate thought-provoking discussions of literature, for example, by asking students to reflect on the ethical dilemmas of characters. In science and technology, students can consider the implications of technological advances as well as social and political priorities in practice today. In history, contrasting accounts of the same event can be shared and the underlying ethical perspective of each perspective probed.

Teachers can assist students in discerning personally held values by identifying and defining such concepts. Give students the following list. In small groups ask them to define and give examples of how such values are expressed in daily life.

Some Common Values

Altruism	Honesty	Compassion
Humility	Consideration	Integrity
Courage	Interdependence	Courtesy
Justice	Creativity	Kindness
Determination	Love	Dignity
Loyalty	Diligence	Mercy
Empathy	Patience	Enthusiasm
Peace	Excellence	Respect
Faithfulness	Responsibility	Forgiveness
Self-discipline	Friendliness	Tolerance
Generosity	Trust	Helpfulness
	Truthfulness	

Students can identify which values they currently hold and which ones they might like to adopt. By using the goal-setting processes mentioned earlier, students can select a new value to integrate into their behavior. Needless to say, the live models that teachers and parents present are far more powerful than any list of terms. School-wide conversations with families and communities can also be held to identify the values that might be inculcated within the school. It may also be necessary to point out to students that if they want to establish and live by a value system, it is necessary to act on such beliefs. Speaking up for one's values, acting on them, and maintaining them over time is indicative of a person whose life is founded on personal integrity.

As students clarify and express the values they hold, they will also confront the value systems of others. Learning to defend one's beliefs without diminishing those with different perspectives is an important skill to develop. Classrooms can demonstrate the respectful free speech that democracy requires. Through opportunities to interact with competing value systems, students may find their interpersonal and intrapersonal intelligences are strengthened.

Have you learned lessons only of those who admired you, and were tender with you and stood aside for you? Have you not learned great lessons from those who braced themselves against you and disputed the passage with you?

—Walt Whitman, 1860

Journal Writing

Some years ago, a study of high-achieving students in a Yale University graduating class sought to determine whether there were common denominators for their success. It was discovered that the top 10% of exceptional students were clearly focused on their goals and ambitions. Of those, the top 1% were distinguished by the fact that they took time to write out their goals and ambitions. A follow-up study of the students from that class over the next ten years revealed that those who clearly articulated their vision for the future were among the most successful in their chosen work, and the most successful of those were still taking the time to write out their goals.

Some of the greatest thinkers, inventors, and creative geniuses throughout history have kept journals. Leonardo da Vinci's notebooks are filled with ideas, observations and insights, sketches, and plans for his works of art and inventions. Samuel Pepys is still remembered for the diary he kept in the seventeenth century. Einstein and Schweitzer both maintained journals.

It appears that the simple act of writing moves abstractions into reality. Gabriele Rico, author of *Writing the Natural Way*, noted in an interview that "writing is always there for us to use for the kind of exploration that leads to discovery, recognition, and new learning about ourselves, our feelings, and the world in general."

When students are encouraged to keep journals in any subject-matter area, they often make similar discoveries about themselves. These insights, springing from the boundless resources of intrapersonal intelligence, can be brought into consciousness and reality.

Suggestions for Classroom Journal Writing

There are many ways to incorporate journal writing into the classroom. Some suggestions follow.

Students can be asked once daily or weekly to write about one or more concerns they have about the content or process. Ideally, they should be allowed to keep their journals private while using class time to write. Needless to say, much of the value of personal writing lies in the students' confidence that their journals will be free from grading and public sharing. Periodically, however, ask students to read over their writing from previous days and make observations about their progress, or to quote particular comments they are willing to share with others. Once again, no grades!

Journal writing can easily complement the goals of the teacher and help students maintain records of their progress. Journals can be used to explore thinking about any subject. Sometimes after reading what we have written, we are surprised to learn what we think!

Asking students to write what they know about a subject before beginning its study can establish a baseline of knowledge and an anticipatory mindset. Just three or so minutes of such writing at the outset of a new topic can pay high dividends in terms of student involvement and later reflection on the scope of their learning.

At the end of class, five minutes of journal writing can help consolidate prior learning and review content at an effective time. Teachers can suggest a few questions to "prime the pump." For example, "What did you learn today that was new to you?" "How did you feel about the learning experience?" "How can you apply what you learned to other subjects or in other areas of your life?" "In the light of what you learned today, what do you anticipate you will be learning about next?" "What are a couple of questions that would be appropriate to ask tomorrow?" "What can you add to the subject from your personal experience?"

Later on, after students are used to journal writing, the teacher can suggest that they do a five- or ten-minute "fast-write." A "fast-write" consists of writing as quickly as possible everything they can remember about what they just learned. Or, students can make a mindmap or cluster before they write. For many, as discussed previously, this process can springboard them into accessing feelings, insights, and connections that may have been unacknowledged. Also, it may be useful to create a format for journals such as using the left page for mindmaps, and the right page for writing. Some people combine the two on the same page.

Many teachers and students have found that journal writing yields significant improvement in understanding and retention that can result in increased scores on both standardized and perfor-

mance measures. In addition, students identify their emotional reactions and insights into classroom learning.

Journals for Personal Insight

Keeping a journal is also one means for probing intrapersonal intelligence. Students can explore facets of their identities through writing processes that emphasized self-awareness and acceptance. To do so, teachers can assign journaling sessions where older students consider their self-awareness. Simple processes follow:

1. Ask students to write ten "I am" sentences that address personal understanding. In preparing to write, students can consider the knowledge gained from life experiences, interactions with others, from their world views, and from qualities they would like to develop.

2. To foster self-acceptance, ask students to identify positive qualities they already possess and others they might like to change. After the ten "I am" sentences are written, ask students to classify the sentences according to several categories: 1) their physical attributes, 2) emotional attributes, 3) mental qualities, 4) roles in relationship to others such as sister, son, or friend. Students can evaluate their responses in terms of what is or is not growth-promoting. Then additional statements can be written that include "I lack . . . ," then the ideal correlate "I will . . . ," onto "I want to . . . ," and finally "I am."

3. Students might also reflect on other aspects of self-acceptance such as images they attempt to live up to, constant changes they must cope with, and the answers to some of life's questions they must live without. They might also evaluate their own level of self-esteem and identify how it could be improved.

4. Explain to students that self-actualization consists of capitalizing on one's strengths and abilities, making decisions in one's and

others' best interests, and remaining flexible and open to life's possibilities and events. As students ponder their ability to self-actualize, they can describe their potential, how they plan to actualize it, and how such actualization may ultimately benefit others. To help students work toward such possibilities, ask them to specify their goals and the steps they might take to achieve them.

5. After any or all of the above activities have been completed, students can specify what they would be willing to share with a small group of classmates. In small groups, students can share, discuss, and receive feedback on their journal entries and perhaps commit themselves to some form of personal growth.

Getting to Know Oneself through Others

Gardner maintains that the personal intelligences are inextricably linked and that under ordinary circumstances, neither can develop without the other. It is through relationships with others that we gain knowledge of ourselves. Observing how others respond to us provides much information that shapes our sense of self. When intrapersonal intelligence becomes well developed, such self-knowledge is often used to balance out personal goals with those of the larger community. Ultimately, by knowing ourselves well, we are able to contribute to the betterment of others. Our sense of self, as Gardner suggests, results from a fusion of one's interpersonal and intrapersonal knowledge.

Many of the strategies suggested elsewhere in this book yield intrapersonal insights. Whenever students interact with others, their intrapersonal knowledge can be enhanced by reflecting on what they learned. Simple questions can be asked that promote self-awareness. For example, what feedback did they receive from others? How did they respond to it? Was the feedback accurate? Why or why not? What did the students learn about themselves from their own reactions to the activity? Which of these reactions do they feel good about? What is one thing they might wish to improve?

Teachers can also develop activities that encourage students to consider their growing sense of self. Some suggestions follow.

Gaining Intrapersonal Insights from Interpersonal Feedback

1. As a group ice breaker, ask students to interview each other. The information gained from such interviews can be used to introduce everyone to the class. Interview questions might consist of:

   What would your life motto be?

   What three wishes would you like granted?

   What values guide your behavior?

   Who is your hero or heroine?

   What is one of your fears?

   If you could change anything about yourself, what would it be?

   If you could change anything about the world, what would it be?

   When the introductions are being made, classmates should feel free to ask additional questions of the student being introduced.

2. In pairs, students might explore personal perceptions of one another. Topics that can guide such conversations might include:

   Who I think I am

   Who you think I am

   Who I think you think I am

   Who you think you are

   Who I think you are

   Who you think I think you are

   When the conversations are complete, ask students to write in their journals how their self-perceptions compare with the perceptions of others.

3. Students can select an object that has some special meaning in their lives. Perhaps the object has affected their personal development, perhaps it has sentimental value, or maybe it is a symbol of their future. Students can bring their objects to class, describe what they mean, and tell a story of the role such items represent in their lives. Again, classmates should be able to pose questions at the end of the brief descriptions.

4. Students can write character sketches of themselves. Since these will be shared with the rest of the class, fictitious names are necessary to keep the writings anonymous at first. In their character descriptions, students can include a variety of details about themselves, their behaviors and the reasons for such actions, their desires and goals, and their perceived impact upon others. On an agreed-upon date, the anonymous descriptions can be brought to class with the students' real names written and concealed on the backs of their papers. The teacher can then organize students into small groups, hand out character descriptions of those in the group, and have the students read and discuss the writings. Each group should determine whose descriptions they are reading and explain the reasons for their matches or mismatches.

Reflecting on the Wonder and Purpose of Life

▪ ▪ ▪ ▪ ▪ ▪ ▪ ▪ ▪ ▪ ▪ ▪ ▪ ▪ ▪ ▪ ▪ ▪

Life for all of us is a Great Mystery. The big questions like, "What is the universe?" "Where does it come from?" "Who am I?" "What is my purpose?" are the questions we all come face to face with eventually.

—Herbert Martin, Professor, Department of Teacher Education, California State University, Sacramento

The word *education* evolved from the Latin *educare*, which means to draw out or lead forth. The original definition of the word, then, suggests that schooling can facilitate the expression of what is contained within one's mind, heart, and the deepest recesses of being. Both children and adults seek meaning in their experiences and answers to humanity's ageless questions. All of us must arrive at our own explanations of life's mysteries, but it is possible for classrooms to create the conditions for wonder and awe to flourish. Encouraging the expression of students' insights and helping them grapple with meaning-making educates in relevant and profound ways.

How can we cultivate a sense of wonder in children? How can we assist them in expressing their insights and posing big questions? One answer is to expose them to a curriculum enriched with all eight intelligences. Language can be used to reflect and discuss feelings, thoughts, and ideals significant to each student; math reveals numerical principles in operation throughout nature and on a universal scale; games evoke challenge and delight, while relaxation and visualization ready our bodies and minds for contemplation; gardening or caring for animals reveals the interdependence of life; dance, the visual arts, and music all express insights through the symbol systems of the arts; and the personal intelligences provide opportunities for interaction which enable us to know and understand others and ourselves better. Teaching and learning through all the intelligences let us perceive through multiple lenses the wholeness within. Such holistic teaching also enables children to discover an inherent area of personal interest and fascination that may spark a lifetime of personal or professional pursuit.

Some teachers desire to encourage students to wonder, question, and forge meaning in their lives. We offer processes below that tap students' imaginations and encourage them to ponder life's possibilities.

Classroom Activities to Nurture a Sense of Wonder

1. Students can develop their own original poems, myths, legends, and tall tales to explain the mysteries of life.

2. They can write, draw, or compose songs about events that changed their lives and what was learned from such experiences.

3. Teachers can suggest that students travel into time to view themselves and personal concerns from a distant perspective. Suggest that they create future newspaper headlines that refer to their achievements.

4. Engage in classroom discussions about what is important and of value in life.

5. Ask students to identify the qualities, values, and actions featured in stories, movies, or the news.

6. Show students works of art and ask them to respond in verbal or nonverbal ways.

7. Suggest that students write a letter to an unknown person introducing themselves with descriptions of their appearance, activities, interests, significant people in their lives, and their hopes and dreams for the future. This letter may be to a prospective penpal, employer, or someone they would like to meet.

8. Have students create self-portraits by drawing a diamond shape, circle, or crest, and dividing it into a number of parts to include any of the following: their physical attributes, intellectual qualities, artistic skills, emotional characteristics, social qualities, fears, wishes and dreams they hold, major turning points, and essential values. Students can then draw or write in each section what is most descriptive of them and share their self-portraits with classmates if desired. The same activity may also be done in the future tense by drawing the attributes and qualities they hope to acquire a year from now or five years from now.

9. Students might be encouraged to pay attention to their intuitive hunches while using reason to check the accuracy of their intuitions.

Finding Purpose in School and Life

When planning lessons to teach any topic or concept, educators should reflect on an important question: "So what?" Students want and deserve to know the relevance of what they are learning in their lives. They wonder, "What can I do with this information?" "Can it be used outside of school?" "How will it benefit others?" When beginning a new lesson or unit, teachers can engage their classes in discussions of the larger purpose underlying coursework. In addition to the instructor's perspective, students can articulate the meaningfulness of classroom assignments for them. Ideally, each student should be able to identify one valid reason for investing time, energy, and effort in school work. In fact, Howard Gardner has asserted that all educational endeavors should begin with existential questions, such as "Who are we? Why are we here?" He realizes, however, that standards and testing diminish the interests in existential concerns. If interested in reading an interview with Gardner on teachers.net, go to http://teachers.net/archive/gardiner092899.html.

Some teachers are interested in addressing one of the greatest questions of all—the purpose of life—with their students. Some begin such discussions by defining the concept of purpose that compels us to act. It is a process that continues to unfold throughout our lives. Purpose offers a sense of direction and a means of contributing to the betterment of others.

One way for students to tap their own sense of purpose is through written exercises that explore intrinsic motivators. To prepare students, ask them to get paper and a pencil and relax quietly in their seats. Explain that you will ask a series of questions that explore one's inner sense of direction. As you pose the questions, students should write down key words and phrases or make note of any fleeting images that appear. Explain that you will ask the questions slowly, providing time for them to seek answers from within:

- What are you good at?
- What have you always loved?
- What do you care for the most?
- What have you always known?
- What do you feel compelled to do?

After asking such questions, suggest that students continue to sit for a moment or two in silence, noting their ideas or images. Then organize them into pairs or small groups to share any insights they want to volunteer. For those who did not tap any inner drives during the exercise, suggest that they create answers that appear most appropriate for them. Students may also discuss what aspects of their schooling contribute to their perceived life purpose.

It may seem that adolescents and teenagers would benefit most from reflecting on life purpose, but young children often posses a very strong sense of direction. In fact, Walters and Gardner (1986) claimed that some children have a "crystallizing experience" at a very young age. During such moments, they become intrigued about a topic or field such as the joy in solving mathematical problems or in playing beautiful music. Such moments often ignite a lifelong dedication to a career or avocation. Frequently, young children value acknowledgment from adults who make them believe their childhood dreams will come true. Educators can open the doors to wonder.

Self-Directed Learning: An Intrapersonal Learning Approach

Self-directed learning is an outstanding example of intrapersonal education since it is founded upon student choice and autonomy. Some conventional educational approaches are based on autocratic principles where teachers serve as authority figures and infrequent opportunities exist for student participation in decision-making. In self-directed classrooms, however, the student rather than the teacher is the central decision-maker, and self-motivation and self-discipline are the keys to success. With guidance from teachers, students select and manage their own learning processes, including the topic to be studied, the goals to pursue, the learning strategies to apply, and the resources to utilize. They also have say about ways to demonstrate and assess their accomplishments. In self-directed learning efforts, the teacher's role shifts from teaching content to teaching learning processes so that students can design and manage some of their educational experiences.

Some teachers use self-directed learning as a primary mode of instruction, and others include it once or twice during an academic term. Most self-directed lessons or units are organized with a learning contract. Frequently, the contracts are negotiated with the student, family, and teacher. One such sample contract follows.

As is evident from the contract, students determine what and how to learn, a time frame, ways to demonstrate their newly acquired competence, and persons to verify their skills. The teacher's role consists of working with individuals and small groups, diagnosing student abilities, negotiating contracts, arranging contacts for the students to pursue, and helping students problem-solve around planning, managing time, and utilizing resources.

SELF-DIRECTED LEARNING CONTRACT

Name: _____

Project Topic: _____

Goals: (What do you want to learn?) _____

_____

_____

Learning Strategies: (How are you going to learn about it?) _____

_____

_____

Resources: (Who and what will provide information?) _____

_____

_____

Tasks and Timeline: (What will you accomplish when?) _____

_____

_____

Demonstration: (How will you demonstrate what you have learned?) ___

_____

_____

Evaluation: (What criteria should be used to evaluate the quality of your work?) _____

_____

_____

Since motivation to learn springs primarily from the needs, interests, and aspirations of students, teachers who use self-directed learning do not need to rely on material rewards or competitive activities. When students have a choice about what they want to study, they typically pursue their interests with enthusiasm.

Teachers and students need to make gradual adjustments as they move into self-directed for-mats. Many students are unfamiliar with exercising choice and control over their learning, and some teachers find it difficult to let students decide what they will study and to take responsibility for the results. Most classrooms are not prepared for the networking and integration of community resources that are required for independent learning. For those teachers interested in working with this intrapersonal approach, some practical suggestions follow.

Suggestions for Implementing Self-Directed Learning

1. Encourage students of all ages, from kindergarten through high school, to suggest topics of personal interest to study throughout the school year.

2. Teach independent learning skills include decision-making, problem-solving, goal-setting, time management, and self-evaluation.

3. Enlist both school and community resources for students to access.

4. For primary-age children, teachers can establish learning centers in the classroom and let students select one to work at during "choice time."

5. For elementary through high school students, independent projects can be assigned every other month or so. The projects can be organized with learning contracts.

6. For elementary through secondary level students, the school schedule might be reorganized so that a portion of the day is dedicated to traditional academics and the other to self-directed learning.

7. Some schools attempt to create a complete self-directed learning program with support from families and administration. The traditional subjects, grading systems, and learning activities are replaced with those developed by the students, teachers, and parents together. If possible, children of mixed ages, or even children and adults, have opportunities to study together. Students should have access to the school's playground, library, laboratories, classroom, and community resources, within democratically determined guidelines.

   In such programs, long-term concentration, focused interest, enjoyment, and imagination are encouraged. Frequently, tutorials or apprenticeship options are established based on student interests. For assessment, teachers and others meet frequently with students who exhibit what they have learned and identify what they next wish to pursue.

8. When adopting self-directed learning, it is important to anticipate the challenges of such approaches. At the outset, when students assume responsibility for their learning, they often experience great enthusiasm. Yet when they confront the enormity of planning their learning, they typically feel overwhelmed and need assistance with scheduling and problem-solving. Teachers, too, often have difficulty shifting from dispensing information to facilitating and monitoring student efforts.

While an ultimate goal of any educational experience is to produce capable, independent learners, it is ironic that many students never exert choice or control over their learning while in school. All K–12 classrooms will benefit by implementing some self-directed options so that students develop into autonomous learners who can nurture their personal and professional growth throughout their lifespans.

Technology That Enhances Intrapersonal Intelligence

Many new kinds of technology develop the intrapersonal ability to think about thinking, to bring the inner world of feelings and ideas into the outer world of experience, and to use higher-order thinking skills such as decision-making and problem-solving. These tools help people to pursue a line of thought in greater depth and to brainstorm creative options.

As increasing numbers of classrooms become centers for inquiry, many teachers and students are discovering ways to explore and develop intelligence and build "mental models" that visualize connections between ideas and their broader topics. Hypermedia presents multimedia material in ways that are similar to the processing of the human brain, making connections between ideas and images just as hypertext does with words.

Computer programs such as "Inspiration" or "Kidspiration" are thought processors that capture ideas and perceive relationships by combining graphics with text. Such programs facilitate individual brainstorming, and as ideas are generated, they can be clustered into mindmaps or traditional outlines. They allow students to manipulate ideas in whatever ways best suit their thinking, and personal ownership of the educational enterprise is nurtured as students actively develop their own learning and understanding. See www.inspiration.com.

Following are additional sites about other graphic organizers that help students to brainstorm, organize, plan, create, see relationships between ideas, discover patterns, clarify thinking, and process, organize, and prioritize new information: Graphic Organizer Index at www.graphic.org/goindex.html, www.graphic.org, and www.ncrel.org/sdrs/areas/issues/students/learning. The SCORE Language Arts Teacher Activity Bank illustrates tools for metacognitive journaling, learning logs, reflective journals, and speculating about effects. See www.sdcoe.k12.ca.us/score/actbank/torganiz.htm.

Individual student learning or personal growth plans, developed collaboratively by student and teacher, also encourage the development of intrapersonal intelligence. They can be facilitated through computer programs that make possible ongoing modifications or revisions, as well as the recording of accomplishments in the form of electronic or multimedia portfolios of student work.

Intelligent tutoring systems are very different from earlier models of computer-assisted learning in that they offer students choices in how to learn any topic, keep track of the students' preferred ways of learning, and eventually offer information in forms that make it possible for students to learn through their strengths and to exercise and improve less well-developed skills.

Doing research on the Internet facilitates the ability to focus on a desired outcome, pose well-defined and limited questions, and follow through with the exploration of specific or related topics. Search engines that are fast and accurate can facilitate this process. See www.searchenginewatch.com for a listing of search engines and suggestions for searching the Web. Among the recommended search engines are All the Web-FAST search, one of the largest indexes at www.alltheweb.com, Alta Vista, one of the oldest web crawlers at www.altavista.com, Ask Jeeves at www.askjeeves.com, and Google, one of the largest collection of Web pages at www.google.com.

Clearly, there are many successful ways to help students develop intrapersonal intelligence without such tools as the above, but they do offer both students and teachers a variety of intriguing opportunities to explore the development of the human mind and intelligence They also offer students more choices in how to learn and can help them to become independent learners throughout life.

Summary

In his book *On Becoming a Person* Carl Rogers (1961) describes one aspect of intrapersonal intelligence as it develops throughout life. He writes:

> Becoming a person means that the individual moves toward being, knowingly and acceptingly, the process which he inwardly and actually is. He moves away from what he is not, from being a facade. He is not trying to be more than he is, with the attendant feelings of insecurity or bombastic defensiveness. He is not trying to be less than he is, with the attendant feelings of guilt or self-deprecation. He is increasingly listening to the deepest recesses of his psychological and emotional being, and finds himself increasingly willing to be, with greater accuracy and depth, that self which he most truly is.

To gain deep self-knowledge and to gain peace with that knowledge requires considerable life experience. Intrapersonal intelligence develops gradually over time, and in the classroom, intrapersonal processes require time in planning and teaching as well as time to unfold within the learner. Yet teaching to nurture knowledge of oneself is critically important since such knowing underlies success and fulfillment in life. This chapter has addressed numerous aspects of intrapersonal intelligence including 1) establishing an environment to nurture the sense of self, 2) self-esteem enhancers, 3) setting and achieving goals, 4) thinking skills, 5) emotional skills, 6) journal writing, 7) getting to know oneself through others, 8) reflecting on the wonder and purpose of life, 9) self-directed learning, and 10) intrapersonal forms of technology. For the reader to summarize, reflect, and synthesize the content of this chapter, we offer the following opportunity for reflection.

 APPLYING INTRAPERSONAL INTELLIGENCE

1. Important ideas or insights gleaned from this chapter:

_____
_____
_____
_____
_____

2. Areas I'd like to learn more about:

_____
_____
_____
_____
_____

3. Ways I can use this information in my teaching. Please note that all of the strategies mentioned in this chapter are listed below with space provided to note how each strategy might be incorporated into classroom instruction:

INTRAPERSONAL STRATEGY	CLASSROOM APPLICATION
Establishing an Environment to Nurture the Sense of Self	_____
Characteristics of Schools That Nurture Self-Esteem	_____

INTRAPERSONAL STRATEGY	CLASSROOM APPLICATION

Self-Esteem Enhancers: Learning to Love Oneself

Compliment Circles _____

Individual Acknowledgment _____

Peer Support _____

Guidelines for Enhancing Self-Esteem _____

Setting and Achieving Goals

Challenging Students to Learn _____

Olympian Goal-Setting _____

Thinking Skills

Metacognition _____

Emotionally Intelligent Education

Engaging Feelings in the Classroom _____

Establishing an Environment that Permits
Emotional Expression _____

Identifying Feelings _____

Expressing Emotions _____

Educating for Human Values _____

Journal Writing

Suggestions for Classroom Journal Writing _____

Journals for Personal Insight _____

Getting to Know Oneself through Others

Gaining Intrapersonal Insights from
Interpersonal Feedback _____

Reflecting on the Wonder and Purpose of Life

Classroom Activities to Nurture a Sense of Wonder _____

Finding Purpose in School and Life _____

Self-Directed Learning: An Intrapersonal Learning Approach

Suggestions for Implementing
Self-Directed Learning _____

Technology That Enhances Intrapersonal Intelligence

_____

INTRAPERSONAL REFERENCES

Costa, A. (2001). *Developing Minds: A Resource Book for Teaching Thinking.* Alexandria, VA: ASCD.

Fassler, J. (2001). *Helping Children Cope.* iUniverse.com. www.iuniverse.com.

Fuller, R. (1988). *Ball-Stick-Bird Publications.* Williamstown, MA: Author.

Gardner, H. (1993). *Frames of Mind: The Theory of Multiple Intelligences.* New York: Basic Books.

Glasser, W. (1998). *The Quality School.* New York: Harper Perennial.

Goleman, D. (1995). *Emotional Intelligence: Why It Can Matter More Than IQ.* New York: Bantam Books.

Jewett Jarratt, C. (1994). *Helping Children Cope with Separation and Loss.* Boston: Harvard Common Press.

Knake, B. (1989). *The Inside World.* Mt. Vernon, WA: Author.

MacLean, P. (1990). *The Triune Brain in Evolution.* New York: Plenum Press.

Rogers, C. (1961). *On Becoming a Person.* Boston: Houghton Mifflin.

Trelease, J. (2001). *New Aloud Handbook.* New York: Penguin.

Trelease, J. (1993). *Read All about It!: Great Read Aloud Stories for Preteens and Teens.* New York: Penguin.

Walters, J., & Gardner, H. (1986). The Crystallizing Experience: Discovery of an Intellectual Gift. In *Conceptions of Giftedness,* R. Sternberg and J. Davidson (Eds). New York: Cambridge University Press.

8

The World around Us
NATURALIST INTELLIGENCE

Human welfare is dependent upon the interrelationships
of all living things.

—Gregory Bateson, *Mind and Nature*

RACHEL CARSON'S LEGACY

Rachel Carson was a writer, scientist, and, long
before the word was popularized, an ecologist.

*R*achel developed a lifelong love of
nature and in her later years reflected that
there was: "No time when I wasn't interested
in the out-of-doors and the whole world of
nature."

An award-winning author as a child, Rachel
stunned and disappointed her friends when
she changed her college major from English to
zoology, a field considered inappropriate for
women in 1932. Upon her graduation from
Johns Hopkins University, Carson was hired by
the U.S. Bureau of Fisheries and wrote radio
scripts on marine topics. Desiring to advance

in her career, she took civil service exams to
become the first woman biologist employed by
the Bureau of Fisheries. For her position as
chief of all publications, Carson wrote pamphlets on conservation and natural resources
and edited scientific articles. In her free time,
she authored the books *Under the Sea* (1941),
The Sea Around Us (1952), a New York Times
best-seller for 81 weeks, and *The Edge of
the Sea* in 1955, another New York Times
best-seller.

In all of her writing, Carson attempted to
teach others about the beauty and wonder
of the living world. She also emphasized that
humanity was one part of the greater whole
of nature, but that we distinguished ourselves
by our power to alter nature, in some cases,
irreversibly.

Although her previous writing made Rachel
Carson well known, her book *Silent Spring*
(1962) altered the course of human history
by launching a worldwide environmental
awareness. *Silent Spring* documented the
negative consequences of pesticide use.
Carson challenged the commonly accepted
practices of agricultural scientists and the

RACHEL CARSON'S LEGACY . . . continued

government and called for changes in synthetic chemical usage. Within the book's first year, more than a quarter of a million copies were sold. U.S. Supreme Court Justice William O. Douglas called it "the most important chronicle of this century for the human race." *Silent Spring* led to regulation of pesticide use in the United States and ultimately changed the way we view the natural world.

Rachel Carson received numerous awards for her work, including the Schweitzer Medal of the Animal Welfare Institute and the National Wildlife Federation Conservationist of the Year. Carson was also the first female recipient of the National Audubon Society's Audubon Medal, the group's highest award for conservation achievement. The 4500 acre

Rachel Carson National Wildlife Refuge near Wells, Maine, was named after her in 1970. Out of 508 refuges in the United States, the Rachel Carson Refuge is one of only three named after women. In 1980, she was posthumously awarded the highest civilian decoration in the nation, the President's Medal of Freedom. In the speech that honored her, Rachel Carson was described as:

A biologist with a gentle clear voice, she welcomed her audiences to her love of the sea, while with an equally clear voice she warned Americans of the dangers human beings themselves pose for their own environment. Always concerned, always eloquent, she created a tide of environmental consciousness that has not ebbed.

DEFINITION: Understanding Naturalist Intelligence

In 1995, Howard Gardner expanded upon his original list of seven intelligences by adding an eighth: the naturalist intelligence. Originally, Gardner included the naturalist as part of logical-mathematical and visual-spatial intelligences. However, based on the criteria he established for identifying an intelligence—which include core skills and operations, an evolutionary history, a symbol system, developmental timetables, and individuals who excel at or are severely deficient in these capacities—Gardner hypothesized that the naturalist deserved recognition as a distinct intelligence. He described the core capacities of the naturalist as one who "is able to recognize flora and fauna, to make consequential distinctions in the natural world, and to use this ability productively (in hunting, in farming, in biological science)." Further, naturalists are often skilled at identifying members of a group or species, distinguishing among the members or species, recognizing the existence of other species, and perceiving the relationships among several forms of life.

All of us use skills of the naturalist intelligence when we identify people, plants, animals, and other features in our environments. By interacting with our physical surroundings, we develop a sense of cause and effect and perceive predictable patterns of interaction and behavior such as seasonal weather and corresponding plant and animal changes. Through the perceptual skills of the naturalist we compare data, classify characteristics, extract meaning, and formulate and test hypotheses.

Gardner theorizes that the naturalist intelligence evolved from the needs of early humans whose survival depended on recognizing helpful or harmful species, changing weather conditions, and food resources. At the dawn of the twenty-first century, however, the environment for many of us varies greatly from what existed a thousand or even a hundred years ago. Few of us have easy access to large stretches of undeveloped land with diverse flora and fauna. Today, children and youth often spend their time indoors or on blacktopped pavement with few opportunities to interact with nature. Yet, such interaction is not a requirement to develop this intelligence. The skills of observing, classifying, and categorizing can be developed and applied to artificial objects. This is the case when children sort sports cards, stamps, or jewelry. Developing the skills of the naturalist is not dependent on direct interaction with the natural world, and neither is it dependent on visual observation, as many might assume. Gardner notes that blind individuals can discriminate among species or human-made items by touch, and others may do so through sound.

The naturalist intelligence is evident in many areas of scientific inquiry. Entire sciences such as biology, botany, zoology, or entomology are dedicated to this intelligence. Such sciences investigate the origins, growth, and structure of living things.

They have also yielded elaborate classification systems of plants and animals.

Naturalist skills extend beyond taxonomies to include the ability to work effectively with a variety of plants and animals and to discern patterns perhaps in any area of human endeavor. Gardner speculates that art work and spiritual practices involving aspects of the natural world exhibit the perceptual skills of the naturalist. He also wonders if, perhaps, his own identification of the theory of multiple intelligences emerged out of the pattern-seeing and classifying capacities of the naturalist.

Every culture values individuals who can identify helpful or harmful species or who can categorize their properties and uses. So, too, do cultures value the skills of the cook, gardener, farmer, and hunter, all of which draw upon the naturalist intelligence. Some individuals with highly developed naturalist intelligence create products or theories that cross cultural boundaries and endure for generations. Examples of those whose knowledge of the living world and its creatures is outstanding include Charles Darwin, George Washington Carver, Rachel Carson, Luther Burbank, and Jane Goodall.

Such individuals' curiosity and detailed analysis help us perceive phenomena in the infinite space of the macrocosm as well as in the microcosm of a single cell.

✓ CHECKLIST: Naturalist Intelligence Qualities

We are all born as naturalists eager to explore the world through our senses. With the inherent faculties of the human mind and body, we experience our environments through our sensory perceptions, through active observation, and by reflecting on and questioning our perceptions.

Children express this intelligence in many ways. Some want to understand how things work, others may be fascinated with how things grow, some desire to explore natural settings and care for their inhabitants, and still others delight in classifying objects and identifying patterns. Some students stand out in their ability to note and memorize distinctions, their love for the natural world, and/or a desire to interact with its creatures or systems. Although it is not feasible to capture the broad range of naturalist expression in a single list, some suggested descriptions follow. It is likely that a person with well-developed naturalist intelligence:

1. Explores human and natural environments with interest and enthusiasm.

2. Seeks out opportunities to observe, identify, interact with, or care for objects, plants, or animals.

3. Categorizes or classifies objects according to their characteristics.

4. Recognizes patterns among members of a species or classes of objects.

5. Pursues learning about life cycles of flora or fauna or the production of human-made objects.

6. Wants to understand "how things work."

7. Is interested in how systems change and evolve.

8. Shows interest in the relationship among species and/or the interdependence of natural and human-made systems.

9. Uses tools such as microscopes, binoculars, telescopes, observation notebooks, and computers to study organisms or systems.

10. Learns taxonomies for plants and animals or other classification systems for linguistic structures or mathematical patterns, e.g., Fibonacci numbers or fractals.

11. May express interest in careers in biology, ecology, chemistry, zoology, forestry, or botany.

12. Develops new taxonomies, or theories of life cycles, or reveals new patterns and interconnections among objects or systems.

Naturalist Learning Processes

Our primary goal in this chapter is to suggest instructional strategies that integrate naturalist thinking skills into a variety of disciplines. This integration is easy to accomplish since Gardner suggests that essential capacities of this intelligence include observing, reflecting, making connections, classifying, integrating, and communicating perceptions of the natural and human-made world. Such thinking skills can enrich study in all disciplines.

Naturalist activities make classroom learning investigative and personal. Many of the following strategies are essentially founded on a single, interdisciplinary question, which is, "Why is this item (a math fact, a leaf pattern, a line of a poem, etc.) like that?" This question, which can be posed repeatedly in different subjects, encourages students to construct meaning for themselves. Once they begin to formulate their theories about why things appear as they do, students can compare their ideas with those of their classmates and with accepted disciplinary knowledge. Through such classroom investigations students gain a general knowledge of the world, how it works, and broad frameworks and structures for understanding it.

We acknowledge that environmental education plays an important role in developing the naturalist intelligence. It is beyond the scope and intent of this chapter to address this area with any specificity. Instead, we concur with Rachel Carson's assertion that:

> If a child is to keep alive his inborn sense of wonder . . . he needs the companionship of at least one adult who can share it, rediscovering with him the joy, excitement and mystery of the world we live in.

The following activities are offered to support teachers in nurturing the excitement and mystery children experience when exploring natural and human-made worlds.

Establishing a Naturalist Learning Environment

It is not necessary to have ready access to wetlands and natural refuges to develop naturalist thinking. Students can easily explore the interior and exterior of their schools, their homes, refrigerators, grocery stores, water puddles, their hands, or the broad expanse of the sky. They can travel undersea or to mountaintops through diverse technology options.

It is also unnecessary to assume that a naturalist environment is limited to something "out there" or the world of nature. Instead, by broadening our concept of environment we can approach learning and teaching as understanding the connectedness of things. Edward T. Clark (1991), a former professor of environmental education and author of award-winning articles, suggests an alternative conceptual framework for environment:

> When "environment" is understood as the entire context of our lives, as the interconnectedness among biology, technology, and culture, then environmental education must be seen as the larger picture that gives meaning to all studies.

The Big Picture

One way to help students perceive the larger picture and the connectedness of things is to share a single image with them, the famous photograph of earth from space. This powerful image shows the planet as a single, interconnected system. All natural and human phenomena are subsystems of a larger, planetary system. Just as a person's heart and lungs are subsystems of a single body, so too are natural and

human-made systems part of a larger system, that of the earth. All systems are interdependent. All academic disciplines, while systems unto themselves, are part of a larger system of the human endeavor to understand our experiences and our relationship to the environment.

To begin glimpsing academic interconnectedness, teachers can refer to the image of earth in space and ask students to brainstorm how their studies fit into the large, planetary system. They might push further by considering how current topics are dependent on and interconnected with others.

Students can perceive relationships through developing their naturalist thinking skills. As the reader will find later in this chapter, suggestions are offered for explicitly developing observing, categorizing, and investigating skills. Before we outline these processes, however, we recommend that students actively take charge of their immediate classroom environments. Leaving behind sedentary exploration, students can assume responsibility for their learning and that of others through becoming curators of their own disciplinary-based exhibits. They can transform their classrooms into student-created museums.

Classroom Museums

The word *museum* evolved from the Greek myth of the nine Muses. The Muses knew all of human knowledge and categorized it into the arts and sciences. Thus, "museum" originally referred to a place of inspiration and study. Today, most dictionaries define "museum" as an institution that displays or preserves valuable objects.

Although we typically think of museums as buildings with valuable collections of art, science, or history, classrooms can be transformed into similar places of inspiration and study. To do so, students assume the roles of collectors, researchers, and curators. As "curators," their roles shift. No longer recipients of knowledge, students become curators who create environments for inquiry and learning.

Additionally, by gathering and displaying collections, students use many naturalist thinking skills. They perceive and process information, categorize and prioritize data, and apply the theories learned in class in highly personal ways. Some simple steps are suggested below for creating a classroom museum.

To Create a Classroom Museum

1. With your students, review a major concept that they have been studying.

2. Assign students the task of individually or collaboratively creating displays that reveal their understanding of the concept.

3. Specify the content criteria of a successful display, which can include any or all of the following:
   - A definition of the concept
   - Three or more examples of the concept that are written, drawn, or photographed
   - A brief explanation as to why and how the concept functions as it does
   - A description of how it is similar to and different from other concepts students have studied
   - An explanation of the concept's relevance in the lives of the students
   - A brief brochure or recording that guides the viewer through the display

4. Specify the visual criteria of a successful display, which may include any or all of the following:
   - The capacity of the display to communicate the concept
   - Its effectiveness at attracting viewer attention
   - Its visual appeal and interest
   - An appropriate selection of items
   - A logical sequencing of the content
   - The quality of its framing, mounting, or other display features

5. Assign students the responsibility of collecting, researching, and creating their displays. Provide butcher paper, poster board, colored markers, and magazines for those who require such materials.

6. Identify the wall, desk, or table space that will be made available for the displays. Ask students to determine their space needs ahead of time so that on the assigned day the collections can be mounted easily.

7. Assign half of the students to serve as curators to present their displays on a predetermined day. Once the displays are mounted, the audience members of the class can tour the collection and provide written or oral feedback based on the suggested criteria to each "curator." On a second predetermined day, student roles switch.

If desired, the teacher may keep the collections displayed in the classroom for a week or more, and, perhaps, institute a series of museum exhibits for the most important concepts students are to learn. Other classrooms and parents can be invited to see the exhibits. If feasible, students might attend field trips to nearby museums, meet local curators, and learn how professional exhibitions guide visitors to popular artifacts and teach information in exciting formats.

Naturalist Curriculum Themes

Concepts that emerge from the naturalist sciences can support and enrich the study of other disciplines. For example, when considering a single natural phenomenon, that of the seasons, there are numerous interdisciplinary connections that can be made. In social studies, students can explore seasonal employment issues, rural and city traffic patterns, recreational activities, religious festivals and holidays, and political events. Similarly, a health class might address seasonal physical and emotional conditions, sleep patterns, or the availability of fruits and vegetables. By working with natural science themes, students experience a greater sense of connectedness with the broader environment.

Natural Science Themes

Some possible naturalist themes are:

Interdependence

Change

Adaptation

Balance

Resources

Diversity

Competition

Collaboration

Interrelationships

Cycles

Patterns

Population

Nature as Curriculum

In addition to integrating natural science themes **into** the curriculum, curriculum can **emerge** from natural phenomena. When planning a single lesson, unit, or year-long curricular focus, we can ask, "What is the role of nature in the topic I am about to teach?" If we do, students can contemplate why early civilizations evolved in certain geographic locations, or how weather influences architecture, world economies, food, and clothing design. By bringing nature center stage into the classroom, students and teachers alike may realize a deeper sense of interconnectedness with the world around us.

Supradisciplinary Themes

As most high school journalism students know, five simple questions must be answered in any article. These include: What happened? Where? Who was involved? When did it happen? Why? Similarly, author Marion Brady (1995) claims that to understand an experience requires information about 1) time, 2) environment, 3) participants, 4) action, and 5) the motive, if people are involved. An experience is meaningful once we know who did what, when, where, and why. Brady suggests that all disciplinary knowledge, in fact, reality itself, is organized through a conceptual structure that encompasses five basic components:

Time

Environment

Participants

Action

Motives

Brady's supradisciplinary view of reality provides a foundation for any general education curriculum. Its simple framework makes searching for patterns, structures, and relationships manageable. Students can identify the five areas in any or all of their studies. Additionally, they can investigate interactions among the five categories and the resultant systemic changes caused by such interactions. By teaching common elements that underlie human experience and disciplinary study, students can make sense of how the world works. Like naturalists, they will connect their observations by perceiving complex interrelationships.

Improving Observation

When teachers assign interpreting a poem, remembering the steps for multiplying fractions, or drawing portions of a still life painting, they may be disappointed with weak observation skills. While careless observation may result from too much television, too little motivation, or a lack of imagination, it is likely that such a shortcoming is not entirely of the students' doing. On a daily basis, our senses record more data than we consciously acknowledge. We can only employ our observations as naturalists if we value, notice, and record them. Our perceptions can be strengthened with open-ended and novel experiences. The following activities grab student attention.

Sightless Observations

Ezra Pound described genius as "the capacity to see ten things where the ordinary man sees one." Sometimes, we can heighten our sensory perception by actually removing one! In the following two warm-ups, students are not allowed to use their sense of sight so that they can "observe" their environments through other senses. They "see" as naturalists do with all sensory organs and with concentration and persistence.

A Blindfolded Walk

Identify safe, uncluttered locations for brief, five-minute blindfolded walks. The best routes are outside on school grounds; however, school hallways or aisles in the classroom will do. Divide students into pairs and give each a blindfold. Assign one student to serve as the leader and the other, who will be blindfolded, to be the follower. The roles will switch so that each student has the opportunity to be both leader and follower.

Once students are gathered at the designated location, one from each pair should be blindfolded. The leader slowly and carefully guides the blindfolded student along the walkway. The follower should be instructed to use her senses of touch, smell, and hearing to explore the environment. Once back at the starting point, the follower removes the blindfold and the roles are reversed. When both students have been leader and follower, they can discuss their sightless observations. Sample questions include:

- What were student reactions to this activity?
- What sense did they rely on the most to gather data?
- What did they notice that might have gone unnoticed if they had relied on vision?
- How many different objects did they encounter?
- Can they describe any object's characteristics?

To extend this further, students can write about their reactions to leading and following, the characteristics of their leaders, and reactions evoked by their experiences. The teacher could provide a map of the route and students might draw items they encountered and determine the number of steps or units of measurement along the way.

Mystery Bags

Another "sightless" activity consists of gathering natural objects such as a pinecone, shell, feather, flower, and vegetable, and placing each in a paper bag out of the class's view. Select one bag for the first round of questioning.

Divide the class into groups of three or four and select one observer from each group. The observers come to the front of the class and silently look into the bag without revealing clues about its contents.

Students then return to their groups. Other group members attempt to guess the object in the bag by asking the observer "yes" or "no" questions. After guessing the object, a new observer is selected and a second round begins with a different object. Debrief with questions such as:

- Which questions were the most helpful?
- Which questions were the least helpful?

- Which characteristics helped you identify the object?
- What did you learn about the object that you did not know before?

To extend this activity, students can make a chart of efficient questions, write responses to the above questions, or create their own "mystery bags" for classmates.

The thinking skills involved in "mystery bags" include recognizing patterns, identifying characteristics, inferring, and hypothesizing. By writing concepts on notecards and placing the cards in bags or simply handing them to students, this game and its thinking processes can be extended to any academic topic. For example, in math, students might guess different kinds of mathematical or algebraic equations, units of measurement, or geometric shapes. Similarly, in social studies, the same process can be used to identify famous individuals, events in history, or concepts such as democracy and industrialization.

Looking Closely

To develop naturalist skills, it is necessary to go beyond casual looking to active interrogating. Students can learn to ask: "What am I seeing?" "How can I describe my observations?" "What is happening?" "Why?" Through observing and intentional questioning, both adults and children are able to construct meaning and generate new questions to pursue.

Looming Large

Hand lenses or jewelers' loupes are small, inexpensive tools that magnify objects. They enable teachers to bring new visual worlds into the classroom. By using a magnifier with common or unusual everyday objects, student attention is immediately focused and visual experience is intensified and heightened.

Jewelers' loupes are shaped much as top hats and are noticed in the eyes of jewelers who use them to analyze gemstones. Inexpensive 5× loupes can be purchased in classroom sets. One outstanding resource for finding loupes and other naturalist learning materials is Kerry Ruef's *The Private Eye*.

Developing the Interdisciplinary Mind through Observation

In *The Private Eye*, Ruef (1998) outlines an interdisciplinary approach to using loupes and higher-level thinking skills. This curricular format consists of a four-step process:

Step 1: Students observe everyday objects through loupes to heighten visual awareness, observation skills, and to nurture wonder and excitement about the natural world.

Step 2: They create analogies of their magnified observations to personalize their learning and strengthen concentration.

Step 3: They draw what they see through the loupes at differing scales to gain aesthetic appreciation.

Step 4: They theorize "Why is this object like that?" to learn how function drives form in nature, and to practice theorizing as scientists.

Inferring and Theorizing

After a few enthusiastic years of piloting Ruef's processes in the Seattle School District, K–12 teachers have found that everyday objects, a jeweler's loupe, and simple questions develop "gifted results" in their students. Some interdisciplinary examples of their classroom projects follow.

Language Arts Write nonfictional descriptions of observations or use them to jump-start story ideas.

Geography/Science Observe a seed pod and determine how and where it travels.

Art Draw, paint, or sketch a magnified thumb print as a work of art.

Vocational Education Let a nail rust in the rain. Observe what happens. Study the chemical process of rust and research why metal bridge girders are coated.

Math Draw an object to different scales of magnification with precision.

Social Studies Read and decode road maps with loupes.

Drawing as Close Observation

I have learned that what I have not drawn, I have never really seen, and that when I start drawing an ordinary thing, I realize how extraordinary it is.

—Frederick Franck in *The Zen of Seeing*

Whenever we draw, we intensify our concentration. In so doing, we blend inner, mental imagery with external imagery, resulting in close observation. Drawing is an effective means of recording, interpreting, and magnifying our observations. Many students, after eight or nine years of age, will claim that they can't draw, but most enjoy doing so if time is dedicated to the task and concerns about what things should look like are minimized.

There are some simple tips for making drawing a pleasant experience for students of all ages. First, you may want to explain some drawing fundamentals. One method of teaching the essentials of drawing has been developed by Mona Brookes (1996). In her book *Drawing with Children* she explains that there are only five basic shapes to master in order to draw any item. These five shapes include a dot, straight line, angled line, curved line, and circle. Brooke's technique can assist students in drawing elements of nature.

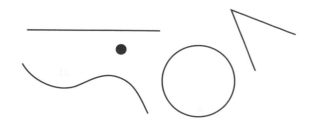

One of the first steps in freeing our drawing abilities is to forego stereotyping, and therefore, "non-seeing, self-talk" when we draw, such as, "This is an eye" or "Here is a branch." Instead, by concentrating on the curves, angles, circles, dots, and straight lines of an eye or a branch, for example, we can perceive and reproduce a more accurate representation of any object.

An easy way to jump-start student skills is to ask them to sketch quickly a simple item from memory such as an apple or pencil. Then display an apple or pencil and ask students to draw the item by observing its five basic shapes. Most will experience dramatic results.

There are countless drawing processes that refine observation skills. Some are: 1) drawing a close-up view of part of an object, 2) using a magnifying tool and drawing what is observed, 3) drawing an item from a distance or from different angles or perspectives such as the side, back, or top. Another effective strategy is to have students cut small cardstock frames approximately 2'' × 3'' or 4'' × 6'' in size. They can use the frames to define a drawing space, to eliminate visual distraction while heightening the visual focus. Whenever students draw any item and they think they are done, they can be asked to look again, to add more details, to move closer to what they are observing, and in so doing, to understand and question what they see.

Field Logs

For a naturalist, an important part of interacting with nature is keeping a record of one's encounters. By maintaining a field log, data, sketches, questions, and reactions can be reviewed at a later time and shared with others. Since naturalists often ask questions about what they observe, it's important to create a format for log-keeping that captures both facts and ponderings. One possibility is a double-entry log that looks like:

DETAILS AND FACTS ABOUT WHAT I OBSERVED	QUESTIONS, THOUGHTS, AND FEELINGS ABOUT WHAT I OBSERVED

Keeping a log of one's observations requires effort and practice. It is helpful to begin by observing a single, brief scene or event and gradually extending log-keeping to more open-ended experiences. Students can modify the format in ways that are most helpful for them. For example, some like to include a column or pages for quick artistic sketches.

What to Observe While in the Field

If possible, students should have opportunities to practice using field logs in a natural environment. Perhaps there are green spaces around the school, in local parks, or in nearby neighborhoods. Whether taking a walk as a class or assigning one as homework, here are some questions that will direct student log-keeping and sketching while in the field.

- What is the temperature, humidity, and sunlight like in this area?

- What is the local terrain like? Is it hilly, grassy, or flat?

- Describe the quality of the soil. Is it rocky, dark, sandy, or muddy?

- How many plants and animals are there? Are they of the same kind?

- Do they appear healthy?

- What does their presence tell you about the local environment?

- Why do you think these plants and animals live in this habitat?

- How do the plants and animals of one area differ from those in another?

- Sketch one or more plants or animals for further study.

- What is something you wonder about from your observations?

Once back in the classroom, help students identify the flora and fauna they observed and encourage their researching answers to individual questions.

Dialogue Logs

Occasionally, teachers and students find it motivating to use "dialogue logs." These logs invite dialogue between the log-keeper and a teacher or classmate. The reader reacts to the observations and questions written by the log-keeper. Dialogue logs can be formatted to include a column for responses or the respondent might simply write reactions in the margins or the back side of the page. When considering the use of dialogue logs, it is important to guarantee students the right to privacy of any pages they do not want to share.

Field logs do not need to be limited to recording data and questions solely about natural phenomena. They can document classroom interactions, problem-solving processes, and student reactions to content they are learning. Some teachers find that logs serve as informal assessment tools because they provide insight into students' content knowledge and problem-solving approaches.

Perceiving Relationships

Our ability to discern relationships hinges on three essential cognitive processes: 1) noticing similarities and differences, 2) classifying objects according to various criteria, and 3) perceiving interrelationships. Many naturalists are highly skilled at such processes. They are systems thinkers who are fascinated with how things interrelate. At the same time, they like to think in the particular. They want to know the names of living things, their individual characteristics, and their places in the larger web of life. The following activities engage students in the naturalist thinking processes of comparing and contrasting, classifying, and perceiving interdependence.

Noting Distinctions among Similar Items

This activity sensitizes students to subtle differences among similar objects. Students will compare and contrast two items that, at first glance, appear alike. To begin, provide each student with a copy of the Compare and Contrast Chart form on the next page. Review the chart with students, explaining that the first step is to write the name of the items they are observing (stones, feathers, apples, etc.) at the top of the chart. Next, to distinguish the paired items from one another, students should invent an individual name for each of the two objects. Third, they will list the items' similarities, and next, identify specific characteristics to compare such as shape, length, weight, color, markings, and size. Lastly, the students will complete the "Differences" portion of the chart.

Students can work in pairs or in small groups for this activity. Give each group two items such as two carrots, apples, feathers, seashells, stones, or bird feathers, and have them complete the chart.

Then debrief the activity using the following questions as a guide. If desired, students may first discuss their charts in small groups, and then proceed with a whole-group discussion.

- What was their initial impression of the paired items?

- How did their impressions change?

- Which senses did they use to observe the paired objects?

- Were there more similarities or differences among the items?

- What do they assume caused the similarities?

- What do they assume caused the differences?

- Is there a way they can verify their assumptions?

To continue to refine observation skills the teacher may want to rotate a variety of paired objects among students. After a couple of such observations students can reflect on any perceived changes in their ability to observe details.

Similar processes can be used throughout the curriculum. For example, teachers can make copies of the chart and have students compare and contrast the elective and appointive offices of state government, nouns and verbs, or herbivores and carnivores. Also, note that another Compare and Contrast Matrix can be found in the visual-spatial intelligence chapter.

It's Classified!

Classifying is a fundamental cognitive process that refers to sorting objects, events, living things, and phenomena into clusters according to their common characteristics. An additional aspect of classification is giving a label to a cluster of items that communicates its essential characteristics as is evident in the Periodic Table of Elements. Through

COMPARE AND CONTRAST CHART

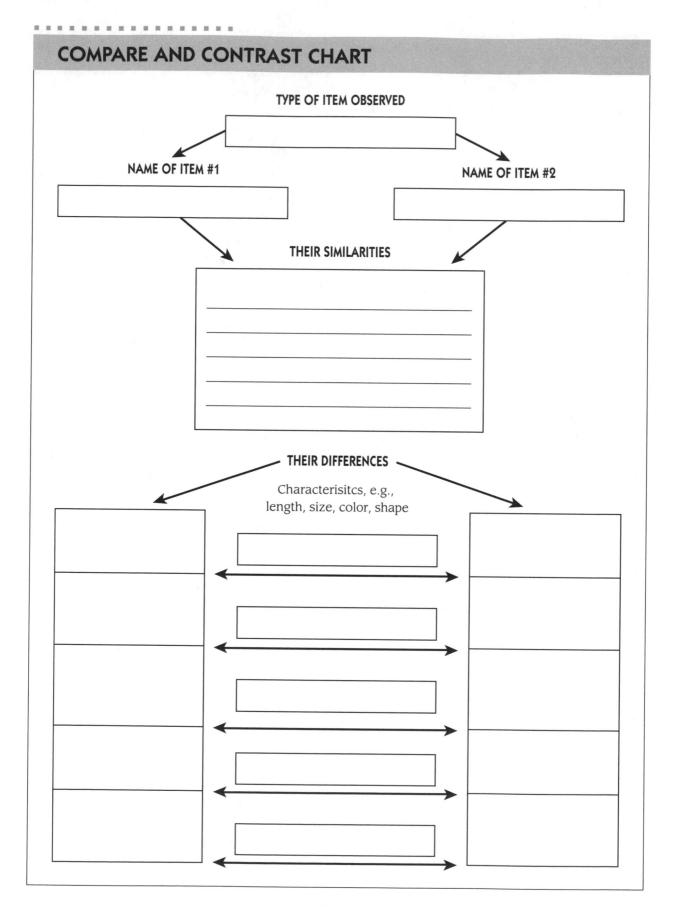

TYPE OF ITEM OBSERVED

NAME OF ITEM #1

NAME OF ITEM #2

THEIR SIMILARITIES

THEIR DIFFERENCES

Characterisitcs, e.g.,
length, size, color, shape

classification, the complexity of the environment is reduced. Objects are identifiable, attention is focused, data are organized, and relationships can be perceived.

Biologists have developed classification systems that provide an orderly arrangement of all living things. For thousands of years people have tried to classify animals and plants. Early classification systems likely divided living things into two groups: 1) useful, and 2) harmful. As more living things were discovered, new ways to sort phenomena were invented. Aristotle devised a system to categorize animals as those with backbones and those without. He divided plants by size and appearance, which resulted in classifying herbs, shrubs, and trees. Aristotle's scheme was used for approximately 2000 years.

The basic design of modern classification came from the Swedish naturalist Linnaeus who during the 1700s separated plants and animals according to their structure and gave distinctive names to each species. His classification of plants and animals continues to be used today and is referred to as a taxonomy. Like adults, many young children are fascinated with learning the names of natural phenomena in the environment. In fact, some may demonstrate an unusual amount of knowledge about a particular natural object such as spiders or dinosaurs and spontaneously offer information or teach others about what they know. Activities are suggested below that engage students in classifying and labeling, and in so doing, improve their content knowledge and the use of an important cognitive process.

Making Collections

David Attenborough (1989) in his book, *Life on Earth*, tells the story of 24-year-old Charles Darwin who as a naturalist on the HMS *Beagle* set sail for South America in 1831. In a forest outside of Rio de Janeiro, Darwin in a single day in one small area:

> collected sixty-eight different species of small beetles. That there should be such a variety of species of one kind astounded him . . . he was deeply puzzled by this enormous multiplicity of forms.

Twenty-eight years later, Darwin (1859) published *Origin of the Species by Means of Natural Selection.*

One hands-on way to teach classification and nurture close observations of natural and human-made phenomena is by making collections. Students can create collections of flora or fauna, books, math problems, science facts, food preferences, automobiles, music, or whatever is most appropriate for the content to be taught. Once their "specimens" are gathered, students can begin classifying them through numerous categories.

Students as Collectors

There are four simple steps in making collections. Briefly, these include:

1. Identifying what will be collected
2. Securing appropriate collection containers or books
3. Collecting responsibly
4. Classifying and labeling one's collection

Before students begin individual collections, it may be helpful to make a class collection together. For example, each student might bring a single flower or leaf to class. The teacher can provide a container, perhaps an oblong box divided into twenty to thirty areas for student specimens. Once the items are brought to class, they should be identified and labeled according to their common and scientific names, all of which can be found in a variety of guides. Students can then suggest categories for organizing the collection. One or two can be given the task of sorting according to an identified category. Then, as a class, students may want to classify the types of foliage found and create bar graphs or pie charts of the ratio of one type of plant to the rest of the population.

The four steps for creating collections are described below.

Step 1: To begin collecting, it is necessary to decide on the appropriate collectables. In social studies, this might consist of photos or handwritten cards of cities, states, countries, famous women, or different governmental structures. In science, "trading cards" might be drawn of cells, clouds, stars, or galaxies. In math, students might collect receipts, temperature charts from the newspaper, stock market listings, or advertisements.

Step 2: Find appropriate containers for student collections. These may include notebooks, egg cartons, small shoe or cardboard boxes (perhaps divided into sections with strips of cardboard), plastic containers, jewelry boxes, or handmade blank books. Scrapbooks work best for flat items such as pressed flowers or leaves, trading cards, stamps, and pictures.

Step 3: When students are ready to start collecting, review proper etiquette. When collecting natural specimens, students should refrain from removing items from protected lands or private property, avoid poisonous plants or animals, wear gloves or other gear as needed, and be respectful of all life forms. With human-made items, students should ask for permission before gathering specimens from homes, schools, or elsewhere.

Step 4: Once the specimens are collected, students should organize them into different categories such as seeds, flowers, leaves, or bark. There is no limit to the number and types of sorting categories. For collections that are other than flora and fauna, some categories might include age, variety, brand, function, accomplishments, country of origin, team, and batting averages. Natural objects might be sorted by function, size, shape, color, age, or variety.

The specimens should be placed thoughtfully and artistically into containers. Labels should be made for individual items. If working with flora or fauna, students should label their specimens with both their common and scientific names. There are dozens of guides available in libraries and bookstores to aid in identifying plants and animals. The Roger Tory Peterson series is well known, but there are others on birds, trees, insects, flowers, mushrooms, mammals, and endangered animals. The Audubon series entitled *First Field Guides* are excellent resources as well.

Multisensory Collections

Not all collections need to be visual ones. Some might consist of smell, taste, touch, or sound collections. For example, an eleventh grade chemistry class studied major teas of the world. These included Asian black and green teas and popular herbal teas. Students created adjectives for the taste and smell of the different teas to evaluate and classify them. They also consulted old tea books to see what criteria others had developed for judging teas. We can heighten our sensory awareness and expand our vocabularies when relying on other sensory systems.

More Classifying Suggestions

As mentioned in the visual-spatial intelligence chapter, the use of graphic tools can help learners quickly grasp a concept and the relationships among its subordinate ideas. Classification systems are effectively communicated through a visual medium. Since taxonomies branch out like family trees, they can be visually displayed in such a format. A sample "Classification Tree" follows.

Classification Tree

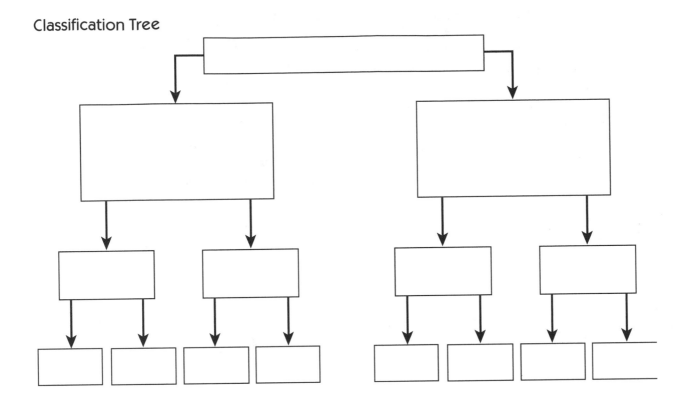

Classification trees are not only helpful for recording and reading taxonomies, they can also be applied to other data as the following geography classification tree demonstrates.

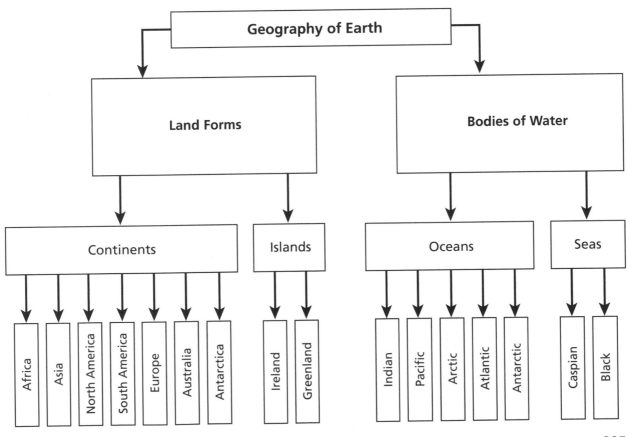

Real and Imagined Classes of Animals

Students eagerly engage in classifying tasks that address intrinsically interesting topics. One such topic is animals. Many students (and adults!) are fascinated with animals, their behaviors, and how best to care for them. The chart below is another iteration of a graphic classification tool. What varies is how the students may use it.

To teach animal classification, give students copies of the following chart. Working in small groups of three or four, ask students to brainstorm familiar animals and to keep their lists confidential. After identifying animals and their attributes, all students with the exception of one, should fill out the charts by inserting their selected animals. One student in each small group should be instructed to leave the "Animal" column blank but fill in the attributes portion of the chart. Groups then exchange their incomplete charts and attempt to identify each other's animals by the attributes only. Once the small groups have completed this activity, the whole class can review the charts for accuracy and fill in any areas left incomplete.

ANIMAL	HABITAT	PREDATORS	FOOD	CARNIVORE OR HERBIVORE	SIZE (S, M, L)	COLOR
1						
2						
3						
4						
5						
6						
7						
8						
9						
10						
11						
12						
13						
14						
15						
16						
17						
18						
19						
20						

Inventing Creatures

Students can also invent their own animals for classification. Working independently or in small groups, ask students to imagine creatures by responding to the following questions:

How does it move?

How is it segmented?

What are its sensory organs?

What kind of skeletal system or soft body structure does it possess?

What is its body covering?

Once the above decisions have been made, students can draw their creature, label its attributes, name it, and classify it according to scientific taxonomy. More than likely, this will be an engaging and worthwhile experience for students.

Understanding Interdependence

No living thing, whether plant or animal, lives alone. Each life form is dependent on other living and nonliving things. For students to grasp this concept quickly, ask them to identify some of the living and nonliving things on which their lives depend. This is a task far easier said than done due to countless interrelationships!

Elsewhere in this book, we have recommended actively involving students in processes that demonstrate interconnections. For example, in the interpersonal intelligence chapter, we suggested classroom-based cooperative learning techniques, service learning in a local community, and a youth summit process for an environmental educational project. Learning about interdependence among people is critical, but it is also important to understand the role of interdependence among diverse life forms. One way to introduce this concept is through a food chain.

Food Chains as Examples of Interdependence

You may want to explain the basic components of a food chain to students before engaging them in the activities that follow. Explain that food chains exist when the living things in one ecosystem (organisms that live in a particular area together) feed on another. Usually the larger animals feed upon the smaller ones, thus making a chain. For example, a cougar might eat a deer that ate grass that took its nutrients from the soil that developed from decaying plants and animals. There are three main roles in food chains:

- the producers such as grass and plants that make food

- the consumers are the ones who eat food

- the decomposers are the fungi and bacteria that break down dead plants and animals to return nutrients to the soil

Nearly all food chains begin with the sun since it produces the energy that plants need to grow. A typical chain would go from the sun to plants to plant eaters to carnivores.

Understanding Food Chains

Students can create simple food chains with a few manipulatives. They might label note cards with producers, consumers, and decomposers evident in their local surroundings and arrange them in the correct order. They may go on field trips to observe simple food chains in action. For example, students might observe grasshoppers that eat leaves and frogs that eat grasshoppers. You can also show students the diagram on the following page and ask them to identify how many food chains are represented.

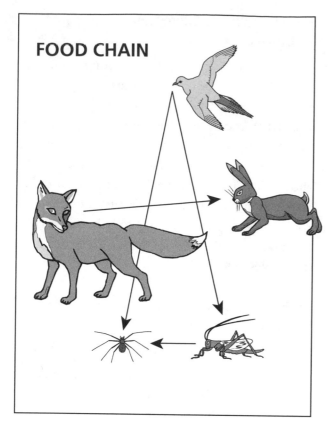

FOOD CHAIN

- College and universty departments of biology, forestry, zoology, marine biology, environmental science, ecology
- County cooperative extension services
- Environmental organizations
- Forest industries
- Landscape designers
- Museums
- National, state, and local parks
- Nature centers
- Nurseries
- State departments of agriculture, forestry, or natural resources
- Wildlife refuges
- Zoos

Of course, teachers and students can put the Internet to effective use for further information on nearly any topic. Additionally, new technology programs, several of which are described later in this chapter, can motivate students to explore the wonders of the natural world.

Students can then draw food chains they are aware of and perhaps reflect on, in a poem or a picture the interconnectedness of life.

Forging Community Relationships

As every teacher knows, students frequently raise questions that lack easy answers! Since very few people, if any, excel at all eight intelligences, it is helpful to contact experts who can answer student questions and serve as mentors to budding naturalists. Most communities have access to one or more of the following organizations. Students might research local phone numbers and specific individuals to contact. A variety of relationships can be forged between one's classroom and:

- Aquariums or oceanariums
- Botanical gardens or arboretums

Hypothesizing and Experimenting

Simple observations in the natural environment can lead to very big questions. For example, one day on a stroll through the Philadelphia Zoo, the famous naturalist Loren Eiseley pondered why ducks in the pond had such beautiful markings. Moving from this observation and question, Eiseley next began questioning the concept of natural selection and if it played any role in the ducks' colorful feathers. Naturalists use their observations to generate both questions and possible explanations, and they are often interested in pursuing answers to their questions.

Students can engage in posing questions and seeking answers to their questions through a variety of classroom experiments. In the logical-mathematical chapter, we described the scientific method and offered sample hypotheses for students to pursue. Certainly, the same procedures can be applied to studying natural phenomena. Some sample experiments with plants follow:

Planting Questions in the Classroom

1. Students can experiment with different ways to grow plants from seeds, bulbs, and cuttings. They can identify methods that foster or impede growth.

2. Compare plants grown in fertilizer to those without. Students can guess how much fertilizer is required to affect plant growth. To answer this question, it will be necessary to perform a controlled experiment and others to test the variables.

3. Compare the rate of growth among plants exposed to different variables. Students can ask, "What effect does humidity, heat, or water have on plants?" Again, it will be necessary to conduct a controlled experiment and to test one variable at a time.

Students usually enjoy the hands-on opportunities that classroom research provides. Typically however, classrooms don't undertake research projects frequently. What can be done on a daily basis is to teach students to ask questions and to promote their innate curiosity.

Developing a Questioning Frame of Mind

The inquisitive mindset of naturalists can be nurtured in our students by posing questions that can't be readily answered. To do so, students can learn about the debates and open-ended questions in disciplines we teach. At the outset of the school year, one or two questions can be identified for year-long consideration. For example, students might be asked how imagination enriches our lives or what it would take for their school to be an environmental self-sustaining facility. Students can articulate their opinions or hypotheses at the outset of an instructional unit, and then revise their hypotheses as studies progress. In doing so, they develop a questioning frame of mind in environments that respect mystery and discovery.

Naturalist Learning Centers

Classrooms can reflect the natural world by including simple naturalist centers. Such centers teach students about natural phenomena and encourage them to create extensions between the life sciences and other curricular areas. They also encourage observation, exploration, and experimentation. A corner of a classroom usually makes a good location for a naturalist center. It can be easily established with a table. If possible, it is beneficial to have a window nearby for growing plants or a shelf space for display or storage. Encourage students to display artifacts they discover at the center. If possible, make simple reference books available at the center to extend student interests or to help them find answers to questions as they arise. New activities can be added twice monthly to sustain and pique curiosity. Students can produce summaries or drawings from the information they collect at the center or make entries in their individual logs. Instructions for materials usage and appropriate behavior should be reviewed before students begin working at this center.

Standard equipment at naturalist centers consists of simple, easy-to-find items. Some possibilities include:

Equipping a Naturalist Center

Collecting Tools:
paper and plastic cups
plastic wrap
clear sorting containers
tweezers
eyedroppers

Observing and Measuring Equipment:
jeweler loupes
magnifying glasses
thermometers
microscopes
binoculars
spoon and cup sets
scales
rulers
calculators

Animal Equipment:
cages, boxes, tubs
insect cages or jars
bird houses
aquarium

Gardening Equipment:
egg cartons
milk cartons cut in half
plant pots
potting soil
garden tools
terrarium

If Desired, Water Table Equipment:
tubes
plastic containers
sieves
funnels
sponges, corks, washers
food coloring

Recording Materials:
markers
note cards
tape recorder
camcorder
paper
sketch pads

Specimens:
rocks
shells
seed pods
sand dollars
twigs
preserved insects
fibers
grains
seeds
leaves
bones
feathers

With a classroom naturalist center established, students can pursue a variety of activities that extend to any discipline. Some samples follow that engage students in the naturalist skills of observing, recognizing patterns, classifying, and experimenting.

Naturalist Center Activities

1. Ask students to place specimens under the microscope or look at them with a jeweler's loupe. To categorize, recognize patterns, and make analogies and inferences, students can answer questions such as:

   What else does this remind me of?

   How does this compare with . . . ?

   How is this similar to . . . ?

   Why is this the way it is?

A variation is to suggest that students make personal collections of at least three items from the naturalist center. Inspired by their collections, they can write similes that relate an item to content they are studying such as:

For social studies: The veins in this leaf branch out and multiply like the population of North America during colonial times.

For science: The fuzz on the bark looks like iron filings lined up by a magnet's attraction.

2. At the center, plant a variety of seeds such as grass, pumpkin, sunflower, or dried beans. Have students select a seed, and predict and then measure how much it grows during a two-week period. Ask whether they anticipate a relationship between the size of the seed and its speed of germination. Students might also conduct experiments of their choice such as how air and light affect the germination and growth of plants. Their hypotheses can be tested against their observations and school textbooks. The skills of predicting, observing, and verifying can be transferred to other disciplines such as story plots, musical compositions, historical events, and weather or seasonal patterns.

3. Ask students to observe a variety of specimens at the naturalist center. Instead of identifying the objects by their common names, such as rocks, feathers, or seeds, have them invent original names for each item. In so doing, they experience objects as if they were discovering them for the first time. Explain that scientists usually name things in the following ways:

Naming Objects
- after themselves
- after the place where the object is found or lives
- after a color or texture
- after something the object looks like or reminds the scientist of

After this activity, students often develop a greater interest in taxonomies and how objects assumed their names. Teachers may suggest that they consider categories in a variety of disciplines, such as the parts of speech or elements of the periodic table, and hypothesize reasons for such classifications.

Outdoor Naturalist Activities

Being outdoors is an effective way to enter the naturalist's world. Such opportunities provide students with experiences they typically long for: to be outside, move, interact, and reflect. The possibilities for outdoor activities are endless. We suggest three that are manageable for most classrooms.

Nature Walk

Identify an approximate thirty-minute outdoor walk that is conveniently located. It can be on or off school grounds. Before leaving the classroom, review the following items that students will be expected to note on their walk:

1. Observe a natural item that is smaller than one's hand. Sketch it.

2. Observe an item that is larger than a house. Take some time to let the image soak in. Quickly sketch the outer edges of the item.

3. Try altering your visual perspective. Look sideways, zoom in and out. Jot down a few notes about the change in perspective.

4. Listen to a distant sound and another nearby. Jot down descriptions of what was heard.

5. Touch something rough and something smooth. Write brief descriptions of the subsequent sensations.

Once students have completed their walk, bring them back to the classroom and ask them to reflect on the following:

Which sensory experience did they like the most and why?

What was an unexpected experience they had?

What did they find challenging?

What questions arose from this activity?

What did they learn about the way naturalists think and work?

Where else might they use some of the activities during their walk to enhance their learning?

Adopt a Tree

Select a tree on the school property for students to visit frequently during the school year. They can make predictions of the changes the tree is likely to undergo throughout the year and then observe and record what actually occurs. Students can collect and draw leaves, twigs, buds, and insects from the tree, classify these items, and identify related food chains. They can create comparisons between the life cycle of the tree and seasonal changes in human behavior.

A Quick Quadrat

Sixth grade teacher Maggie Meyer in Lacey, Washington, uses a process called "A Quick Quadrat" with her students. A quadrat refers to a square used by scientists for data collection. The goal of this activity is to enhance observation and data gathering skills. Before going outdoors, students should be organized into pairs. Each pair receives a piece of yarn cut into a forty-inch length with the ends tied together. While seated, the students practice making ten-inch squares on their desktops. Together, the whole class next predicts what items they will find outdoors in their quadrats. These predictions are listed on the blackboard for later comparison.

Once outside, the teacher should lead students to a preselected spot that offers the greatest variety of natural objects. There, students construct their quadrats. If it is helpful, they may use toothpicks to mark and hold the corners of their squares. On data sheets, each student lists what she observes, the number of items in her quadrat, and draws one or more of the items.

Once back in the classroom, the students share the results of their data-gathering with the whole class by responding to several questions:

What items were found?

What student predictions were correct?

What was incorrect?

What could explain such discrepancies?

Why were some items clustered together in the quadrats?

What was especially interesting about their quadrats?

Other observations of their choice

There are many extensions of A Quick Quadrat to other subject areas. The students might construct graphs or make pictographs of the data. They could make up math story problems or create art displays. They could write fictional or nonfictional explanations of how an item appeared on the school grounds or how these items are connected to the larger environment around their school.

Learning Naturally

At a time when technological equipment is part of the envionment of increasing numbers of schools, it is critical to make the natural environment accessible as well. In some school communities, students take part in planning their learning environments through a unique participatory and systemic design process developed by New Orleans architect Steven Bingler. Bingler fosters communication among educators, psychologists, architects, urban planners, software designers, students, parents, and representatives from community businesses and not-for-profit organizations. Bingler believes that the outcome of such community engagement will be "a new kind of learning environment that spans a spectrum of learning as rich and varied as the life-long learners who create and use it."

Several school districts are already under way with this process. At the Lincoln High West Campus School in Stockton, California, the students decided that the richest learning environment they could imagine would be in the form of a farm. As planning for the new school evolved, it became clear that a rustic setting, where students were surrounded by the beauty and peacefulness of nature, was what they ultimately wanted in their new school. When completed, the school will be set in a rustic environment, but will also include an extensive computer and technology center with teleconferencing capabilities, an auditorium, and large meeting rooms. A business conferencing center will provide income to support the cost of the school and a fitness center located on site will also be a community resource and generate additional income.

After hearing about the planning process for Lincoln High School, the Western Placer School District, north of Stockton, decided to embark on a district facilities plan with wide participation from the students and community. A local real estate developer has donated 170 acres of real estate to the district and 2,000 mandarin orange trees. The orchard will eventually provide an annual income of $400,000 for the school district. A planned innovative environmental studies curriculum will equip students to manage the project while receiving hands-on science education in a natural setting.

Such integration of nature and academia is not occurring only in rural settings. In Minnesota, an innovative school design project resulted in the Zoo School, which is located within the boundaries of the 200-acre Minneapolis Zoo. The zoo donated the land for use of the two-year public

high school, and zoo scientists teach courses. Admission to the school is highly competitive and students are admitted in part on the basis of their essays explaining their desire to attend. Social studies, English, and environmental science are combined in an integrated thematic curriculum. Many students who have not done well in other school settings excel at the Zoo School, which allows them to participate actively in innovative ways of learning in this unusual setting where the naturalist intelligence flourishes.

Technology That Enhances Naturalist Intelligence

A symposium was held recently in Japan on the effects of multimedia technology on human development. During the first day, presentations were given on learning through new technologies, "edutainment," designing and utilizing new kinds of learning spaces, using the Internet, virtual reality projects, science education in the Internet Age, growing up in a multimedia environment, and the future of "cyber-child" research. At the end of the day, a Japanese teacher in the audience asked to speak. She said, "Last week we had a beautiful snowfall in Tokyo, and I remembered as a child being so excited about playing in the snow, feeling snowflakes on my face, making snow people, and tossing snowballs. I looked out of my window, and there were no footprints in the snow!" Many educators, like this teacher, have growing concerns about the numbers of children who spend their free time indoors watching television, playing techno-games, or working on their computers without an appropriate balance of outside activities.

As electronic technologies become increasingly available and integrated into our lives, it is essential that they do not replace human interaction and experience in the natural world. They are, however, excellent tools that facilitate scientific investigation, exploration, and other naturalist activities. Telecommunications technologies help students to understand the world beyond their own immediate environment, and show them how their actions affect their world. As you will see in the examples that follow, these tools make it possible for students to understand real experiences in greater detail and depth.

Handheld computers are being used in many schools to bridge between the classroom and field experiences. In one Chicago suburb high school, teachers note that hand-helds have increased productivity and efficiency across all disciplines, including language arts, the sciences, and social studies. A biology teacher "beams" assignments to her students' handheld computers via infrared ray, and the students then use their computers to collect data in the field and input the data into the school computer. They process the data, discuss it with classmates, and write reports on their return to the classroom.

In another project, twenty sixth grade students in Arizona used a variety of scientific instruments to measure soil and water temperature, wind speed, and soil composition. They also used mobile computers connected to a wireless local area network and walkie-talkies to collaborate with each other and communicate the data they collected. The students, teachers, and technicians were divided into three groups to gather data in different locations. They communicated the data to another base-camp group that provided equipment, coordinated the activities, and transmitted the findings to yet another group in the school fifteen miles away where students built a database of the results. A naturalist worked with this group to increase their understanding and offer further information which they communicated back to the students in the field.

Although it is not possible for students to actually explore some sites such as the depths of the Mediterranean Sea, the cones of active volcanoes,

the Galapagos Islands, or Iceland, they may have a nearly real experience through the JASON Project, previously mentioned in the kinesthetic intelligence chapter. Through this project, millions of students have actually interacted with explorers at such sites. Founded by Dr. Robert Ballard, who discovered the wreckage of the *Titanic* and who remains an active participant in the project, the JASON Project brings real excitement to science classes. Using technology, students participate in an annual scientific expedition over a two-week period tied to a year-long curriculum. Students and teachers accompany the JASON scientists to the expedition site and serve as peer role models online and during the live broadcasts. At the primary interactive sites (PINS), students can access a network of museums, educational institutions, and research organizations via satellite links to communicate with scientists; operate robots and scientific equipment via live remote control; and see and participate in live, up-to-the minute coverage of expedition activities. See www.jasonproject.org.

Another example of virtual expeditions, the National Geographic's Amazon Quest is one of several projects organized by explorer Dan Beuttner. In an area where more than fifty still "uncontacted" indigenous tribes are located, the Amazon experience helps students understand the challenges of indigenous people. With the help of wireless computers, a satellite dish, and a portable electrical generator, Beuttner and his team broadcast live interviews, post movies and field reports from remote areas, and interact with thousands of students in their classrooms. Every day students are asked to discuss and vote on an ethical dilemma faced by the Amazon Quest expedition, such as whether or not to buy products that encourage the killing of endangered animals. Beuttner says, "Our goal is to use technology not only to put people in the driver's seat but to put them in position where they can make real discoveries and indeed direct an expedition thousands of miles away." See www. nationalgeographic.com.

Another project that involves students in doing "real work" virtually, was the Salmon Summit, a collaborative learning experience for students from schools in Alaska, British Columbia, and the state of Washington. Students spent five months studying every aspect of the Pacific salmon in their own regions and investigating how the fish could be protected. They then switched roles and became representatives for each other's jurisdictions, drafting Statements of Concern on behalf of those areas. The research and the online collaborative work of the students led to the Pacific Salmon Summit in March of 2002. At that time all the students met face to face in Vancouver, British Columbia, to negotiate a Joint Statement of Concern and Plan of Action as representatives of the United States and the Canadian federal government. It was possible for online visitors to watch, listen, and participate in summit activities in real time. Numbers of student projects using language arts, the visual arts, science, and math were other outcomes of this project.

Numerous CD-ROMs that offer both content and process are also available, such as Videodiscovery's Digital Library of science media for students at all levels. The library includes 30,000 images and movies, along with comprehensive descriptions and classrooms lessons. Their Health Sleuths "mysteries" are standards-based, offer problem-solving challenges and strategies, promote critical reasoning, and are fun, engaging, and stimulating. The Earth Science series includes geology, oceanography, meteorology, and astronomy. Along with helping students to master content in engaging ways, there is in each program an emphasis on the development of higher-order thinking skills. See www.videodiscovery.com.

Before concluding this brief review of electronic technologies that enhance the development of naturalist intelligence, let us turn to the most basic of nature studies: the study of human nature and the ecology of the brain. Until recently, most studies were done in surgery or by observation of brain-injured people. Now it is possible not only to see the structures of the brain with noninvasive technologies such as PET and CAT scans, but also to watch brain activity through functional MRIs. We are just beginning to understand what this information tells us about individual differences in learning. An informative, colorful, and interesting website on this topic is Dr. Eric Chudler's Neuroscience for Kids at http://faculty.washington.edu/chudler/neurok.html. Also see New Horizons for Learning's "News from the Neurosciences" on their website at www.newhorizons.org.

Other recommended websites related to developing the naturalist intelligence include: WISE, a Web-based inquiry science environment at http://wise.Berkeley.edu; The Exploratorium's Institute for Inquiry at www.exploratorium.edu/IFI/index.html; TERC (a math, science and technology teaching and learning site) at www.terc.edu; the Electronic Journal of Science Education Archive Page at http://unr.edu/homepage/jcannon/ejse/ejse.html; the Lawrence Hall of Science at www.lhs.Berkeley.edu; the Center for Science Education at www2.edc.org/cse; and the SCI Center (for high school science instruction) at www.scicenteratbscs.org.

Important electronic tools that enhance the development of this intelligence, in addition to those previously mentioned, include Inspiration and Kidspiration at www.inspiration.com, IHMC Concept Map Software at http://cmap.cognist.uwf.edu, and FileMaker Pro at www.filemaker.com/products.

The tools and resources mentioned are but a few examples of rapidly escalating ways to enliven, activate, enrich, and deepen real learning through technology. They also offer tools and opportunities to exercise naturalist intelligence in projects that require identifying patterns and connections in nature, comparing data, classifying, making comparisons, and formulating and testing hypotheses. The walls of science classrooms are indeed coming down as a whole world of learning becomes accessible to students and teachers who can partner with scientists and explorers in discovering and constructing knowledge about our planet and its inhabitants.

Summary

I wanted to know every strange stone, flower, insect, bird, or beast.

—George Washington Carver

George Washington Carver is an example of a naturalist much needed in our contemporary world. Humanity needs the skills of those who observe, perceive connections, make and test hypotheses, and communicate ways to improve the quality of life. Carver was not only a naturalist, an artist, and an inventor; his work was motivated by compassion for others. As biographer Gene Adair (1989) writes in *George Washington Carver, Botanist*, Carver explained,

The primary idea in all of my work was to help fill the poor man's empty dinner pail. My idea is to help the "man farthest down." This is why I have made every process just as simple as I could to put it within his reach.

Carver's goals mirrored the efficiency of nature itself. Who knows what any of us might discover if we were to act upon his advice to

. . . begin now to study the little things in your own yard, going from the known to the nearest related unknown . . . .

The activities in this chapter highlight some of the skills and attitudes of the naturalist through observing, questioning, and experimenting. It should be noted that naturalists also possess a profound respect for and love of nature. They feel a strong obligation to and responsibility for the natural world. To summarize, reflect, and synthesize the content of this chapter, the following is offered.

 APPLYING NATURALIST INTELLIGENCE

1. Important ideas or insights gleaned from this chapter:

_____

_____

_____

_____

2. Areas I'd like to learn more about:

_____

_____

_____

_____

3. Ways I can use this information in my teaching. Please note that all of the strategies mentioned in this chapter are listed below with space provided to note how each strategy might be incorporated into classroom instruction:

NATURALIST STRATEGY   CLASSROOM APPLICATION

Establishing a Naturalist Learning Environment _____

    The Big Picture _____

    Classroom Museums _____

Naturalist Curriculum Themes

    Natural Science Themes _____

    Nature as Curriculum _____

    Supradisciplinary Themes _____

Improving Observation

    Sightless Observations _____

    Looking Closely _____

    Drawing as Close Observation _____

    Field Logs _____

Perceiving Relationships

    Noting Distinctions among Similar Items _____

    It's Classified! _____

    Making Collections _____

    More Classifying Suggestions _____

    Understanding Interdependence _____

    Forging Community Relationships _____

Hypothesizing and Experimenting

    Planting Questions in the Classroom _____

    Developing a Questioning Frame of Mind _____

Naturalist Learning Centers

    Equipping Naturalist Centers _____

    Naturalist Center Activities _____

    Outdoor Naturalist Activities _____

Learning Naturally _____

Technology That Enhances Naturalist Intelligence _____

NATURALIST REFERENCES

Adair, G. (1989). *George Washington Carver, Botanist*. New York: Chelsea House.

Attenborough, D. (1989). *Life on Earth*. Boston: Little Brown and Company.

Boyer, E. (1995). "The Educated Person" in J. Beane (Ed.)*Toward a Coherent Curriculum: The 1995 ASCD Yearbook*. Alexandria, VA: ASCD.

Brady, M. (1995). "A Supradisciplinary Curriculum" in J. Beane (Ed.) *Toward a Coherent Curriculum: The 1995 ASCD Yearbook*. Alexandria, VA: ASCD.

Brookes, M. (1996). *Drawing with Children: A Creative Method for Adult Beginners Too*. New York: Jeremy Tarcher.

Budwig, L. (1992). "Breaking Nature's Silence: Pennsylvania's Rachel Carson." *Pennsylvania Heritage*, Vol. XV111, No. 4.

Carson, R. (1956). *The Sense of Wonder*. New York: Harper and Row.

Clark, E. T. (1991). "Environmental Education as an Integrative Study." In Ron Miller (Ed.) *New Directions in Education*. Brandon, VT: Holistic Education Press.

Eiseley, L. (1959). *The Immense Journey*. New York: Vintage Books.

Gardner, H. (1995). "Are There Additional Intelligences? The Case for the Naturalist Intelligence." *Harvard Project Zero*. Cambridge, MA: President and Fellows of Harvard College.

Gardner, H. (1998). "Are There Additional Intelligences? The Case for the Naturalist, Spiritual, and Existential Intelligences" In J. Kane (Ed.) *Educational Information and Transformation*. Englewood Cliffs, NJ: Prentice Hall.

Lear, L. (1998). *Rachel Carson: Witness for Nature*. Springdale, PA: Rachel Carson Homestead Association.

Meyer, M. (1998). *Learning and Teaching through the Naturalist Intelligence*. Available online at www.newhorizons.org.

Ruef, K. (1998). *The Private Eye: Looking/ Thinking by Analogy*. Seattle, WA: The Private Eye Project.

9

Curriculum Development
THROUGH THE MULTIPLE INTELLIGENCES

Ultimately, a full understanding of any concept of any complexity cannot be restricted to a single model of knowing or way of representation.

—Howard Gardner, *The Unschooled Mind*

THE ART IN SCIENCE

". . . four hundred conference-goers jumped to their feet in a standing ovation for the science students-turned-actors."

A junior high science class undertook a study of geologic eras and the evolution of plant and animal life. The teacher organized the curriculum thematically, calling the unit Origins, intending to spark student interest in the beginnings and transformations of the planet as well as its life forms. At one point in the unit, students were required to participate in individual or small group projects. To initiate their research, students posed questions to organize and focus their efforts. Numerous resources both inside and outside of the class were pursued in search of answers. At the end of two weeks, the projects were shared with classmates; it was then that the real work

began. Appreciative of the quality and content of one another's work, the students objected to bringing their work to closure. Deciding that their material was interesting and well presented, the class wondered how best to share their learning with others.

The idea of a play, of combining the projects into a single cohesive drama to be shared with other classes and parents, was

THE ART IN SCIENCE . . . continued

suggested and readily embraced. The reports were reformatted into small improvised scenes. Each scene began with the questions that initiated student research and the small vignettes were sequentially arranged according to a geologic timeline. The set consisted of a large, unfolding scroll, 100 feet in length, featuring scenes of plant and animal life, odes to prehistoric events, and geologic graffiti. A choreographer from the local community assisted in the creation of a dance entitled "In the Beginning" and a musician parent working with a group of volunteers composed a song called "Backwards and Forwards in Time."

The resulting play, entitled "Life and Everything You Wanted to Know about It," was performed for other classes and parents, and eventually for an international educational conference where four hundred conference-goers jumped to their feet in a standing ovation for the science students-turned-actors.

There were numerous ingredients that made the Origins unit a success. Students learned and interacted with their material in numerous modes. They told stories and drew timelines; they painted, sang, and danced the content. They were mentored by others more skilled than themselves, and they received feedback from parents and community members on their efforts.

When provided with open-ended learning experiences, students are capable of perceiving concepts through numerous lenses and applying what they learn in fresh contexts, instead of simply imitating what was taught. In addition, when the multiple intelligences are incorporated into curricular units, it is likely that at least one mode will facilitate learning for each student.

Previous chapters surveyed environmental factors and teaching strategies to expand instructional repertoires while providing students with options to increase the likelihood of their learning. This information would be incomplete without reflecting on an additional aspect of professional practice: curriculum development. Just as Gardner's theory has profound implications for pedagogy, it offers equally provocative options for lessons, units, and school programs.

Implications of the Theory of Multiple Intelligences for Curriculum

· · · · · · · · · · · · · · · · ·

Many educators interpret Howard Gardner's work as suggesting numerous entry points into classroom lessons. The multiple intelligences are typically perceived as instructional processes to enhance student learning in any discipline. Yet the theory's application has taken many forms in classroom and schoolwide curriculums.

For example, some teachers maintain that the Theory of Multiple Intelligences suggests early talent development. They assert that each student's gifts should be nurtured as soon as they appear. Others maintain that MI mandates broadening the curriculum to accommodate an array of courses, especially in the visual and performing arts. They argue that the arts deserve equal time in the curriculum. Such is the case at the Key Learning Community, the nation's first MI school. There the curriculum expanded to feature visual arts, music, creative dramatics, and dance for every student, beginning in kindergarten. In addition to the elementary teachers who serve as generalists, the Key Learning Community also employs teachers licensed in specialized arts areas to ensure that students receive quality arts instruction.

After exposure to Gardner's work, some teachers begin questioning the purpose of schooling. They ask, What are schools for if not to engage the greater capacity of each student? Gardner himself has sketched an "individual-centered curriculum" in which schools ideally provide educational options responsive to each student. Likewise, some teachers who desire to identify and nurture the intelligence strengths of each student establish apprenticeship or mentoring options for their students.

Yet other educators perceive Gardner's work as underscoring the importance of in-depth student

TEACHING

&

LEARNING
THROUGH
THE

MULTIPLE INTELLIGENCES

understanding. Ensuring that students understand and can apply their knowledge in new situations is not an easy educational goal to achieve. Project-based teaching, providing multiple entry points into content, and reducing the pressure for coverage are some methods educators adopt to attain the goal of educating for understanding.

Howard Gardner himself has stated that in terms of curricular modifications, the Theory of Multiple Intelligences is like a Rorschach test. Individual teachers and entire schools may go about applying MI in diverse and even conflicting ways. Gardner asserts that one application of his theory is not necessarily "right" and another "wrong." Typically, both approaches can be justified and prove appropriate for their settings.

As the brief examples of curricular adaptations show, MI theory can be applied as a discipline-based model or as a pedagogical method. It is interesting to note that the multifaceted intellect has spawned entire disciplines from each intelligence. For example, literature springs from our linguistic capacities just as mathematics and earth sciences do from our logical and naturalist intelligences.

Thus, conventional disciplinary-based programs are rooted in the multiple intelligences. At the same time, Gardner's theory can be interpreted and applied as an instructional tool.

This chapter explores diverse multiple intelligences curricular models. Educators who are considering adopting MI theory may want to reflect on those models that appear beneficial for their students and communities. The ones described in this chapter include:

Lesson Planning through the Multiple Intelligences

The Theory of Multiple Intelligences suggests that teachers integrate multimodal learning strategies into their lessons. Since most teachers are comfortable working with two or three intelligences, attempting to add additional modes necessitates some risk-taking and flexibility. The rewards for such efforts are tangible, however. It is gratifying to observe students' enthusiasm, engagement, and achievement as well as the enhancement of their intellectual capacities.

Numerous strategies have been described in previous chapters that can be incorporated into daily or weekly lessons. It should be stated at the outset that there is no need to attempt lessons with all eight capacities. The authors recommend that three or four modes be used as windows into content. This effort provides students with several opportunities to access information and it challenges teachers to work in new ways. Teachers often report that thinking in multiple modes for lesson planning becomes second nature during or soon after the first year of attempting to do so.

To begin lesson planning, educators can identify a concept to teach and the intelligences most appropriate for communicating such content. To infuse variety into classroom lessons, the following Instructional Menus help teachers brainstorm options to expand pedagogical repertoires.

Although these menus provide instructional options, teachers have found other uses for them. Some give students copies asking them to identify ways to proceed in learning. Doing so removes some of the responsibility for multimodal teaching from the instructor and places it on, in many cases, the "eager" shoulders of the students.

INSTRUCTIONAL MENUS

LINGUISTIC MENU

Use storytelling to . . .

Conduct a debate about . . .

Write a poem, myth, legend, short play, or news article about . . .

Relate a short story or novel to . . .

Give a presentation on . . .

Lead a class discussion on . . .

Create a radio program about . . .

Write a newsletter, booklet, or dictionary about . . .

Invent slogans for . . .

Make an audiotape of . . .

Conduct an interview of . . . on . . .

Write a letter to . . . about . . .

Use technology to write . . .

Others of your choice . . .

LOGICAL-MATHEMATICAL MENU

Create story problems for . . .

Translate . . . into a formula . . .

Create a timeline of . . .

Design and conduct an experiment on . . .

Invent a strategy game that . . .

Use a Venn diagram to explain . . .

Make up syllogisms to demonstrate . . .

Make up analogies to explain . . .

Use . . . thinking skills to . . .

Design a code for . . .

Categorize facts about . . .

Describe patterns or symmetry in . . .

Use technology to calculate . . .

Others of your choice . . .

KINESTHETIC MENU

Role play or simulate . . .

Create a series of movements to explain . . .

Choreograph a dance about . . .

Invent a board or floor game of . . .

Make task or puzzle cards for . . .

Build or construct a . . .

Attend a field trip that will . . .

Make simple manipulatives for . . .

Devise a scavenger hunt to . . .

Make a model of . . .

Use hands-on materials to . . .

Design a product for . . .

Use technology to play . . .

Others of your choice . . .

VISUAL MENU

Chart, map, cluster, or graph . . .

Create a slide show, videotape, or photo album of . . .

Design a poster, bulletin board, or mural of . . .

Use a memory system to learn . . .

Create artwork that . . .

Make architectural drawings for . . .

Create advertisements for . . .

Vary the size and shape of . . .

Color code the process of . . .

Invent a game to demonstrate . . .

Illustrate, paint, sculpt, or construct . . .

Use the overhead projector to teach . . .

Use technology to draw . . .

Others of your choice . . .

MUSICAL MENU

Give a presentation with musical accompaniment on . . .

Write song lyrics for . . .

Sing a rap or song that explains . . .

Indicate the rhythmical patterns in . . .

Relate the lyrics of a song to . . .

Explain how a piece of music is similar to . . .

Present a short class musical on . . .

Make an instrument and use it to demonstrate . . .

Use background music to enhance learning . . .

Collect and present songs about . . .

Write a new ending to a musical composition to explain . . .

Create a musical collage to depict . . .

Use musical technology to . . .

Others of your choice . . .

INTERPERSONAL MENU

Conduct a meeting to . . .

With a partner, use "out-loud problem-solving" to . . .

Act out diverse perspectives on . . .

Participate in a group to . . .

Intentionally use . . . social skills to learn about . . .

Do a service project for . . .

Teach someone else about . . .

Collaboratively plan rules or procedures to . . .

Address a local or global problem by . . .

Give and receive feedback on . . .

Using one of your strengths, assume a role in a group to accomplish . . .

Create a culturgram or systems wheel (see interpersonal chapter) of . . .

Use technology to interact with . . .

Others of your choice . . .

INTRAPERSONAL MENU

Describe qualities that will help you successfully complete . . .

Create a personal analogy for . . .

Set and pursue a goal to . . .

Describe how you feel about . . .

Explain your philosophy about . . .

Describe your personal values about . . .

Use self-directed learning to . . .

Write a journal entry on . . .

Explain the reason to study . . .

Do a project of your choice on . . .

Receive feedback from another on . . .

Self-assess your work in . . .

Use technology to reflect on . . .

Others of your choice . . .

NATURALIST MENU

Collect and categorize data . . .

Keep a journal of observations about . . .

Compare weather phenomena to . . .

Invent categories for . . .

Explain how a plant or animal species resembles . . .

Make a taxonomy of . . .

Use binoculars, microscopes, magnifiers, telescopes to . . .

Identify the relationships between . . .

Care for plants or animals to learn about . . .

Describe the cycles or patterns in . . .

Specify the characteristics of . . .

Attend an outdoor field trip to . . .

Use technology to explore . . .

Others of your choice . . .

Other teachers use the menus for homework. For example, a teacher might distribute a single list such as the musical one and ask that students do their homework musically for a week. Then on Fridays, students review or share their musical studying with classmates. At the beginning of the following week, students receive a different menu and again are directed to study according to that list's options. By rotating through the eight intelligences during the course of eight weeks, all students can be challenged to confront their weaknesses and enjoy working through their strengths. Further, some teachers encourage students to identify their favorite homework strategies for the ninth week. Teachers then have opportunities to observe student preferences and to glimpse the areas in which students are motivated to take risks. Parents frequently report that they seldom have observed their children so engaged with homework. The multimodal requirements create new challenges that many students enjoy undertaking.

Teachers have also used the menus for assessment options. After reviewing the menus, students select how they will demonstrate their learning. As long as the criteria are clearly specified for quality work, knowledge, and skills, students can communicate their achievement through charts, movement sequences, role-plays, or original songs.

Whether used as instructional, assessment, or homework tools, the menus and the learning activities described earlier in this book teach students that the eight intelligences are effective problem-solving strategies for educational and real life challenges.

A Lesson Planning Matrix

There is no single, preferred model of multiple intelligences–based lesson design. Teachers are highly adept at creating approaches that best suit their preferences and those of their students. When beginning to approach MI as an instructional framework, realistic expectations must be set. For secondary level educators working within the confines of fifty-minute class periods, it is unlikely that several areas will be addressed within a

single period. Rather, including strategies from a few intelligences during one to two week's time is manageable. Elementary school teachers may find that over the course of two days many intelligences can be integrated into classroom activities. Other teachers have eased into MI-based instruction by identifying one intelligence to highlight each day. After a few days, the students have worked in several modes. Some teachers let students continue work in an intelligence of their choice on a predetermined day of class.

It is important to note that though the multiple intelligences provide an effective framework, it is not desirable to turn Gardner's theory into a rigid pedagogical formula. One teacher who wanted to teach all content through eight modes admitted that he occasionally "tacked on" activities to complete his daily lessons. This practice ceased when students complained that some lesson components were "really stretching it." What is most important in MI instruction is that the tools of instruction are appropriate for the content. This is not to say, however, that a teacher should consistently avoid an intelligence because it is out of his comfort zone. Instead, teaming with a colleague can enhance the learning options of both students and teachers.

A few educators prefer to develop a latent capacity before applying it to classroom instruction. Some, for example, have identified drawing, movement, or musical activities to study formally or informally. Once confidence is gained, the teachers share with students what they have learned or infuse their new skills into classroom lessons.

One of the authors directed a mid-career teacher preparation program in which students were required to select a latent intelligence to develop over a year's time. Additionally, the preservice candidates were asked to incorporate their budding capacities into classroom instruction during their student teaching practicum. It was inter-esting to observe the choices adults made about which intelligences to develop. One year, out of the forty students in the program, two chose to improve linguistic skills through taking speech lessons and surveying children's literature. Six dove into logical-mathematical intelligence through attending math phobia classes, reviewing math curriculums, and studying problem-solving models. Five reviewed environmental education programs for classroom use. Ten pursued visual art courses. Six experimented with kinesthetic intelligence through physical education programs. Eight took vocal or instrumental lessons. Two studied collaborative learning processes, and one engaged in extensive journal writing. Educators who are willing to continue to enhance their human capacities become important role models for others since they practice what they hope to nurture in others.

A lesson planning matrix is suggested on the next page as one option for organizing multiple intelligences instruction. Please note that both the lesson's objective and outcome can match a state's curricular standards. The matrix also asks that the stated outcome be directly assessed so that teachers know if their students have met the specified learning targets. The reader will note that two completed lessons are also provided. The first on photosynthesis incorporates all eight intelligences; the second lesson suggests the use of six.

As evident in the sample lessons, the same concept can be taught in several ways. Clearly identifying the outcome or curriculum standard ahead of instruction avoids a common problem in MI-based teaching. Teachers often enjoy brainstorming multimodal experiences and can find themselves far afield of the original objectives. Students can get lost in engaging, but fragmented experiences. As with any instructional method, it is essential that educators determine what is of greatest value for students to know and then pursue the teaching of those concepts in a cohesive manner.

LESSON/UNIT PLANNING WITH THE MULTIPLE INTELLIGENCES

Lesson/Unit Title: _____

Lesson/Unit Objective (May be a state standard): _____
_____

Anticipated Learner Outcome (May be a state standard): _____
_____

Classroom Resources or Materials: _____
_____

LEARNING ACTIVITIES

LINGUISTIC	MATHEMATICAL-LOGICAL

VISUAL-SPATIAL	BODILY-KINESTHETIC

MUSICAL	INTERPERSONAL

INTRAPERSONAL	NATURALIST

Lesson/Unit Sequence: _____
_____

Assessment of Learner Outcome or Standard: _____
_____

SAMPLE ONE: LESSON/UNIT PLANNING WITH THE MULTIPLE INTELLIGENCES

Lesson/Unit Title: ___Photosynthesis: Converting Sunlight to Food___

Lesson/Unit Objective (Standard): ___Students will learn the process of photosynthesis as one___ example of life processes

Anticipated Learner Outcome: ___Students will explain the process of photosynthesis and relate___ the concept of transformation to their own lives

Classroom Resources or Materials: ___Displayed posters or charts of the process of photosynthesis, a variety of___ musical tapes or compact discs and player, water color supplies, science textbooks, previously planted seedlings

LEARNING ACTIVITIES

LINGUISTIC

Preview key vocabulary and read textbook section describing photosynthesis

MATHEMATICAL-LOGICAL

Create a timeline of the steps of photosynthesis. Label the flow of matter and energy.

VISUAL-SPATIAL

With watercolors, paint the steps of photosynthesis.

BODILY-KINESTHETIC

Role play the "characters" involved in the process of photosynthesis.

MUSICAL

Create a musical collage with different musical selections representing the steps involved in photosynthesis.

INTERPERSONAL

In small groups, discuss the transformative role of chloroplasts in photosynthesis and draw parallels to students' lives.

INTRAPERSONAL

Write a journal entry that reflects on a personally transformative experience and compare it to photosynthesis.

NATURALIST

Compare seedlings growing in sufficient light to those growing without adequate light.

Lesson/Unit Sequence: ___1. Linguistic activity 2. Logical-mathematical activity 3. Bodily-kinesthetic activity___ 4. Visual-spatial activity 5. Naturalist activity 6. Musical activity 7. Interpersonal activity 8. Intrapersonal activity

Assessment of Outcome: ___1. Grade mathematical timeline and/or painting for the effective display of photosynthesis___ processes based on the steps of photosynthesis and quality of presentation. 2. Ask students to evaluate one another's role-plays and/or songs.

SAMPLE TWO: LESSON/UNIT PLANNING WITH THE MULTIPLE INTELLIGENCES

Lesson/Unit Title: ___Solving Algebraic Equations___

Lesson/Unit Objective (Standard): ___Students will develop algebraic sense through learning to___ solve algebraic equations

Anticipated Learner Outcome: ___Students will be able to explain and apply the concepts of solving equations___

Classroom Resources or Materials: ___Textbooks, colored markers, tape and cassette player for___ "Oh Susannah" or other song

LEARNING ACTIVITIES

LINGUISTIC	MATHEMATICAL-LOGICAL
In pairs, students read, discuss, and outline textbook information.	In small groups, students develop flow charts for solving equations.

VISUAL-SPATIAL	BODILY-KINESTHETIC
Teacher and students color-code the steps of solving algebraic equations. Students solve "colored" equations.	N/A

MUSICAL	INTERPERSONAL
Students compose song lyrics to the tune of "Oh Susannah" that explain vocabulary terms such as sets, exponents, factors, variables, constants, etc.	N/A: Included in other activities but the social skills of listening well, participating, building on each other's ideas are stressed.

INTRAPERSONAL	NATURALIST
Individually, each student identifies two variables in her life and explains how they function similarly to an equation.	In pairs, students create algebraic equations based on variables in nature such as rabbits and foxes or caterpillars and leaves.

Lesson/Unit Sequence: ___1. Visual-spatial activity 2. Linguistic activity 3. Logical-mathematical activity___ 4. Musical activity 5. Naturalist activity 6. Intrapersonal

Assessment of Outcome: ___1. Assess flow charts for accuracy of problem-solving equations. 2. Provide students with___ algebraic equations and ask them to follow color coding process to solve the problems. 3. Ask each student to create one equation and an answer sheet for others to solve.

Interdisciplinary Units

Traditionally, the academic disciplines have been taught without meaningful connections to one another or to students' lives. With MI-based teaching, discrete subject matter distinctions begin to dissolve, enabling teachers to plan interdisciplinary units if desired. Math, reading, music, art, movement, nature studies, and cooperative and independent work and related state standards can be woven into teaching any topic.

A group of middle school teachers in the Seattle School District expressed a desire for an all-purpose matrix for lesson planning as their schools embraced interdisciplinary instruction. In addition to the multiple intelligences and the corresponding curriculum standards they might encompass, the teachers wanted to include critical and creative thinking skills, parent involvement, student choice, and real world connections in some of their units. The matrix they used to organize curriculum planning follows:

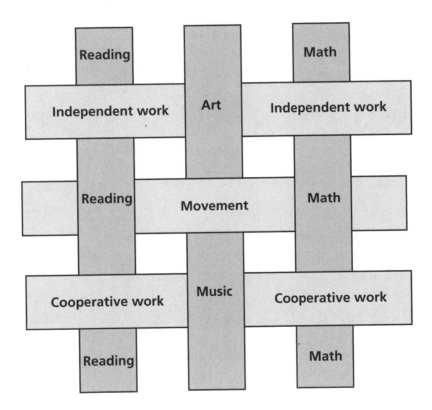

INTERDISCIPLINARY PLANNING THROUGH THE MULTIPLE INTELLIGENCES

Theme: _____ Resources and Materials: _____

	LINGUISTIC PROCESSES OR STANDARDS	MATHEMATICAL PROCESSES OR STANDARDS	VISUAL PROCESSES OR STANDARDS	KINESTHETIC PROCESSES OR STANDARDS	MUSICAL PROCESSES OR STANDARDS	INTERPERSONAL PROCESSES OR STANDARDS	INTRAPERSONAL PROCESSES OR STANDARDS	NATURALIST PROCESSES OR STANDARDS
OBJECTIVES								
STUDENT OUTCOMES								

Unit Sequence: _____

HIGHER-LEVEL THINKING SKILLS • Analysis • Synthesis • Evaluation	CREATIVE THINKING SKILLS • Fluency • Flexibility • Elaboration • Originality	REAL WORLD CONNECTION PROCESSES	PARENT/FAMILY COMMUNITY OPTIONS	STUDENT CHOICE OPTIONS	ASSESSMENT PROCESSES	RESOURCES NEEDED

Unit Closure: _____

Interdisciplinary Planning with Developmental Sequences

The preceding interdisciplinary matrix provides students with numerous enriched learning opportunities. At times, however, teachers may want to focus on in-depth sequential knowledge and skill development in one or more intelligences. To plan such a unit, teachers identify what the student should be able to do by the end of the unit, what the developmental tasks are in the targeted intelligence(s), and the specific activities to be undertaken. A sample is shown on the facing page.

When extensive planning is undertaken (see page 263) as the interdisciplinary units require, it is useful to share such work with other colleagues. In fact, some teachers and schools create portable lessons that are boxed with all the necessary resources, a brief teacher's guide, and an inventory list for refurbishing supplies. Many schools and districts catalog the portable lessons, making them available to interested colleagues, and preventing the proverbial, time-consuming re-invention of the wheel.

Interdisciplinary Schoolwide Approaches at the Secondary Level

Many multiple intelligence programs around the country are housed in elementary schools; yet, Gardner's theory can be applied easily at the secondary level since all of the intelligence experts in a junior or senior high school are readily identified by the subjects they teach. To achieve greater depth in content knowledge and to decrease students' fragmented curricular experience, teachers can plan schoolwide interdisciplinary units.

At the New City School in St. Louis, teachers of fifth- and sixth-graders have used 90-minute blocks for their basic skills subject areas. The teachers split their block time in three equal ways: 30 minutes of direct instruction, 30 minutes of cooperative learning, and 30 minutes of independent learning. When planning the blocks, the teachers review the eight intelligences to see if they are incorporated into all lessons during a week's time. Without making major curricular changes, the time blocks are becoming much more interdisciplinary in nature.

Teachers at any middle, junior, or senior school can meet once annually to identify the major units each covers during the year. It is helpful to chart the topics month-by-month on a large calendar so that everyone can see what is taught when. After learning about one another's curriculum, teachers find it easier to align units that are mutually supportive and to teach them concurrently. For example, the history department in a high school teaches a consumerism unit each spring. The math department usually covers percentages, ratios, and probability in the fall. By shifting such math topics to the spring and adding lessons on stocks and bonds, the two departments can enrich one another's content. To extend such collaboration further, the art department could have students study commercials and create packaging for consumer products. In language arts, students can reflect on potential or real purchases in class journals. Consider what such products reveal about their value systems. English teachers might also oversee independent learning projects of students' choice. PE classes could study the claims and actual results of diverse fitness programs. In science, small groups of students could consider the environmental effects of consumerism. In music classes, songs could be analyzed for the societal values they promote and students could compose lyrics addressing consumerism issues. In industrial arts, display cases could be built for the school's student store, and in life skills, students could compare natural versus synthetic products. By tapping the inherent resources of a high school staff, multiple intelligence–based, interdisciplinary units naturally emerge.

IINTERDISCIPLINARY UNIT PLAN WITH DEVELOPMENTAL SEQUENCES

Theme: _____ Resources and Materials: _____

	LINGUISTIC SKILLS	MATHEMATICAL SKILLS	VISUAL SKILLS	KINESTHETIC SKILLS	MUSICAL SKILLS	INTERPERSONAL SKILLS	INTRAPERSONAL SKILLS	NATURALIST SKILLS
STUDENT OUTCOMES								
DEVELOPMENTAL TASKS								
ASSESSMENT MEASURES								

Unit Sequence: _____

Unit Closure: _____

IINTERDISCIPLINARY UNIT PLAN WITH DEVELOPMENTAL SEQUENCES

Theme: Colonial Life in America   Resources and Materials: Quilt and music supplies, cleared space for dance, research project format and resources for biographies, geometric shapes

	LINGUISTIC SKILLS	MATHEMATICAL SKILLS	VISUAL SKILLS	KINESTHETIC SKILLS	MUSICAL SKILLS	INTERPERSONAL SKILLS	INTRAPERSONAL SKILLS	NATURALIST SKILLS
STUDENT OUTCOMES	Write a biographical character sketch	Apply geometric shapes to quilting	Dance a reel or traditional square dance	Make a quilt or wall hanging	Provide musical accompaniment	Gain diverse perspectives on land use	Conduct a research project of one's choice	Explain how colonists used native plants or animals
DEVELOPMENTAL TASKS	1. Choose an individual from colonial America 2. Gather information from three sources 3. Write draft according to teacher criteria 4. Solicit teacher and peer feedback 5. Rewrite draft	1. Using colored construction paper, cut out squares, rectangles, trapezoids, and right, isosceles, and scalene triangles 2. Arrange in quilt patterns 3. Identify geometric parts, congruent angles, and symmetry	1. Walk through steps of the Virginia Reel or a square dance 2. Perform steps with music 3. Practice dance 4. Perform dance for another class	1. Transfer construction paper quilt designs to fabric 2. Learn piecing and quilting techniques 3. Sew a quilt or wall hanging together	1. Listen to music of colonial America 2. Select a simple classroom instrument 3. Practice playing the instrument 4. Practice playing accompaniment for colonial song	1. In pairs, role play a European colonist and an American Indian 2. Discuss land use concerns 3. Join another pair 4. Identify diverse points of view	1. Identify an interest about colonial times 2. Use a variety of resources to learn about topic 3. Follow research format provided by teacher 4. Identify and prepare a product or form for sharing research	1. Use the Internet or reference materials to identify plants or animals indigenous to one or more of the 13 colonies 2. List ways colonists used the plants or animals 3. Make a small notebook of sketches or written descriptions of the plants or animals and explain how they were used by the colonists
ASSESSMENT MEASURES	Submit final copy of character sketch that meets criteria	Submit a quilt pattern with identified geometric shapes	Perform dance for others	Display sewn quilt or wall hanging	Accompany a recorded song with an instrument	Orally explain two diverse perspectives of land use	Present independent research project according to teacher format	Turn in plant or animal notebook

Unit Sequence: Concurrent through centers

Unit Closure: Colonial fair for another class

One Seattle high school with a highly diverse student population decided to pilot a schoolwide MI week on the topic of international awareness. The literature teachers introduced short stories from the cultures of their immigrant students. Business education teachers addressed international trade issues. Math teachers taught lessons on foreign currency. PE teachers taught games from around the world, and in science, students studied local and global environmental issues. Social studies teachers surveyed diverse forms of government and civil rights issues. Health teachers covered a unit on infectious diseases while art and music teachers engaged students in visual media and ethnomusicology.

During the planning stages for their MI week, the teachers grew so excited with the possibilities for their units, they decided to invite parents to the event as well. Realizing that many parents would not be able to attend school during the day, they changed the week's schedule, starting daily at 3:00 PM and ending at 9:00 PM. Not only was the event a huge success with the students, the school had literally hundreds of parents attending classes with their children. It was the first time that the high school experienced enthusiastic parent participation, especially among immigrant families.

Short-term efforts such as the above introduce teachers to interdisciplinary collaboration without making extensive year-long commitments. Further, secondary teachers work in their content areas without dedicating extensive planning time for new lessons. Nevertheless students benefit from viewing a topic or theme through numerous perspectives and perceiving the connections among formerly distinct subject areas. After such units are taught and assessed, many teachers appreciate the in-depth learning their students underwent. Some secondary teachers claim that interdisciplinary units improve instruction and learning.

Intelligence Teams

Rather than teaming based on content areas, some schools feature "intelligence teams" in which teachers identify and contribute based on their intelligence expertise. Such teams typically consist of two to four educators, each of whom assumes responsibility for one or more intelligences in lesson planning or daily instruction. Working with theme-based or traditional curricula, such teachers serve as resources for one another.

There are countless ways teacher teams self-organize to incorporate the intelligences into school programs. For example, at the Key Learning Community in Indianapolis, Indiana, specialists in the eight intelligences work directly with teachers to infuse each capacity into daily instruction. At Wheeler Elementary in Louisville, Kentucky, teachers have formed grade-level teams, each assuming responsibility for one or more intelligences. Students rotate among classrooms, working with teachers who assume responsibility for providing all students at the same grade level with opportunities for full spectrum learning. Another more common option includes teachers who co-plan multiple intelligence–based lessons while maintaining responsibility for instruction in their self-contained classrooms. In some cases, teams divide instructional tasks by having four teachers assume responsibility for two intelligences.

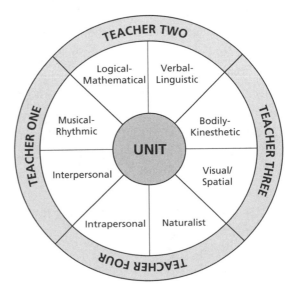

The Benefits of Teaming

Such teaming provides numerous benefits. When working together, coordinating lessons, sharing successes, and addressing challenges, the aggregate accomplishments of the teams far outweigh solitary efforts at improving instruction. When teachers collaborate, they avoid being scrutinized by others for teaching differently, and they reap the benefits of collective practice. Increased dialogue about teaching, education, and one's own personal and professional strengths ensues, and resources are pooled. When planning lessons together, teachers have opportunities to reflect on and refine what, why, and how they are teaching. Students also have much to gain from increased professional dialogue. More students in more classes benefit from the combined expertise of the intelligence teams, and teachers begin assuming responsibility for promoting the growth of their colleagues just as they do for their students.

Some teams find that lessons including several of the intelligences not only provide greater depth in content, they also require more time to teach. Important implications for curricular programs subsequently emerge. Teachers ask, "What are the truly essential concepts my students should acquire?" "What can I omit from the curriculum; what should be retained or added?" "What should a student be able to do by the end of grade level?" "How can student choice be worked into the classroom?" "How many themes should be taught in a school year?" By addressing such questions, teacher teams begin rethinking their school's curriculum. Over time, program-wide changes may come about that respond to notions about what to keep in the current curriculum, what to change, how to assess student work, and what connections to make among subject areas. Multiple intelligences teaching often becomes a driving force for significant curricular reform within a school.

Curriculum Development for Intelligence Development

While most teachers use MI theory as a teaching tool to improve learning, a few have another goal. They want to develop the individual intelligences themselves. This is no small undertaking since each intelligence contains a complex cluster of knowledge and skills and most curriculums are so overcrowded they preclude additional goals. Nevertheless, some educators are forging ahead, trying to develop their students' intelligences in a variety of ways.

Some teachers identify one or more intelligences to emphasize throughout their semester or year-long courses. For example, one middle school teacher integrated one aspect of kinesthetic and musical intelligences, dance, into all her classes. She selected the following core movement elements and skills to guide her efforts:

1. Basic locomotive movements such as walking, running, sliding, skipping, moving forward, backward, diagonally, and turning.

2. Steps, positions, and patterns from different dance styles or traditions

3. The cultural and historical context of selected dances

These three core "intelligence" components regularly appeared in lessons. For example, when students were learning about platonic solids in geometry, they improvised "dances" using basic locomative movements. In social studies, students learned folk dances of Germany and Scandinavia and the social context for such dances. Classroom exercise breaks or transitions often featured movement skills.

Multiple Intelligence Outcomes

One of the authors developed eight, year-long intelligence outcomes that he wove throughout the curriculum when he taught a multi-age classroom of third, fourth, and fifth grade students. These goals included:

Linguistic Intelligence

The writing process

Logical-Mathematical Intelligence

Pattern identification in mathematical processes

Visual-Spatial Intelligence

The use of color, shape, and design

Kinesthetic Intelligence

Eye, hand, body coordination through juggling

Musical Intelligence

Two-part rhythms

Interpersonal Intelligence

Conflict mediation

Intrapersonal Intelligence

Personal goal-setting

Naturalist Intelligence

Identification of seasonal changes in exterior and interior environments

Taking such efforts one step further, some schools have identified multiple intelligence outcomes around which they mold their entire programs. Such schools have determined the essential tasks, achievements, and habits of mind all students should exhibit. Curriculum and assessment are driven by the MI outcomes. One example of such planning in action is at New City School, a K–6 school in St. Louis. There, they have determined that the personal intelligences are the two most important capacities, and as a result emphasize these throughout all classroom and school-wide curriculum. A different example of an MI outcomes program is evident at the K–11 program at Key School in Indianapolis. The Key Learning Community states that upon graduation each student will demonstrate the following core abilities:

- Communicates clearly in written form
- Is verbally articulate in two languages
- Sings or plays a musical instrument proficiently
- Uses math and logic in applied areas
- Uses technology as a tool for inquiry and communication
- Recreates the three-dimensional world through the visual or practical arts
- Is physically fit
- Selects applied area for inquiry, reflection, and apprenticeship
- Participates in stewardship activities demonstrating a shared relationship with nature
- Expresses capacity to care about global issues
- Participates in groups and organizations in the larger community
- If 18, is an active, registered voter

When attempting to develop intelligence, educators are no longer teaching through the intelligences. They are teaching for intelligence.

A Learning Center's Instructional Format

One of the authors taught a successful public school MI classroom for ten years before becoming a curriculum specialist for his district. The program consisted of eight learning centers for mixed-age elementary students. Initially, the centers were named after Gardner's intelligences; they later took the names of individuals who were exemplars of a particular intelligence. The names of the centers changed on a yearly basis. At the beginning of each school year students studied the eight "intelligence experts," and learned how the eight developed and used their intelligences. In this way, eight geniuses became mentors in absentia to the elementary children. The chart that follows describes the names of the centers.

EIGHT LEARNING CENTERS BASED ON THE THEORY OF MULTIPLE INTELLIGENCES

WILLIAM SHAKESPEARE CENTER

(other individuals include Maya Angelou, Li Po)

Linguistic Intelligence

ALBERT EINSTEIN CENTER

(other individuals include Marie Curie, Stephen Hawking)

Logical-Mathematical Intelligence

PABLO PICASSO CENTER

(other individuals include Diego Rivera, Frank Lloyd Wright)

Visual-Spatial Intelligence

MARTHA GRAHAM CENTER

(other individuals include Jim Thorpe, Wilma Rudolph)

Kinesthetic Intelligence

RAY CHARLES CENTER

(other individuals include Kitaro, Carmen McRae)

Musical Intelligence

MOTHER TERESA CENTER

(other individuals include Mahatma Gandhi, Florence Nightingale)

Interpersonal Intelligence

EMILY DICKINSON CENTER

(other individuals include Anne Frank, Sigmund Freud)

Intrapersonal Intelligence

JANE GOODALL CENTER

(other individuals include Rachel Carson, George Washington Carver)

Naturalist Intelligence

The curriculum was thematically organized and much of it was taught through the learning centers. Also at the outset of the school year, students listed topics they wanted to study. Their teacher reviewed the classroom textbooks and district and state standards. He then identified themes that integrated student interests with external curricular requirements. Thematic units were planned that spanned four to six weeks and covered such topics as "Art around the World," "What Things Exist in Space?" "Our Planet's Problems," and "Life in Ancient Civilizations." Though student learning objectives were deliberately taught in the thematic units, they did not necessarily follow textbook sequences.

Once a theme was identified, the teacher divided it into a series of specific lessons. For example, a unit on outer space might include lessons on galaxies, the solar system, comets, planets, and satellites. Each day the instructor presented one aspect of the unit, beginning with a morning "main lesson" which gave an overview of the topic for that day. Students then divided into small groups to work at the centers where they learned about the topic in eight ways. They read, wrote, listened, sang, built, acted, collaborated, invented, made books and models, conducted research, solved problems, and completed art and environmental projects. Some students preferred to move through the eight centers in an orderly, structured way. Others enjoyed traveling more randomly. All students were required to complete certain tasks during the day but each did so in his or her own way.

The lesson shown below is an example of how one aspect of a unit on space on the topic of comets was presented in multiple ways.

Because of the daily variety of student activities, review and practice were no longer monotonous or repetitive tasks. Skills were learned and applied in numerous modes. The work at the centers enabled children to make informative, multimodal presentations of their studies to classmates or others. It was the norm rather than the exception for students to sing, dance, draw, role play, observe, calculate, and write what they learned. It also was the norm for each child to experience some form of daily academic success, since there were opportunities to learn through their strengths. In the ten years since this program was implemented, not a single student has failed to find at least one area in which to excel.

The main lesson and the center time consumed the first half of the school day. At the end of the center experiences, time was set aside to share individual and group center work. On a voluntary basis, students sang or played songs, read poems, displayed artwork, or explained games they had made. Classmates critiqued each other's products, and discussions were frequent about what constituted quality work, and what the students were interested in pursuing next.

A SAMPLE LESSON USING EIGHT CENTERS

MAIN LESSON: "COMETS"

The teacher gives a short lecture with pictures and diagrams describing comets, their size, composition, and orbits. He also includes a kinesthetic demonstration where students portray the sun and the different parts of the comet and "walk" through the comet's orbit around the sun.

CENTERS:

Martha Graham Center: Students make their own comets with sticks, marshmallows, and ribbons for comet tails. Then, as comets, they walk through an elliptical orbit, keeping their tails pointed away from the sun.

Pablo Picasso Center: Using glue and glitter, students make comets on colored paper, correctly labeling all the parts.

William Shakespeare Center: Students read about comets from science textbooks, library books on astronomy, or encyclopedias, and answer questions about their reading.

Ray Charles Center: Using the melody to "Twinkle, Twinkle, Little Star," small groups compose songs about comets which must contain several facts.

Emily Dickinson Center: Individually, students write about how a person's life might resemble a comet.

Albert Einstein Center: Using graph paper and rulers, students draw a series of comets to different scales: with the tail 10× as long as the head, 50× as long, 100× as long, and 500× as long.

Mother Teresa Center: In their groups, students create a game show about outer space that includes visuals and fact cards. Questions presented to the "contestants" must call on higher-level thinking skills.

Jane Goodall Center: Since using telescopes to observe comets is not feasible, provide students with pictures of comets and their orbits. Ask students to categorize the comets by their similarities.

The remainder of the school day was dedicated to independent projects with students pursuing their own interests. The combination of centers in the morning and independent projects in the afternoon provided both structure and flexibility in the daily routine. Additionally, it enabled the teacher to guide the academic and personal growth of the students.

Because of their afternoon project work, students acquired important self-directed learning skills. They learned to ask researchable questions, to identify numerous resources, to create realistic timelines, and to initiate, implement, and bring closure to a learning activity. Students were responsible for initiating, completing, and presenting one project per month. Time was set aside for project presentations the last week of the month. The topics were as numerous as the modes students used to present their ideas to classmate and others. The academic and multifaceted communication skills developed during the centers emerged in highly personal ways through the independent projects.

For their projects, students frequently selected classroom topics to explore in greater depth. Since they were also free, however, to work on noncurricular topics, some studied a single area of personal interest for months at a time. For example, one girl was fascinated with mechanical processes, and did her monthly projects on how things work. Such freedom of choice enabled students to deepen their understanding of school curriculum or to enhance an intelligence of their choice. The achievement gains of the students as measured by standardized tests were impressive. Though they represented diverse ability levels, at the end of the first year the students scored at or above grade level in the basic skills. Their thinking skills, however, were the highest in the school district. Parents clamored to have their children placed in the MI classroom, and it was featured in newspapers throughout the country and included in research studies of Harvard's Project Zero. Classrooms that adopted the model proliferated.

Numerous challenges confront a teacher who attempts to engage several intelligences as daily classroom centers. Although planning is initially a challenge, teachers report the task gradually becomes easier through ongoing practice and by developing a repertoire of instructional approaches. Teachers also learn shortcuts to daily planning, such as providing long-term projects at one or two of the centers or asking students to take charge of planning certain centers.

Many teachers have found it helpful to create plans for a week at a time whenever possible. This frees the instructor to focus on the daily topics and projects at hand. A sample weekly planning grid is shown on the next page.

In centers-based programs, as students work at the centers and on their projects, teacher time can be spent conferring with individuals or small groups. Time can be used to informally assess student work, give feedback for improvement, tutor those with reading or math difficulties, assist gifted students with challenging extensions, and work with small groups to design structures, create dances, and plan projects. In summary, the four main components of this classroom model are as follows:

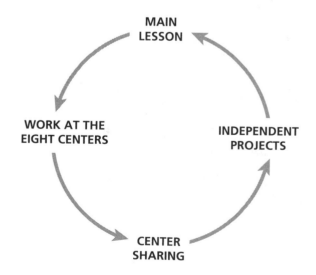

WEEKLY PLANNING GRID

Date: _____

	MONDAY lesson	TUESDAY lesson	WEDNESDAY lesson	THURSDAY lesson	FRIDAY lesson
PICASSO CENTER (Spatial Intelligence)					
MARTHA GRAHAM CENTER (Kinesthetic Intelligence)					
RAY CHARLES CENTER (Musical Intelligence)					
MOTHER TERESA CENTER (Interpersonal Intelligence)					
SHAKESPEARE CENTER (Linguistic Intelligence)					
EINSTEIN CENTER (Logical-Mathematical Intelligence)					
EMILY DICKINSON CENTER (Intrapersonal Intelligence)					
JANE GOODALL CENTER (Naturalist Intelligence)					

Although most classrooms featuring centers are elementary ones, some teachers at Lincoln High School in Stockton, California, have used centers based on the intelligences. Fewer centers were set up on a daily basis due to limited classroom space. Students selected which centers to work at each day and then regrouped to discuss their experiences. The teachers found that the use of centers decentralized the classroom and added flexibility that many students require for effective learning.

The role of classroom teacher in such a model shifts from being a director to serving as a facilitator, guide, and resource provider. In addition, new teaching competencies frequently develop. Skills emerge enabling one to observe students through multiple lenses. Planning diverse approaches to teaching often results in new creative capacities within oneself. One teacher after working with the multiple intelligences approaches asked, "Who is changing the most, the students or myself?"

Project Spectrum

Another approach to center-based teaching was used at Project Spectrum, an early childhood decade-long research effort at Harvard and Tufts Universities. Project Spectrum, which ran from 1984 to 1994, sought to develop curricular alternatives that responded to the diverse interests and abilities of young children. In a Spectrum classroom, children interacted with a variety of materials and studied at numerous centers on a daily basis. Rather than attempting to access each of the eight intelligences directly, centers were established to reflect respected social roles, or in Gardner's terminology, "adult end states." *End states* are skills useful not only in school programs, but also in significant adult roles. Spectrum students, by working at centers on "end state" activities, experienced using an amalgamation of intelligences. For example, at the science center, termed the "naturalist's corner," various plant and animal specimens were available for observation and comparison. This center engaged sensory and logical-mathematical capacities as well as the skills in which naturalists typically engage.

There were eight centers in a Spectrum classroom. These centers and the key abilities they tapped are described below:

Art Center: Visual arts perception, production, and composition

Language: Storytelling, reporting, and wordplay

Math: Numerical reasoning, spatial reasoning, and problem-solving

Mechanical: Fine motor skills, visual-spatial abilities, problem-solving with mechanical objects, and understanding of causal relationships

Movement: Body control, sensitivity to rhythm, expression, generating movement ideas, responsiveness to music

Music: Music perception, production, and composition

Science: Observations, identifying similarities and differences, hypothesis formation and experimentation, interest in knowledge of natural environment or scientific phenomena

Social: Understanding of self, others, assumption of various social roles: leader, facilitator, caregiver, friend

Adult end states shifted to match the focus of center activities. For example, at the language center, the skills of a storyteller, novelist, reporter, lawyer, playwright, and poet were profiled at different times. To further clarify adult roles, Spectrum featured Connections, a community mentoring program for young children. Students worked with local adults from various professions under consideration in the classroom. In this way, children could gain insight into the materials and skills they encountered at school.

The curriculum at Project Spectrum was presented in theme kits that drew on the full range of intelligences. Some themes included "Night and Day" or "About Me" that easily accessed all eight intelligences. The thematic format enabled children to perceive relationships among the disciplines and to examine a topic from multiple perspectives. In an effort to expand the sphere of learning for children, curriculum linkages were made between home, school, and community. Suggested activities that complemented classroom lessons were given to parents. Also, local museums were asked to make museum exhibits more accessible to children. Through integrating the resources of home, school, and community, Project Spectrum students were able to internalize deep understandings of their learnings. For additional information on Project Spectrum, three books may be ordered from the Project Zero eBookstore online at www.Harvard.edu/eBookstore. They are also cited in this chapter's reference list.

Curriculum Bias

Over the years, numerous curriculum trends have proliferated, each with its own philosophic assumptions, goals, and teaching and learning processes. With the advent of Gardner's theory, educators can analyze any curricular model through eight lenses to see if it accommodates the full range of human capacities. When one does so, it may become apparent that some programs have a strong bias by addressing one or two intelligences and excluding others. For example, collaborative learning relies heavily on interpersonal and linguistic intelligences. To ensure that students gain access to subject matter through other modes, the cooperative processes can be adapted to include kinesthetic, visual, musical, logical, naturalist, and intrapersonal processes. With such enhancement, students can learn through their strongest intellectual entry points.

In surveying curricular trends such as writing across the curriculum, integrated technology, and others, biases appear inherent in their formats. In fact, one may ask whether curriculum theorists generate models that reflect their individual intelligence strengths! When a teacher, school, or district is considering curriculum adoption, it may be wise to pose several questions about any program. The following questions help to reveal a model's strengths and weaknesses:

- What is the philosophical perspective promoted by the curriculum?

- What are its assumptions?

- What are the main components of the curriculum (i.e., procedures, assessment, and materials)?

- Which intelligences are emphasized?

- Which intelligences must students possess to succeed?

- Which intelligences are required of the teacher?

- Which intelligences are overlooked?

- How might the curriculum be adapted to include multiple intelligences?

When integrating Gardner's theory into school programs, it is unnecessary to discard current or new programs. Just as teachers adapt individual lessons and units, department or schoolwide programs can also be enhanced. In fact, it is inadvisable to discard what is working well or has the potential to do so. Instead, maintain curriculum that is successful and work to increase its success.

Project-Based Curriculums

▪ ▪ ▪ ▪ ▪ ▪ ▪ ▪ ▪ ▪ ▪ ▪ ▪ ▪ ▪ ▪ ▪

Noting that most productive human work occurs in the form of meaningful and complex projects, Gardner recommends that curriculums feature projects to prepare students for their adult lives. Students readily gain knowledge and skills when they are acquired in realistic contexts through active exploration of their environments and through participation in real world experiences. Whether community service programs, school trips, or laboratory experiments, projects involve students in efforts that are personally relevant and of value for others. Open-ended in nature, a project poses multiple solutions and engages students in a "whole" situation, one that encourages discovery of its parts, relationships, meaning, and resolution.

John Dewey claimed that schooling should ideally consist of a total and continuous experience rather than a series of abstract, fragmented courses taught by several educators. Dewey objected to curriculums that were organized for the convenience of adults, and stressed the value of real world experiences that engaged children's multifaceted natures. In *School and Society*, Dewey (1899) wrote,

> No number of object lessons, got up as object lessons for the sake of giving information, can afford even the shadow of a substitute for acquaintance with plants and animals of the farm and garden acquired through actual living among them and caring for them. No training of the sense organs in school, introduced for the sake of training, can begin to compete with the alertness and fullness of life that comes from daily intimacy and interest in familiar occupations. Verbal memory can be trained in committing tasks, a certain discipline of the reasoning powers can be acquired through lessons in science and mathematics; but after all, this is somewhat remote and

shadowy compared with the training of attention and of judgment that is acquired in having to do things with a real motive behind and a real outcome ahead.

Although most schools are not organized around what Dewey would call a continuous, total experience, many teachers use projects to blend classroom with real life experiences. For example, one fifth grade class wanted to travel to Washington, D.C., to see the government at work. To achieve their goal, the students developed a business plan for a recycling project for fundraising. They had to determine how many residents lived in their town, how many cans were used in the average household per week, how many people would participate in recycling, and how much the projected collection of cans would weigh to estimate their revenues. Expenses also had to be deducted from their proceeds. By planning and implementing this complex, real world project, the students achieved their goal of visiting Washington, D.C.

Primary students at Project Spectrum studied local birds and their nesting habits for one classroom project. They designed and built bird houses and then observed whether their designs successfully met the needs of the birds or whether modifications were required.

Middle school students in Lakewood, Washington, learned biology concepts through a project that involved solving a mock crime. Students conducted investigations, gathered evidence, and attempted to solve the crime. Once the crime was solved, students analyzed the problem-solving approaches that led to the correct answer.

High school students in Palo Alto, California, wanted to determine the use of a piece of property in a redevelopment section of their city. The students prepared videotape documentaries to present to the city council as a way to propose their land use recommendations.

Other high school students in Ithaca, New York, became concerned about cancer therapies after a classmate was diagnosed with leukemia. The students undertook research projects, conducted interviews of medical personnel, and made hospital visits to understand the disease and identify traditional and nontraditional healing approaches.

Such projects typically span two weeks to two months in length. Some teachers include three or more projects in a year, claiming students cover more information than with conventional approaches. Projects are frequently interdisciplinary in nature and draw on a wide range of intelligences in their execution. Many high schools require senior projects for graduation. Guidelines for implementing projects into the curriculum follow.

Guidelines for Effective Projects

1. Identify important concepts or practices and determine an open-ended project that encompasses such knowledge.

2. Involve students in planning the various aspects of a project including the criteria for assessment. At times, students should also create their own projects.

3. Identify and provide needed materials. Also tap knowledgeable community members, parents, or older students as resources.

4. Guide students through the stages of initiation, implementation, refinement, presentation, reflection, assessment, and planning for new and subsequent pursuits.

5. Select student drafts and final work as documentation during and upon completion of the project.

6. Ask students to think back over their learning processes and identify their growth as learners as a result of their projects.

7. Have students present their projects to an audience of classmates, parents, community members, or others who will support and offer constructive criticism of their efforts.

8. Assess the project from numerous perspectives. Gardner has recommended the following:
   - How well the project was planned, presented, and executed
   - Accuracy
   - Challenge level
   - Creativity and originality
   - Use of resources
   - Feedback from knowledgeable individuals about its quality
   - The quantity of student learning
   - The quality of student reflection

9. When students have completed their projects, ask them to reflect on what their work reveals about them—their interests, strengths, challenges, whether they are independent or collaborative workers, and what interests emerged that might be addressed in the future.

Project-based learning skills must be explicitly taught. Students usually require guidance in how to proceed. In Bruce Campbell's (1994) book, *The Multiple Intelligences Handbook: Lesson Plans and More*, he outlines eight steps for teaching students how to carry out projects and recommends that each student have a project videotape to record each presentation. This can be used to share with others, as a tool to self-assess, and as a way to capture students' growth over time.

Project-based classrooms vary from conventional ones. Students become the active initiators of their own learning, making school more lively and relevant. For most students, projects foster their academic and personal strengths, and develop skills for managing the numerous real life projects they will undertake during their adult years.

EIGHT STEPS FOR DOING PROJECTS

1. STATE YOUR GOAL.

"I want to understand how visual illusions work."

2. PUT YOUR GOAL INTO THE FORM OF A QUESTION.

"What are visual illusions and why do they fool our eyes?"

3. LIST AT LEAST THREE SOURCES OF INFORMATION YOU WILL USE.

Library books and Internet resources on visual illusions

Eye doctors or university professors

Prints of M.C. Escher's work

The art teacher

4. DESCRIBE THE STEPS YOU WILL USE TO ACHIEVE YOUR GOAL.

Ask the librarian to find books on visual illusions and read them for relevant information

Research visual illusions on the Internet

Talk to the art teacher and others about visual illusions

Study Escher's work

5. LIST AT LEAST FIVE MAIN CONCEPTS OR IDEAS YOU WANT TO RESEARCH.

What are visual illusions?

How is the human eye tricked?

How are they made?

Who are some artists who have made visual illusion art?

How can I make visual illusions?

6. LIST AT LEAST THREE METHODS YOU WILL USE TO PRESENT YOUR PROJECT.

Explain what optical illusions are.

Make a diagram of how the human eye works.

Make posters with famous optical illusions.

Try to make optical illusions of my own.

Hand out a sheet of optical illusions for class members to keep.

Have the class try to make some.

7. ORGANIZE THE PROJECT INTO A TIMELINE.

Week 1: Access a variety of resources.

Week 1: Interview adults.

Week 2: Look at different kinds of optical illusions.

Week 2: Try to make my own optical illusions.

Week 2: Make diagram of the eye.

Week 2: Make handouts for class.

Week 3: Practice presentation.

Week 3: Present to class.

8. DECIDE HOW YOU WILL EVALUATE YOUR PROJECT.

Practice in front of my parents and get their feedback.

Practice in front of Matt and John and get their feedback.

Ask class for feedback on my presentation and visuals.

Fill out self-evaluation form.

Read teacher's evaluation.

Analyze videotape of my presentation.

Apprenticeships

Some teachers and schools who want to nurture individual student talent establish mentoring or apprenticeship programs. Apprenticeships offer students powerful opportunities to work with older students or adults who have demonstrated expertise in a discipline or craft. When mentored, students can perceive where their classroom efforts are headed and the positive adult end states they may attain. School apprenticeships usually occur in one of two formats: as part of the regular curriculum or as extracurricular enrichment. Some examples follow.

Sample Programs That Are Part of the Regular School Day

Many schools encourage cross-age tutoring programs in which older students assist younger ones with school assignments. Not only do positive relationships develop among the students but academic skills are reinforced for both, and the older students usually appreciate contributing to their school in concrete ways.

The Center for Arts Education in New York City established arts-related mentoring for students in several city K–12 schools. For example, at PS 102 in East Harlem, artists mentor elementary students in the visual and performing arts. Parent workshops are also offered that parallel what students learn in class. Similarly, at Martin Luther King (MLK) High School in New York, artists provide residencies for students who use opera to integrate literature and history. English language learners at MLK participate in residencies that explore collections of European masterpieces.

The Key School in Indianapolis features PODS in which elementary students are mentored by teachers, parents, or community members in crafts or disciplines of their choice. Each student attends a pod four times weekly to work on material related to one or more intelligences with the goal of gaining real world skills. Since the pods are open to any student in the school, they consist of children of varying ages. Pod topics included architecture, cooking, gardening, the Sing and Song Pod, Logowriter, Imagine Indianapolis (a city planning pod), and Young Astronauts.

Extracurricular Apprenticeships

Mentoring can also occur outside of the typical school day. For example, the PTA of an elementary school organized a once-weekly after-school enrichment program offered by parents throughout the school year. Similarly, to address their student latchkey problem, elementary teachers at another school created eight after-school clubs, each dedicated to one of the eight intelligences. Most of the clubs meet weekly and provide an engaging alternative to being at home alone for young students.

The award-winning "Breakout" program at Skyview Junior High in Bothell, Washington, encourages each student to pursue a personal interest and to become an expert on that topic. The main goal of "Breakout" is for students to make a difference in their community. Some choose to work in local hospitals, nursing homes, or schools. Others fundraise for causes of their choice, hold debates, make presentations, create pieces of art that communicate their interests, write short stories, make videos, or design computer software. A mentor is assigned to each student, who assists and tracks student progress and evaluates it on completion. While students pick the content of their community project, the teachers select the skills they must address. These cut across all disciplines and include interviewing, notetaking, statistical analysis, goal-setting, and performance techniques in the arts.

Another approach to apprenticeships is evident at the Key Learning Community. There, seniors must undergo 180 hours of mentoring by a community expert. They then must demonstrate what they learned in community forums. For more information on Key's high school apprenticeship program go to www.ips.k12.in.us/mskey/students/ns/apprentice.

Some enterprising elementary teachers who had centers-based MI classroom models decided that they would seek out community members to mentor their students. In recruiting local citizens, the teachers explained that they would name their classroom centers after those who agreed to work with the students. The school received numerous offers and the students benefited from real life mentors who shared their expertise on a twice-monthly basis in the classroom.

Apprenticeship Possibilities

Gardner has suggested that schools personalize their programs for students by offering apprenticeships during the elementary and middle school years. The apprenticeships he has recommended would not track students into careers at an early age, but instead, they would contribute to a well-rounded liberal arts education. Apprenticeships would consume approximately one third of the student's schooling experience and each student ideally would participate in three:

1. One in an art form or craft
2. One in an academic area
3. A third in a physical discipline such as dance or sports.

Students would have input into the apprenticeships they undertook. Through them, students might learn an important lesson frequently overlooked in today's fast-paced society: that one gains mastery of a valued skill gradually, with effort and discipline over time. If apprenticeships did become a norm of schooling, they would enable students to graduate with significant skills and knowledge to use positively in their communities.

Teaching for Understanding

▪ ▪

In nearly every student there is a five-year-old "unschooled" mind struggling to get out and express itself.

—Howard Gardner, *The Unschooled Mind: How Children Think and How Schools Should Teach*

In the first five years of life, the young child amasses a wealth of information—and misinformation. The young "intuitive learner" as Gardner refers to children of this age, develops comprehensive, "homespun" theories to make sense of the world. In *The Unschooled Mind*, Gardner (1991) suggested that such early notions later supersede instruction in schools. When confronted with rote learning and uninspiring educational experiences, a student's early theories, scripts, and stereotypes hold sway; they do not readily dissolve with instruction. Education should preserve the positive attributes of the youthful mind but also revise the misconceptions students harbor. This can happen only when educators teach for understanding.

What is understanding? David Perkins, Co-Director with Howard Gardner of Project Zero at Harvard University, has addressed the enigmatic nature of human insight. Perkins (1991) contrasts understanding with knowledge. When a person knows something, it is inferred that he has mentally stored that information that can readily be retrieved. By contrast, when a student understands something, it is assumed his skills surpass memory and retrieval. Perkins maintained that understanding refers to what individuals can do with information, rather than recite it, and that insight involves action rather than possession. When students understand something, they can explain concepts in their own words, apply information appropriately in new contexts, and make fresh analogies and generalizations. Indeed, many new assessments ask that students solve problems, make graphs, or write responses to guage whether they understand disciplinary concepts.

How can we promote educational understanding? To move beyond the possession of information to truly understanding it, there are several approaches to pursue. Gardner (1999) summarized some of his thinking on this topic in *Intelligence Reframed: Multiple Intelligences for the 21st Century*. Several components of teaching for understanding are explained below. These can be woven into the planning of major instructional units during a school year.

Principles of Teaching for Understanding

1. Educators can identify essential skills, knowledge, and outcomes for students to tackle. We can ask, "What core ideas and issues are most crucial for students to know?" In many cases, we can use state standards to identify core concepts, but at the same time, instead of trying to cover a breadth of topics, we should strive for depth. For example, in social studies, standards can coalesce around concepts such as democracy, and in the sciences, on change and evolution. In math and music, students can study patterns and transformation, and personal identity and values in literature. Most concepts can be taught through diverse modes and media.

2. Once timeworthy concepts are determined, teachers can address how best to present them to their students. Some teachers organize curriculum around broad themes. Yet the question can be asked, "If we want to teach thematically, where do themes come from?" The Key Learning Community suggests identifying themes through conversations with diverse groups: teachers, scholars, experts, business and government leaders, personnel in cultural institutions, parents, and students. By identifying themes with community involvement, it is easier to gain acceptance of an innovative curriculum while also encouraging community members to participate. Sample themes from the Key Learning Community include:

Changes in Time and Space
The Renaissance Past and Present
Working in Harmony Here and Now
Working in Harmony with Other Cultures
Working in Harmony in Nature
Let's Make a Difference

Some teachers prefer organizing curriculum around open-ended questions for students to answer by the end of a unit. For example, the Montana Office of Public Instruction's program, *Framework for Aesthetic Literacy* (1994), suggested that K–12 English and language arts be taught through the visual and performing arts. Each unit begins with a focus question that provides the cohesive glue for the students' work. A sampling of some of the *Framework for Aesthetic Literacy* questions include:

What is beauty? Who determines the standards for what is beautiful?
What does the past tell us about the present?
How do the arts reflect their cultures?
What can we learn from misfortune?
Why do authors write what they do? How do they do it?

By working with such open-ended questions, students not only acquire basic skills, they also deepen their understanding by generating and defending their answers to some of life's most interesting questions. Pursuing worthwhile questions also addresses students' concerns about why they should bother studying in the first place.

3. Once teachers have identified core concepts and how to present them to students, a road map is needed to guide the instructional journey. The ultimate destination should be identified first. This can be done by specifying, before the unit begins, what students should know and be able to do as a result of their studies. Rubrics, completed work samples, or grading criteria make the hoped-for outcomes concrete and tangible.

Once the outcomes are clarified, the sequence should be mapped out. What will students do when? What essential content or standards will be taught? Which intelligences will serve as entry points into content, for processing content, and for demonstrating knowledge of it? How will such experiences help students reach the specified learning targets?

4. In addition to teacher-directed instruction, students benefit from occasionally determining aspects of classroom curriculum. If a goal of K–12 education is to nurture lifelong learners, students need opportunities to acquire and apply self-directed learning skills. This can be accomplished through encouraging student projects or through setting personal academic goals, both of which can enrich a unit's study. Through self-initiated academic experiences, students deepen their understanding of content while also learning to be autonomous learners, thinkers, and creators.

5. Another strategy for educating for understanding is to offer students access to experts who embody the knowledge and practices of the unit's content. By spending time with such individuals, students will grow in skills more readily than they would by completing work sheets or answering questions at the end of a book's chapter. Such real world examples reinforce the relevance of their studies.

6. All students should use higher-level thinking skills throughout the unit. They should generalize what they learn, provide examples, connect the content to their personal experiences, and apply their knowledge to new situations. For example, in a unit on the criteria of living things, students can be introduced to a bacteria or virus and asked to determine whether the organism is alive. They could also explain the organism's potential impact on health, compare and contrast it with similar entities, and apply knowledge about the organism and criteria of life to similar issues.

7. Assessment is multidimensional and integrated throughout the unit. Students should help establish the criteria for assessing their work before they begin their studies. Additionally, student work should be assessed through multiple lenses: with the teacher informally and formally assessing the students, students assessing each other and themselves. In addition, students should give their teachers feedback on each unit, suggesting ways to improve the learning of future classes.

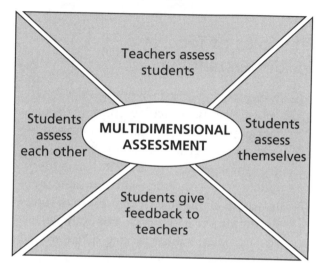

A Rubric for Education for Understanding

The above components of education for understanding may be interesting in theory, but what would they look like in practice? The authors have developed the following rubric that some teachers use as a guide for curriculum development or as a tool for peer feedback when reviewing one another's unit plans or when observing in a colleague's classroom.

Education for Understanding Curriculum Development Rubric

Two sample rubrics follow. The first outlines an elementary unit on the theme of immigration. The second blank matrix is provided for those teachers interested in planning units that incorporate components of education for understanding.

EDUCATION FOR UNDERSTANDING
CURRICULUM DEVELOPMENT RUBRIC

Theme or Guiding Question _____

Essential Content _____

Outcomes

1. _____
2. _____
3. _____
4. _____

ROAD MAP OF UNIT	MI-BASED LEARNING	THINKING SKILLS	REAL WORLD APPLICATIONS	PROJECTS

MULTIDIMENSIONAL ASSESSMENT

Peer and Guest Speaker Assessment _____

Student Self-Assessment _____

Teacher Assessment _____

EDUCATION FOR UNDERSTANDING
CURRICULUM DEVELOPMENT RUBRIC

Theme or Guiding Question ____Immigration: What do immigrants experience as they become American citizens?____

Essential Content ____Social studies standards of immigration and citizenship____

Outcomes

1. ____Students will define immigration____
2. ____Students will define citizenship____
3. ____Students will describe one family's experience of traveling to the U.S.____
4. ____Students will explain the steps of becoming a U.S. citizen____

ROAD MAP OF UNIT	MI-BASED LEARNING	THINKING SKILLS	REAL WORLD APPLICATIONS	PROJECTS
Establish background knowledge of immigration and citizenship	Visual posters of definitions	Compare and contrast similarities and differences	Invite guest speaker to tell her story of journeying to the U.S.	Per predetermined criteria, students complete projects that could consist of map-making, radio show, or service activity to educate others about immigration and/or citizenship
Make timeline from guest speaker's presentation. Research additional information. Conduct conference call with guest speaker to verify accuracy of timeline.	Timeline	Sequencing and researching Verifying data	Guest speaker gives feedback on accuracy of timeline and auxiliary student research	
Watch and summarize Steven Spielberg's videotape of immigration called An American Tale.	Written summary or song lyrics about story	Identify main ideas and supporting details		
Read A Very Important Day by Marissa Moss.	Small group role-plays of becoming a U.S. citizen	Elaboration		
Students conduct interviews and later present stories of local immigrants	News articles or flow charts	Understanding point of view Analyzing	Interviews of local immigrants	

MULTIDIMENSIONAL ASSESSMENT

Peer and Guest Speaker Assessment ____Feedback on role-plays, songs, and timelines____

Student Self-Assessment ____Growth in knowledge about immigration and citizenship____

Teacher Assessment ____Informal assessment of posters, timelines, role-plays, and interviews. Summative assessment of projects.____

Summary

Educators who are considering adopting a multiple intelligences approach should clarify what the concept means to them. There are numerous curricular implications of such a goal. Some of these include multimodal lesson design or deepening discipline-based study. For other teachers an MI approach may refer to project-based learning or apprenticeship opportunities, and for still others it means endeavoring to more effectively teach the "five-year-old mind" so that education results in genuine understanding.

APPLYING THE MULTIPLE INTELLIGENCES IN YOUR CLASSROOM

1. Important ideas or insights gleaned from this chapter:

   _____

   _____

2. Areas I'd like to learn more about:

   _____

   _____

3. Ways I can use this information in my teaching. Please note that all of the strategies mentioned in this chapter are listed below with space provided to note how each strategy might be incorporated into classroom instruction:

CURRICULUM STRATEGY	CLASSROOM APPLICATION
Lesson Planning through the Multiple Intelligences	_____
Instructional Menus	_____
A Lesson Planning Matrix	_____
Sample Lessons	_____
Interdisciplinary Units	_____
Interdisciplinary Planning through the Multiple Intelligences	_____
Interdisciplinary Planning with Developmental Sequences	_____
Interdisciplinary Schoolwide Approaches at the Secondary Level	_____
Intelligence Teams	_____
The Benefits of Teaming	_____
Curriculum Development for Intelligence Development	_____

CURRICULUM STRATEGY	CLASSROOM APPLICATION
A Learning Center's Instructional Format	
Project Spectrum	
Curriculum Bias	
Project-Based Curriculums	
Guidelines for Effective Projects	
Eight Steps for Doing Projects	
Apprenticeships	
Sample Programs That Are Part of the Regular School Day	
Extracurricular Apprenticeships	
Apprenticeship Possibilities	
Teaching for Understanding	
Principles of Teaching for Understanding	
A Rubric for Education for Understanding	
Education for Understanding Curriculum Development Rubric	

▪ ▪ ▪ ▪ ▪ ▪ ▪ ▪ ▪ ▪ ▪ ▪ ▪ ▪ ▪ ▪ ▪ ▪

CURRICULUM DEVELOPMENT REFERENCES

Campbell, B. (1994). *The Multiple Intelligences Handbook: Lesson Plans and More.* Stanwood, WA: Campbell and Associates.

Chen, J., Isberg, E., & Krechevsky, M. (1998). *Project Zero Frameworks for Early Childhood Education, Vol. 2, Early Learning Activities.* New York: Teachers College Press.

Chen, J., Krechevsky, M., & Viens, J. (1998). *Project Zero Frameworks for Early Childhood Education, Vol. 1, Building on Children's Strengths: The Experience of Project Spectrum.* New York: Teachers College Press.

Dewey, J. (1899). *School and Society.* Chicago: University of Chicago Press.

Framework for Aesthetic Literacy: Montana Arts and English Curriculum. (1994). Helena, MT: Montana Office of Public Instruction.

Gardner, H. (1989). *To Open Minds: Chinese Clues to the Dilemma of Contemporary Education.* New York: Basic Books.

Gardner, H. (1991). *The Unschooled Mind: How Children Think and How Schools Should Teach.* New York: Basic Books.

Gardner, H. (1999). *Intelligence Reframed: Multiple Intelligences for the 21st Century.* New York: Basic Books.

Krechevsky, M. (1998). *Project Zero Frameworks for Early Childhood Education, Vol. 3, Preschool Assessment Handbook.* New York: Teachers College Press.

Perkins, D. (1991). "Educating for Insight." *Educational Leadership. Volume 49* No. 2 October, 1991.

10

Dissolving
the Boundaries
ASSESSMENT THAT ENHANCES LEARNING

Unless assessment is placed in the context of authentic domains
and social environments, we doubt it can adequately represent
human intellectual performance.

—Howard Gardner, *Multiple Intelligences: The Theory in Practice*

ASSESSING SUCCESS

Gabriel experienced little success throughout his elementary and middle school years. Labeled by teachers as a poor student with a negative attitude, Gabriel readily accepted his instructors' appraisals.

*H*is low expectations of any future academic accomplishments were evident in his statement to his math teacher on the first day of high school when Gabriel blatantly suggested, "Give up on me." Knowing that first impressions mattered, the teacher quickly responded, "I'm not intending to give up on you!" Gabriel retorted cynically, "It's just a matter of time."

The teacher already knew that Gabriel scored at the third or fourth grade level on standardized math tests. What he didn't know, however, was how he might work with this recalcitrant student. To learn more about Gabriel, the teacher informally observed him both inside and outside of class. In the hallways, the boy was animated, often talking with several students and jocularly swatting and

slapping his friends. Noting whom Gabriel spent time with, the teacher later approached the boys, asking them to tell him about Gabriel. The teacher learned that Gabriel held a job at a local grocery store, and that he enjoyed skateboarding. This information inspired ideas about how to engage him in math.

The next day, the teacher suggested to his ninth grade math class that they had the option of replacing some textbook work with math projects. When the class unanimously voted in favor of real world projects, the teacher explained that the students would have to research information about products or concepts they found interesting, and identify some prespecified mathematical principles as evident in their topics. The students spent the rest of their math class brainstorming criteria for assessing their projects. Since Gabriel spent the hour with his head down, looking bored and disengaged as usual, the teacher approached him individually just as the bell rang. "Gabriel, I know you're good at skateboarding. Your friends tell me so. Why don't you do a project on skateboards? You could even bring one or two skateboards to school to do a demonstration for the class." In response to the teacher's well-meant suggestion, Gabriel shrugged and walked out of the room.

The projects weren't due for two weeks and the teacher did not know whether Gabriel was working on one until another student in the class blurted out, "Wait until you see what Gabriel's doing!" The teacher's spirits rose—perhaps, after all, he was choosing to participate.

As the appointed day drew closer, students began signing up to present their work. When Gabriel said he wanted to do his first, he quickly informed to the teacher that he "simply wanted to get it over with."

Students created score sheets for assessing each other's projects. The teacher explained he would use the same form. On project day, Gabriel was the first to share his work. He displayed one chart that compared several brands of skateboards in relation to performance, cost, and design; another diagram gave a statistical analysis of top ranking skateboarders and their abilities; and a third revealed the results of a survey he conducted of fellow classmates and their attitudes towards skateboarding. Without using appropriate math terminology, Gabriel nevertheless explained that skateboarding involved several mathematical principles, including those of physics, symmetry, probability, and mathematical thinking and problem-solving skills. When students and the teacher handed Gabriel their assessment sheets evaluating his project, his slight smile went unnoticed by most except the math instructor.

The project assignment was the first time Gabriel chose to participate in his math class. His involvement not only enhanced his self-image, but also revealed an effective mathematical thinker. By the end of the semester, on a standardized test, Gabriel's math scores had improved significantly. Though his participation in class remained somewhat inconsistent, neither Gabriel nor his teacher talked again about giving up.

A Nation Assesses

In recent decades, reliance on standardized testing had increased, as have concerns about its impact on educational resources and curricular and instructional practices. Additionally, critiques of standardized tests have focused on their tendency to overassess rote knowledge while underassessing what students can do with their knowledge.

Norm-referenced, multiple-choice tests are quick and efficient to administer, but policymakers have reconsidered their value. New state assessments, though not yet perfected, are emerging that attempt to yield more genuine pictures of student learning than possible with short-answer evaluations. Numerous teachers and districts now work with portfolios and performance-based tasks. Admittedly still in the developmental phase, new forms of assessment are fraught with questions about time, reliability, and manageability. Yet many educators, acutely aware of the deficiencies and limitations of standardized measures, believe that new approaches to assessment will capture more of what students know and can do both within and outside of school.

Admittedly, assessment is a complex issue and one that evokes extensive debate. It is not the goal of this chapter to address controversies with standardized testing. Instead, we review research and strategies from Gardner and others that show how assessment can improve teaching and learning.

Through Project Zero, Howard Gardner and others studied classroom assessment and determined that effective monitoring of student work cannot exist in a vacuum. The classroom itself can be transformed so that meaningful assessment takes place. It is not enough to change current evaluation procedures. Instructional practices can be altered so that an effective assessment culture emerges in our schools. In many cases, assessment occurs at the end of a unit of study and emphasizes grading and accountability. Although such summative evaluation practices serve important roles at times, they do not necessarily improve learning.

When teachers integrate active performance assessments throughout their units they say many changes ensue. When students actively demonstrate what they are learning, their motivation and achievement increase (Campbell, 2002). Further, teaching practices transform and more equitable participation of all students is evident.

Principles to Guide Classroom Assessment
1. Assessment Captures Growth over Time
2. Assessment Is Multidimensional
3. Asssessment Informs Instruction
4. Informal Assessment Is Important
5. Students Are Active Self-Assessors

Assessment of the Intelligences
Measuring Intelligence at Project Spectrum
Working Styles
Spectrum Reports
Perceiving Student Strengths

Assessment through the Intelligences
Sample Verbal-Linguistic Assessment Approaches
Sample Logical-Mathematical Assessment Approaches
Sample Visual-Spatial Assessment Approaches
Sample Bodily-Kinesthetic Assessment Approaches
Sample Musical Assessment Approaches
Sample Interpersonal Assessment Approaches
Sample Intrapersonal Assessment Approaches
Sample Naturalist Assessment Approaches

Processfolios
Processfolio Guidelines

An Assessment Schedule
Schoolwide Assessment Processes
Multiple Intelligences Report Cards

Our goal is to offer an array of tools to expand the assessment repertoires of classroom teachers. We do not suggest that these techniques apply across all districts or the nation for high-stakes policy decisions about schools and those who study in them. Rather, we encourage teachers to create diverse assessment measures that require students to use and not simply recall their knowledge. In doing so, students will be better prepared for state assessments that feature mixed formats and performance-based tasks.

Principles to Guide Classroom Assessment
▪ ▪ ▪ ▪ ▪ ▪ ▪ ▪ ▪ ▪ ▪ ▪ ▪ ▪

Two significant research studies at Harvard Project Zero were undertaken in the 1980s and 1990s that addressed assessment. One was Project Spectrum, already mentioned in Chapter 9, and the second was Arts PROPEL. Between 1986 and 1991, Arts PROPEL, a pilot approach to teaching and assessing in the arts and humanities, was field tested by Harvard Project Zero, by Educational Testing Service, and by teachers, administrators, and students in Pittsburgh, Cambridge, and Boston. The two main goals of Arts PROPEL were to observe how students learn in the arts at the middle and high school levels, and to devise evaluation methods that enhanced learning and assessed achievement. Arts PROPEL initially assumed its work had relevance for secondary level arts instruction, but its implications appear appropriate for elementary grades and for other academic subjects. Similarly, the work from Project Spectrum for early childhood education appears to have important implications for the upper grades as well.

It should be noted that the name PROPEL was an acronym for three roles students should play in assessment: PRO is for *production* (and includes an R for *reflection*), PE is for *perception*, and L is for the *learning* that results. PROPEL and Project Spectrum principles can guide teachers interested in changing their assessment procedures. Below are sample assessment tools and examples that bring each assessment principle to life.

1. Assessment Captures Growth over Time

Frequently, student work is assessed in an isolated, snapshot manner, eclipsing a long-term perspective of academic growth. The portfolio is one tool that effectively offers longitudinal perspectives of student work while encouraging ongoing reflection of classroom learning. Depending on their use, portfolios provide evidence to students, teachers, parents, and others of both academic and intrapersonal growth.

Students, when given the opportunity, often enjoy assuming an active role in evaluation by determining their own longitudinal, academic gains. This can be achieved by asking students to contrast their former knowledge with their current skills and comprehension. Students can reflect on their growth in each subject matter area by reviewing the contents of their portfolios, journals, or several samples of their work. To aid such reflection, teachers might pose the questions in the following box for students to consider.

Even second or third grade students can respond to similar questions when encouraged to reflect on their progress. Such skills develop, however, only when teachers ask reflective questions. Others can also reinforce such thinking. Parents and others can pose the same questions listed below. In fact, it is often beneficial for student, teacher, and parent to compare and contrast responses to the same set of questions.

STUDENT REFLECTION ON ACADEMIC GROWTH

In reviewing samples of your work during the last few months, please respond to the following questions:

- What samples of your work did you review? When were the assignments completed?
- How has your work changed? How does it differ from before? What evidence do you have of such change?
- What did you learn that you didn't know previously? When and how did you learn this new information? Did your new learning contradict or affirm your prior knowledge?
- How have you used your new knowledge in this class, in other classes, and outside of school?
- Do the changes in your work affect how you see yourself as a mathematician, writer, artist, etc.?
- Have you achieved an adequate knowledge and skill level? If not, how might you gain additional information in the future?
- What other comments might you make about your work over the last few months?

2. Assessment Is Multidimensional

Typically, letter grades or scores provide the student, teacher, and others with little information about achievement. Traditional measures such as numerical percentages simply state whether a student has scored low, average, or high in a subject matter area. This unidimensional view does not convey what was accomplished and what was challenging. For example, in a math class, a student could receive a C grade. This single score would not indicate that the student performed at a superior level in mathematical thinking and problem-solving, above average on daily assignments, yet failed most tests and quizzes due to test anxiety. If the C grade were replaced with multiple indicators, meaningful and relevant interventions would be possible. One alternative math assessment might appear as follows.

MATHEMATICS QUARTERLY ASSESSMENT

Student name: _____   Date: _____

Major concepts studied: _____

_____

STUDENT PERFORMANCE CHECKLIST

	Strong	Adequate	Poor
Comprehension of math processes, e.g., quadratic equations			
Interpretation of problems			
Problem-solving of text problems			
Problem-solving of open-ended, real world problems			
Performance on assignments			
Performance on tests			

Narrative comments: _____

_____

_____

Identified student strengths to build on: _____

_____

_____

Recommendations for strengthening skills: _____

_____

_____

In contrast to most reporting measures, this assessment tool identifies student strengths and weaknesses, and recommends options for ongoing learning.

Another approach to multidimensional assessment is to gain feedback on student performance from numerous sources. In fact, assessment can ideally consist of three perspectives: 1) assessment of content and skills, 2) interpersonal assessment from peers, parents, or knowledgeable community members, and 3) intrapersonal assessment from students who are responsible for assessing their achievement.

One of the authors developed the report card on the facing page for elementary students that incorporates all three perspectives. This report augmented the school's traditional trimester evaluation of student progress.

3. Assessment Informs Instruction

A frequent criticism of standardized or traditional assessment is that it focuses instruction on memorization and recall. When assessment addresses essential and important aspects of learning, it can influence and improve instruction in positive ways.

As most educators would agree, one of the greatest obstacles to effective learning is the pressure to cover content. Frequently, we are asked to survey a smorgasbord of topics. Many teachers, when teaching through the multiple intelligences, however, claim that learning slows down, that less content is covered but what is studied is done so in greater depth and increased student understanding. Today, we can take solace in the fact that our society is immersed in the information age. Since more information is available than we could ever access or use in each discipline, it becomes impera-

tive to identify what is most essential for students to know, and what behaviors will benefit them as adults.

In some cases, teachers are determining what is most important to teach by following the principle, "If it is important enough to teach, it is important enough to assess." For example, the Northwest Regional Educational Laboratory (1998) has identified the traits of an effective reader. Some teachers use the traits to both teach and assess reading skills. Sample skills include decoding, comprehension, realizing context, making interpretations, synthesizing ideas, and critiquing.

Assessment consists of a five-point scale ranging from a low skill level of 1 to a high of 5 to score each reading skill evident in student work. The curriculum in such cases integrates what students are to learn and how they will be assessed. Students know in advance not only what their task is, but the standards for their reading.

Just as essential classroom curriculum can be identified, schoolwide outcomes can also be specified to guide curriculum development and assessment in each subject area. For example, a middle school might select the following outcomes as integral to all subject areas: identifying a problem, accessing information and resources, learning disciplinary content, considering diverse perspectives, collaborating on projects, reflecting on one's growth, and effectively managing one's behavior. To help students achieve these outcomes, each classroom, as part of its curriculum, might feature open-ended problems, group and independent projects, access to technology, multicultural issues, portfolios, and positive discipline strategies. Each teacher in each discipline would then teach to and assess the same outcomes. A particularly inspirational example of integrated K–12 outcomes is evident in the curriculum of the Chugach, Alaska, school district. In this case teachers have identified

DIFFERENT PERSPECTIVES REPORT CARD

Name: _____ Date: _____

How are you doing in the following categories?

Write one sentence in the box under "self," describing your progress in each area.

Then, ask a classmate to evaluate your performance in the second column.

Next, take it home and ask a parent or other adult to assess your work in the third column.

Compare and contrast everyone's opinion of your progress. Do you agree or disagree with their comments? Write your reactions to this feedback on the back of the card and place the card in your portfolio when completed.

	SELF	CLASSMATE	ADULT
LANGUAGE ARTS reading writing speaking listening			
VISUAL AND PERFORMING ARTS music movement drawing			
MATH computation problem-solving			
CENTERS WORK completing tasks working with others			
INDIVIDUAL PROJECTS research planning presenting			

all knowledge and skills their predominantly Alaska Native students should master at each academic level and how each level integrates with the next for all elementary through secondary years. Students know what is expected of them at all times and many are mastering the content in their early teens and entering college sooner than their counterparts in other schools.

Another way that assessment can inform instruction is through specifying the standards by which students will be assessed. Grading criteria are most meaningful when democratically determined by teachers and students together. Students gain insight into both assessment and learning when they participate in discussions about what constitutes good work. Ideally, high standards in any classroom should address both the knowledge of content and the processes of learning. Typical tests tend to overemphasize factual knowledge with little focus on the thinking and learning processes. The example below shows how grading criteria can include both content and process.

Traditionally, assessment has been viewed as a way to gather data about student comprehension and performance. It also indicates, however, the quality of instruction and reveals how effectively students were taught in the first place and what additional instruction they need. Teachers can hold discussions or seek written feedback from students at the end of major curriculum units to learn what was effective and ineffective. Additionally, teachers can observe when students struggle with concepts and plan to reteach the topics through different intelligences. It is also beneficial to evaluate students multimodally so they can demonstrate what they have learned in several ways.

SCIENCE ASSESSMENT

Name: _____   Date: _____

PROCEDURES	COMMENTS
Understands target concept	
Makes a meaningful prediction	
Selects an effective approach	
Uses correct equipment	
Analyzes data	
Measures accurately	
Graphs data appropriately	
Seeks peer help if needed	
Records observations	
Considers next steps	
Cleans up after experiment	
Other	

Rather than being concerned that all students master all concepts at the same rate, or that some need more help than others, teachers and schools can create support structures to ensure greater student success at varying times. At the beginning of any term, teachers might specify what concepts will be learned and what assignments will be required. Students can be free to work at their own pace while completing curriculum projects in a timely manner. Other resources such as computer-assisted instruction can be made available. By having binders or notebooks of student assignments from previous years, students can consider how their predecessors approached similar topics, how they problem-solved, and how they brought their projects to fruition. Cross-age tutoring with older students or community volunteers often increases achievement. In Washington State, students from a rural high school tutored children from an elementary school, some 35 miles away, by fax. Homework halls, phone hotlines, or centers in community agencies can also provide significant support.

Teachers can also begin to rethink instruction and assessment by reflecting on valued social roles that adults assume. What are the projects or tasks performed by accountants, historians, journalists, naturalists, artists, musicians, or social workers? What content knowledge and abilities do they each possess? Are there implications for classroom instruction and assessment? Typically, vocational education programs have addressed this issue successfully by identifying performance tasks that cover essential content while providing students with increasingly complex projects such as building a usable structure in carpentry. Debate and arts programs are often structured similarly.

Even with preschool and primary-age students, assessment can highlight skills relevant to rewarding adult roles or endstates. For example, at Project Spectrum in language arts, a child's ability to tell stories or provide descriptive accounts of experiences (the skills pertinent to journalists or novelists) was assessed rather than the repetition of a series of sentences. When grounded in real world activities, assessment is more meaningful to the child, teacher, family, and ultimately, society.

4. Informal Assessment Is Important

Formal and informal types of assessment are valuable. Teachers know much more about their students than is typically recorded with traditional paper and pencil measures. Students are informally assessed daily by teachers who regularly observe their participation in classroom interactions. At times, such informal knowledge can be made explicit through simple observation checklists such as the example shown on the next page.

In addition to observation, teachers can hold small- or whole-group sessions where students critique quality work as well as consider the effectiveness of instruction. Such discussions do not leave a paper trail, but instead yield insight into student perceptions of their work, classroom experiences, and accomplishments and frustrations.

OBSERVATION CHECKLIST

Teacher: _____ Class: _____ Date: _____

TARGET SKILLS

Ratings: + = Frequently
          ✓ = Sometimes
          o = Not Yet

NAMES OF STUDENTS						COMMENTS
1.						
2.						
3.						
4.						
5.						
6.						
7.						
8.						
9.						
10.						
11.						
12.						
13.						
14.						
15.						

5. Students Are Active Self-Assessors

If a goal of K–12 education is to develop autonomous, lifelong learners, students need opportunities to manage their own learning and to determine their achievement. When given opportunities to do so, students can evaluate their strengths and weaknesses, evaluate what they have learned, and document their use of appropriate thinking and learning processes. They can capture such data in journals, peer assessment sessions, checklists, exhibitions, informal student/teacher discussions, or portfolios. One example of active student reflection is evident in the portfolio reflection sheet on the facing page.

When students are asked to reflect on their work, they become active learners. They construct an understanding of the subject matter. They perceive and begin to internalize standards that are relevant and meaningful. They realize the choices they made in their work and the options they rejected. They also acquire the skills for ongoing growth outside of school wherever self-initiated and open-ended activities occur.

PORTFOLIO ITEM REFLECTION

Name: _____ Date: _____

Description of the portfolio selection:

Why did you select this sample from your portfolio for reflection?

What content knowledge did you acquire while working on this piece?

What did you learn about yourself as a historian, biologist, etc.?

If you were to continue working on this selection, what would you add, delete, or change? Why?

What problems did you encounter with this selection? How did you resolve them?

In what ways does your selection meet the specified grading criteria for this assignment? In what ways does it not meet such criteria? Identify any ways it may have surpassed such criteria.

What else would you like to research because of what you learned from this assignment?

By extending these five principles of assessment into classroom procedures, the line between assessment and learning blurs and dissolves. Information about students is valuable when it is gained over time during their involvement in learning. Assessment that occurs when work is completed is often too late to be helpful. Multimodal or "intelligence fair" measures can occasionally be employed to avoid overreliance on linguistic or quantitative means. Assessment can become less threatening, less decontextualized, and assume its rightful place as a partner in learning. In such environments, student work is not done once and thrown away. Students can continue to refine their learning by resubmitting their work for suggestions and critique. They can review it for evidence of what was learned and has yet to be learned. Assessment, when thoughtfully used, ceases merely to reflect learning—it enhances learning.

Assessment of the Intelligences

Project Spectrum, a laboratory preschool at Harvard, was dedicated, in part, to exploring the development of the multiple intelligences in young children. Originally, Gardner intended to create seven instruments at Project Spectrum to assess the intelligences he had identified at that time. He quickly realized, however, that since intelligence does not exist in a vacuum, any attempt at gauging human capacities would necessarily have to measure prior life experiences and other influences. Prior learnings, the environment, heredity, and cultural values, all shape and mold the capacities an individual develops. Because of the interplay among biological, environmental, and cultural potentials, Gardner decided it made little sense to consider intelligence in the abstract.

Measuring Intelligence at Project Spectrum

To measure the multiple intelligences of Spectrum students, Gardner and his colleagues decided to immerse children in a year-long, enriched environment and assess the capacities they demonstrated in a natural context. Mara Krechevsky (1998), Director of Project Spectrum, worked extensively with a comprehensive approach to assessing individual intelligences of her students. Children's unique cognitive profiles were determined in part through a variety of processes:

- The classroom environment featured engaging materials, games, and learning opportunities for each of the eight intelligences.

- Several forms of documentation were used consisting of score sheets, observation checklists, portfolios, and tape recordings.

- Information was gathered over time in context in the child's environment.

- Intelligences were tapped directly through each particular medium rather than assessing abilities through conventional linguistic and mathematical means.

- Children's strengths were emphasized.

- Assessment was embedded in real world activities useful both in and outside of the school setting.

One sample assessment activity used in a Spectrum classroom was the bus game. This game identified a child's ability to use a notational system, perform mental calculations, and organize number information for one or more variables. Using props, the game featured a cardboard bus, a game board with bus stops, adult and child figures who got on and off the bus, and sets of colored chips. The adult supervising the activity assumed the role of the bus driver, while the student being assessed served as the conductor. To play the game, the child kept track of how many people got on and off the bus at each stop. The bus trips became increasingly more challenging. At the first stop, for example, people could only get on the bus. At the second, they could get on or off. The student was also asked to count the number of adults and children on the bus. For some trips, the chips were used to keep track of the numbers, while on others the child was asked to count in his head.

In this game, students were assessed on their ability to organize numerical information efficiently in a real world situation, but quantitative skills were only one aspect of logical intelligence measured. Students were also assessed on their abilities to create notational systems and code different kinds of information. As the child assumed the role of a conductor, he practiced the skills needed by an adult in such a job. Such assessment procedures have meaning for the child, the teacher, the child's family, and the community at large.

Other games and activities totaling some fifteen measures in all have been developed at Project Spectrum are available in the book *Project Spec-*

trum: Pre-School Assessment Handbook (1998). All of the measures are "intelligence fair" since they avoid hypothetical situations and abstractions and provide children with challenging concrete tools to manipulate in each intelligence area. For example, physical skill is measured, in part, with an obstacle course; mathematical intelligence is assessed through the bus, treasure hunt, and dinosaur games. Other Spectrum tasks include: storytelling and reporting for linguistic intelligence, using portfolios for art, analyzing interpersonal interactions and intrapersonal awareness with a classroom model and events, singing, playing, and learning new songs for musical intelligence, participating in creative movement curriculum for kinesthetic intelligence, completing assembly tasks and observations for additional logical-mathematical activities, and conducting environmental projects for naturalist activities.

Working Styles

When assessing individual intelligences, Project Spectrum researchers discovered the importance of considering the "working styles" of children when they worked with tasks of the different intelligences. Some students demonstrated the same working style across several intelligences, but styles of others appeared influenced, in part, by the task at hand. Some children, for example, were focused and reflective when working in their areas of strength, and distractible and impulsive in areas that proved more challenging. Working styles refer to the behaviors and attitudes toward learning. They may provide insight into approaches to tasks that can either help or hinder learning. Student working style characteristics noted at Spectrum included:

Easily engaged . . . . Reluctant to engage
Confident . . . . Tentative
Playful . . . . Serious
Focused . . . . Distractible
Persistent . . . . Frustrated by task

Reflective . . . . Impulsive
Apt to work slowly . . . . . Apt to work quickly
Conversational . . . . Quiet

Responds to visual, kinesthetic, or auditory stimuli
Demonstrates planned approach
Brings personal agenda or strength to task
Finds humor
Uses materials in unexpected ways
Has pride in accomplishment
Pays attention to detail
Is curious about materials
Is concerned with correct answer
Focuses on interaction with adult
Transforms the task or material

When Spectrum teachers observed students in action, they identified the distinctive styles the children exhibited. It should be noted that there were no negative or positive connotations attached to the working style descriptions. Of course, not all characteristics were evident in a single learning activity. The concept of working styles may have important implications for educational interventions.

Spectrum Reports

Spectrum tasks were implemented over the course of a year. During this time, the working styles of each child were also observed. At the end of the year, a Spectrum Report summarized all information gathered about a child. The document described the child's personal profile of strengths and weaknesses and suggested activities at home, school, or in the community to enhance strengths and bolster weaknesses. Such informal recommendations were offered to help students and families make informed choices about future educational options. A sample Spectrum Report follows.

Harvard's Spectrum program has been adapted in several ways. Teachers and researchers from around the country have used the program with

SPECTRUM REPORT

Greg

Greg has shown a strong ability and interest in many of the Spectrum activities presented to the class this year. He has distinguished himself in the areas of visual arts and numbers.

Greg's efforts in the area of visual arts are impressive for a child his age. What is most striking is his comfort and effectiveness in using a wide variety of media. These include paint, markers, collage, wood, and styrofoam. In drawings, Greg has shown an unusual sensitivity to color, composition, and detail. His drawings consist of both complex representations and designs. In one drawing, Greg drew an extremely detailed underwater scene including a half dozen distinctively different fish, an underwater vehicle, a whale spouting water, and flecks of "super red fish food." In another drawing, he drew a Native American with his donkey after carefully looking at a similar picture on the wall of the classroom. He added stripes of face paint in alternating colors and a large headdress complete with dozens of feathers. Greg's use of space is also very effective. He uses the whole page for his compositions, relating individual parts to one another and to the page as a whole. Greg's 3-D sculptures are outstanding as well. He exhibits

an understanding and awareness of design and composition "all the way around" his creations. Informal observations of Greg in the classroom have shown that he can spend a long time working on a single painting or drawing and that he enjoys reworking many of them over and over again.

Greg has revealed a strong competence with numbers and number concepts. When playing the Dinosaur Game, a Spectrum activity centered on numbers and number concepts, his counting was a bit inconsistent, but he understood the strategy component of the game. When given the choice of a die that had five out of six signs meaning that he could move his gamepiece forward, or five out of six signs meaning he could move backward, he chose the die that would help him to win and articulated the reason for the choice. He also correctly chose the move that would be most beneficial to him and the move that would be least beneficial to the adult, his opponent in the game.

Whereas earlier in the year Greg appeared to have some difficulty counting accurately while playing the Bus Game in the spring he exhibited an outstanding facility with numbers for a child his age. He devised a successful method of using different colored chips to help him keep a running tally of figures entering and exiting a toy bus at a series of station stops. Later in the activity, he was able to calculate in his head the number of figures entering and exiting the bus at the various stops.

Greg has also demonstrated a strong interest in the Discovery Area of the classroom. At the very beginning of the year, Greg helped to dig up animal bones in the playground. He spent a lot of time looking at the bones and trying to figure out how the pieces fit together. This interest has persisted throughout the entire year. Greg often brings in an assortment of his pets from home to put in the discovery area and tell the children about during "Show and Tell." In addition, he made a remarkably accurate sculpture of a bone out of clay. Based on these observations, we feel that Greg might enjoy additional opportunities to explore the natural world. The Children's Museum and the Museum of Science both have excellent displays and resources in this area.

In an activity which involved taking apart and reassembling two small food grinders, Greg showed a competence with and understanding of mechanical objects. He approached the task in a straightforward, serious, and focused manner and completed it with very little help from the adult. Greg was attentive to detail and demonstrated an understanding of the causal connection between the various parts of the objects.

One activity in which Greg was not initially eager to participate was creative movement. He had some difficulty with the structure of the movement sessions earlier in the year. He would usually choose to be in the "audience" rather

than participate and would sometimes disrupt the group and express his disdain for the movement activities. As the year progressed, Greg became an active member of the creative movement sessions. He generated some inventive movement ideas for the group and participated willingly in most of the group's activities.

Greg revealed strengths in many areas throughout the course of the year. He was enthusiastic and energetic in his approach to many of the Spectrum activities. He showed that he was capable of extremely focused work in areas of particular interest to him such as the visual arts and natural science. There were, however, some activities in which Greg chose not to engage. For example, he chose not to participate in the two music activities and the storyboard activity. He expressed an interest in the materials themselves, asking how things were made and where things came from, but did not always show an interest in the structured activities related to the materials.

As the year progressed, Greg became comfortable with the one-to-one format of the Spectrum activities. This enabled him to share his ideas more freely and make apparent the strengths and interests he had in a variety of areas.

average, gifted, and at-risk children from four to eight years old. Spectrum has also forged new links among schools, museums, homes, and local communities to enhance children's learning. For example, Spectrum developed a curriculum for preschoolers at The Children's Museum in Boston to make museum exhibits more accessible to young children. "Connections," Spectrum's community mentor program, enabled young children to work with professional adults who exemplify different intelligences in their jobs. Spectrum approaches seek to increase academic achievement, enhance self-esteem, and ease school adjustment.

Perceiving Student Strengths

A fundamental implication of Gardner's work concerns how we perceive our students. Even though educators want to identify student strengths, doing so has proved challenging for several reasons. We can appreciate, at least theoretically, that students possess individual cognitive profiles with varying strengths. And yet, when trying to put such notions into practice, it can be difficult to observe children through a multiple intelligence lens. The initial challenge we often face is looking beyond our inherent strengths to perceive those that may be unfamiliar. Additionally, when we consider how students fare in school, we usually think in traditional ways such as how they perform in basic skill areas. These challenges are exacerbated by the fact that most teacher development efforts at both the pre-service and in-service levels emphasize how to educate for traditional literacies. There is little work being done to teach teachers how to acknowledge talents across content areas. We need tools to expand our observation skills and to identify and document diverse capacities.

Many educators wish there were simple checklists that could readily indicate the intelligence strengths of their students. In fact, several such multiple intelligence checklists have been developed. Educators should use them with caution, if

at all, since they do not adequately reflect the numerous facets of each intelligence, nor do they use "intelligence fair" measures to assess student strengths.

Even when teachers have embraced the belief that all students possess strengths, it remains all too easy to limit the perception of talent to linguistic and logical-mathematical skills. One study made this phenomenon clear. Campbell (2000) explored the beliefs of elementary and secondary teachers after they had learned about Gardner's theory. All teachers claimed that MI had a significant impact on their conceptions of intelligence. Yet, when asked to describe the characteristics of intelligent students, many offered traditional descriptors. For them, bright students were quick thinkers, knew large amounts of content, and were usually highly verbal.

How can we go about counteracting traditional notions? How can we broaden our perception of student strengths? Some suggestions follow.

Approaches to Perceiving Student Strengths

1. Enrich your classroom environment with manipulatives, art supplies, musical instruments, hands-on math activities, books and book-making materials, and other items to engage several intelligences. Provide students with free time and observe what they enjoy doing the most.

2. Survey parents to determine student interests and strengths. Learn what students like to do outside of school as one way to identify interests and talents.

3. Interview teacher specialists such as PE, art, music, librarians, and technology personnel to learn if they have identified students with evident strengths in their programs.

4. Provide students with self-directed learning opportunities and independent project work to pursue their interests. Observe their choices.

5. Determine how to enhance your instruction with movement, music, the visual arts, cooperative learning, and self-reflection. Observe student reactions and engagement.

6. Offer students in-school or out-of-school mentoring or apprenticeship opportunities to deepen their knowledge and skills.

7. Videotape students in action in the classroom. Later observe the tape either alone or with another colleague to learn about diverse students' strengths.

Some teachers choose to learn about selected intelligences they have not previously used. For example, several teachers decided to collaboratively read the document entitled, *Dance, Music, Theatre, Visual Arts: What Every Young American Should Know and Be Able to Do in the Arts* published in 1994 by the National Standards for Art Education. This booklet provided insight into the content and skills of several intelligences. This enabled them to infuse new instructional strategies into classroom lessons. One teacher after reading the dance standard for choreographic principles that states—"Create a sequence with a beginning, middle, and end both with and without a rhythmic accompaniment. Identify each of these parts of the sequence"—asked small groups of students to create a movement sequence or "dance" of formulas for volume in her math course. She could offer this window into math with some degree of confidence even though she had not formally studied dance. She also had an opportunity to observe which students greeted this activity with enthusiasm and skill.

Once teachers have identified student strengths, students can be encouraged to further develop their strengths while also using talents to ameliorate weaknesses. For example, if a student is strong mechanically, but weak linguistically, she might write a book explaining how to put together a clock or other object of her choice.

Assessment through the Multiple Intelligences

Just as students benefit from learning multimodally, they also benefit from demonstrating their knowledge in diverse ways. The Theory of Multiple Intelligences offers a framework for both instruction and assessment. Some students find it easier to share what they have learned through charts, role-plays, songs, journals, models, checklists, or cartoons rather than solely through paper and pencil means. All students may find multiple assessment options motivating and challenging.

When offering multimodal assessment options, it is critical that the criteria for quality work be clarified before students begin their assignments and that the same criteria be used for assessment.

Suggestions for assessing through each of the eight intelligences are summarized in the chart below. The descriptions of sample assessment tools that follow include job roles or endstates, as referred to at Project Spectrum. These adult roles serve to guide the type of performance assessments for each intelligence area.

Sample Verbal-Linguistic Assessment Approaches

Culminating Essay A culminating essay reviews what students have accomplished with a project or curriculum unit or what they have learned at the mid- or end point of a grading period. Essays ask students to construct meaning from their course-work, to interpret their experiences, and to reveal their mastery of content and process knowledge. When assigning a culminating essay, students should be familiar with proper essay formats, the concepts or processes they are expected to address, and the criteria by which they will be assessed. A sample planning form follows.

CULMINATING ESSAY PLANNING FORM

Student Name: _____

Date: _____ Class: _____

Concepts: What was (were) the main principle(s) or concept(s) you learned during this unit (i.e., platonic solids, causes of pollution, the legislative process)?

_____

_____

Learning Processes: In reviewing your work, what learning or thinking skills did you use to complete this unit (i.e., express ideas clearly, interpret and synthesize information, consider multiple perspectives)?

_____

_____

Essay Format: Use standard essay format: an introductory paragraph, three to five paragraphs for the body of the essay, and a concluding paragraph.

	SCORES		
CRITERIA FOR ASSESSMENT	**Not evident**	**Evident**	**Well Done**
Are the essential concepts well described?			
Are diverse perspectives explored?			
How well is the information synthesized and interpreted?			
How well is the essay format followed?			
Is the essay well written in terms of mechanics and style?			

Other Linguistic Assessment Approaches journals, logs, portfolios of written work, word-processor products, newspaper articles, magazines, brochures, advertisements, discussions and debates, and storytelling.

Linguistic Job Role Students could be asked to assume the role of newspaper editor and writer and write feature articles and letters about the topic being studied.

Sample Logical-Mathematical Assessment Approaches

Scoring Sheets Numerical scoring sheets provide feedback on student work through number scales that range from 1 to 3 or 5 per criterion. The teacher, or the teacher and students together, can determine the qualities that should be in academic work. A numerical point spread can be assigned to each criterion indicating exceptional work, above average work, average work, and incomplete work. It is often helpful to work with a 4-point spread since 4 does not easily correlate with the five traditional grades of A, B, C, D, and E.

Such score sheets can be used to evaluate portfolios, products, essays, content skills, and process skills such as problem-solving, collaborative learning, and goal-setting. Since these measures are criterion-based, student work is not compared with that of others. Instead, it is scored on the basis of preestablished criteria. Students might be given the option to revise their work to earn higher scores.

A sample numerical scoring tool is shown below. It was jointly developed by a teacher and

---

POETRY ASSIGNMENT NUMERICAL SCORE SHEET

Name: _____   Date: _____

Class: _____   Period: _____

Ranking system: 0 = skill not evident
1 = minimal skill evidence
2 = effective demonstration of skill
3 = highly effective skill demonstrated

POETRY COMPONENTS					STUDENT SCORE	TEACHER SCORE
Craftsmanship	0	1	2	3		
Sensory imagery	0	1	2	3		
Word or language play	0	1	2	3		
Provocative ideas	0	1	2	3		
Cohesive theme	0	1	2	3		
Overall effect of poem	0	1	2	3		
Total score						

high school students in a creative writing course. The class identified the poetry components as criteria for assessment.

As evident in the score sheet, both teacher and student assign scores that each deems appropriate for the assignment. After the score sheet has been returned, students can reflect on any discrepant criteria.

Other Logical-Mathematical Assessments
Out-loud problem-solving, staging a trial, doing surveys, outlining or charting what has been learned, playing puzzles or games, making timelines, and interpreting data.

Logical-Mathematical Job Role
Students might be asked to bid on a job that is related to their studies such as surveying a geographic region, buying or selling of goods, or performing statistical analyses. They can numerically chart their data.

Sample Visual-Spatial Assessment Approaches

Concept Maps or Mindmaps Concept maps or mindmaps (also see Chapter Four) can reveal what students know before, during, and after a unit of studies. The maps begin with a major concept, key words are brainstormed, and a clustering of related ideas follow. One example of an evaluation mindmap is included below.

Sample assessment criteria for visual concept maps or mindmaps might consist of the following:

A clear, central focus

Adequate number of key concepts, ideas

Appropriate detail

Pertinent examples

Accurate relationships among data

Neatness, clarity, and legibility

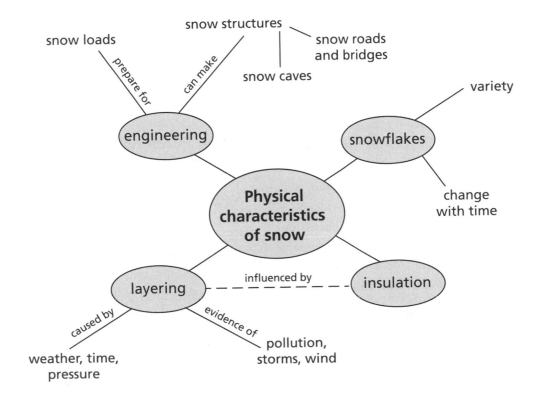

Other Visual-Spatial Assessment Approaches

Students can use flow charts, three-dimensional models, photographic essays, videotapes, collages, scrapbooks, mobiles, or art work.

Visual Job Role Students might assume the roles of artists to create public art that communicates an aspect of their studies.

Sample Bodily-Kinesthetic Assessment Approaches

Exhibitions Academic progress can be assessed through exhibitions where students demonstrate their knowledge of a subject matter area. Exhibitions typically involve students in developing products or giving presentations. While some high schools use exhibitions as comprehensive, interdisciplinary activities seniors must complete to graduate, others use them as performance assessments to document what students have learned and whether they can apply their knowledge. Such exhibitions consist of group projects, dramatic skits, presentations, portfolios, integrated art and writing products, or constructed models. Evaluation of exhibitions frequently involves the teacher, students, a family member or guardian, and in some cases, experts from the community. Some exhibitions are presented at parents' nights, or for school board members and administrators, other classrooms, or general community members. Exhibitions often diminish the importance of standardized test scores as indicators of student success. When community members actually see what students have accomplished, they find such presentations more meaningful and relevant than unidimensional scores on a computer printout.

Two sample classroom exhibitions and one interdisciplinary, end-of-the-year senior exhibition follow. In many cases, students must develop their own formats for their exhibitions, and they can choose to work independently or with a partner.

Some classroom time is provided so that the teacher and adult volunteers may serve as resources for students, but most of the work is completed outside of school to encourage effective time management. Typically, such assessments require anywhere from one week to two months of preparation time.

Sample Classroom Exhibitions

1. Students compose a portrait of themselves as able learners for a specific subject matter area. They must identify, select, and present evidence that they have learned and can apply the content, skills, and appropriate behaviors of a specified discipline both in and outside of school.

2. Based on their study of contemporary world problems, students could identify an issue of crucial importance and provide a rationale for their selection. Additionally, they must demonstrate knowledge of how others have attempted to resolve the issue, the reasons for success or failure of previous efforts, and specify the contributions they hope to make to ameliorate the problem. To fulfill the above requirements, students are required to submit a videotape or other visuals, one shoe box diorama, one skit, and one written paper.

Sample Interdisciplinary Senior Exhibition Required for Graduation

Students must identify and explain a particular behavior pattern evident in the insect world, in animals, in humans, and in literature. They must draw from their knowledge of coursework in science, social studies, literature, and health as well as their own observations and reflections about behavior. Students may select a format of their choice (written, artistic, graphed, etc.) to explain the selected behavior. References must be made, however, to learning gleaned from science, social studies, literature, health, personal observations, and reflections.

Criteria for evaluation of the exhibitions might include:

Knowledge of the discipline(s)
Supporting evidence from diverse subjects
Supporting evidence for student opinions
Appropriateness of format
Ability to narrow a broad topic into a workable one
Execution of the project
Ability to apply content knowledge outside of school
Resourcefulness
Inventiveness
Time management

Other Bodily-Kinesthetic Assessment Approaches Model building with manipulatives, making a product or game, doing a simulation, role-play, pantomime, or dance.

Bodily-Kinesthetic Job Role Students might assume the role of product or model designers and submit samples of their work to a panel.

Sample Musical Assessment Approaches

Musical Contracts Working independently or in small groups, students can select musical approaches to demonstrating content knowledge. The teacher should clarify what students must address, such as the theoretical concepts of democracy or evolution, or writing procedures such as rules for comma or semicolon usage. In the sample assessment tool shown on the following page, a range of options provides choices that may prove challenging to some students and highly motivating to others. Assessment criteria are also included.

Other Musical Assessment Approaches Dances that illustrate concepts, songs, sound scripts, musical mnemonics, and advertisements.

Musical Job Role Students might serve as composers or producers who are responsible for creating appropriate musical scores to accompany coursework.

Sample Interpersonal Assessment Approaches

Peer Problem-Solving In pairs, students can work on content area problems identified by the teacher. One student can attempt to solve the problem through thinking out loud while the other observes, listens, and questions the problem-solving strategies. Roles are then reversed using the same problem or a new one. After both have thought through their problems they give each other feedback on problem-solving strategies.

Peer problem-solving emphasizes thinking through a problem and not just providing the right answer. By receiving feedback on their thought processes, students can learn diverse strategies to use in the future. It should be noted that before students work in pairs, they should be reminded to be supportive listeners and conversationalists. After all, most great discoveries involved much trial and error.

A sample form for guiding students through this process is shown on page 307. Teachers may find it helpful to conduct a trial run with the class so that the steps of the process are clear before students work with partners.

Other Interpersonal Assessment Approaches Students can use collaborative learning, interviews, service projects, teaching others, and leadership opportunities.

Interpersonal Job Role Students might role play interviewing for jobs that are related to course content.

MUSICAL ASSESSMENT CONTRACT

Name (s): _____   Date: _____

Your assignment is to demonstrate your knowledge of the following concepts:

_____

_____

Through one type of musical activity (Please check one):

____ Make a musical collage using diverse musical selections that reveal your knowledge of the concepts studied

____ Choreograph a dance that addresses the concepts

____ Perform a dance

____ Create and perform on a keyboard an original song or rap about the concepts

____ Create and perform a song with percussion

____ Create and perform a song with an instrument of your choice

____ Create a song to sing without accompaniment

____ Write lyrics to the melody of a song you already know

____ Find prerecorded songs or compositions that address the concepts. Identify what ideas the recordings addressed and didn't address.

Prepare to turn in on (date) _____

With one of the following products (Check one):   ____ live performance

____ audiotape

____ music video

You will be assessed on the following	Low		High	STUDENT SCORE	TEACHER SCORE
Demonstrated knowledge of concepts that included at least 10 important facts	1	2	3		
Included a minimum of three examples to enrich concepts	1	2	3		
Extended the concepts beyond this class	1	2	3		
Well-presented performance	1	2	3		
Other:					

PEER PROBLEM-SOLVING ACTIVITY

For this activity, you will work in pairs. Your goal is to learn how you and your partner problem-solve and so this activity is not focused on a single correct answer. After the teacher provides the problem and organizes the pairs, follow these steps:

1. For the first round, one student assumes the role of the "problem-solver" while the other becomes the "listener."

2. The problem-solver begins by thinking through the problem out loud so the listener can determine how the problem is being addressed. In addition to words, the problem-solver may also graph, chart, walk through, or draw his thinking methods while explaining to the listener what he is doing.

3. While the problem-solver is working, the listener should ask questions about the thinking strategies being used. The listener does not offer suggestions or advice about ways to proceed.

4. If the problem-solver gets stuck, the listener should summarize the thinking methods used so far. This sometimes helps to jump-start thinking.

5. When the problem-solver solves the problem or stops working on it, the listener describes what she observed about the other's methods.

6. For the second round, the roles are reversed and the same procedure followed.

7. When the second round is completed, both students should complete the chart below. The written feedback should be shared with one another. The teacher will explain whether the written information should be turned in.

Partner's name:_____   Your name: _____

1. I noticed this person solved problems by _____

_____

_____

2. This person seemed to get stuck when _____

_____

_____

3. This person got unstuck when _____

_____

_____

4. My feedback was (check one) _____ somewhat helpful or _____ very helpful.

5. My feedback would be more helpful if I _____

_____

Sample Intrapersonal Assessment Approaches

Reflective Journal Students can maintain journals to track content they are learning and their attitudes toward the subject. Teachers can encourage many ways to reflect in addition to writing. For example, the only words in Picasso's journals were laundry lists, Jung filled his journals with mandalas, and Einstein computed abstract equations. Sometimes students resist maintaining journals because they lack ideas about what to write, draw, or equate in them. Teachers can jump-start reflection by suggesting prompts such as those below.

> Key ideas I've learned about this topic
>
> Questions I have are
>
> One thing I discovered is
>
> What frustrates me is
>
> If this topic had a sound it would be _____ because
>
> What I feel good about is
>
> I could use some help with
>
> If I could change one thing about this topic it would be
>
> One thing I would like to master is
>
> When I work with others in this class, I
>
> My attitude toward this class, when drawn, would look like
>
> This topic connects to other subjects at school because
>
> The best part about class today was
>
> What I feel most confident with is
>
> At first I thought _____ , but now I think _____
>
> My personal goal for today, this week, this unit, is

Rather than establishing criteria to assess journal reflections, students might identify entries to share with the teacher or a classmate who, in turn, writes responses. This reflective dialogue provides intrapersonal feedback on what students are learning, struggling with, succeeding at, and enjoying. Such written reflections also provide teachers with insight into classroom learning and assessing.

Other Intrapersonal Assessment Approaches Participating in entry and exit interviews; writing editorials, awards, autobiographical sketches, or memoirs; setting and achieving goals; and managing self-directed projects.

Intrapersonal Job Role Students could simulate expert witnesses in mock trials where they testify for or against ethical issues in their studies.

Diverse assessment approaches give students options for expressing their knowledge. Further, such multimodal tools can be integrated into regular classroom experiences rather than appearing as sporadic events at the end of units. Instruction and assessment can blend and enhance each other. Instead of making students anxious about evaluation, such strategies can heighten motivation and enjoyment in learning.

Sample Naturalist Assessment Approaches

Observational Checklists Just as teachers use observational checklists for formal or informal assessment, so, too, will students find them helpful. Checklists are flexible tools that are easily adapted for multiple purposes. For example, students can self-assess their progress with individual checklists, or they can conduct peer assessment of others' skills.

Checklists typically focus on three kinds of observable skills: process skills such as mounting a slide on a microscope, content knowledge such as multiplying fractions, or thinking skills such as making predictions or supporting claims with evidence. To make checklists, the teacher, or in some cases the students, should specify exactly what skills are to be assessed.

Most checklists are constructed with a list of observable actions that can be marked as present or absent, with a yes or no, or as observed or not observed. Either the characteristic is evident or it is not. For example, a student does or does not use a prewriting technique before writing an essay. Checklists should be completed during the course of a targeted activity or shortly thereafter.

A sample observational checklist follows. It assesses whether students understand a short story and its elements of fiction, and whether appropriate social skills are used during small group discussions. To use this checklist or an adaptation, each student should be assigned one classmate to observe. Review its contents before proceeding so that everyone knows what knowledge and skills to assess.

Other Naturalist Assessment Approaches A written, sketched, or photographed observation journal; identifying and categorizing a unit's content; describing the characteristics and functions of data; and conducting hands-on experiments or environmental projects.

Naturalist Job Role Students could serve as amateur zoologists to determine appropriate habitats for local endangered species for a biology course, an earth science unit, or as a community service project. Additionally, they can conduct observations of natural phenomena such as weather forecasts or of human behavior inside or outside of school.

SHORT STORY DISCUSSION CHECKLIST

Your name: _____   Title of story: _____

Name of peer you are observing: _____

During a small group discussion, observe your assigned classmate to assess participation according to the following items. Circle either "evident" or "not evident" for each action below:

E	NE	Distinguishes between main and minor characters.
E	NE	Identifies one or more strategies used by the author to develop the main characters.
E	NE	Explains a character's thoughts, feelings, motives, and behaviors.
E	NE	Describes the setting and its appropriateness for the story.
E	NE	Sequences the major events in the plot.
E	NE	Identifies the conflict(s) a character encounters.
E	NE	Links ideas in the story to personal knowledge or experiences.
E	NE	Identifies the author's theme, message, or purpose in writing the story.
E	NE	Asks thoughtful questions about the story.
E	NE	Builds on others' comments in the small group discussion.

After the small group discussion has ended, pair up with the classmate you observed. Share your completed checklist and discuss the observations you made. If the student desires, she can respond to your assessment by writing comments on the back of the form.

Processfolios

Although the portfolio has gained popularity as an assessment strategy, Gardner (1991) has recommended the use of processfolios. Noting that portfolios typically contain completed work, processfolios, by contrast, offer insight into both the processes and products of student learning. They document initial goals, drafts, and revisions; they include early as well as later works, and journals entries, photographs, or other items that influenced student work.

Rather than serving as storage devices, processfolios give students and teachers the means to dialogue about learning and development. When used throughout a term, they serve as assessment tools that are inherently integrated with academic work. Ongoing dialogue about the contents of processfolios with teachers, students, parents, and outside experts transforms classrooms into laboratories that promote acquisition of knowledge and skill, and that reflect on the meaning of course work for a student's life.

To fit their classroom needs, teachers should establish guidelines for processfolios. Arts PROPEL teachers and researchers (1991) identified several procedures suggested below.

Processfolio Guidelines

1. To begin their processfolios, give students folders and ask them to describe their attitude and knowledge of the subject matter at the outset of the course. Students can also be asked to begin annotated tables of contents.

2. Lessons and units to be taught have clear instructional objectives. The criteria teachers establish to assess processfolios can consist of quantitative scores and qualitative comments. There should ideally be a reference group against whom students are being assessed. For example, the reference group might consist of 1) other students of the same grade level, 2) past student performances, or 3) expectations of community members who have expertise in the area being assessed.

3. During the course of their studies, students and teachers select items to include in processfolios that reflect course goals. Such items may include drafts, revisions, journal reflections, multimedia entries, and final products. To guide the selection of processfolio entries, teachers can request pieces that:

   Show accomplishments

   Reflect change or growth

   Reveal student risk-taking

   Compare satisfying and unsatisfying learning experiences

   Indicate student working styles

4. Student journal entries can accompany each selection in the processfolio. The reflections might consist of written or taped justifications for selected work, what has been most beneficial and challenging in their studies, and how students apply subject matter content outside of school. Such journal entries can provide rich opportunities for dialogue.

5. When students and teachers review processfolios together, both accomplishments and next steps can be discussed. During the review, student strengths, weaknesses, goals, and learning strategies should be identified so that students perceive their overall accomplishments, their challenges, and next steps to pursue.

6. It may be necessary to adjust how processfolios are reviewed according to the size of the class. In a small classroom, individual conferences between students and teacher can be easily arranged, whereas in larger classrooms, peer group feedback may be more practical. A limited number of issues should be pursued in any session so that students are not overwhelmed with too much feedback.

7. If desired, several people can be involved in the evaluation of processfolios, including the teacher, the student, classmates, parents, and

community experts. The evaluation must be closely linked with the original instructional goals. The emphasis on what and how a processfolio is assessed will vary from teacher to teacher and from classroom project to project. The staff at Arts PROPEL suggested the following topics to consider in assessment:

Craftsmanship
Ability to set goals
Pursuit of learning over time
Risk-taking and problem-solving
Use of the tools of the content area
Care and interest evident in work
Ability to assess own work
Ability to grow from constructive feedback
Ability to work independently
Ability to work collaboratively
Ability to access resources

Processfolios contribute numerous benefits to a classroom. Not only do they serve as ongoing, natural forms of assessment, they also encourage students to be active learners who are aware of their academic development. By assuming responsibility for self-assessment of both the products and processes of learning, students may be encouraged to initiate change and growth not from external rewards or pressures, but from an intrinsic desire to do so.

An Assessment Schedule

So far in this chapter we have reviewed numerous principles and forms of assessment. Teachers typically spend a great deal of time planning their curriculum and multimodal lessons. The authors suggest that the same kind of effort might go into planning a comprehensive assessment system. Assessment can be as varied and well-thought out as any unit of study. Teachers can step back and reflect on the timing and types of assessment tools they use. To support such reflection, a sample assessment calendar is suggested below. It emphasizes the importance of the personal intelligences in evaluation by placing increased responsibility on students as assessors of their academic gains.

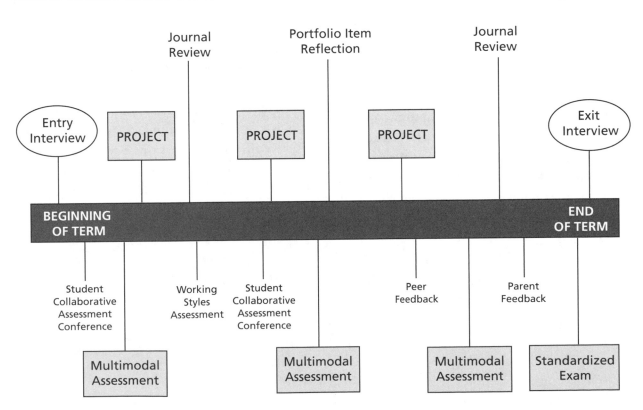

As the schedule suggests, to begin a marking period, whether a quarter, trimester, or semester, the teacher can establish baseline data about each student. Such information informs future curricular decisions and provides a reference point for gauging student growth at the end of the term. Entry interviews provide one means for getting to know students' knowledge, attitude, and skill levels at the outset of a marking period. A sample entry interview form is provided on the facing page.

To conduct entry interviews, students can write their own responses, be queried by peers or classroom volunteers, and, in the case of young children, dictate their answers to older students or adults. Entry interviews provide valuable additions to student processfolios.

As noted on the assessment calendar, before any kind of assessment is undertaken, the authors recommend that students and teachers conduct Collaborative Assessment Conferences. The notion for such conferences was developed by Seidel (1991). They involve students and teachers in democratically deciding what assessment should ultimately look like. It is also effective for teachers to show samples of work from previous classmates so that students have tangible images of the standards they should meet.

The ongoing curriculum will provide numerous opportunities for assessment. Over the course of the marking period, teachers might assess students through any of the intelligences using the assessment tools suggested earlier in this chapter or others better suited to their needs.

In addition to multimodal assessment, the working styles of students, such as those observed at Project Spectrum, might also be identified. During informal conferences with students, teachers can share their observations, and discuss whether such approaches to learning are beneficial or whether other behaviors might be more helpful.

As mentioned in the curriculum development chapter, projects provide students with opportunities to develop the skills they will rely on as adults. The authors recommend that two or three projects be conducted during a marking period or the course of a year. As a result, three projects are included in the assessment calendar. Student presentation of projects is one form of assessment used effectively at the Key Learning Community. Three times yearly, students complete projects that are videotaped and that become part of their permanent school record. Such videotapes provide ready evidence of student knowledge, skills, and growth over time. Whether teachers decide to create video archives of student projects as done at the Key Learning Community, the evaluation form on the page 314 may prove useful in assessing student projects.

Another intrapersonal form of assessment is the class journal, notebook, or learning log. If students maintain such documents, teachers periodically can request that students review such items in search of significant learning. Such reflection, perhaps occurring once or twice a term, actively engages students in summarizing and synthesizing both the process and content of their studies.

ENTRY INTERVIEW

Name: _____   Date: _____

Class: _____   Period: _____

Interviewer's Name: _____

1. Have you had a class with similar subject matter before? If yes, what was it?
   (Or, if the student is in an elementary grade, mention some things he is likely
   to learn this new term and ask what he has learned at home or elsewhere.)

2. What did you learn before that will help you in this class?

3. Aside from content or facts, what did you learn about studying, thinking, or learning
   that could help you in this class?

4. How do you use what you learned previously inside and outside of school?

5. What interests you about this subject matter or grade level?

6. What do you hope to learn?

7. What would you like to be able to do with your learnings from this class or grade level?

8. Is there something you would like your classmates to know about you?

9. Is there something you would like your teacher to know about you?

10. Is there any other comment you would like to make?

PROJECT EVALUATION

Name: _____   Project: _____

Research question: _____

TEACHER AND PEER ASSESSMENT

Research:	Excellent	Satisfactory	Needs Work
Used at least five sources	3	2	1
Documented sources of information	3	2	1
Gathered interesting and new information	3	2	1
Identified new topics to pursue	3	2	1

Presentation Skills:			
Was well prepared and organized	3	2	1
Content was well-thought out	3	2	1
Demonstrated good delivery skills	3	2	1
Used multiple modes	3	2	1

STUDENT SELF-ASSESSMENT

1. Please explain what you learned about doing a project: _____
   _____
   _____

2. Please explain what you learned about doing a presentation: _____
   _____
   _____

3. Please explain what was the most difficult part of this project: _____
   _____
   _____

4. Please explain what was the most enjoyable part of this project: _____
   _____
   _____

5. If you did this project over, what would you do differently? _____
   _____
   _____

During the course of their work or at the end of a class, students benefit from feedback offered by adults other than their teachers. Students can take their processfolios home to discuss with relatives or other adults. To shape the feedback students will receive, teachers can develop questionnaires to accompany student work home. A sample is provided below.

After discussing their work with adults, students typically experience a range of reactions to such feedback. It can be helpful to give students an opportunity to reflect on their discussions. The questionnaire that follows on the next page is one way to debrief.

FOLDER REVIEW

Student: _____ Date: _____

Class or subject matter area: _____

Adult reader: _____

Enclosed, you will find samples of this student's work from _____ (class or subject area). We believe that it is important for students to receive feedback on their academic efforts from numerous sources, and we invite you to become part of our assessment team. Please review the work included in this folder, and consider constructive, encouraging comments to make to the student. The following questions may serve as a guide for your discussion. We also ask that you jot down your responses to these questions so that the student can later include your feedback in his or her work folder.

1. What piece or pieces of work tell you the most about this student's knowledge?

2. What strengths do you see in this student's work?

3. What areas of improvement might be addressed?

4. Have you noticed the student applying knowledge gained from this class outside of school? If so, how?

5. Based on the kinds of work you have observed, what suggestions do you have to improve the curriculum?

6. What other comments would you like to make?

**Thank you for your time to contribute in meaningful ways
to this student's academic progress!**

STUDENT RESPONSE TO FEEDBACK

Student Name:_____ Date: _____

Please take a few minutes to reflect on the feedback you received from a parent or another adult about your academic work by responding to the following questions.

1. What was your general reaction to sharing your work with an adult outside of school?

2. Do you think your discussion gave you helpful feedback on your progress? Why or why not?

3. What do you think the adult learned about you as a student?

4. What did the adult not understand about your work that you would have liked him or her to know?

5. What did you learn about yourself as a student?

6. What surprised you most about the conversation?

7. What might have made the conversation better?

8. Would you like to share your work again in this manner? Why or why not?

Schoolwide Assessment Processes

In addition to the suggested assessment calendar for individual teacher use, some schools specify assessment approaches that can be adopted by any teacher or used by all in a building.

Such a comprehensive approach, one that highlights the personal intelligences, is evident in an elementary school's recommended schoolwide practices.

Ultimately, each teacher must decide how best to assess student learning in the classroom. Realistically, both standardized and alternative forms of evaluation will co-exist in most classrooms. By expanding the assessment repertoire, students will have multiple opportunities for demonstrating what they know. They also may feel a keener sense of ownership in learning if they collaborate with their peers and teachers about what constitutes good work in the first place.

RECOMMENDED SCHOOLWIDE ASSESSMENT APPROACHES

Teachers, parents, and students can all be actively involved in assessment as follows:

TEACHER EVALUATION	STUDENT EVALUATION	PARENT EVALUATION
Portfolios	Portfolio	Portfolio
Anecdotal reports	Anecdotal self-assessment	Observations made while in classroom or at home
Interviews	Self-reflection	Goal-setting with child
Multimedia performance assessments with specified criteria	Evaluation of one's own and peer projects	Review videotapes of projects
Mental notes from "kid watching"	Interest inventories	Formal and informal conferences with teacher or student
Checklists	Peer evaluation	Participation in classroom and schoolwide meetings
Teacher-made tests	Evaluation of teacher	Program surveys
Analysis of standardized test results	Analysis of performance on test	Phone contacts
Report cards	Evaluation of course	Written comments on report cards

Multiple Intelligences Report Cards

Some educators working extensively with the multiple intelligences have found that traditional report cards do not adequately reflect what their students are learning and have subsequently devised new report cards. Using such measures, however, typically requires the education of parents, administrators, and others so that they understand the rationale for such changes. When teaching, one of the authors wrote a brief parent newsletter each month explaining his academic goals, philosophy, and some of the learning experiences students had in his class. When he subsequently experimented with a new report card, parents willingly considered the alternative since they already understood the teacher's philosophy and procedures. The report card that was used is shown on the facing page.

One goal of the report card was to show the developmental progression of children's skills in several intelligence areas. Each quarter, the bar graphs were filled in with one color up to the level at which the child was performing. The next quarter, the bar graphs were completed in a different color to represent growth during the second term. If little or no growth occurred during a term, a vertical line was drawn to represent the static nature of work in that area. If a student's skills were to slip backwards, an arrow would be drawn to represent the regression.

Another example of a multiple intelligences report card is in use at the Key Learning Community. Each quarter, teachers assess student accomplishments in all eight intelligences while also recording intrapersonal progress in project presentation, POD choices (student or small group mentoring activities), and in flow activities. Flow at the Key Learning Community consists of a classroom that students visit four times weekly to pursue activities of their choice. Teachers observe and record what students select. Such observations result in a profile of each child that shows what she chooses to do when given free choice.

Another unique area assessed at Key Learning Community is POD participation. Four times weekly, each student attends a POD of her choice to work on material related to one or more intelligences. On the school's report card PODS are assessed by the primary intelligences they engage.

To learn about Key Learning Community's assessment practices and their K–12 MI program in general, go to www.ips.k12.in.us/mskey/aboutus/aboutus.htm. At the school's website, you'll find explanations of their assessment practices and catch a glimpse of their report card.

MULTIPLE INTELLIGENCES REPORT CARD WITH DEVELOPMENTAL INDICATORS

Name: _____

	Novice	Apprentice	Practitioner	Scholar

READING
(Linguistic Intelligence)

WRITING AND SPELLING
(Linguistic Intelligence)

MATH AND SCIENCE
(Logical-Mathematical Intelligence)

VISUAL ARTS
(Visual-Spatial Intelligence)

MOVEMENT ACTIVITIES
(Kinesthetic Intelligence)

BUILDING ACTIVITIES
(Bodily-Kinesthetic Intelligence)

MUSIC SKILLS
(Musical Intelligence)

GROUP WORK
(Interpersonal Intelligence)

REFLECTIVE THINKING
(Intrapersonal Intelligence)

ENVIRONMENTAL ACTIVITIES
(Naturalist Intelligence)

RESEARCH
(Project Preparation Skills)

PRESENTATIONS
(Project Demonstration Skills)

Novice: recognizes concepts, begins to develop skills

Apprentice: acquires increasingly complex skills through guided practice

Practitioner: works independently and accurately with knowledge and skills

Scholar: demonstrates mastery of concepts and practices, applies in new settings

Colored bars demonstrate beginning points in each area as well as level of progress to this point in time. The longer the line, the greater the improvement.

Summary

Positive assessment cultures develop in classrooms where assessment is perceived as an integral component of learning. When tests are demystified, students will engage freely in public discussions about what constitutes good work. Students are capable of using predetermined assessment criteria to inform their ongoing work and to deepen their content knowledge. The boundaries between instruction and assessment can dissolve when students reveal what they know through project presentations, exhibitions, or other multimodal means. When students are demonstrating what they learned, accurate data can be simultaneously gathered without taking additional time from teaching and learning.

It is not realistic to assume that performance-based approaches to assessment will completely supplant standardized measures. Single-snapshot testing sessions can also contribute helpful data about learning and teaching. It is important, however, to use multiple tools and to clarify the purposes and processes of each for students.

Many of the strategies in this chapter tap teachers' extensive clinical judgments and acknowledge the quantity and quality of professional knowledge they possess about their students. Through reliance on informal, formal, and diverse means of assessment, teachers can teach students how to evaluate themselves. Fostering the ability to direct and redirect their own educational efforts, students can achieve a major goal of education—learning how to learn and how to improve one's learning.

APPLYING ASSESSMENT INFORMATION

1. Important ideas or insights gleaned from this chapter:

_____

_____

_____

_____

_____

_____

2. Areas I'd like to learn more about:

_____

_____

_____

_____

_____

_____

3. Ways I can use this information in my teaching. The strategies mentioned in this chapter are listed below with space provided to note how each strategy can be incorporated into classroom assessment.

ASSESSMENT STRATEGY	CLASSROOM APPLICATION

Principles to Guide Classroom Assessment

1. Assessment Captures Growth over Time

2. Assessment Is Multidimensional

3. Asssessment Informs Instruction

4. Informal Assessment Is Important

5. Students Are Active Self-Assessors

Assessment of the Intelligences

Measuring Intelligence at Project Spectrum

Working Styles

Spectrum Reports

Perceiving Student Strengths

Assessment through the Intelligences

Sample Verbal-Linguistic Assessment Approaches

Sample Logical-Mathematical Assessment Approaches

Sample Visual-Spatial Assessment Approaches

Sample Bodily-Kinesthetic Assessment Approaches

Sample Musical Assessment Approaches

Sample Interpersonal Assessment Approaches

Sample Intrapersonal Assessment Approaches

Sample Naturalist Assessment Approaches

Processfolios

Processfolio Guidelines

An Assessment Schedule

Schoolwide Assessment Processes

Multiple Intelligences Report Cards

ASSESSMENT REFERENCES:

Campbell, L. (2002). *Mindful Learning: 101 Proven Strategies for Student and Teacher Success.* Thousand Oaks, CA: Corwin Press.

Campbell, L. (2000). *The Unspoken Dialogue: Beliefs about Intelligence, Students, and Instruction Held by a Sample of Teachers Familiar with Multiple Intelligences Theory.* Unpublished doctoral dissertation. Santa Barbara, CA: The Fielding Institute.

Campbell, L., & Campbell, B. (1999). *Multiple Intelligences and Student Achievement: Success Stories from Six Schools.* Alexandria, VA: ASCD.

Harvard Project Zero and Educational Testing Service (1991). *Arts PROPEL: An Introductory Handbook.* Available from Harvard Graduate School of Education.

Gardner, H. (1993). *Multiple Intelligences: The Theory in Practice.* New York: Basic Books.

Krechevsky, M. (1998). *Project Zero Frameworks for Early Childhood Education. Vol. 3, Preschool Assessment Handbook.* New York: Teachers College Press.

National Standards for Arts Education. (1994). *Dance, Music, Theatre, Visual Arts: What Every Young American Should Know and Be Able to Do in the Arts.* Reston, VA: Music Educators National Conference.

Northwest Regional Educational Laboratory (1998). *Traits of an Effective Reader.* Portland, OR: Author.

Seidel, S. (1991). *Collaborative Assessment Conferences for the Consideration of Project Work.* (Working paper). Cambridge, MA: Project Zero. Harvard Graduate School of Education.

11

Lessons Learned

Do not then train youths to learning by force and harshness,
but direct them to it by what amuses their minds so that
you may be better able to discover with accuracy the peculiar
bent of the genius of each.

—Plato

EDUCATING FOR INTELLIGENCE

*S*ince Howard Gardner first published *Frames of Mind: The Theory of Multiple Intelligences* in 1983, educators have readily perceived implications of his work for their professional practice. These implications include the very topics this book addresses: how to perceive and nurture diverse student strengths, how to teach to reach all students, how to develop multiple intelligences–based curriculum, and how to better assess student learning.

Since the mid 1980s thousands of teachers (Campbell, 2000) claim to have adopted MI theory in their programs. While distinct from one another, these efforts appear to share similar characteristics and have learned much about transforming their offerings. This final chapter surveys what has been learned during the last 20 years since Gardner created his theory, what student achievement results have been realized, and what steps have been taken to translate Gardner's work from psychological theory into educational practice in rural, suburban, and inner-city classrooms.

Linking Students and Their Talents

▪ ▪ ▪ ▪ ▪ ▪ ▪ ▪ ▪ ▪ ▪ ▪ ▪ ▪ ▪ ▪

One of the most provocative implications of the Theory of Multiple Intelligences is the responsibility of educational institutions to engage each student's talents. Somewhere in their schooling, it is vital that students discover at least one strength and be encouraged to pursue their interests. Such pursuits not only nurture joy in learning—they also fuel the persistence and effort needed for disciplinary mastery and inventiveness. Conversely, if students do not discover one or more talents, they may never develop a love for learning and instead travel aimlessly through school or abandon formal education altogether.

How can schools nurture critical linkages between students and their talents? As emphasized in this book, no formula exists for adopting MI; however, there are steps teachers and schools can take to initiate such efforts. Educators can identify where multiple intelligences components exist in curricular and extracurricular programs. They can increase the availability of such offerings for all students. For example, when, as is often the case, the visual arts and music are offered as separate subjects for only a few students, efforts can be made to infuse the arts throughout the curriculum. Opportunities for personalizing education for each student should be promoted. The school's technology systems and software programs can be surveyed for the intelligences they engage and those they overlook. Plans can be made to expand the technological options. Teachers can evaluate their strengths and team plan with other colleagues to compensate for less-developed MI skills. Project-based and hands-on learning can become preferred instructional methods. Discussions with parents and local community members might uncover apprenticeship opportunities for students. By taking stock of their existing programs and determining what to strengthen or add, schools can offer multiple intelligences options to everyone.

Lessons Learned from MI Programs

▪ ▪ ▪ ▪ ▪ ▪ ▪ ▪ ▪ ▪ ▪ ▪ ▪ ▪ ▪ ▪

During the last two decades, MI theory has been used to organize daily instruction, revamp school programs, improve student achievement, and engage the community in K–12 education. Teachers implementing MI options have experienced successes and encountered challenges, and much can be learned from their efforts. The lessons they have learned fall into five areas: 1) enhancing perceptions of students, 2) transforming instruction, 3) making curricular adaptations, 4) implementing new forms of assessment and student results, and 5) developing incremental changes in professional practice. These lessons and their related student achievement results are described in the following sections.

LESSON #1: Students Are Multitalented

Imagine what it would feel like if others perceived you as multitalented? This is the daily experience of students in MI classrooms and schools. For example, at the K–6 New City School in St. Louis, Missouri, at EXPO Elementary in Minneapolis, Minnesota, at Skyview Junior High School in Bothell, Washington, and at the K–12 Key Learning Community in Indianapolis, Indiana, teachers assume that all students are bright. Such beliefs have profound implications for student and teacher dynamics. Positive teacher regard raises expectations. Students respond to the perceptions of those around them by transforming their sense of self and their beliefs about what they can achieve. With the current emphasis on standards and high stakes testing, it may prove worthwhile to reflect on the precursor to academic success—the belief that it is possible to succeed.

Numerous studies have shown that teacher beliefs affect student achievement outcomes (Campbell & Campbell, 1999). Educational mandates since the 1970s, in fact, have been nearly cliché in their call for teachers to maintain high expectations. What is typically lacking, however, is much specificity about the beliefs or the expectations teachers could adopt. Though expected to develop the intellectual potential of their students, the nature of such potential has seldom been addressed. Gardner's theory provides one model of intelligence that teachers have embraced, and when they do they begin to perceive diverse student strengths (Campbell, 2000).

In addition to what educators believe, researchers at Project Spectrum (Krechevsky, 1998) and teachers at six MI-based schools (Campbell & Campbell, 1999) claimed that nearly all students did exhibit intellectual strengths. This phenomenon provides teachers and students with options when learning becomes stymied. Teachers can tap strengths to overcome deficits. For example, a second grade student at Russell Elementary in Lexington, Kentucky, was not making adequate progress in reading. Her teacher, however, knew that she was artistically skilled. Subsequently, the teacher helped the student apply her perceptual and motor skills to word recognition and spelling with positive results.

LESSON #2: Instructional Repertoires Expand

A second implication of the Theory of Multiple Intelligences concerns instruction. Each of the chapters on the eight intelligences in this book describes ways to enhance our instructional repertoires. While MI affirms that content can be taught in numerous ways, educators must ultimately develop methods that are appropriate for their students, their subject areas, and their settings. MI theory offers a mental checklist for reflecting on the multimodal nature of instruction.

Teachers have devised several ways to enrich instruction. For example, some adopt multimodal or arts-based pedagogy, others emphasize self-directed projects, and still others promote apprenticeships. Unlike many educational innovations, MI does not prescribe a specific pedagogy. As a result, teachers creatively adapt their instruction to reflect enhanced beliefs about human capacities. Doing so also mitigates concerns about limiting the range of teaching practices to accommodate standards-based mandates. Students can master standards and other educational goal through enriched pedagogy.

Supporting Instructional Changes

Many teachers, nevertheless, find it daunting to change instructional practice. This labor-intensive task can be rendered manageable with helpful support. Some strategies used at MI sites are listed below.

- Schoolwide study groups can read Gardner's works or watch videotapes of MI programs. For example, the staff at New City School in St. Louis conducted study groups for a year or more before creating an MI school.

- Staff members who are highly skilled in diverse intelligences can provide experiential workshops for their colleagues.

- Building specialists in PE, the arts, or reading can be tapped for input into curriculum development or to provide in-class instruction to students.

- Experts such as professional artists, accountants, or environmentalists can mentor teachers or students.

- Visits to MI sites to see how others use MI theory can be instructive.

Creating Time for Multiple Intelligences

The demands of daily teaching are such that it is difficult to find time to transform classroom or schoolwide practices. Rather than finding time, however, some schools *create* time through implementing diverse time management strategies. Some include:

- Providing full day releases: Substitutes can be hired to release teachers, or teachers can be paid for working during vacation.

- Altering the school's schedule: Each school day can be lengthened by a few minutes to accrue a partial day for planning once or twice monthly. Or, in team teaching situations, team members might alternate between teaching and planning. Scheduling can also be changed so that several teachers share the same planning time. Further, the school's calendar can be reworked to provide more teacher planning days.

- Inventing time: Student teachers, parents, community members, volunteers, or administrators assume teacher tasks or classes to free teachers to work together during the school day.

- Using faculty meetings differently: One or more faculty meetings a month can be dedicated to co-planning or problem-solving issues of pedagogy, curriculum, and assessment.

- Providing credit for time: Teachers can be compensated with in-service credit for their efforts. University faculty can develop courses that include practicums for educators to reflect on and apply new instructional approaches.

Many Faces of MI

Teachers have found numerous ways to integrate MI into instruction. In fact, there may be as many models of MI teaching as there are teachers! Many use the intelligences on a daily basis as entry points into content. For some, this means using classroom learning centers that are dedicated to different intelligences. Others enhance direct instruction with multimodal or artistic components. Some team with colleagues to enrich students' learning. Some schools make a building-wide commitment to teach with MI on a daily basis or

for targeted occasions. One example of an MI special event occurs at an elementary school each spring. There, the school features an MI week. The curriculum is thematically structured and highlights a culture represented among the school's student body. Teachers identify what and how they will contribute to the theme based on their individual strengths and interests. Students spend the week in multiage groups rotating throughout the building with obvious enthusiasm for the event.

One important caveat from MI-based instruction is that the theory should not become a rigid pedagogical formula. For lesson planning, teachers have found it helpful to first identify what they want to teach and what students should be able to do with such instruction (Campbell, 1997). When these goals are clearly in mind, appropriate MI strategies can be selected for instruction.

Benefits from MI Instruction

Meeting the challenges of teaching in multimodal ways is worth the effort for both teachers and students. Some teachers appreciate having the theory's language to guide and explain their work. Some say MI validates how they have always taught, and others claim it grants permission to teach in new ways. Many also appreciate the opportunities they have to develop their creativity and latent intelligences. All take satisfaction in teaching students in ways that are motivating, engaging, and worthwhile.

There are also student achievement gains that reinforce the value of MI. Many individual schools attribute their students' elevated achievement scores to MI instruction. For example, the award-winning Eugene Field Accelerated School in Jefferson City, Missouri, claimed that their students' strong performance on standardized measures was due to the "staff's focus on and implementation of multiple intelligences in every classroom" (Missouri Department of Elementary and Secondary

Education, 1998). Likewise, Wheeler Elementary in Lexington, Kentucky, was recognized as a Blue Ribbon School of Excellence by the U.S. Department of Education and was identified by *Redbook* magazine as one of the nation's best schools. A study of 41 MI schools conducted by Kornhaber, Fierros, and Veenema (in press) found that half of the schools reported improvements in standardized test scores which they attributed to their adoption of MI. Additional benefits included improved student behavior and parent participation.

One MI model called Different Ways of Knowing created by the Galef Institute has been adopted by over 400 schools across the country. A study conducted by the American Research Institute showed that, in many cases, students made strong gains in language arts, math, and social studies (American Association of School Administrators, 2001). While additional studies are needed, the few that do exist suggest that MI programs can enhance student achievement.

LESSON #3: MI School Curriculums Differ

Aside from instructional changes, MI theory has inspired curricular adaptations as well. These range from modest to dramatic changes. Typically, MI curriculum (as described in Chapter 9) encompasses interdisciplinary or project-based models, apprenticeships, arts programs, or intelligence-based programs such as those at Key Learning Community and the New City School.

The majority of MI efforts across the country are focused in individual teachers' classrooms and are interdisciplinary or thematic in nature. Less common are entire schools dedicated to MI. Nevertheless, such programs do exist. It is interesting to consider what prompted disparate schools from the east to west coast, large and small, located in rural, suburban, and inner city environments to

select MI as their focus. In a study of six schools embracing MI theory (Campbell & Campbell, 1999), two primary motivators were evident. MI proved compelling because such sites wanted 1) to dramatically increase student achievement and MI was selected as the means to do so, or 2) to implement a "state-of-the-art," research-based program, and Gardner's theory was perceived as anchored in cognitive sciences research.

The schools crafted curriculums to meet their students' and community's needs. Those wanting to improve achievement such as Russell Elementary School in Lexington, Kentucky, and Lincoln High School in Stockton, California, believed that student gains would be realized if learning were made memorable. To do so, curriculum and instruction were made multisensory and experiential in nature. As a result, Russell Elementary School adopted a strong arts emphasis and dedicated a significant portion of each school day to the arts. Lincoln High School created Integrated Studies classes that were team taught and blended two or three subjects together thematically. Lincoln teachers also implemented rigorous projects in which students must ask questions about the world and pursue interdisciplinary answers. Once students have arrived at reasonable answers, they must inform or influence others.

Schools founded as MI programs or as research-based models have developed curricular approaches to suit their needs. Sites such as the large, diverse inner city school, EXPO for Excellence in Minneapolis, the suburban Skyview Junior High School in Bothell, Washington, and the K–12 magnet Key Learning Community in Indianapolis all promote thematic, project-based curriculum. Interestingly enough, these three sites also offer some form of apprenticeship. Gardner has suggested that schools personalize their instruction for students through apprenticeships offered by skilled youth or adults. The purpose of such apprenticeships is not to track students into careers but instead to immerse them in real world tasks so that they can see the application of academics outside of school.

Curricular Apprenticeships

At the elementary level, EXPO students are taught by building specialists for one to four weeks at a time in ways that deepen and expand on classroom themes. The specialists communicate that visual, verbal, musical, or kinesthetic extensions of studies are valid and important and should be accomplished with skill. Additionally, EXPO students participate in multiage electives three times a year where teachers provide offerings according to their avocational interests. Selecting such electives can be a daunting task since students have as many as thirty to choose from. Sample electives include "Team Sports," "Hmong Literacy," or "Animals in Nature and Art."

Student apprenticeships are also promoted at Skyview Junior High School through its award-winning Breakout! program. This interdisciplinary project is required of all ninth graders. The students must be mentored by local community members and find a way to contribute to the well-being of others. The apprenticeships are organized with a twenty-page passport that specifies requirements students must meet. Sample Breakout! efforts have included making works of art, producing videos or CDs for local agencies, fundraising for a performance center, and spearheading a wetlands rehabilitation project.

Schools that integrate apprenticeships into their curriculums have done so in diverse ways. In some cases, apprenticeships are part of the regular school day and are taught by building teachers or specialists. In others, they are structured as extracurricular programs with specific goals and purposes clearly delineated. However they are organized, apprenticeships can deepen students' disciplinary knowledge and skill, provide opportuni-ties to apply knowledge in new settings and contexts, and to contribute meaningfully as citizens in their communities.

Human Development as a Curricular Goal

Perhaps the least common MI curricular approach is the one that strives to develop each student's intellectual strengths. At such sites, the schools' missions, goals, and programs accommodate individual student interests and personal goals. Instead of emphasizing curriculum development, such schools emphasize human development.

Key Learning Community in Indianapolis is committed to enhancing each student's intellectual strengths. While all Key students learn academic content through several intelligences, they also identify their strengths and how such skills can guide their life choices. At Key, students have numerous opportunities to develop their talents. For example, students select their electives in multiage pods which meet daily. The pods provide instruction in areas where students demonstrate interest and promise. Students also attend the Flow Room several times weekly to immerse themselves in self-selected activities they find personally motivating, challenging, and gratifying. Because of the extensive curricular time dedicated to student choice at Key, teachers have less time to teach the traditional basic skills. They capitalize on the time for basic skill instruction by seeking highly effective ways to teach the traditional literacies. This dedication, however, to an intelligence-based model rather than a basic skills model is successful academically since all but a handful of students at the Key score at or significantly above grade level on standardized test scores.

Other examples of personalizing education in MI programs are evident. For example, New City School, Russell Elementary School, and EXPO for Excellence School all emphasize the significance of the personal intelligences. In some cases, students in collaboration with their teachers and family members set year-long goals that are reinforced at school and at home. For example, EXPO students and families meet with teachers at the beginning of each school year for goal-setting conferences. Students' strengths, challenges, and interests are identified and three or four MI-related goals are identified for implementation. During the school year, students are encouraged to pursue their goals and document their progress toward achieving them. In early spring, student progress is reviewed and adjustments are made. At the end of the school year, parents review student portfolios and ascertain what was accomplished. Though the goal-setting is time consuming for the staff, the teachers say it makes a significant difference in student behaviors and academic success. It also helps the school actualize its goal of developing self-directed learners.

Some schools take another approach to promoting human development. For example, at Russell Elementary School, students learn and practice character skills once weekly to ensure well-developed inter- and intrapersonal capacities. Such skills include following directions, asking for help, recognizing the feelings of others, and being honest. The character program is part of Russell's schoolwide Respect and Responsibility Plan and is reinforced by all teachers in all classrooms.

The staff at New City School has written two books on the importance of teaching curriculum through the personal intelligences. In their 1996 book entitled *Multiple Intelligences: Teaching through the Personal Intelligences* they assert that being able to read, write, and compute does not guarantee success. People who are considered successful are those who "can work well with others, know their own strengths and weaknesses and navigate to areas where they are productive." Their curriculum integrates problem-solving and thinking skills that focus on student attitudes and reactions to and processes of learning disciplinary content. New City's ultimate goal is to create thoughtful, respectful, and contributing members of society.

As evident in the above examples, some MI teachers and schools expand their curriculums to encompass the traditional disciplines. By providing explicit instruction in inter- and personal intelligences, students can develop significant skills that will serve them well in and out of school.

Lesson #4: Assessment Transforms

The Theory of Multiple Intelligences has spawned extensive dialogue about assessment—assessment of student work and assessment of human intelligence. In terms of classroom assessment, if all content does not need to be taught in the same way, why should assessment be uniform? Gardner (1999) addressed this question by calling for more assessment options.

An observation that can be made about the assessment practices of teachers and schools adhering to MI theory is that both the products and processes of student learning are considered important. Capturing such data occurs through processfolios, student logs, or interviews and discussions about assignments and student thinking about such work. Another significant change is that assessment becomes integrated with instruction, and that students assume active roles as self- and peer-assessors. When students brainstorm criteria for a classroom project, for example, apply the criteria to guide their project work, and use the criteria to assess their completed assignments as well as those of their peers, the distinction between learning and assessing blurs. Other assessment changes include the development of new MI report cards and videotaped archives of student presentations over time that document growth in skills and knowledge.

Standardized tests and state assessments are typically administered alongside the MI performance-based measures. This is important because educational innovations are considered worthwhile if students perform well on standardized tests. In a case study of six MI schools (Campbell & Campbell, 1999), it was found that students at all six sites outperformed their peers in basic skills areas on district, state, and standardized tests. This is significant since the teachers at the schools did not teach to such tests and, instead, remained focused on their curriculum. Additionally, the students at the schools represented a highly diverse group in terms of socioeconomic, language, racial, and ability indicators. Though more studies are certainly needed, it is worth noting that most teachers at the MI sites downplayed the test results. They expressed concern that the scores might eclipse the real work they undertook to provide personally relevant education, to develop a range of intellectual competencies, and to assist students in using and applying skills in real world settings. One thing the scores do convey, however, is that rather than thwarting basic skill achievement, adopting MI enhances traditional measures of student success.

Intelligence Testing

When Gardner's book *Frames of Mind* was released, he was approached about the possibility of developing tests to measure each of the seven intelligences. Rather than creating another battery of paper and pencil tests, Gardner and his colleagues established the Spectrum classroom, an enriched preschool environment filled with materials and resources to engage the different intelligences. The assumption of the researchers was that children would find the environment comfortable and inviting and would naturally interact with the materials that were present. The quality and sophistication of the children's interactions over time would reveal their strengths as well as areas that would benefit from an additional emphasis. Eventually, as the books from Project Spectrum show, a curriculum and assessment procedures consisting of games and problem-solving tasks were devised.

Spectrum assessments were brought to children in a familiar environment and proved capable of providing a cognitive profile at a given moment in time. As Gardner (1999) readily asserted, it is important not to overemphasize any kind of intellectual profile because abilities readily change.

Culturally Fair Intelligence Testing

Although it is unlikely that most teachers will be interested in formal intelligence testing of their students, there has been, nevertheless, fascinating work with intelligence testing in Arizona. Federal grants through the United States Department of Education have funded efforts to identify minority, economically disadvantaged students as gifted. In one study, June Maker, a researcher from the University of Arizona, collaborated with Navajo communities to identify underrepresented gifted students. Maker's premise was that Navajo children do exhibit giftedness even though they are routinely assessed below the 50th percentile on some school records for ability and achievement. Maker devised problem-solving tasks according to Gardner's model of the (then) seven intelligences. Before she began such work, there had never been a single American Indian child identified as gifted from the Chinle Boarding School, one of her Arizona pilot sites. After she assessed the students with tools such as tangrams and storytelling, Maker identified eighty-five students at the boarding school with high potential.

The researcher says she learned many things about working with Navajo students. Significantly, she observed that the students performed better when tested in small groups than when tested individually. Her small group evaluation contrasts greatly from the individualized assessment conducted at Project Spectrum. Maker's approach has raised the question of whether intelligence testing or perhaps any form of standardized testing should be administered in *culturally fair* ways. In addition, Maker observed the value of first engaging the Navajo students in three-dimensional tasks such as bead work or sculpting before proceeding onto evaluation activities. By initially working in their areas of strength the students were motivated to tackle additional tasks both in and out of their comfort zones. Maker has also stated that based on her experiences, Gardner's model of intelligence does not appear to be biased toward any cultural, ethnic, or linguistic group. The models that likely need changing are limited beliefs and practices that cause students to be overlooked as competent and talented individuals.

Bridging Strengths with Weaknesses

Teachers and schools working with MI theory base their practices on the assumption that all students are talented. This has profound implications for special education students. In fact, when a teacher at EXPO for Excellence was asked how many special education students she had in her class, she said she no longer perceived students as having deficits. Instead, she looked for strengths, always found them, and used such talents strategically.

Many MI teachers and schools replace remediation with enrichment. Some administrators say that active learning makes it nearly impossible for students NOT to learn. This does not mean that special services are completely eliminated. However, how they are handled varies significantly from the norm. For example, at one MI school, when teachers refer students for special services, they must first provide assessments of the students' strengths as well as reasons for the referral. Subsequent special education interventions are based on bridging student strengths with weaknesses. This could occur by using kinesthetic and visual strategies to remember core concepts or by color-coding steps of a problem-solving process. In addition to improving learning, other benefits have been reported for special education students. Kornhaber, Fierros, and Veenema (in press) found that 32 out of 41 MI schools claimed students with learning disabilities were motivated, made positive social adjustments, and exerted more effort in MI-based programs.

LESSON #5: Professional Practice Appears to Transform Developmentally

Some MI teachers experience a developmental progression in implementing Gardner's ideas. Although no one individual's experience will adequately explain anyone else's, some teachers appear to confront challenges in a similar sequence. The initial hurdle encountered by MI educators is to determine why and how MI is appropriate. Is the theory to be used to support goals such as teaching for understanding or to prepare students for the workplace? Once a core purpose is made explicit, then curricular and instructional decisions can be made. Some teachers may decide to use learning centers, or project-based options or multimodal direct instruction—a common challenge is to begin teaching content in new ways. In fact, for many MI educators extensive time is given to adapting or creating new instructional strategies. New classroom resources such as manipulatives, art, and music supplies are gathered. Typically, assessment techniques are also reconfigured.

Teachers often report that, after the first year, lesson planning in new ways becomes second nature. Some experience the development of their own latent abilities and, just like students, are willing to take risks to tap underdeveloped intelligences. Teachers soon devise ways to shorten lesson planning time by creating occasional long-term projects for students or by teaming with others.

Teachers notice that their student observation skills become more finely tuned, and they endeavor to teach students through their strengths. Their ability to teach students self-directed learning skills improves and some have the confidence to share MI efforts with colleagues formally or informally. Some become dissatisfied with traditional reporting measures and develop new reports for parents and students that more accurately reflect what was taught and learned.

Some teachers find an MI challenge that extends beyond their teaching and assessing to include community members as mentors in the classroom or to connect students with learning in their communities. Many teachers who have worked with the Theory of Multiple Intelligences perceive significant changes in their professional role in the classroom. Instead of dispensing information, they serve as facilitators, coaches, resource personnel, tutors, motivators, and networkers to promote diverse forms of intellectual growth. Frequently, experienced MI teachers are called on to share what they have learned with others and to help support schoolwide or district-level change.

Similarities in Multiple Intelligences Schools

Though MI schools are distinct from one another, there are striking similarities that have emerged among diverse school programs. It is as if each school identified fundamental principles to put into place whether the site was large or small, rural or inner city, elementary or secondary. During the last twenty years of MI program implementation, the following eight core components have become evident in schoolwide models.

Characteristics of Multiple Intelligences Schools

1. Teachers believe students are intellectually competent in multiple ways and communicate such beliefs to students.

2. The school's mission, environment, and curriculum promote intellectual diversity.

3. Teachers use multimodal, active learning methods.

4. Students have opportunities to improve their weaknesses by tapping their strengths.

5. A curricular goal of teaching for student understanding emerges. The curricular scope is narrowed to enable students to achieve in-depth knowledge of core disciplinary concepts.

6. Students develop autonomous learning skills through initiating and completing projects of their choice.

7. Individual talents of students are identified and nurtured. Students participate in extra-curricular, mentoring, or apprenticeship programs of their choice.

8. In collaboration with the teacher, students identify the criteria by which they will be assessed. Students receive feedback and evaluation from numerous sources: their teachers, peers, or others, and from self-reflection. The processes and products of learning are assessed. Assessment data including that from standardized tests and state assessment measures are analyzed and used to guide student and classroom achievement goals.

As is evident in the above characteristics of MI schools as well as in the programs described earlier, many of the schools' efforts are guided in large part by students' individual talents and interests. Opportunities for gaining general knowledge and specialization, for creative exploration and disciplined skill-building, and for student choice and required study, ebb and flow throughout the school years. When educational institutions transform their environments, instruction, curriculum, and assessment to accommodate intellectual diversity, joy in learning and schooling for intelligence can be realized. And yet, it is the interaction between the teacher and students that is the critical link in student achievement. Those who teach in multiple intelligences–based schools must necessarily continue as learners themselves, discovering latent abilities, expressing and refining their talents, and identifying new ones to develop. Ultimately, the greatest influence on student learning is what teachers model in their beliefs, words, and behaviors.

What Are Our Next Steps?

Gardner's work acknowledges that human development is more complex and flexible than many psychologists or researchers had previously theorized. As we contemplate how to respond to the numerous implications of the Theory of Multiple Intelligences, we can begin looking at our students with a new curiosity and appreciation. We can explain to them and to colleagues and parents that each of us possesses a unique cognitive profile of individual gifts. We can offer pre-service and in-service staff development to expand our vision of what it means to be human and what it means to be educated. We can design educational programs that nurture individual differences through holistic offerings and personalize education for each student. We can share ideas with each other and discuss our successes and failures. As educators, we can create learning communities that are self-transforming through reflection and informed response. We can act on the fact that school does not have to be the way we remember it.

We can also reflect on the question: What is the mission of education? There is currently no agreement about the fundamental purpose of education in the United States. Some claim it is to educate for basic skills literacy. Some say it is to prepare graduates to compete in a global market place. Others maintain that we must emphasize our cultural heritage. Some of us suggest that a mission for education could be to develop the full spectrum of human capacities, to identify the strengths our students possess, and to develop such talents during the K–12 years. All children and adults deserve opportunities to explore their capacities and pursue their interests so that they may become gifted in their own right. Society could only benefit from the contributions of a highly talented citizenry.

To transform schooling as we have known it to what it might become requires the support of administrators, families, business leaders, and policy makers. All must acknowledge that education is the single most important responsibility of any society and invest the time, money, and creativity to develop human capacity as the world's top priority. One example of human development as a governmental priority was pioneered in Latin America. During the 1980s the small country of Venezuela pursued the goal of increasing the intelligence of every Venezuelan citizen. Military, media, business, and educational organizations all participated in this venture. Luis Machado, the Minister for the Development of Intelligence in Venezuela, stated:

> Today a society of and for intelligence can be consciously and humanly planned. This is not a theory; it is a reality that transforms . . . . In possession of more developed minds, people will be able to find within themselves the elements needed to build a new society.

Surely, if an entire nation can strive to enhance the intelligence of its citizenry, we in our classrooms, schools, districts, and states should pursue no less.

Part of Howard Gardner's definition of intelligence includes the ability to solve problems. The authors refrain from recommending specific approaches to implementing the Theory of Multiple Intelligences. It is through problem-solving how to better meet the needs of their educational communities that teachers will create effective models while simultaneously developing more of their inherent capacities. Instead of offering prescriptions, we conclude this book with questions, that when answered by local communities, may indicate ways to enhance human intellectual competencies. Such questions include:

> How might teachers, students, school administrators, families, and community members become informed about human competence and its implications for educational practice?

What should the mission of local educational programs be and how might schools express such missions?

How can pre-service, in-service, and staff development programs promote teaching and learning strategies that develop students' basic skills and individual gifts?

How can school environments be enriched and enriching?

How can we learn to perceive the full spectrum of student intelligence?

How might assessment and instruction be integrated to benefit learning?

What essential concepts should students learn?

What role might MI theory play in improving student achievement?

Which community members might serve as mentors or provide apprenticeships?

How can educators combine effective educational strategies with practical and intelligent uses of technology?

And finally, how might you use the information in this book to support your work as an educator?

■ ■ ■ ■ ■ ■ ■ ■ ■ ■ ■ ■ ■ ■ ■ ■ ■ ■ ■

LESSONS LEARNED REFERENCES

American Association of School Administrators. (2001). *An Educator's Guide to Schoolwide Reform*. Available online at www.aasa.org/ issues_and_insights/district_organization/ reform/overview.htm.

Campbell, L. (2000). *The Unspoken Dialogue: Beliefs about Intelligence, Students, and Instruction Held by a Sample of Teachers Familiar with Multiple Intelligences Theory*. Unpublished doctoral dissertation. Santa Barbara, CA: The Fielding Institute.

Campbell, L., & Campbell, B. (1999). *Multiple Intelligences and Student Assessment: Success Stories from Six Schools*. Alexandria, VA: ASCD.

Campbell, L. (1997, Sept.). Variations on a Theme: How Teachers Interpret MI Theory. *Educational Leadership, 55*(1), 14–19.

Faculty of the New City School. (1996). *Multiple Intelligences: Teaching through the Personal Intelligences*. St. Louis, MI: The New City School.

Gardner, H. (1999). *Intelligence Reframed: Multiple Intelligences for the 21st Century*. New York: Basic Books.

Gardner, H. (1983). *Frames of Mind: The Theory of Multiple Intelligences*. New York: Basic Books.

Kornhaber, M., Fierros, E., & Veenema, S. (in press). *Multiple Intelligences: Best Ideas from Theory and Practice*. Boston, MA: Allyn & Bacon.

Krechevsky, M. (1998). *Project Zero Frameworks for Early Childhood Education. Vol. 3, Preschool Assessment Handbook*. New York: Teachers College Press.

Missouri Department of Elementary and Secondary Education. (1998). *MI Way of Learning*. Available online at www. succcesslink.org/best/b7.html.

Name Index

Subject Index

environment for, 156–159
learning processes in, 155–156
technology that enhances, 180–181
Interviews
distinguished from conversation, 17–18
effective skills in, 18
Intrapersonal intelligence, xxi, 185–215
assessment of, 308
checklist of qualities, 187–188
definition of, 187
learning processes in, 188–189
technology that enhances, 214–215
Intrapersonal learning approach, 212–214

Jigsaw, 160
Jingles, 16
Journal writing, 22, 207–209
for personal insight, 208
reflective, 308
suggestions for, 207–208

Keyboarding, 26, 143
Key Learning Community, 279, 318, 328
Key words, notetaking with, 104
Kinesthetic flow charts, 81
Kinesthetic intelligence, 63–89
assessment of, 304–305
checklist for, 66
definition of, 65
learning environment for, 67–68
learning processes in, 67
technology that enhances, 88–89

Laban Movement Analysis, 73
Language, intelligence and, 2
Language arts
blending with visual arts, 118
creative movement in, 74
writing in, 22
Language-rich environments, 2
Language skills, improving with music, 138–139
Learning centers, 267–272
Learning disabled, 41
Learning naturally, 242–243
Learning styles, 167–168
Learning through an Expanded Arts and Academic Program (LEAP), 117–119
Lectures, listening to, 11
Linguistic intelligence, xx
Listening, 3
keys to effective, 6, 7
to learn, 6–12
to lectures, 11
to music, 133, 134–137
to poetry, 8–9
to stories, 6–8

Listening Guide, 12
Listening skills, 5
Literacy, 3
in four disciplines, 117
Literature, 18–21
containing emotional issues, 205
cooperative discussions of, 161
Logic, 33
deductive, 35, 36, 37–39
inductive, 35, 36, 39–40
teaching of, 35–36
Logical-mathematical intelligence, xx, 31–59
assessment of, 302–303
checklist of qualities, 33
definition of, 32
learning environment for, 34–35
learning processes of, 33–59
technology that enhances, 57–59
Logs, 22
dialogue, 230
field, 229–230
see also Journal writing

Main idea, getting, 42
Manipulatives, 77–79
junk drawer, 78
Mathematical intelligence. See Logical-mathematical intelligence
Mathematical probability, 52–53
Mathematical thinking processes, 44–48
Mathematics, 33
across the curriculum, 56
art and, 118–119, 120
assessment of, 289
creative movement in, 74–75
music and, 140
songs for, 137
TPR games for, 82
writing in, 22
see also Logical-mathematical intelligence
Mathematics education, 35
Mathematics instruction, 33
Measurement, 49–50
Mediated Learning, 40, 41–42
Mediated Learning Experience (MLE), 41–42
Memorization, 110–111
in drama, 69
of poetry, 16–17
Memory
improving, 16–17
rote, 109
working, 42
Mentoring, 277–278
Metacognition, 199
Mindmapping, 105–106, 303
Mindscaping, 108
Misspelling, 112
Mnemonics, 110

Moral intelligence, xxi
Movement, creative, 73–75
Movement theorists, 73
Multicultural classroom, 171
Multicultural education, 177–180
Multiculturalism
music and, 139
resources for storytelling, 10–11
Multidimensional assessment, 280
Multilingual classroom, 162
Multiple intelligence-based schools, 323, 325
characteristics of, 332
curriculum differences in, 327–329
Multiple intelligence instruction
apprenticeships, 277–278
benefits of, 326–327
developing individual intelligences, 266–267
human development as curricular goal, 328–329, 333
implications of, 251–252
instructional menus, 252, 253, 254
integrating, 326
learning center-based programs, 267–272
lesson planning, 252–273
organizing, 255–258, 325–326
supporting changes in, 325
teaching for understanding, 278–282
teaming, 265
using interdisciplinary units, 259–265
see also Curriculum
Multiple intelligences
categories of, xxi, 300
criteria for identifying, 220
Multiple Intelligences, Theory of (MI)
implications of, 324, 325
understanding, xix
see also Multiple intelligences
Multiple intelligences programs, lessons learned from, 324–332
Multiple perspectives, 168–173
Murals, 118
Museums, classroom, 224–225
Music
across the curriculum, 139–140
art and, 143
background, 132–133, 138
basic components of, 129
expressing feelings through, 129, 204
importance of, 130
improving language skills with, 138–139
introducing into the classroom, 132–134
and learning skills, 137–140
listening to, 133, 134–137
math and, 140
and multiculturalism, 139
and reading comprehension, 138

Credits

Excerpts from "Notes for a Preface" in *Complete Poems*, on page 1 Copyright © 1950 by Sandburg, Carl, and renewed 1978 by Margaret Sandburg, Helga Sandburg Crile, and Janet Sandburg. Reprinted by permission of Harcourt Brace and Co.

The poem entitled "The Intelligence Rap" on page 9 is printed with permission of Lisa and Shawna Munson.

Portions of the text entitled "Categories of Writing" on page 21 were adapted from James Britton's *Language and Learning*. Copyright © 1970 by James Britton. Reproduced by permission of Penguin Books, Ltd.

Part of the section entitled, "Mediating Learning", referring to the Building Blocks of Thinking developed by Katherine Greenberg, Ph.D. on pages 41–43 was adapted from the Cognitive Enrichment Network (COGNET) funded in part by the U.S. Department of Education Follow Through Program (Grant # S014C10013), The University of Tennessee Follow Through Sponsor Project, Katherine H. Greenberg, Ph.D., Director.

"The Questioning Strategies Bookmark" on page 45 was developed by Jay McTighe of the Maryland State Department of Education. Reprinted by permission.

"Classroom Zones" on page 68 is printed with permission from Dr. Ann Taylor, Professor of Architecture at the University of New Mexico, and originator with partner, George Vlastos, of Architecture and Children, 111 South Jackson, PO Box 4508, Seattle, WA.

Text sections entitled "Understanding Bodily Knowing" on page 73 and "Introduction to Creative Movement Activities" on page 74 were contributed by Peggy Hackney. Printed with permission.

"Elements of Dance Warm-Ups" on page 75 and "A Sequence for Learning through Dance" on page 76 are printed with permission from Debbie Gilbert, Executive Director of Very Special Arts in Washington State, and Co-Director with Joanne Petroff of the Whistlestop Dance Company, PO Box 20801, Seattle, WA. 98102.

The text section entitled "Task Cards" on page 77 is adapted from Kenneth and Rita Dunn's book, *Teaching Students through their Individual Learning Styles*. Copyright © Allyn and Bacon. Reprinted/adapted by permission.

"Visual Chart Starters" on pages 102–103 contains a section on "thinking frames" developed by Beau Fly Jones, Program Director of the North Central Regional Educational Laboratory, 1988. Copyright © North Central Regional Educational Laboratory. Reprinted by permission.

The two "concept maps" on pages 104 and 105 are from the book, *Learning How to Learn* by Joseph Novak and Bob Gowin,1984. New York: Cambridge University Press. Copyright © Cambridge University Press. Reprinted with the permission of Cambridge University Press.

The "cluster" and student writing sample in the section entitled "Clustering" on page 107 is taken from Gabriel Rico's book, *Writing the Natural Way*, 1983 published by Jeremy Tarcher. Copyright © by Jeremy Tarcher and The Putnam Publishing Group. Reprinted with permission.

"Mindscaping" on page 108 is adapted from *Mapping Inner Space* by Nancy Margulies, Zephyr Press, 1990. Copyright © by Nancy Margulies. Reprinted by permission.

The "multiplication art card" on page 109 was made by Suni Deardorff. Printed with permission.

"Learning to Think like an Architect" on page 116 contains adaptations of Ann Taylor and George Vlastos's Architecture and Children Curriculum, School Zone Institute, 111 South Jackson, PO Box 4508, Seattle, WA. Printed with permission.

"Art as an Instructional Tool", "Blending the Visual and Language Arts", and "Integrating Art and Math" on pages 117–119 contains information from an article entitled "Teaching the Basic Skills Through Art and Music" which appeared in the April, 1992 issue of *Phi Delta Kappan* . The article was written and copyrighted by Jodi Dean and Ila Lane Gross of Learning through an Expanded Arts Program (LEAP). Used by permission. All rights reserved.

The song, "Everyone is Differently Abled" on page 128 contains words and music by Danny Deardorff and Lorraine Bayes from the album "All of Us Will Shine" and the video "Let's Be Friends" by Tickle Tune Typhoon Productions, Copyright © 1987. All rights reserved. Used only by permission.

"Songs for the Sciences" on page 136 contains lyrics from Sing A Song of Science by Kathleen Carroll, creator of *Brain Friendly Teaching and Learning*, 1990. Copyright © by Kathleen Carroll. Reprinted by permission.

The section entitled "Teaching Reading Musically" on page 138 is adapted from the work of Sheila Fitzgerald, Ph.D. Michigan State University. Reprinted by permission.

"Introducing the Concept of Musical Notation" on page 142 is adapted from *See with Your Ears* by Don Kaplan, Lexicos, PO Box 296, Lagunitas, CA 94938. Copyright © 1983 Don Kaplan.

"Collaborative Learning" on pages 159–162 contains information adapted from *Cooperation in the Classroom* by David Johnson and Roger Johnson, Interaction Book Company, 1987. Copyright © David and Roger Johnson. Reprinted by permission.

"Reflecting on Service Learning" on page 165 was written by Kate McPherson,Director of Project Service Learning and author of *Enriching Learning through Service*. Printed by permission.

"Local and Global Problem-Solving" on pages 173–176 is adapted from the *Our Only Earth Series* by Linda MacRae-Campbell and Micki McKisson. Copyright © 1990, 1992 Zephyr Press. Used with permission of publisher.

"Teaching with a Multicultural Perspective" on pages 177–178 is adapted from James Banks' *Multiethnic Education: Theory and Practice*. Third Edition. Boston: Allyn and Bacon. 1994. Printed with permission.

"Understanding Cultural Diversity through the Arts" on pages 178–179 is adapted from *Strategies for Culturally-based Art Education: A Qualitative Methodology* by E.M. Andrews, 1980, and *The Innovation Process of Cultually-based Art Education: A Qualitative Analysis of the In-service Programming and Implementation Processes of an Innovative Multicultural Art Curriculum in Canada* by E.M. Andrews, 1983. Reprinted by permission.

Quotes from "The Inside World" by Bill Knake on page 186 are reprinted with permission of Bill Knake.

The information on the Apollo program on page 190 was contributed by Brad Greene who may be contacted at the William Glasser Institute, 22024 Lassen St., Ste. 118, Chatsworth, CA 91311, phone: 800-899-0688 or online at www.wglasser.com.

"Olympian Goal Setting" on pages 197–198 is adapted from the work of Marilyn King and her "Dare to Imagine" program. Reprinted by permission.

The section entitled "Principles of Assessment" on pages 287–295 is adapted from the work of Arts PROPEL of Harvard Project Zero and the Educational Testing Service. Printed with permission.

The information on "Working Styles" on pages 297–299 and the Project Spectrum sample report card on page 298 was reprinted with permission of Mara Krechevsky of Harvard Project Zero.

The portion of the text entitled "Multiple Intelligences Report Cards" on page 318 contains a report card from Bruce Campbell's book, *The Multiple Intelligences Handbook: Lesson Plans and More*. Copyright © 1994 Campbell and Associates, Incorporated, Stanwood, WA.